Anglo-American Antiphony

Anglo-American Antiphony

THE LATE

ROMANTICISM OF

TENNYSON AND EMERSON

Richard E. Brantley

UNIVERSITY PRESS OF FLORIDA

Gainesville Tallahassee Tampa Boca Raton Pensacola Orlando Miami Jacksonville

Library of Congress Cataloging-in-Publication Data
Brantley, Richard E.
Anglo-American antiphony: the late romanticism of Tennyson and
Emerson / Richard E. Brantley.
p.   cm.
Includes bibliographical references (p.) and index.
ISBN 0-8130-1247-3 (alk. paper)
1. Tennyson, Alfred Tennyson, Baron, 1809–1892—Criticism and
interpretation.   2. Emerson, Ralph Waldo, 1803–1882—
Criticism and interpretation.   3. Literature, Comparative—
English and American.   4. Literature, Comparative—American
and English.   5. Romanticism—United States.   6. Romanticism
—England.   I. Title.
PR5592.R63B73   1994   93-30648
821'.8—dc20

The painting of Tennyson by Samuel Lawrence is reproduced by
permission of the National Portrait Gallery, London. The
photograph of Emerson is reproduced by permission of the
Houghton Library, Harvard University.

The University Press of Florida is the scholarly publishing
agency for the State University System of Florida, comprised of
Florida A & M University, Florida Atlantic University, Florida
International University, Florida State University, University of
Central Florida, University of Florida, University of North Florida,
University of South Florida, and University of West Florida.

University Press of Florida
15 Northwest 15th Street
Gainesville, Florida 32611

For our daughters
JESSICA AND JUSTINE

and *in memoriam*
RABUN LEE BRANTLEY, JR.
(1933–1956)

Contents

Prelude

"Have American philosophers and critics no home to go to," asks Denis Donoghue, "no intellectual tradition of their own?" American critical theory, when "bearing the names of Heidegger, Adorno, Benjamin, Foucault, Derrida, de Man, Deleuze, Lyotard, Blanchot, and other daunting sages," derives from France or Germany,[1] but it need not be so. My homegrown critical method (distinct from theory, if theory means only abstract contemplation or top-down imposition) derives from my Anglo-American heritage, the broadly experiential common ground of empiricism and evangelicalism. My religious as well as philosophical mode of criticism is perhaps most appropriate for interpreting such mid-nineteenth-century authors of British and American extraction as Alfred, Lord Tennyson (1809–1892), the Poet Laureate of England, and Ralph Waldo Emerson (1803–1881), the Sage of Concord. This diptych of Anglo-American letters follows intrinsically Anglo-American, empirical-evangelical ways of "fighting the good fight." While hardly blind to pain and sorrow, Tennyson and Emerson envision a better future through material "progress" and the social gospel. (Hence they tend to be blind to industrial threats to nature.) Their shared empirical-evangelical approach to experience leads them to the philosophically theological, satisfyingly complex claim that humankind unites with God in world and word and thus harmonizes with the universe.

Norman Maclean, long-time professor of Romanticism at the University of Chicago, concludes in *A River Runs Through It and Other Stories* (1976) that the faith held in common by a Presbyterian minister and his remaining son is: "You can love completely without complete understanding."[2] Without a more than partial understanding, however, faith gives way to forlorn hope. "For Maclean," writes Ralph C. Wood, "life remains a mysterious 'it,' a vast impersonal process wherein, as David Hume once said, 'man matters no more than an oyster.'" But Maclean was "not content with this hard creed." His "residual faith caused him subtly to modify" it, for "the doubt-wracked life toughens true faith." Wood concludes that Maclean "spent his career teaching a paradoxical truth not found in most books: that the intellectual life is immensely important and yet supremely unimportant when set beside the task of ordinary living."[3] This experiential balance finds its binational counterpart in the empirical-evangelical, more Arminian than Calvinist sensibility prevalent throughout the Anglo-American world from at least 1750 to 1850. The secular-sacred vision shared by Tennyson and Emerson is just such a balance: it is more optimistic than pessimistic and more Late Romantic than pre-Modernist, for it not only testifies to "the substance of things hoped for [and] the evidence of things not seen" (see Hebrews 11.1) but also explores the role of the physical senses in spiritual experience.

My chosen diptych of Anglo-American letters reflects an optimism that can make sense even for our world if we, like the laureate and the sage, can focus on the moral relation between humankind and what the journal *Ultimate Reality and Meaning,* with refreshing if bald intrepidity, calls "the totality of existence."[4] The search for "ultimate" reality and meaning, of course, should cultivate "proximate" plays of skepticism. Nevertheless, spatial models such as milieu, horizon, and context, temporal models such as origin, cause, and the ultimate/final, and personal models such as God, self, soul, and spirit can still form ways of knowing and believing. The desires that people live by, regardless of whether they adumbrate the heaven to which one might want to go, constitute "heaven" in the here and now, for natural-spiritual experience is still conceivable.

I dedicate this book of my mellow years to our daughters, Jessica and Justine. Pertinent to my dedicatory impulse are the concerns of my friend and colleague Melvyn New. In *Telling New Lies: Seven Essays in Fiction, Past and Present* (1992), New asks how parents and teachers are to "instruct the next generation" if we have "spent all our truth" and how we are to fulfill our own "need for belief" when "valid skepticism demonstrates the lie in every human construct." Suggesting that "the loss of a providential god weighs heavily on the culture" in which we live, his diagnosis of current ills—the loss of "the sense of presence in the course of secularizing our societies" and the "ever-increasing need for and fear of union (sexual, intellectual, emotional)"—is acute. Careful to stipulate that our "critical act" is "a dance with truth" rather than a "march toward it," he argues that twentieth-century criticism must distinguish "lies of art" from "lies of power" in the same way that "an earlier time tried to distinguish the voice in the whirlwind from the voice of the serpent." Finding in joy "another name for Religion" (Nietzsche's phrase), New vows "never to surrender" the moment of "faith" or "grace" in each "formulation of art." He upholds the belief that "the moment of sufficient presence otherwise missing from human life" is available through the particular joy of reading; Nietzsche, after all, declares that "we negate and must negate because something in us wants to live and affirm—something that we perhaps do not know or see as yet—this is said in favor of criticism."[5] The objective of my criticism, for anyone interested in what we might pass on to the children, is to draw out the truth and grace and joy of life as well as of art.

Having tried to acknowledge lies of power, art, and even faith, and to tell the big difference between the lies of power and those of art, I aspire, above all, to "snatch a grace beyond the reach" of art and criticism.[6] My "believing" as well as "understanding" criticism, my "second naiveté," forms my hermeneutic circle: "believe in order to understand; understand in order to believe."[7]

To Jessica, Justine, and my students, Shelley's *Adonais* (1821) speaks out loud and bold:

> Clasp with thy panting soul the pendulous Earth;
> As from a centre, dart thy spirit's light
> Beyond all worlds, until its spacious might
> Satiate the void circumference: then shrink
> Even to a point within our day and night;
> And keep thy heart light lest it make thee sink
> When hope has kindled hope, and lured thee to the brink.
>   (stanza 42, lines 417–21)

This advice, written in reaction to the death of Keats at age twenty-five, implies that while "the lie in every human construct" may be seductive, the truth and grace and joy of life as well as of art retain resonance. To follow Shelley's advice, I explore how his lesson of this- and otherworldliness applies to the works of Tennyson and Emerson; I also ask whether the lesson is yet worthy to be taught. Since it entails the recovery of at least biological plenitude if not Providence, the compatibility between criticism and affirmation may yet turn out to enhance knowledge as well as belief. Then critical understanding will indeed not only thrive itself but also help the next generation thrive.

Shelley's combination of this- and otherworldliness coalesces not only philosophy with faith but also philosophical theology with literature.[8] While I try to keep in view the range of critical perspectives from the four-fold method of medieval exegesis to deconstructive aporia's suspension of infinite meanings, I entertain unity among once closely allied philosophy, religion, and literature, for only half-jokingly claiming *e pluribus unum* as the motto of my British-American critical method, I recuperate the unitary criterion for both the form and the content of Tennyson's and Emerson's works and ideas. Recognizing that skepticism is itself belief, they reconcile radical doubt with belief. While they do not exactly "define" the noumenal bases of human constructs, they sound them out. Thus they collapse distinctions between the secular and the sacred.

I dedicate this book, moreover, to the memory of my brother Rabun Lee Brantley, Jr., who died in an automobile accident during the spring of his senior year at Washington and Lee University. The previous fall, on September 30, 1955, the twenty-two-year-old English major had written to me: "Reading everything you can get your hands on will be the most valuable thing you can do toward getting a good education. It is important to read more and more advanced books as it is easy to drift and follow the paths of least resistance. The harder books will often contain the most enjoyable reading." Then eleven, I was too young to understand what he meant by "enjoyable." Even now, "enjoyable" might seem a light term to describe such experiences as reading Tennyson's *In Memoriam A. H. H.* (1850), written in reaction to the death at age twenty-two of Tennyson's friend Arthur Henry Hallam, and Emerson's *Experience* (1844), written in reaction to the death at age five of Emerson's son, Waldo. Such works lead me back to the untimely death of one who had been in life a mystery of experience and sophistication to a younger brother just beginning to grasp the possibilities of the written word. But I believe Lee knew how art instructs: through the grace and even the pleasure of "thoughts that do often lie too deep for tears."[9]

On February 24, 1956, his twenty-third birthday and my twelfth, Lee had given me the novels of Sir Walter Scott, and this first introduction to "serious" reading has become "the fascination of what's difficult." [10] The book you hold fulfills the odyssey of reading foretold by one who died even younger than Keats but who recognized, with Keats, that grave yet emotionally rich works are "enjoyable." In "On Sitting Down to Read *King Lear* Once Again" (1818), Keats announces that

> once again, the fierce dispute
> Betwixt damnation and impassion'd clay
> Must I burn through; once more humbly assay
> The bittersweet of this Shakespearean fruit.
>
> (lines 6–9)

Finally imploring Shakespeare, however, to "give me," "when I am consumed in the fire" of *King Lear*, "new phoenix wings to fly at my desire" (lines 13–14), Keats finds presence and mystery even in tragedy. Works by Tennyson and Emerson contain divine comedy alongside emotionally rich *gravitas*.

Reading, Lee knew, is not simply a matter of letting the words wash over the mind; it rouses one to the good fight. Whenever either Jessica, now twenty-three, or Justine, now fourteen, derives a "momentary stay against confusion," [11] an earnest of truth, grace, and joy, from the act of reading, she profits from Lee's precocious lesson of complexity and paradox. May she then imagine him as the eternally young proto-teacher who leads us to the joyful wisdom that reading contributes to living. One's close reading, of course, does not customarily juxtapose such scattered bits of truth, grace, and joy as these:

> Worlds of wanwood leafmeal lie.[12]
> After the first death, there is no other.[13]
> . . . gaiety transfiguring all that dread.[14]

Nevertheless, even such odd associations lend meaning (if not structure) to life, juxtaposing and sometimes even compounding life with art. The "utmost ambition" of poetry, after all, is "to lodge a few poems where they will be hard to get rid of," namely, in the memory,[15] and wrestling with literary accounts of pain or sorrow yields genuine, albeit fragile, affirmation of the joyful dread (or dreadful joy) of living. Let us once again burn through Tennyson's and Emerson's "Fierce dispute / Betwixt damnation and impassion'd clay" and assay their fruitful bittersweetness, for then we may retain just what we need of their tragicomic vision, their combination of understanding with faith.

The University of Florida Division of Sponsored Research supported this project during the summer of 1992. At the 1993 meeting of the Southeastern American Society for Eighteenth-Century Studies at the University of Alabama at Birmingham, I presented "The Empirical Procedures of Tennyson's *In Memoriam*: The Eighteenth-Century Context." This paper appears here in chapter 2 as "Empirical Procedures." I published "The Evangelical Principles of Tennyson's *In Memoriam*" in *English Romanticism: Preludes and Postludes* (East Lansing, Mich.: Colleagues, 1993). This article appears here in chapter 3 as "Evangelical Principles." I thank the editor, John A. Alford, for his permission to reprint it.

I am happy to acknowledge this book as a function of my membership in the Department of English at the University of Florida. My indebtedness to works by Ira Clark, Norman Holland, Brandon Kershner, David Leverenz, David Locke, William Logan, Brian McCrea, Joan New, Melvyn New, James Twitchell, and Gregory Ulmer is explicit. I also thank many in the department and university whose works I did not happen to cite. Carl Bredahl, Patricia Craddock, Alistair Duckworth, John Van Hook, Anne Goodwyn Jones, John Leavey, John Perlette, Robert Ray, John Seelye, and R. A. Shoaf come quickly to mind.

Since much of what and how I think, like much of who I am, derives less from the evidence on which my formal arguments stand and less from the logic of their assumptions than from people, I attempt to pass along what I understand from the teaching model demonstrated by the late T. Walter Herbert, who was Distinguished Service Professor of English at the University of Florida. Herbert's humanist tradition of open mind and warm heart was relatively free of system. He never let me forget Keats's "Negative Capability," the state when one is "capable of being in uncertainties, Mysteries, doubts, without any irritable reaching after fact and reason." I strive to impart to my students and even to inspire in them (as they inspire in me) this awareness of value amidst multiple perspectives, consciousnesses, and cultures. The mutuality of teaching and learning can thus combine the spirit of skeptical counterinterpretation with a sense of traditional presence. Since Herbert was more likely to expect truth, grace, and joy than to suspect false consciousness (after the manner of Marx, Nietzsche, or Freud), the method that I share with him can now seem positively innovative.

Because Diana Brantley's solutions to problems of procedure and principle have toughened this text, her near influence is always telling. Harold Bloom and Robert Detweiler read the complete manuscript with generosity and in detail. Many excellent staff members at the University Press of Florida have expertly facilitated its progress through to publication. I extend particular thanks to Deidre Bryan, Judy Goffman, Enid Hickingbotham, and Larry Leshan. Walda Metcalf, associate director and editor-in-chief, offered me, once again, her customary mixture of astute professional guidance and hearty common sense. The good offices of these people can help readers be either constructively skeptical about this volume or enthusiastic about it—or both.

Theme and Variations

Mutually contradictory principles of knowing, according to Immanuel Kant, are ultimately irreconcilable. However, according to G. W. F. Hegel, they merge into a higher truth that supersedes them. The continuous "unification" of empiricism and evangelicalism can produce a synthesis. Although empiricism is "natural" and evangelicalism is "spiritual," the great principle of empiricism, that one must see for oneself and be in the presence of the thing one knows, applies as well to evangelical faith. Each of these two methodologies operates along a continuum that joins emotion to intellect; each code of experience joins externality to words through "ideas/ideals of sensation," that is, through perception-cum-grace. While *empiricism* refers to immediate contact with and direct impact from objects and subjects in time and place, *evangelicalism* entertains the notions that religious truth is concerned with experiential presuppositions and that experience need not be nonreligious. On the basis of the experiential common denominator between empiricism and evangelicalism, through the "both/and" logic of philosophical theology, I argue that Alfred, Lord Tennyson (1809–1892), the Poet Laureate of England, and Ralph Waldo Emerson (1803–1882), the Sage of Concord, theologize empiricism. They ground transcendentalism in the world, balance religious myths and religious morality with scientific reverence for fact and detail, and ally empirical assumptions with "disciplined" spirit. Above all, they share the simultaneously rational and sensationalist reliance on experience as the avenue to both natural and spiritual knowledge.

The empiricism and the evangelicalism of Anglo-American culture, like the responsively chanting, antiphonal voices in a divided chancel choir, sometimes alternate; antiphony denotes, however, the accompaniment of one voice by another in another octave. The "Agnus Dei" of Giuseppe Verdi's *Requiem* (1874), for example, features a contralto who undergirds, yet also hauntingly seconds, the floating line of the soprano. Similarly, through the antiphonal, nonunisonary "unity" of resonant doubleness, Anglo-American empiricism sometimes achieves simultaneity with Anglo-American evangelicalism. Since the empirical-evangelical dialectic, if not the empirical-evangelical synthesis, of the Anglo-American world produces harmony through an opposition of voices, the resulting accord is not only more agreeable but also more complex than mere homophony or univocity alone could be. This genetic trait of Anglo-American sensibility, this generic component of Anglo-American relations, constitutes the interdisciplinary methodology to which Tennyson and Emerson self-consciously (with irony), consciously, or unconsciously contribute. This book, besides exploring the empirical-evangelical dialectic of the Anglo-American world, sounds the empirical-evangelical antiphon of that world.

I seek, thereby, to establish a single, yet twofold, theme of Anglo-American Romanticism. In *Wordsworth's "Natural Methodism"* (1975), I used the theology of John Wesley (1703–91)—founder of British and American Methodism—to gloss Wordsworth's British Romanticism. Wesley's evangelical versions of practical charity, reciprocal covenant with the Holy Spirit, conversion, spiritual perfection, and the emblematic and typological "reading" of the Book of Nature influenced not only Wordsworth's themes but also his symbology, structure, tone, irony, characterizations, and narrative patterns.[1]

In *Locke, Wesley, and the Method of English Romanticism* (1984), I used Wesley's philosophical theology to gloss British Romanticism in general. Wesley absorbed and spiritualized the empiricist epistemology of John Locke (1632–1704) and then, through the complex process of cultural osmosis, passed on to William Blake, William Wordsworth, Samuel Taylor Coleridge, Percy Bysshe Shelley, and John Keats a method for both their natural observation and their "spiritual experience."[2]

In "The Common Ground of Wesley and Edwards" (1990), I sought to show how Wesley and Jonathan Edwards (1703–58), leader of the Great Awakening in America, are even more similarly empirical than similarly evangelical. Far from just validating spiritual insights by borrowing from sense-language, Arminian Wesley and Calvinist Edwards speak literally to experience in general, including empirical observation, scientific method, and apprehension of God in nature and the Spirit.[3] Thus their shared methodology, harking back to the epistemology of Locke, not only links sense to reason and matter to mind but, more importantly, aligns nature with grace.

In *Coordinates of Anglo-American Romanticism: Wesley, Edwards, Carlyle, and Emerson* (1993), I explored how Wesley and Edwards provide an inter-disciplinary framework for interpreting a premier Anglo-American pairing of Late Romantic writers. The creative tension between empiricism and evangelicalism—the sparks that fly from coordinates on the arc—illumi-nates the noble, yet neglected, Anglo-American sensibility represented especially well by the mutual, cross-pollinating prose works of Thomas Carlyle (1795–1881), the Sage of Chelsea, and Emerson.[4]

Now I will describe another ample arc of Anglo-American Romanti-cism, for I will interpret especially notable nineteenth-century poetry as well as prose against the background of similarly notable (because simi-larly nuanced and even pre-Romantic) prose of the eighteenth century, namely, the "empirical" methodology developed in tandem by Wesley and Edwards. The Lockean basis of their evangelical faith heralds the broadly experiential (empirical-evangelical) vision shared by Tennyson's *In Memo-riam A. H. H.* (1850) and the prose of Emerson's prime (1836–52), so that the Late but not belated Romanticism shared by Tennyson and Emerson, like that same Romanticism shared by Carlyle and Emerson, is an Anglo-American dialectic of desire for and trust in experience as the best means of knowing what is true, whether naturally or supernaturally.

The prologue to *In Memoriam*, the especially auspicious beginning to Tennyson's commemorative verses on Arthur Henry Hallam, conceives of experience as both "natural" and "spiritual"; the elegist, indeed, conflates empiricism with Christ-centered faith ("thee" refers to Christ):

> We have but faith: we cannot know,
>   For knowledge is of things we see;
>   And yet we trust it comes from thee,
> A beam in darkness: let it grow.

3

Let knowledge grow from more to more,
   But more of reverence in us dwell;
   That mind and soul, according well,
May make one music as before,

But vaster.
(lines 21–29)[5]

Insofar as "it" (lines 23, 24) refers at once to "knowledge" (line 22) and to "faith" (line 21), empirical philosophy and experiential faith can seem to form an identity; the "things we see" (line 22), after all, can seem just as much the gift of God as faith itself. "Faith," therefore, while differing markedly from the "things we see," can seem dialectically involved with sense experience. Moreover, both "knowledge" (line 25) and "reverence" (line 26) appear to increase—for later can seem better—and in their interaction with one another, as well as in their joint interaction with and combined effect on the world, "mind" and "soul" (line 27) also seem increasingly one. This "identity" of the prologue, this natural-spiritual scope, is potentially more resonant, if not potentially more capacious, than old cosmologies. The quintessential poem of Victorian *Zeitgeist* emerges as the new, the philosophically and theologically current, *Divina Commedia*, for like the natural-cum-spiritual paradigm that Tennyson announces at the outset, the dual methodology or synthesis/antiphony of *In Memoriam* is precisely its continuous formation of an empirical-evangelical congruency on the hardly just contingent (the more ordained than contingent) ground of experience.

   Coordinates of Anglo-American Romanticism, by focusing on the empirical-evangelical dialectic of Emerson's *Nature* (1836), argues that *Nature* "not only arrays idealistic philosophies alongside material ones but also draws sympathetically on the Christian-moral interpretation of life."[6] Thus, while highlighting "the pure empiricism of *Nature*'s materialist perspective," I also drew out "the specifically evangelical quality of its Christian-moral view," and I concluded that *Nature*, "more than exclusively idealistic, if not sometimes almost Christian," employs "empirical-evangelical strategies within its actual-ideal language." I now assert that Emerson's monograph puts forward a unique set of insights on which he bases the ingenious but cohesive variations of his subsequent career, for I now specifically argue that his empirical-evangelical imagination, his unity of opposing

4

perspectives, underlies seven of his other frequently anthologized works, namely, *The American Scholar* (1837), *The Divinity School Address* (1838), *Self-Reliance* (1841), *The Over-Soul* (1841), *The Poet* (1844), *Experience* (1844), and *Fate* (1852). On the empirical end of his scale of criteria are the physical senses, the sense-based reason, the awakened consciousness, the understanding, radical skepticism, inductive method, subject-object inter-action, and "nature-culture coevolution." (I adapt for my purposes the "gene-culture coevolution" of E. O. Wilson.)[7] On the evangelical end of his scale are personal conversion, immediate as well as traditional revelation, the religious affections, practical charity, moral action, the goal of spiri-tual perfection, and millennial expectation. His intensely methodological doctrine of the "spiritual sense," while employing Berkeleyan immateri-alism or the proportional analogy between sense, perception, and ideas, and ideas in the mind of God, emphasizes the physical senses as atten-dants on or preconditions for faith, as though natural experience becomes, or combines with, spiritual experience; this doctrine bridges Emerson's natural/spiritual kinds of experiential grounding. He does not so much mix as unify epistemology and religious methodology, for what seems his violent yoking together of disparate themes is his experientially generated continuum that joins scientific method and rational empiricism to natural and revealed religion. His hope for prosperity, justice, serenity, and joy, accordingly, is at once natural and spiritual.

Thus the laureate and the sage represent not simply their national lit-eratures, respectively, but Anglo-American literature as well. In an age of what Paul Ricoeur calls "the hermeneutics of suspicion"[8] or what might be called the latter-day Marxist-Nietzschean-Freudian academic enterprise of detecting false consciousness, I find that the empirical-evangelical dia-lectic of Anglo-American sensibility holds to the moment-by-moment (or at least momentary) efficacy of a consciousness more trustworthy than illu-sory, more true than false. The Anglo-American sensibility that underlies the main poem of Tennyson's midcareer and the prose of Emerson's prime reflects not only the anxiety but also the mutuality of influence. With more awareness of worldview than of those who create worldviews and hence with no blooming "anxiety of influence,"[9] Tennyson and Emerson are nonetheless descended from the intellectual as well as charismatic Anglo-American diumvirate of Wesley and Edwards. *In Memoriam* is similar to the essays not so much because Tennyson influences Emerson as because this poem and these essays receive empirical-evangelical cross-pollinations on both sides of and in both directions across the Atlantic. If Lockean elements common to the theologies of Wesley and Edwards illuminate certain key resemblances between the literatures of England and the United States during the early modern era, this phenomenon emerges not just because Tennyson and Emerson richly reflect an Anglo-American heritage of philosophical theology but also because that heritage itself is rich.

Insofar as Berkeley, Kant, Cassirer, and Gombrich all said that there is no substance as substrate, no pure given, no absolute immediacy, no innocent eye, and no perception without conception,[10] empirical-evangelical ideas may seem exclusively cross-cultural, rather than at all self-evident or universally true. Not even modern science enjoys any special privilege, according to Nelson Goodman, who argues, "contrary to common sense," that there is no unique, real world that "preexists and is independent of" human mental activity and human symbolic language.[11] In the perennial debate between common sense and philosophy, Jerome Bruner and Carol Fleisher Feldman come down squarely on the side of Goodman, for they conclude that "we are never in contact with some sort of aboriginal reality independent of our own minds or the minds of others who preceded us." According to them, the "intellectual vigor" of modern physics is "precisely its sensitivity in choosing appropriate *theoretical* descriptions to interpret particular observations" (my italics).[12] Even neo-empiricist philosopher of language W. V. Quine grants to Goodman that since "physical theory" is "ninety-nine parts conceptualization to one part observation," nature is a "poor candidate" for the "real" world.[13] Goodman's preaching to the converted, however, courts at least enough opposition to ask "Is not 'belief is all' a belief?" Those steeped in the virulent, if now cliché-ridden, anti-mimeticism that dates back at least to Roland Barthes's *S/Z* (1970)[14] may need to realize that a belief in realism, if not mind-independent reality itself, underlies recent experiments not only in science and mathematics but also in theology, literature, and literary criticism. By briefly rehearsing such experiments, I further introduce my full argument concerning Tennyson and Emerson; I also further clarify and further make explicit my assumptions concerning such philosophical, religious, and literary issues as scientific rhetoric, representation, the pure given, expression, artful versus artless "art," language as the real, the real in language, and, clearly not least, the language of the real.

6

I generally concur, in so doing, with the "reference criticism" of Edouard Morot-Sir. Conceiving of all scientific, religious, moral, and artistic value judgments as positive or negative reference, his work takes the side of modern realists against such idealists as Bergson, Heidegger, Chomsky, and Rorty. Morot-Sir grants priority to reference as the *act* by which signs make sense and by which they exist. "Any linguistic expression," he writes, "belongs to the *experience* of reference" (my italics).[15] While he assumes that reference is the center of human cultural existence, I assume that it is also the center of human natural/biological existence, for my assumptions enforce such belief beyond belief as that philosophical, religious, and literary experiences are grounded in and refer to natural (as well as spiritual) existences beyond culture.

My view that empirical if not evangelical ideas are not just cultural or cross-cultural but even derive, if not from the self-evident and true, then from the evident and perceivable, may be further clarified by a brief overview of the recent, magisterial work by David Locke. Addressing himself to "the problematics of representation," "writing without expression," "the rhetoric of science," "the art of artless prose," "the putative purity of science," and "writing as reality," Locke maintains that science is "not some privileged verbal shorthand that conveys a pure and unvarnished scientific truth" but *writing* that must be *read*. Nothing in the "literary critical armamentarium," he observes, is to be "ruled off-limits" in the study of scientific texts. Representation theory, expression theory, evocation theory, art-object theory, artifact theory (social milieu), and instrumentality theory (signifying systems) are all as applicable to scientific texts as to literary ones. Scientists, historians, philosophers of science, and literary scholars must realize, if they have not already done so, that science is not "the empty vessel into which the content of . . . scientific thought is poured" but "patterns of signs" and "intricate interpenetrating laceworks of codes." "The day of the overarching framework, the prepared ground, the universally acknowledged basis for argument," Locke carefully states, "seems, at least for now, to be behind us," and he adds that "lacking a grand synthesis, one must aim for discrete (and discreet) analysis."[16]

Thus *Science as Writing* contributes at once to the theory of science and to the theory of literature. Locke points to the crucial connection between authorial voice and experimental method and results. He observes that the very artlessness of scientific writing requires great skill. Neither mystical nor antiscientific, he is as much at home with Derrida as with Darwin,

Watson, Crick, Einstein, or Galileo, but Locke does not simply argue that scientific writing is a linguistic or cultural construct. He asks whether scientific language is as "cultural" as literary language and whether it is fictional, narrative, and polysemous. However, he concludes that just as science can be personal without losing any of its importance as knowledge beyond language, so scientific writing can be rhetorical, that is, different from science itself, without losing any of its accessibility to scientific knowledge. Perhaps the most intriguing question Locke raises is, "Does scientific discourse, in any sense, *constitute* the reality scientists investigate in their work?" Scientific arguments, he answers, are properly conceived of as "newly emerging entities that generate their own context, create their own space as they unfold, just as, Einstein says, the masses of the universe generate their own special matrix by virtue of their existence."

Scientists now making similarly objectivist claims appear to think, despite such arguments as those of Goodman and Derrida, that while neither culturally nor naturally predetermined, things are as much naturally as culturally determined. Gerald Edelman's theory of "neural Darwinism," first published in 1978, holds that the meaning of any particular pattern of activity in the brain is "determined by the immediate environmental setting of the organism and the selection of particular circuits over others at any one time." The biological mechanisms of brain- or nerve-mapping creates generalizations constantly " 'revised' or updated by new experiences" so that "new ways of behaving" do not rely exclusively on "the precision of innate rules or programs." [17] Thus nature is "always already" in the affair of culture. Edelman's scientific version of absolute immediacy is matched by Ronald de Sousa's scientifically based argument that such limbic emotions as fear, love, and hate perform a decidedly precultural function in their precise determination of perception, recognition, and recollection. [18] The arch-adaptationist views of E. O. Wilson and Richard Dawkins, though controversial in the field of evolutionary biology, have by no means been rejected; despite Stephen Jay Gould's opposition to the view that not just human intelligence but social organization and the control of nature are "inevitable consequences of long-term natural selection forces," R. C. Lewontin, for one, is by no means entirely certain that such forces do not in fact govern a continuum that indissolubly joins nature to culture and vice versa. [19]

Stephen Toulmin, attacking scientific foundationalism, argues that the

8

Cartesian "quest for certainty" and its "accompanying deification of reason" have betrayed us into "overreaching ourselves"; Toulmin elevates Montaigne's acceptance of "ambiguous surfaces" over Descartes's attempt to dispel ambiguity. Toulmin's "way forward" is the reappropriation of Montaigne's "more modest, skeptical, and tolerant outlook," for Toulmin expects that a subtler, more supple science will play the "game" of "influence, not force," and his notion of influence as both salutary and surprising, both concrete and unpredictable, informs my conviction that the evangelical as well as empirical near-influence on Tennyson and Emerson is both telling and just as subtle as Toulmin might wish it to be.[20]

Another, still bolder "way forward," however, is through Hans Moravec's vision that in the coming "post-biological" age we will not only download our minds into computers and so achieve immortality, but also retrieve minds already dead and thus have to count the cost of never losing anything. "In the present condition," Moravec concludes, "we are uncomfortable halfbreeds, part biology, part culture, with many of our biological traits out of step with the invention of our minds."[21] But he is as far as possible from denying the nature-culture continuum that I assume exists. He envisions a nature become culture, and rather than either lamenting or gloating over "the end of nature,"[22] Moravec defines the coming culture as new nature.

The view recently developed by Wilson Coker and Peter Kivy, that music is representational, has been out of fashion since at least the late eighteenth century, if not before,[23] but their view finds recent counterparts in the various flirtations with a quite un-Cartesian (because more objective than subjective) view of mathematics, namely, that math is "out there" rather than solely "of the mind." Michael Guillen, observing that the history of so-called "self-contained" mathematics is actually an "unruly gate-crashing," points out that the Pythagoreans resented the intrusion of irrational pi, and that although the imaginary numbers of sixteenth- and seventeenth-century mathematics predicted Einstein's universe, they met with universal disdain at the time.[24] According to Guillen, irrational pi and imaginary numbers can and should be thought of as looming up from without. Keith Devlin, after pointing out that it took several thousand hours for a computer at Concordia University, Montreal, to answer "no" to the question whether a finite projective plane of order-10 exists, concludes that mathematics is rapidly turning into an empirical science where "results

9

are only probable to varying degrees," and where proofs are becoming too lengthy and complex for the human mind to "see" their validity.[25] It is hard, accordingly, for Martin Gardner "to comprehend how mathematicians who pretend that mathematical structure is not 'out there,' independent of human minds, can view successive enlargements of the [Mandelbrot-set] and preserve their cultural solipsism."[26]

Religion, etymologically, ties together once more, rebridges the realms of dream and experience, and so figures, perhaps even more prominently than empiricism does, in my neo-mimetic, neo-realist peregrinations. "Religious experience," in Wayne Proudfoot's view, while "furtive" and "embroidered" according to "prior conceptual commitments," remains a "lived" construct.[27] Something of this "lived" quality comes across in John J. McDermott's religious-experiential, neo–William Jamesian notion of life as a journey made by transients: "The meaning of a transient's journey is precisely that: the journey itself. . . . We should make our journey ever alert to our surroundings and to every perceivable sensorial nuance. Our journey is a kaleidoscope of alternating experiences, mishap, setback, celebrations, and eye-openers, all undergone on the *qui vive*."[28] D. G. Leahy, in what Thomas J. J. Altizer grandly refers to as a neo-Edwardsean experiential understanding, speaks of "the *material* fulfillment prescinding the matter/form distinction in the form of unreserved anticipation."[29] By way of thus proclaiming the "death" of the Death of God, Leahy concludes that "Time" is for the first time *"absolutely* the place": "The temporality of time is The Place which we, embodying, intimately comprehend as the pure 'at the disposal of another.' *Qui vive?* The person who begins to fabricate an *essentially* new world." Leahy's vocabulary, to say the least, is boldly if not refreshingly essentialist/foundationalist.

Neither scientific-mathematical research nor academic theology, then, is anywhere near abandoning the "inexpugnable realism" that may indeed be "real" enough, as A. O. Lovejoy claimed, to define human nature.[30] Edelman, de Sousa, Wilson, Dawkins, Lewontin, Toulmin, and Moravec on the scientific side, and McDermott, Altizer, and Leahy on the religious side, resist (when one takes them all together) what Stephen Prickett (as though he takes both sides at once) calls "the reductiveness of our modern categories [of theology and science]."[31] Although both categories often insist that experience is *"either* miraculous *or* natural," Prickett advances his biblical as well as Romantic view of experience as *both* miraculous *and* natural. The Bible, he argues (contra Robert Alter and Northrop Frye), is realistic fiction and history, and not just realistic fiction. I would add that Romantic experience, as it is represented by Tennyson and Emerson, is both natural and miraculous because it is both empirical and evangelical.

Consider, accordingly, the third side of my equilateral triangle: literature. The "disengaged, if not sterile" stances of Borges, Nabokov, and Calvino, and their "dry cerebral fondness" for ideas, may well be comprehended according to the presuppositions of continuing, if only residual, Cartesian mathematics, but Italo Calvino's *Cosmicomics* and *Mr. Palomar*, at least, include the experiential-realistic in what only *seems* the mathematically separate and ideal.[32] Moreover, Douglas Hofstadter and Daniel Dennett relate the seemingly dry, seemingly almost mathematical frame of the Modernist/Postmodernist mind to ideas we actually "live by or need to live by"; Hofstadter and Dennett recognize that Calvino, despite his apparently ascetic formalism, not only shows what it means to "share a universe" with dinosaurs and volcanoes, but also "clarifies the features of modern life."[33]

Patrick Suskind's *Perfume* and *The Pigeon* find "freshness of angle" not in "susceptibility to fabulation" but in the "fresh territory" of "the microscopic"; Emmanuel Carrère's *The Moustache* focuses simply on cutting a moustache off; and a new edition of Raymond Queneau's *Pierrot mon ami* makes nothing happen except what John Updike calls the novel's now especially fashionable but still experience-oriented, "banality and cheerful nullity of experience."[34] Updike distinguishes between this French fiction (Carrère, Queneau) with its "mental states" and "life of the mind" and this German fiction (Suskind) with its "microscopic observation," but each of these novels suggests that any given culture refers to something extracultural. Thus recent novels of even the non-Anglo-American world may be said to flaunt once more a realism so microscopic, yet robust, as to be precisely empirical.

The Mezzanine by the American Nicholson Baker preserves, perhaps less unexpectedly, a "core of jubilation" in the "closely observed" worlds of the hero's lunch break, his purchase of shoelaces, and his escalator ride back to work.[35] This novel, in which Baker revives a sense of experience as almost preverbal, is deservedly highly touted.[36] A single thought that comes to the hero "all at once" and "at the foot of the up escalator" is "only the latest in a fairly long sequence" of "inarticulable experiences" so palpably real as to be worthy of his every effort at their articulation.

American poetry is especially well represented for my purposes by the example of William Logan. To be sure, sometimes even critics otherwise admiring of Logan's poetry raise objections similar to those of Dennett and Hofstadter to the works of Calvino, Nabokov, and Borges; G. E. Murray, for example, complains that everything in Logan's poetry "is seen and felt from a distance: experience, location, imagination, even intimacies. It is as if emotion is traded for elegance of style and expression."[37] Thomas Swiss, observing that Logan's too "formally detached" and too "coolly elegant" poems sometimes read more like "literature," adds that their "impenetrable" syntax and "formal" diction sometimes make them hide from "even the most patient reader." All this, however, is a direction in which one might well want to err; the objections to Logan's work redound, finally, to his credit. Although Richard Tillinghast notes that Logan's "urge to conceal" wins out over his "desire to reveal or communicate," Tillinghast concludes that this is as it should be, "since concealment provides mystery and compels fascination," and since concealment is often "the only way to be true to recalcitrant or complex material." Even Murray praises Logan for his "terse and tense structures . . . attempting to comprehend complex physical and emotional interweavings of events, place, and person." Despite his youth, then, Logan's reputation is secure. (In 1989 he received the Peter I. B. Lavan Younger Poets Award from the Academy of American Poets.)

Thomas Swiss's praise of Logan's ability to "move from a striking observation into a poem of wisdom and great feeling" is especially pertinent to my interest in the ideally if not evangelically empirical dimension of Anglo-American literature, for the poems of Logan's fourth volume, *Vain Empires* (1994), approach being both "empirical" and immediately revelatory. "Histoires des Mentalité" proceeds from precise observation to startling revelation:

> Our milk-white daughters dance like social pawns,
> or prawns, in the grand ballroom of the seabed
> where hammerheaded males requite the last *faux pas*.
> There's no escape from sensibility.[38]

"The Shadow-Line," at once lapidary and pellucid, is especially pointed:

> We used to spend summer nights listening to jazz—
> rude subtleties of the horn! Now we discuss

surrendering to what will happen to us,
or ought to, or perhaps already has.

"Florida Pest Control," celebrating Logan's arrival in Florida, encapsulates his secure combination of clarity and surprise:

The houses turn to dust
Beneath us, gnawed by termite,
beetle, or the fear of God.
Only the last can't be exterminated.

This, if not "evangelical," is certainly tough-minded, empirical.

Logan's insights into the poetry of W. D. Snodgrass are especially shrewd (Logan received from the National Book Critics Circle the 1988 Citation for Excellence in Reviewing) and are especially pertinent to my view of Tennyson and Emerson. Hear, first, these lines from Snodgrass's "Song":

Observe the cautious toadstools
still on the lawn today
though they grow over-evening;
sun shrinks them away.

Pale and proper and rootless,
they righteously extort
their living from the living.
I have been their sort.

Logan speaks of "two movements" in Snodgrass's poetry, first "from ignorance outward to knowledge and experience," and second "from observation inward to revelation." [39] This insight constitutes a small essay on and a felicitous axiom regarding Snodgrass's combination of the physical and the moral senses. Logan's axiom is apt, too, for the empirical-evangelical progressions/syntheses that I will trace in works by Tennyson and Emerson.

Samuel F. Pickering, Jr.'s scholarly criticism of Anglo-American children's books both reflects his belief in realism and sharply parallels my representationalist-referentialist assumptions concerning and my empirical-evangelical approach to Romanticism. His *Moral Instruction and Fiction for Children, 1749–1820* (1993) assumes "the importance and presence of Locke," for Pickering reads early children's fiction "almost as educational texts." "In eighteenth-century children's books," he observes, "education determined the progress children made, and success was not a reward for virtue but for a good education of which virtue was simply an important part." Thus George Burder's *Early Piety* (1806) combines the serious, Bunyanesque allegory of the evangelicals with the Lockean appeal to children's delight in change and variety. In early children's fiction it is better to be poor or in a large family than rich or an only child, and Pickering thinks that this emphasis is due to the writers' Lockean conviction that an inauspicious beginning drives home the advantages or necessity of education. Richard Johnson, in *The Foundling; or, The History of Lucius Stanhope* (1798), translates the spirit of Henry Fielding's *Tom Jones* into the educational mood of the late eighteenth and early nineteenth centuries, for such foundlings as Henry in *Henry; or, The Foundling* (1801) become truly noble by being forced to make their way. "Stories which turned loss into gain," Pickering concludes, "can be seen as secularized versions of those evangelical or godly books which celebrated the pious deaths of righteous children." [40]

Despite the evangelical ambivalence about novels, a 1768 children's version of Samuel Richardson's *Pamela* was very popular. "*Pamela*," Pickering's chapter five, explores this popularity. Pamela is a middle-class girl who gives her middle-class values to the aristocratic Mr. B., who, in turn, gives a copy of "Mr. *Locke*'s Treatise on Education" to Pamela after the birth of their son, Billy. Perhaps the most famous of the Pamela figures is Little Goody Two-Shoes, the title of whose story—*The History of Little Goody Two-Shoes: With the Means by Which she acquired her Learning and Wisdom, and in consequence thereof her Estate*—reflects the self-making, Lockean assumptions that underlie her experience. The evangelical Hannah More lamented the fact that too many females tried to imitate the aristocracy, and Pamela, More thought, provided evangelical women with both a model and an antidote. Although Miss Johnson, in *The Mother's Gift* (1787), is not explicitly indebted to *Pamela*, she, like Pamela, is protected by a combination of early education and religion. Like Pamela, too, Miss Johnson finally captivates "a lover, who was less charmed with her person than enslaved by her mind." There are even parallels between Pamela and "godly books in which children saved adults," for example, *The Infant Preacher* (1818) and *The Young Cottager* (1815), for such divine children find a secular counterpart in Pamela's saving of Mr. B.

Locke, while giving doctrinaire religion short shrift, taught practical morality in general and honesty in particular; similarly, early children's books emphasized truthfulness, for example, *Martin and James; or, The Reward of Integrity* (1794) or *The Entertaining History of Honest Peter* (1794). Thus educational progress and moral growth or what one of the stories called "A Knowledge of Letters" and "Virtue" usually went hand in hand. As far back as Dante's *Inferno*, lying was the worst of sins, but the combination of truthfulness with education was a peculiarly Lockean and hence— in Pickering's view—a peculiarly eighteenth- and early nineteenth-century idea for children. "Telling the truth," Pickering concludes, matches "the sturdy individualism that an education based upon Locke seemed to promise." Thus evangelical editions of Lord Chesterfield's letters to his son form an especially interesting focus of *Moral Instruction and Fiction for Children*.

"Servants and Inferiors," Pickering's chapter six, explores the implications of Locke's teaching that the child who treats servants poorly is probably, and properly, destined to unhappiness, failure, and an early death. This teaching is especially prevalent throughout *The History of Tommy Playlove and Jacky Lovebook* (1793). With particular reference to Negro servants, the evangelical Mrs. Pilkington in her antislavery fiction, *A Reward for Attentive Studies; or, Moral and Entertaining Stories* (1800), boldly updates the teaching. (*A Reward for Attentive Studies* anticipates *Uncle Tom's Cabin* by the evangelical Harriet Beecher Stowe.) Perhaps the best book on servants and inferiors is *The Servant's Friend* (1787) by the evangelical Sarah Trimmer. John Newbery, in his introductions to and advertisements of children's books, quotes Locke as an authority on children; accordingly, in Newbery's *The Easter-Gift; or, The Way to be Very Good* (1770), he specifically incorporates Locke's suggestions concerning esteem and grace and especially seeks to teach children good behavior toward servants.

An especially empirical-evangelical theme of Pickering's book is his application of the Lockean-educational context to the ongoing tradition of Christian emblems. The relatively cautious nature of emblem-writing is explicitly, persuasively linked to Locke's doctrine of the tabula rasa, for Appendix A shows how such emblems as the shipwreck, the fight, the garden, the maze, the mirror, and the telescope develop educational as well as moral lessons in early children's fiction.

As for empirical-evangelical applications of Pickering's study to Romanticism, I suspect that *Hamlain; or, the Hermit of the Beach* (1799) pertains to the didacticism, as well as to the exoticism, of Coleridge's *Rime of the*

Ancient Mariner. "If education is a school to fit us for life," writes Hannah More, then life is "a school to fit us for eternity," and one thinks in this connection of Keats's letter on life as a "Vale of Soul-making." According to Jane West, little girls, never members of Parliament, are "legislators in the most important sense of the word," and there are similarly expansive, perhaps even similarly gender-related implications in the definition by the early male feminist (as well as the Romantic poet) Percy Shelley of poets as "unacknowledged legislators of the world." The miraculously nonmorbid lightness of little Elizabeth Villiers's sense of her mother's continuing presence in the letters on her mother's tombstone (see Charles and Mary Lamb's *Mrs. Leicester's School*) match the naturalness with which the girl in Wordsworth's "We Are Seven" continues to "play" with her brother and sister on their tombstones. And finally, just as Pamela saves Mr. B., and just as the divine child in *The Infant Preacher* saves adults, so Madeline, in Keats's "The Eve of St. Agnes," effects the curiously secular/religious conversion of Porphyro, "a famished pilgrim—saved by miracle" (line 339).

Early children's literature, in short, emerges as an important, empirical-evangelical gloss on British Romantic poetry. If the wisdom of the heart is represented by Wordsworth, Blake, and Dickens, and if the wisdom of the head is represented by Sarah Trimmer and Hannah More, Pickering makes no such simple classification. He finds imagination in stories that warn of the dangers of imagination. He counters critics who "celebrate the imagination" in texts that are "not nearly so imaginative" as works by the Trimmers and Mores. He concludes, with refreshing panache, that their wandering plots and marvelously drawn worlds appeal to the imagination more than does the exoticism of the fairy tale, which, after all, may "puzzle and bore rather than awaken."

Pickering aptly calls his book "a covert celebration of imaginative instruction." And, indeed, imaginative instruction may be a fair shorthand way of labeling Anglo-American Romanticism as it is empirically evangelically understandable. My understanding of that Romanticism, at any rate, like Pickering's deep understanding of children's books, assumes the fruitful coexistence of an extensive body of objective truth with the mind-soul. We have had ample study of Locke's political importance, for example, Jay Fliegelman's *Prodigals and Pilgrims* (1982), which explores the implications of Locke's *Two Treatises on Government* (1690) for the growing antiauthoritarianism in eighteenth-century England and America.[41] My own *Locke, Wesley, and the Method of English Romanticism* explores the implications of

Locke's epistemology in *An Essay concerning Human Understanding* (1690), for religious as well as intellectual and literary history. Pickering's *Moral Instruction and Fiction for Children, 1749–1820* is perhaps the single best source for the literary and general importance of Locke's *Some Thoughts concerning Education* (1693). In combination with Pickering's *John Locke and Children's Books in Eighteenth-Century England* (1981),[42] *Moral Instruction and Fiction for Children* suggests very powerfully that finding the ideas of Locke on many pages of late eighteenth- and early nineteenth-century literature— adult's as well as children's—does not exclude but signals the discovery of evangelical religion on those same pages.

Pickering rightly views a line from Wordsworth's "My Heart Leaps Up" (1807)—"The Child is Father of the Man"—as the quintessential poetic version of Locke's doctrine of the tabula rasa. Thus Pickering's emphasis is more Lockean than evangelical. My own view of this line is that it is the quintessential poetic version of the empirical-evangelical rise and progress of the soul. The Lockean-evangelical origin of Anglo-American children's literature prepares for and matures into the empirical-evangelical vision of Anglo-American Romanticism.

In my stance as an intellectual-historian/critic I not only admit to the "inexpugnable realism" that A. O. Lovejoy finds in each human being but, in line with the least that one should learn from the various Postmodernist "gurus of *franglais,*"[43] I play with that realism to the point of being serio-ludic. To the extent that my readings of Tennyson and Emerson are plausible, however, there may well be, with apologies to Berkeley, Kant, Cassirer, and Gombrich, a substance as substrate, an innocent eye, an absolute immediacy, a pure given, and a perception before both conception and words.

Language, indeed, though hardly completely derivative from the external world, may be more dependent on experience than innately determined. Russ Rymer, in his state of the art discussion of the nature-nurture question as it bears on the development of language in individuals, ranges over the linguistic views of Descartes, Locke, Condillac, Chomsky, Catherine Snow, and Lila Gleitman, and concludes with special reference to Victor the Wild Boy of Aveyron and Genie the Closet Girl of Los Angeles by stating that

the organization of our brain is as genetically ordained and as automatic as breathing, but, like breathing, it is initiated by the slap of a midwife, and the midwife is grammar. . . . Language is a logic system so organically tuned to the mechanism of the human brain that it actually triggers the brain's growth. What are human beings? Beings whose brain development is responsive to and dependent on the receipt at the proper time of even a small sample of language.[44]

Neo-empiricist Quine understands rationalist-linguist Chomsky thus: "Chomsky, for his part, argues that we are born with genetically determined 'mental organs,' among them one specialized in language that contains specific 'rule systems' that cannot be derived from the data of experience by 'induction,' 'abstraction,' 'analogy,' or 'generalization,' in any reasonable sense of these terms, any more than the basic structure of the mammalian visual system is inductively derived from experience." Quine answers that "a child initially learns sentences such as 'It's raining' and 'This is red' by conditioning, unaided by auxiliary sentences, and then achieves higher levels of linguistic competence by analogies (from the apparent role of a word in one sentence he guesses its role in another) and by noting how sentences are related to each other (he discovers that people assent to a sentence of some one form only contingently upon assenting to a corresponding sentence of some related form)."[45] "Cut the pie any way you like," declares mathematician Hilary Putnam, "and meanings just *ain't* in the head!"[46] Words may not be so much "of the mind" as locally and flexibly of the brain.

Biologist Gerald Edelman, albeit without addressing the issue of language, implies that there is topologically biological cause for belief in the near influence of nature or body on culture or mind: "The present location of a cell and its present activity provide most of the information on what it is to do next. It is this contingency on position that makes biology into 'topobiology.'" Biologist R. C. Lewontin elaborates: Edelman's "strategy is to push the notion of local positional information to its extreme by supposing that essentially all the action is at the level of small collectives of cells acting as a group on their immediate neighbors. There are no . . . large-scale fields in which the cells are moving. Central planning has been replaced by local initiatives in a kind of perestroika of the protoplasm."[47] Similarly, within the "organism" that I call "eighteenth- and nineteenth-century Anglo-American sensibility" is the good possibility of a near, an empirical-evangelical, influence that proceeds from natural-cultural worlds—through the meanings of words—to words themselves and their resonant effects.

Words, so defended, are potentially salutary, because sufficiently grounded. Vaclav Havel's words—regardless of whether and how much events can lead to words—preceded events, but Havel knows that words determine events for ill as well as good, for his especially striking emphasis on ominous implications within "in the beginning was the word" recognizes that while "Liberty, Equality, Fraternity" brought about the halcyon early days of the French Revolution, the slogan preceded the only "freedom" remaining by the mid-1790s, namely, whether to wear an open or a closed shirt at one's own guillotining.[48] Slogan words, despite all the optimism that socialism had, have come to be used as blunt instruments against enemies of the state, and Havel realizes that an ominous ambiguity hovered over even perestroika. According to Melvyn New, the reader's prime obligation is to separate "lies" of art from lies of power; "power," New adds, "will often speak with the voice of art—is, indeed, art's best mimic, and worst."[49] Power is criticism's "best mimic, and worst," too, for terms that delight me for their evident ground-capacity for lively mind and living faith, namely, *experience, nature, prophecy, committed,* and *Zeitgeist,* served Hitler's cosmic death wish,[50] and these terms are so far from necessarily proceeding from some ontological base to some good effect as to be loose cannons of and vertiginously ungrounded instigators of harm in the realm of nonverbal event. The warnings of Havel and New carry disturbing implications for the relation between history and words, but Havel never loses faith in the efficacious arc from preverbal origins to verbal effects, for he traces his own words back to his as yet unarticulated but authentic experience in jail, which forged his sure to be perennially influential as well as simply timeless letters to his wife.[51] *Experience, nature, prophecy, committed,* and *Zeitgeist* can be efficacious insofar as these words retain their ground-capacity for a lively mind, if not a living faith. When they are more than culturally grounded, they do not necessarily raise the specter of ethnocentrism.

This study of the eighteenth and nineteenth centuries considers "the victors, the charismatic, and accomplished" on the one hand, and what Walter Benjamin, on the other, calls—without Nietzsche's implication of "slave morality"—"the defeated, the humbled, and the powerless."[52] The latter are implied here by the rising tide of largely Christian as well as often intellectual common readers of not only bonnes lettres by Wesley and Edwards but, perhaps more importantly, the belletristic but hardly decadent and even still broadly appealing texts of Tennyson and Emerson. In the view of E. D. Hirsch, Jr., bonnes lettres describe the "grand, broad, and noble conception" of literature that connotes "best thoughts" more than "best manner";[53] this conception adds the hymns of Isaac Watts to the lyrics of Wordsworth and the fiction of Harriet Beecher Stowe to that of Melville. Belles lettres, in Hirsch's view, describe "the narrower, more decadent conception" of literature. "The victors, the charismatic, and accomplished" are embodied here not only by Tennyson and Emerson but also by Wesley and Edwards. Since I have already staked out the common ground of the latter pair, I recapitulate their mutual argument more than I requote it.

Since bonnes lettres of the eighteenth century may seem to play John the Baptist to nineteenth-century belles lettres, I may seem to harbor the naive progressivism of a Whiggish history. "The idea of progress" is "so unfashionable at present as to seem almost laughable."[54] Robert Nisbet and Peter Medawar, however, have carefully defended it.[55] Historians as otherwise diverse as Gertrude Himmelfarb and Lawrence Stone regard as "unfortunate" the principle that "progress" is automatically ruled inferior to the arguments of social-anthropological and demographic-Cliometric histories, for these histories, too, are based on nothing more, if also nothing less, than the given historian's beliefs.[56] Developmental diachronicity if not progress is implied by the learned detail and impressive scope with which scholars still argue that Freudian psychology emerged from Lockean-intellectual trends.[57] I plead innocent to any charges of Whiggish excess. Just as the works of geological science "need not be linked in a continuum of progress . . . but can be spread across a conceptual space" as each geologist "reverts to and complicates" the "eternal metaphors" of "time's arrow" and "time's cycle,"[58] so writings by Wesley, Edwards, Tennyson, and Emerson do not so much "improve" from Wesley and Edwards through Tennyson and Emerson as revert to, and complicate, the perennial themes that spread across the conceptual but also experiential, and indeed geographical, space of the philosophical theology in which I am interested. Belletristic literature that not only comes after but also follows from bonnes lettres may refine, but does not necessarily deepen, the "bonnelettristic" heritage.

While neither empiricism nor evangelicalism is confined to either England or the United States, each method is so characteristic of both countries as to occur simultaneously as well as alternately during the Anglo-American century from 1750 to 1850. "For the [American] middle class with upward longings," sneers Paul Fussell, "the great class totem is 'Mother England,'"[59] and inasmuch as two-thirds of my philosophically theological triangle of Locke, Wesley, and Edwards is British, and inasmuch, too, as the British Locke antedates or enjoys "prior"-ity over the Anglo-American nexus of Wesley and Edwards, I may seem to subordinate American to British sensibility. I share something of German Arciniegas's sense of "A History of the New World in Reverse," however; for just as Arciniegas brings out the hopeful and decisive transformations of Europe by North and South America,[60] so Emerson's contribution to England was philosophically and religiously, as well as politically, more positive than any such contribution made by Tennyson to the United States.[61] Although Locke and Wesley exercised enormous influence on America, Edwards influenced Wesley more than the other way round.[62] However, I do not wish to imply that things American are "better" than things British, for I am not saying so much about the categories "British" and "American" as about the heading "Anglo-American." The "spiritual sense" of the Anglo-American world—that is, its empiricism in combination with its evangelicalism—illustrates that things British and things American coordinate as much as vie with each other.

Daniel Jenkins, in his qualification of Donald Davie's definition of the "Protestant Calvinist aesthetic" as "simplicity, sobriety, and measure," argues (apropos of my interest in evangelicalism in combination with Romanticism) that, in order to achieve needed tension or *contrapposto* in the theological understanding of literary history, one should cultivate the open-endedness, the exhilaration, and the complexity of not only the Romantics but also the Arminian evangelicals.[63] Moreover, in order to achieve *contrapposto* in the *philosophically* theological understanding of literary history, one should cultivate the all but philosophical sophistication of both the Romantics and the Arminian evangelicals.

Davie, replying to Jenkins, graciously concedes that the Arminian Wesleys, brothers John and Charles, "represented originally a just and necessary protest against the inertness that had settled on English Protestantism by the time Watts died." Davie cannot bring himself, however, to do other than blame both the Wesleyan evangelicals and the Romantics for their "pretense of extemporizing in a hortatory tone." Why a Dissenting critic like Davie would necessarily object to hortatory tone is not clear, for although the Wesleys never became Nonconformists, the Methodists did in 1795. The collective tone of not only Wesley and the Calvinist Edwards but also such Anglo-American Late Romantics as Tennyson and Emerson is indeed sometimes hortatory, but it is rarely extemporizing or pretentious. These belletristic figures of Anglo-American literature are so firmly grounded in a broad, inclusive, and flexible concept of experience that they are empirically philosophical as well as evangelically theological.

In line with such religious-historical approaches to Romanticism as those of Stephen Prickett, Bernard M. G. Reardon, and Robert M. Ryan,[64] I argue that the Late Romantic struggle shared by Tennyson and Emerson does not ruin or deconstruct the sacred truths[65] so much as reconstruct or reconstitute them by all experiential means, whether religious or philosophical. Romantic authors, more than authors in general, struggle against religious beliefs as well as against precursors, but Denis Donoghue points out that even the most "successful" of such struggles may issue in pyrrhic victories.[66] I reaffirm my previous affirmation of the philosophical-religious optimism of Romantic literature. Perhaps still practicable is a hermeneutics of discovery.

Finally, most germane to my emphasis on the broadly experiential basis of Anglo-American Romanticism is the distinguished scholarship of Robert Langbaum, who, exploring whether Romanticism extends into the twentieth century, proposes that the phenomenon of Romanticism is not so much a straightforwardly transcendentalizing/spiritualizing reaction against Enlightenment rationality, common sense, and this-worldliness, as it is an evolutionary development of some fundamental epistemological concerns in Enlightenment thought.[67] Romantic writers, like their Enlightenment forebears stretching back to Locke and beyond, cultivate a powerfully skeptical strain in their thinking. They worry about how we know things and how we know that we know them.[68] They are especially inclined to address the problem by applying tests of experience, placing a primary value on empirical evidence at the same time that they half-distrust sensory experience. "We now look downward for the Word," Langbaum states, "downward to the origins of the earth and the cosmos, to our own origins in single-cell organisms hardly distinguishable from inanimate matter, to the unconscious motives that are the real origins of our 'noble' endeavors." This reversal of the "traditional diagram" by which "people looked upward for the truth" has led in literature to "an imagery of regression that has had the effect of renewing spirituality through intensification rather than elevation—a way convincing to modern sensibilities." Robert Browning, for example, believes that "the error of the Darwinians" is that they "think that their knowledge of man's low origins negates his spirituality," but Browning and other Romantics dissolve "the distinction between high and low." [69] Although I follow the direction in Romantic studies thus signaled by Langbaum, I try to broaden the idea of experience he makes central to such studies, for I suspect that the arc of experiential vision from Romantic to Modern retains an at least virtually transcendentalizing/spiritualizing tendency.

I argue, specifically, that the Late Romantic vision shared by Tennyson and Emerson preserves that tendency, along with the post-Enlightenment empiricizing tendency of Romanticism. The comprehensively epistemological dialectic bequeathed by the Wesleyan-Edwardsean Religious Enlightenment to this premier diptych of Anglo-American letters makes its Romanticism at once empiricizing and transcendentalizing/spiritualizing. Experience, according to *In Memoriam* and the prose of Emerson's prime, includes aspirations of imagination as well as workings of consciousness and the unconscious. Thus identification of low "origins" with "spirituality" is of a piece with looking "upward for the truth."

Anglo-American Antiphony: The Late Romanticism of Tennyson and Emerson concludes my tetralogical reaffirmation of the optimism of Romantic literature. My ongoing fascination with the triangle of philosophy, religion, and literature, a case study in the sociology of ideas, focuses on the experiential common ground between, and hence the playful interaction of, empiricism and evangelicalism. The first part of this book, "The Method of *In Memoriam*," will equal the length if not the scope of the second part, "The Method of Emerson's Prose." Each part denominates as Late Romantic the period that extends from about 1830 to 1850. As quintessential spokespersons for middle-brow culture in their age, Tennyson and Emerson were read transatlantically. The poetry of the one and the prose of the other derive in large measure from their shared, "bi-native" tradition of empirical-evangelical prose; the creative tension between the rational empiricism of Locke and the Arminian/Calvinist evangelicalisms of Wesley

23

and Edwards informs, even unconsciously, Anglo-American Romanticism. If the empirical-evangelical arc of method that sparks the most indigenous coordinates of this Romanticism should short-circuit in such pairings of British with American authors as Robert Browning with Emily Dickinson and George Eliot with Herman Melville, that is matter for another treatise. Here I turn my attention to two relatively early nineteenth-century authors who, however great their struggles over blindness and insight, remain insufficiently self-conscious to sustain irony because they are both desirous and expectant of truth and grace and joy.

Exposition the First

THE METHOD OF *IN MEMORIAM*

ONE

Introit

Despite (or because of) the tension and opposition between empiricism and evangelicalism, the one does not exist without the other's being actively present or dynamically near. With regard to art in particular as well as to culture in general, Friedrich von Schiller argues that *Stofftrieb* (material-drive) and *Formtrieb* (form-drive) cooperate to produce *Spieltrieb* (play-drive). Schiller concludes that "we have now been led to the notion of a reciprocal action between the two drives, reciprocal action of such a kind that the activity of the one gives rise to, and sets limits to, the activity of the other, and in which each in itself achieves its highest manifestation precisely by reason of the other being active."[1] The dialectic/"reciprocal action" of empiricism and evangelicalism constitutes the *Spieltrieb* of *In Memoriam*. If the play of this elegy is not exactly seriousness or if the seriousness of the poem is not play, the yoke of the poem, nevertheless, is easy and the burden of the poem is light. *In Memoriam* regards bicultural philosophy/faith as both fully alternating and fully interdependent.

My approach differs from the perhaps too serious, perhaps too unplayful arguments for Tennyson's art as unified: "time and again," declares John R. Reed, Tennyson "exploited" a single moral design;[2] his "awareness of doom," avers William R. Brashear, unequivocally integrates his work;[3] and Tennyson, according to Ward Hellstrom, "consistently endorsed the choice of life over death and involvement over isolation."[4] While I, too, regard Tennyson's art as sufficiently self-consistent, or at any rate well integrated, I seek, nevertheless, to cultivate nuances and to incorporate them into my own synoptic approach to *In Memoriam*, for I draw out the poem's synthesizing, antiphonal power of empiricism-cum-evangelicalism.

My approach differs, too, from the widespread insistence that *In Memoriam* exemplifies "either/or" logic and procedure. W. David Shaw, perceiving that Tennyson either argues through skepticism or affirms through images, does not appear to conceive how or that he might do both,[5] and James R. Kincaid, contending that "the interplay and conflict of the comic and ironic modes" form "the center of Tennyson's major poetry," emphasizes conflict more than interplay. Kincaid, specifically, regards the "dualism" of *In Memoriam* not as a stand-off so much as a hierarchy in which "the values of domestic comedy, of friendship and unremarkable love, are substantiated and *win out over* the arguments of philosophy, science, personal grief, and the ironic perspective" (my italics). Thus "irony's tenuous mixture becomes comedy's pure and triumphant assertion of continuity."[6] This schema leaves little room for even the most tenuous mixture of comic irony or ironic comedy.

A. Dwight Culler, arguing that "Supposed Confessions of a Second-Rate Sensitive Mind Not in Unity with Itself" (1830) is the formative work of Tennyson's career, reads the dramatic monologue as "the portrait of a mind vacillating between two extremes, the intellectual pride of the rationalist and the evangelical's conviction of sin."[7] Notwithstanding the nature of the poem as a dramatic monologue, it boasts a memorable title; the "either/or" logic of this speaker, however, swinging indecisively from "ultrarationalism" to "ultrafidianism," is precisely what *In Memoriam* succeeds in escaping. This elegy, the high watermark of Tennyson's career, envisions a more than predictably antipodal, because strangely whole, encounter between sense-based reason on the one hand and spiritual sense on the other.

Tennyson seeks to reconcile empiricism with evangelicalism. Friedrich Nietzsche, regarding Greek tragedy in particular as well as Greek culture in general, argues that "art owes its continuous evolution to the Apollonian-Dionysiac duality, even as the propagation of the species depends on the duality of the sexes, their constant conflicts and periodic acts of reconciliation." Nietzsche concludes that "the two creative tendencies developed alongside one another, usually in fierce opposition, each by its taunts forcing the other to more energetic production, both perpetuating in a discordant concord that agon which the term *art* but feebly denominates: until at last, by the thaumaturgy of a Hellenic act of will, the pair accepted the yoke of marriage and, in this condition, begot Attic tragedy, which exhibits the salient features of both parents."[8] Nietzsche's tough-minded marriage-metaphor applies to *The Marriage of Heaven and Hell* (1793) by William Blake, to Blake's "sustained tension, without victory or suppression, of co-present oppositions,"[9] and Tennyson's brand of English-language Romanticism similarly maintains "tension, without victory or suppression" between the "co-present oppositions," the strange simultaneities, of empiricism-cum-evangelicalism. Although *In Memoriam* does not apply the metaphor of marriage to the empirical-evangelical relationship, the poem does apply the idea of marriage to that relationship, for Tennyson's reconciliation of these two methodologies envisions a dual methodology.

Perhaps more like Nietzsche's concept than like Blake's, Tennyson's implicit marriage relationship closes in on and is close to not so much a tragic dualism of copresent oppositions as a sweet comedic harmony between them. Thus the interrelation in *In Memoriam* between Dionysiac (if not Apollonian) empiricism and Apollonian (if not Dionysiac) evangelicalism is not only a conflict—a "fierce opposition," a discord, and a yoke—but also a propagation, a reconciliation, a creation, and a concord. Although the tough and tender Romanticism in *In Memoriam*, its synthesis/antiphony of empiricism with evangelicalism, does not fudge the differences between philosophy and faith, neither does that Late Romanticism hedge these "disciplines" about with difficulties. Since many individual sections of *In Memoriam* play on rather than play up the differences between experiential philosophy and experiential faith, Tennyson's poetic argument destroys distinctions between philosophy and faith.

Critics, of course, discern certain Tennysonian dialectics. Valerie Pitt, arguing that "there is in his work a true dialectic, a tension between the insight of the solitary and the sense of the common and the social," adds that "an awareness of the romantic wastes, the fluent and unshaped, appears through, and sometimes is imposed upon, an intense realisation of normal activity and order."[10] Demonstrating that *In Memoriam* "has a dynamic unity of thought and feeling dependent on a dialectical principle of growth and of a single consciousness," Robert Langbaum observes that "the backtrackings, the changes of mood, style and levels of intensity, even the apparent contradictions, are all signs of the genuineness of the experience and coherent aspects of a single developing consciousness."[11] Since *In Memoriam* is a poem of "syntheses," declares Robert Pattison, "it is not surprising to find pagan and Christian myth," specifically the myths of Apuleius and St. John, "united in a single sense." [12] Daniel Albright, against the critical grain of finding dialectic in *In Memoriam*, finds a *failed* dialectic therein:

> Tennyson tried to unite two incompatible poetics, one governed by a heavenly muse who disdained the homely details of life, the other governed by an earthly muse suspicious of the ideal and vague; and because he could not effect a full synthesis, a certain lingering stress can be found everywhere in his work, a headache of inaccurate focus. . . . In *In Memoriam* the elegist is pulled in opposing directions by two muses, Melpomene and Urania, the muse of the commonplace and the muse of the sublime—but, strangely, he is not sure which is the more valuable to him. [13]

I argue that *In Memoriam* effects a full synthesis between Tennyson's earthly muse and his heavenly one. His earthly inspiration of empiricism meets the heavenly afflatus of his evangelicalism on the experiential ground of his commonplace-sublime vision. Valuing both muses equally, Tennyson relates his earthly/philosophical muse to his heavenly/theological muse in just the same way that Wesley and Edwards relate their empiricism to their evangelicalism, that is, by joining the distinctively experiential thesis of their shared Lockean philosophy to the distinctively experiential antithesis of their shared revival faith.

The empirically evangelical synthesis mutually developed by Wesley and Edwards specifically adumbrates the philosophically theologically compositional, empirically evangelically composite *In Memoriam*. As background to this composite, the Cambridge Apostles mixed empirical philosophy with experiential faith; "apostles," after all, is an evangelical name, and these 1820s descendants of Wesley's Holy Club at Oxford during the 1730s not only studied "Descartes and Kant" and "read their Hobbes, Locke, Berkeley, Butler, Hume, [and] Bentham" but also "discussed" such theological and moral questions as "the Origin of Evil," "the Derivation of Moral Sentiments," and, clearly not least (from the evangelical point of view), "Prayer and the Personality of God." [14] Tennyson's interest in proto-evolutionary science long antedated even his relatively early reading of Charles Lyell's all but full-blown evolutionary *Principles of Geology* in 1837. "My father," reported Hallam Tennyson in 1898, "seems to have propounded in some college discussion the theory that the 'development of the human body might possibly be traced from the radiated, vermicular, molluscous and vertebrate organisms.' " [15]

Tennyson saw in evolution if not "a fully proved law" then "a magnificent working hypothesis," but "he could not regard it as a theory hostile to ultimate faith." So reported William Boyd-Carpenter, who interviewed Tennyson concerning his religious views. Boyd-Carpenter added that "far beyond the natural wish to reconcile faith and thought," which Tennyson shared with "all right-thinking men," was his conviction of the "changeless personal relationship between God and man." [16] Tennyson saw a parallel between evolution and the development of the higher criticism in Germany,[17] but a more Lockean than scientific tenor inheres in his characteristic philosophy that "if once we accepted the view that *this life was a time of education,* then the dark things might be found to have a meaning and a value" (my italics).[18] "Victorian humanists, a liberal Anglican like F. D. Maurice, a skeptic like Henry Sidgwick, together with leading scientists, Sir John Herschel and others, thought Tennyson had managed to re-establish the possibilities of faith precisely by taking into account the scientific difficulties . . . 'through almost the agonies of a death struggle.' " [19] The experiential basis of empiricism and evangelicalism enables this dual possibility, this mutuality, of science and personal faith.

"Its faith is a poor thing," writes T. S. Eliot of *In Memoriam,* "but its doubt is a very intense experience." [20] "The whole question of religion versus science," writes Langbaum,

> has ceased to interest us. Most of us never had any faith to lose, and we do not *think* that the lack of religion has left a hole in our lives. As for those who really believe, my impression is that they have long since given up any hope of reconciling their faith with scientific evidence. In this, of course, they are following Tennyson's main prescription, as well as Kierkegaard's (Teilhard de Chardin seems anachronistic in his present-day attempt to reconcile evolution and religion).[21]

Be that as it may, Graham Hough and Eugene R. August accept the affirmation in Tennyson's attempt at just such a reconciliation.[22] Langbaum himself admires Tennyson's reliance on "the testimony of the heart" to help him see "in the natural evolution of species an analogue to social progress and man's spiritual evolution." [23] Kincaid's view that, according to the argument of *In Memoriam*, "faith lives in and is assured by doubt,"[24] is close to mine. So is Timothy Peltason's twofold view, first that "the weirdly faithful agnosticism of the poem—the civil religion of the West for the last two centuries—looks more rigorous and can be looked at more rigorously through the analysis of poetic form"; and second that *In Memoriam* is "about the conditions under which we find ourselves pressed into making new sense of experience."[25] The "new sense" that *In Memoriam* makes of experience is the spiritual sense, that is, the physical senses as both analogues and avenues to spiritual knowledge.

Thus I examine the poem's at once empirical and evangelical formulations of experience. Where Hallam is "The human-hearted man I loved" (*In Memoriam*, 13.11), he is of the natural world, but by the same token of experiential criteria he is also "A spirit, not a breathing voice" (13.12). Tennyson's "reflections on man's relation to God and to nature"—the phrase is George H. Ford's—imply that "nature" and "God" are not only parallel but also intersecting,[26] for "relation," after all, is singular. The empirical-evangelical dialectic of *In Memoriam* tends ineluctably, although not without tension or opposition, toward harmony and wholeness. Comparing *In Memoriam* both to Milton's *Paradise Lost* and to Pope's *Essay on Man* (each of these poems "exactly expressed the character of its period"), Alfred North Whitehead means, according to Langbaum, that *In Memoriam* expresses the "characteristically Victorian controversy between science and religious faith."[27] Ultimately, *In Memoriam resolves* the controversy between science and religion because fundamentally on experiential ground it finds no irremediable controversy between empiricism and evangelicalism. It interrelates them.

TWO

Empirical Procedures

The empirical procedures of *In Memoriam* not only come before but are also more primal if not more primary than the religious principles included in the varied but not finally unintegrated rhetoric of consolation in the poem. These empirical procedures assure a triumph of will that deepens until, by fits and starts from one section of the poem to another, the persona dispels despair through his natural, distinct from his spiritual or natural-spiritual, strategy for recovery from grief. The natural-experiential thesis of *In Memoriam*, quite apart from its synthesis-antiphony of the natural and spiritual kinds of experience—hence quite apart from the full unity of the poem (see my next two sections)—entails more hope than tragedy. Tennyson's human-centered "science" of bittersweet empiricism rises to the challenge posed not only to his faith but also to his philosophy by "Nature, red in tooth and claw / With ravine" (56.15–16).

Tennyson's "strong empirical bias" (Jerome H. Buckley's phrase)[1] includes, of course, his knowledge of nineteenth-century science, which he knew better than did either Coleridge or Carlyle.[2] At Cambridge with its "preeminence in the natural sciences," Tennyson concluded that all branches of knowledge should be subject to "scientific demonstration"; thus he showed "greater receptivity" than did the other Apostles to "the method and intention of the new inductive scientists."[3] One source for his scientific thought, namely, Robert Chambers's *Vestiges of the Natural History of Creation* (1844), "interprets evolution in terms of progress and as evidence of a benevolent Providence,"[4] but the gloomier evolutionary implications of *Principles of Geology* (1830–33) by Sir Charles Lyell, and for that matter of *Origin of Species* (1859) by Charles Darwin, gloss *In Memo-*

riam, too.[5] Alfred North Whitehead, disagreeing (in advance) with the opinion of W. H. Auden that Tennyson is our "stupidest poet,"[6] called *In Memoriam* "a most important reflection of the Victorian mind," and T. H. Huxley, Victorian scientific apologist par excellence, accordingly thought Tennyson a fellow intellectual giant.[7] The "physical realities" of *In Memoriam* (Buckley's phrase) participate in as well as derive from the unflinching evolutionary explorations of Victorian Britain, for after reading Lyell's *Principles*, which espouses "the unorthodox theory of uniformitarian change," Tennyson intuited "the disquieting notion of human evolution, which Lyell himself was reluctant to make explicit."[8] Thus evolutionary science looms so large in the atmosphere of Tennyson's verse that he might almost be said to have contributed to it, and thus, too, Tennyson's tough-minded science can make him seem pre-Modern.[9]

Buckley speaks, moreover, of the "preference in [Tennyson's] verse for microscopic accuracy of detail and precision of image," that is, for the early though still indigenous biology of Erasmus Darwin and astronomy of William and Caroline Herschel.[10] Robert Langbaum, acknowledging the influence of the Herschels on *In Memoriam*, finally sees the poem as more pre–Charles Darwinian than Erasmus-Darwinian or post-Newtonian, for the Herschels "demoted the sun to a minor star in our galaxy and taught the evolution of stars out of nebulae."[11] Regardless of whether Tennyson harked back to the science of the eighteenth century in order to broaden his contribution to evolutionary thought, however, he did indeed hark back to it, and I suggest that he did so in order to relieve his immersion in the cosmic glooms and brightnesses of Victorian evolutionary theory. While the botanical-astronomical values of "microscopic accuracy of detail" and "precision of image" speak eloquently of Romantic particulars, they speak even more eloquently of eighteenth-century sensibility.

Tennyson's "strong empirical bias" includes, above all, neoclassic empiricism based on Locke, for although A. Dwight Culler regards "Locke's empiricism" as "moribund" in nineteenth-century Britain,[12] Hallam Tennyson's account of the Cambridge Apostles so strongly emphasizes the empirical as well as ideal character of their philosophical inquiries that his account deserves repeating here: "These friends [reports Tennyson's son] not only debated on politics but read their Hobbes, Locke, Berkeley, Butler, Hume, Bentham, Descartes, and Kant."[13] The Lockean tenor of

Tennyson's inquiry means, at least, that he observes inductive method, for Carlyle speaks of Tennyson as "carrying a bit of Chaos about him, . . . which he is manufacturing into Cosmos!"[14] The Lockean bent of Tennyson's procedure, finally, is indicated by his assumption of the tabula rasa, his view that even the lowliest experiences can be pivotal if not formative; Roden Noel quotes Tennyson and comments on him thus: " 'I believe that everything which happens to us we remember; it is all stored up somewhere to come forth again upon occasion, though it may seem to be forgotten—even this movement to the window we shall remember.' But he added, 'perhaps not this, so trivial a circumstance!' And now how that very utterance has impressed this circumstance upon me!"[15] The poet accounts for even the unconscious/experiential springs of one's conscious, and hence Lockean/experiential, identity.

The death of Arthur Henry Hallam (1833), like the deaths of species over the course of aeons, can seem an extinction,[16] for Tennyson takes a deeply troubling journey led by his sense-based emotion as well as by his sense-based reason. He also takes, however, sustained and sustaining flights of his sense-based imagination. His natural, distinct from spiritual or natural-spiritual, vision is a nonescapist yet lyric-sweet point of view steeped in the human-centered "science" of bittersweet empiricism that, as I have previously argued, is shared as well by Wordsworth and Keats.[17] Much of *In Memoriam*, indeed, exemplifies what Keats calls "the poetry of earth," which, as Keats declares, "is never dead" (see line 1 of Keats's "To a Grasshopper" [1817]); and much of *In Memoriam*, moreover, locates more happiness than unhappiness in the natural/Lockean world, that is, in what Wordsworth's most strictly Lockean mood describes as the "world / Of all of us, the place in which, in the end, / We find our happiness, or not at all" (*The Prelude* [1850], 10.726–28).[18] Thus the empirical procedures of *In Memoriam* win their way through to a complex and subtle but robust and untroubled tone that runs the full natural gamut from science to philosophy, that is, from tough- to tender-minded attitudes about the nature of nature.

From the beginning of *In Memoriam* through at least sections 55 and 56, Tennyson's tone can be so "disquieting" (Buckley's word) as to constitute his most somber mood. Nature, in shaping the species, shows disregard for as well as indifference to the individual:

> So careful of the type she seems,
> So careless of the single life,
>
> That I, considering everywhere
>   Her secret meaning in her deeds,
>   And finding that of fifty seeds
> She often brings but one to bear,
>
> I falter where I firmly trod,
>   (55.7–13)

Disquiet grows, moreover, in 56, where even the species are insecure:

> "So careful of the type?" but no.
>   From scarped cliff and quarried stone
>   She cries, "A thousand types are gone;
> I care for nothing, all shall go.
>
> "Thou makest thine appeal to me.
>   I bring to life, I bring to death;
>   The spirit does but mean the breath:
> I know no more."
>   (56.1–8)

The processes of nature, then, are blind, deaf, arbitrary, oblivious to humankind, and, worst of all, unintelligent. These famous "evolution" lyrics, according to James R. Kincaid, "do all irony can do to drive a wedge between the unities that man has created: between intellect and emotion, motive and act, God and nature, man and God."[19] Section 56, in particular, presents what Kincaid calls "the nadir of the experience of *In Memoriam*, a vision of hopelessness and waste." Homo sapiens, no more destined to endure than the dinosaur, will leave only a fossil record; our end, horrifyingly, will be as mindlessly violent, as apocalyptically final, as the end of the dinosaur:

> Dragons of the prime,
> That tare each other in their slime,
> Were mellow music match'd with him,
>   (56.22–24)

36

with man-unkind. So scientifically based, so mindless, seems man's inhumanity to man, that Tennyson can only lament: "O life as futile, then, as frail!" (56.25).

In language commensurate with hardened sense-language, Tennyson contemplates his own mortality, for just as he mourns the deaths of individuals and of species, so—in section 50, which addresses God, Hallam, or anyone else who will listen—he updates scientifically, if you will, the old prayer of near desperation about one's own self, namely, "Be with me now and in the hour of my need":

> Be near me when my light is low,
>   When the blood creeps, and the nerves prick
>   And tingle; and the heart is sick,
> And all the wheels of Being slow.
>
> Be near me when the sensuous frame
>   Is racked with pangs that conquer trust;
>   And Time, a maniac scattering dust,
> And Life, a Fury slinging flame.
>   (50.1–8)

Timothy Peltason, failing to acknowledge that this section might be addressed to Hallam, intriguingly speculates that Tennyson has God or the reader in mind; indeed, in echoing *The Cenci* and *Queen Mab*, the section reaches out to Shelley.[20] The section draws, moreover, on Ecclesiastes 12.3–6, where old age is depicted in an allegory as the fading of first one sense and then another. The King James version warns of

> the day when the keepers of the house shall tremble, and the strong men shall bow themselves, and the grinders shall cease because they are few, and those that look out of the windows be darkened, and the doors shall be shut in the streets, when the sound of the grinding is low, and he shall rise up at the voice of the bird, and all the daughters of musick shall be brought low; also when they shall be afraid of that which is high, and fears shall be in the way, and the almond tree shall flourish, and the grasshopper shall be a burden, and desire shall fail: because man goeth to his long home, and the mourners go about the streets: or ever the silver cord be loosed, or the golden bowl be

37

broken, or the pitcher be broken at the fountain, or the wheel broken at the cistern.

Tennyson, similarly, apprehends death as the especially fearful waning of each sensuous power. The fact that he fears death precisely because it deprives him of the physical senses proves the strength, if proof were needed, of his sensationalist epistemology.

The shock of Hallam's death so "stunn'd" the poet from his "power to think" and all his "knowledge" of himself (16. 15–16) that, addressing the phenomenon of fluctuating grief, he asks rhetorically,

> Can calm despair and wild unrest
> Be tenants of a single breast,
> Or sorrow such a changeling be?
> (16.2–4)

His grief varies according to whether "the winds begin to rise" (15. 1) or whether the ocean is "a plane of molten glass" (15. 11). Such apparent correlation between his grief and changeable externality, however, proves illusory:

> Or doth she only seem to take
> The touch of change in calm or storm,
> But knows no more of transient form
> In her deep self, than some dead lake
>
> That holds the shadow of a lark
> Hung in the shadow of a heaven?
> (16.5–10)

The dead, unchanging weight of solipsistic grief underlies the only apparent changeability of grief. This weight of grief would seem to be the very "self" of Tennyson's reality. His lack of sense perception is where his loss shows, for his relation to all objects is destroyed by Hallam's removal. Subject-object coalescence becomes tenuous, at best, when the main object of Tennyson's affections withdraws, and Tennyson withdraws as surely as Hallam does.

Because the persona of the poem can no longer empirically affirm the being of Hallam, the persona pretends to do so through his imagination, for he does not at first seem capable of other than "empirical" means of affirming reality. Awaiting the ship that bears Hallam's body home from Vienna where Hallam died suddenly of an apoplectic stroke, the persona imagines his friend disembarking real and vivid once again, for Hallam would "strike a sudden hand in mine, / And ask a thousand things of home" (14.11–12), and the persona would perceive "no touch of change, / No hint of death in all his frame" (14.17–18). Through such strong memory as would seem to overcome and almost to deny Hallam's absence, the poet still treasures his "look" and his "words" (18.14–16); and even after the body is removed from the ship, during "the ritual of the dead" (18.12), the poet would attempt, in an especially quixotic and bizarre sally of the imagination, to revive Hallam through mouth-to-mouth resuscitation:

> I, falling on his faithful heart,
> Would breathing thro' his lips impart
> The life that almost dies in me;
> (18.14–16)

This vain attempt, however, exemplifies vain imagination, for the poet can no longer sustain the pretense of being in the presence of one whom he loved. Where he cannot empirically affirm Hallam's being, he appears to choose not to affirm it at all, and one feels an especially poignant contrast between Tennyson's desire to see and hear Hallam and the dearth of anyone to see and hear. In this connection one may think of Wordsworth's Lucy, who, since she "neither hears nor sees," and since Wordsworth neither hears nor sees *her,* is dead indeed, that is, so extrinsic to empirical procedures as to seem to exist no longer.[21]

The empirical mode of *In Memoriam* is especially telling and precisely tough-minded in early passages where Tennyson stares at death with courage and without recourse to glib remedy. His meditation on a yew tree in section 2, for example, finds no other consolation than the acute and astringent, and hence salutary, awareness of mortality:

> Old yew, which graspest at the stones
> That name the underlying dead,
> Thy fibers net the dreamless head,
> Thy roots are wrapt about the bones.
> (2.1–4)

Peltason points properly to the "justified pathetic fallacy" of this "fine" section.[22] From one point of view, of course, the tree welcomes and embraces the dead, but it also threatens, entraps, and supplants the dead, for one is reminded, albeit proleptically, of the lament by Thomas Hardy for an English soldier killed in the Boer War (1899–1902): "Drummer Hodge" (1902) chillingly relates that Hodge's "homely Northern breast and brain / Grow[s] to some Southern tree." The final quatrain of section 2 is far from finding in the yew tree any imagery of longevity or hope:

> And gazing on thee, *sullen* tree,
>   *Sick* for thy *stubborn* hardihood,
>   I seem to *fail* from out my blood
> And grow incorporate into thee.
>   (2.13–16; my italics)

This diction, emphatically, grows more negative than merely neutral.

The meaninglessness implied by the stark fact of death is emphasized too by the bleak imagery of section 3, which, reminiscent of T. S. Eliot's "The Waste Land" (1922) or of Robert Browning's "Childe Roland to the Dark Tower Came" (1855), shows how far the natural world in Tennyson's imagination falls short sometimes of even so flawed a divinity as "Crass Casualty" in Hardy's "Hap" (1898):

> "The stars," she [Tennyson's nature] whispers, "blindly run;
>   A web is woven across the sky;
>   From out waste places comes a cry,
> And murmurs from the dying sun;"
>   (3.5–8)

The persona's acquaintances offer such consolations as " 'other friends remain' " and " 'loss is common to the race' " (6.1–2), but the persona rejects these banalities: "And common is the commonplace, / And vacant chaff well meant for grain" (6.3–4). His sarcasm resembles Job's dismissal of the clichés of Eliphaz (see Job 3); the detached generalities of greeting-card verse simply cannot speak to grief as deep as Tennyson's.

The calmness of nature, to be sure, appears to offer "empirical" consolation:

> Calm is the morn without a sound,
>   Calm as to suit a calmer grief,

And only thro' the faded leaf
The chestnut pattering to the ground;

Calm and deep peace on this high wold,
    And on these dews that drench the furze,
    And all the silvery gossamers
That twinkle into green and gold;

Calm and still light on yon great plain
    That sweeps with all its autumn bowers,
    And crowded farms and lessening towers,
To mingle with the bounding main;

Calm and deep peace in this wide air,
    These leaves that redden to the fall,
                    (11.1–14)

This calmness is illusory, for the next lines make an abrupt transition to an ominous, truer calm: "And in my heart, . . . / If any calm, a calm despair" (11.15–16). Thus nature's "calm" is subverted by and fails to correspond with the only calm the poet knows, that is, the calm of tragic nothingness. Thus he refuses consolation from the too obvious "answers" of nature, for the next quatrain, describing the ship's bearing of Hallam's body home, refers to

Calm on the seas, and silver sleep,
    And waves that sway themselves in rest,
    And dead calm in that noble breast
Which heaves but with the heaving deep.
                    (11.17–20)

Just as one reads 11.19 with an emphasis on "dead," so one reads 11.2— "Calm *as* to suit a calmer grief"—with an emphasis on "as"; thus one discerns Tennyson's irony throughout this section. Since the misleading if not deceptive calm of nature masks the worst there is to know, so this calm assuredly fails to satisfy one's need to know the worst.

Peltason, commenting on section 11, acknowledges the "shudder," the "dangerous wavering," in Tennyson's various repetitions of the word "calm."[23] Peltason concludes, however, that "this is not the clear subversion of irony," for he cannot bring himself to think that the word has "suddenly turned against itself and against the lovely serenity of the opening." I, by contrast, see as much bitter irony in Tennyson's various "calm"s as there is, say, in the "sweet"s of canto 1, stanzas 122–27, of Byron's *Don Juan* (1821).

The ironic description of nature in *In Memoriam* section 11 is foreshadowed and carefully prepared for by the especially tough-minded nature language of *In Memoriam*, section 7. Tom Paulin, while registering reservations about Tennyson "as the original National Heritage Poet—all that is bogus, empty, self-parodic, dishonest, false and dead-as-doornails in the culture," "can't let go of *In Memoriam*, 7, one of the saddest love lyrics in the language":[24]

> Dark house, by which once more I stand
>   Here in the long unlovely street,
>   Doors, where my heart was used to beat
> So quickly, waiting for a hand,
>
> A hand that can be clasped no more—
>   Behold me, for I cannot sleep,
>   And like a guilty thing I creep
> At earliest morning to the door.
>
> He is not here; but far away
>   The noise of life begins again,
>   And ghastly through the drizzling rain
> On the bald street breaks the blank day.
>
> (7.1–12)

Ricks's "exemplary edition," as Paulin points out, "sends us to Luke 24.6, the angel before the empty sepulchre: 'He is not here, but is risen.'" Paulin's commentary is worth quoting at length:

> And the notes [by Ricks] point us also to the ghost in *Hamlet* and to Wordsworth's "Immortality Ode"—nowhere else in Tennyson is there such rich and intelligent allusion. Like a scorned, a "guilty" woman, he clutches his grief in the miserable street. This is another version of Patient Griselda. Listening to the poem, you don't notice the barrier of that semicolon in line 9: "He is not here, but far away" is the Empsonian ambiguity which plays over the printed line—he's abandoned me, he's in heaven, his spirit lives, I blame him, though.

It's wonderfully duplicitous, it makes the empty house into a metaphor for the body and Hallam into the risen spirit. Very cleverly, it
changes material reality and doubt into a desolate faith. The printed
stanza, with that abrupt caesural semicolon, seems to take it all away,
so that two very opposite points of view—the materialistic and the
religious—come together in a kind of visionary contradiction. With
its crashing spondees, its deliberate but judicious wrecking of the
otherwise facile metre, the last line is magnificent. Magnificent or just
that shade overdone? But it's unfair to question its crushing finality.
That line and Tennyson's other lovely line, "Break, break, break",
prepare the ground for Christina Rossetti and for Hopkins.

Far from romanticizing the sunrise at Hallam's home on Wimpole Street,
the persona numbly announces, shortly after hearing of Hallam's death,
that

> The noise of life begins again,
> And ghastly through the drizzling rain
> On the bald street breaks the blank day.
>   (7.10–12)

The limping, staggering rhythm of the twelfth line fits the fragmented and
anything but calm (or at best only dead calm) realities of an empty house,
an empty world, and the agitated spirit of a friend left behind, alone and
bereft.

In Memoriam, however—and here is my emphasis—is neither finally
tragic nor often even merely mechanically empirical. Both its theme and
its form resemble the Book of Job more than, say, *De Rerum Natura* by
Lucretius. Individual instances of sudden gains in hope, such as the one
that tacitly occurs between *In Memoriam*, 56 and 57, hark back to the sharp
progress made by the Joban poet in the mysterious interstice between Job
12 and Job 13–14, and between verses 24 and 25 of Job 19. Although I
know of no explicit comparison of *In Memoriam* with the Book of Job, the
parallels between these works are implicit in the helpful discussions by
Kincaid and Culler.[25]

Such instances add up to the gradual progress of three steps forward and
two steps back. Gradual progress, in the cases of both the Joban poet and
the persona of *In Memoriam*, is largely due to the triumphs of their wills.

One cannot, it is true, resist enjoying Edward Fitzgerald's famous objection to the lowest moments of *In Memoriam*: "I felt that if Tennyson had got on a horse and ridden 20 miles, instead of moaning over his pipe, he would have been cured of his sorrows in half the time. As it is, it is about 3 years before the Poetic Soul walks itself out of darkness and Despair into Common Sense."[26] Perhaps Fitzgerald undervalues the senses in which Tennyson's hope *comes* from darkness.[27] Not even the empirical voice of *In Memoriam* succumbs entirely to despair. One thinks, by analogy, of Job's refusal to consider suicide (see Job 3). While I agree with Paulin that *In Memoriam*, 77 "changes material reality and doubt into a desolate faith" and that "the materialistic and the religious" "come together" in this section, I cannot altogether agree with Paulin's rather contradictory point that the "materialistic" and the "religious" of section 7 amount to "very opposite points of view" or to "a kind of visionary contradiction." These "points of view," in the context of the poem as a whole, are not so much "opposite" as joined by synthesis.

Although Tennyson at the beginning emphasizes the "clouds of nameless trouble" that "cross / All night below the darken'd eyes" (4.13–14), and although he thus shares "the dark night of the soul" in which, for example, Gerard Manley Hopkins "wake[s] and feel[s] the fell of dark, not day,"[28] the dawn's return of common day and conscious experience brings consolation and relief to the poet *even* at the beginning, for "With morning wakes the will, and cries, / 'Thou shalt not be the fool of loss' " (4.15–16). Just as Tennyson's "Ulysses" (1842) suggests that the purpose of humankind is "to follow knowledge" across an ever beckoning horizon, so "the overall design" of *In Memoriam* and much of the "poignancy of its separate parts" derive not just from emotion but, more significantly, from "the interplay of idea and emotion" or the "impact upon the lonely self of new knowledge growing from more to more in a troublous and changeful society."[29] Empirical assumptions—that is, ideas of sensation—form Tennyson's sustaining force against strong odds, and this is true from the outset, for Kincaid finds comedy as well as irony in the early sections.[30] Francis P. Devlin's study of these sections finds rebirth and renewal as well as death and separation;[31] section 21, in particular, fights indulgence in grief by advocating scientific as well as political activism. Through two powerful rhetorical questions—

> "Is this an hour
> For private sorrow's barren song,
> When more and more the people throng
> The chairs and thrones of civil power?"

and

> "[Is this] a time to sicken and to swoon,
> When Science reaches forth her arms
> To feel from world to world, and charms
> Her secret from the latest moon?"
>
> (21.13–21)

—a mysterious voice (could it be Carlyle's?) tells Tennyson that even one's most grievous personal loss is hardly the proper occasion for shirking one's work in the world. Although the persona is not quite ready in only the twenty-first of 131 sections to heed fully the genuinely consolatory voice of empiricism, he finds natural reasons, even thus early, to avoid the most paralyzing effects of grief.

Tennyson's hopeful emphasis on the purely natural resources of lyric aspiration is derived from the purely empirical realm, and this particular achievement of his various modes of consolation is perhaps the most genuine and most characteristic achievement of his poem. Using the exclusively natural terms of a pastoral paradise to describe the ideal friendship he enjoyed with Hallam, Tennyson evokes his friend so richly as to make him present once again:

> And we with singing cheered the way,
>   And, crowned with all the season lent,
>   From April on to April went,
> And glad at heart from May to May.
>
> .   .   .   .
>
> And all we met was fair and good,
>   And all was good that Time could bring,
>   And all the secret of the Spring
> Moved in the chambers of the blood;
>
> (22.5–8, 23.17–20)

45

"The force that through the green fuse drives the flower / Drives my green age," writes Dylan Thomas,[32] and in Tennyson's lines there is a similarly boisterous vitality, an "emotion recollected in tranquillity,"[33] that carries over from his time with Hallam to the time of his writing. These lines, although pantheistic enough to revel only chthonically, prepare for the poem's theistic evaluation/valuation of nature. (See my discussion of sections 91, 121, and 130 in chapter four.)

In the famous twenty-seventh section Tennyson casts his bread upon the waters of chance and secular experience:

> I envy not in any moods
> > The captive void of noble rage,
> > The linnet born within the cage,
> That never knew the summer woods;
>
> .   .   .   .
>
> I hold it true, whate'er befall;
> > I feel it, when I sorrow most;
> > 'Tis better to have loved and lost
> Than never to have loved at all.
> > > (27.1–4, 13–16)

"Quoted by now into meaninglessness," writes Peltason, "these lines evidence an important new understanding. The end of experience is not the sum of experience or the only source of meaning. The poet has loved and he has lost, but the second of these has not canceled out the first."[34] Through no more promising a source of buoyancy than sheer existential pluck, Tennyson regains his will to live in the "world / Of all of us." By section 83, therefore, he needs no other resource to generate his resonant, moving expression of hope than just his strong love of nature:

> Dip down upon the northern shore,
> > O sweet new-year delaying long;
> > Thou doest expectant Nature wrong;
> Delaying long, delay no more.
>
> What stays thee from the clouded noons,
> > Thy sweetness from its proper place?

46

> Can trouble live with April days,
>   Or sadness in the summer moons?
>
> Bring orchis, bring the foxglove spire,
>   The little speedwell's darling blue,
>   Deep tulips dash'd with fiery dew,
> Laburnums, dropping-wells of fire.
>
> O thou, new-year, delaying long,
>   Delayest the sorrow in my blood,
>   That longs to burst a frozen bud
> And flood a fresher throat with song.
>   (83. 1–16)

Tennyson sustains this especially lovely lyric simply by wishing for the return of a spring that will bring him the end of grief and a new birth of joy. His persona does not "fling [his] soul upon the growing gloom," as in Hardy's "The Darkling Thrush" (1901), but instead cultivates, for the oddly life-affirming purpose of expressing sorrow anew, the purely natural if not sexually vital "throbbings of noontide" (see Hardy's "I Look into my Glass" [1898]). These surpassingly sweet loco-descriptive lines are more delicate than merely tending toward the diminutive, and they modulate to deep, full passion.

"April is the cruelest month," writes Eliot in *The Waste Land*, and Tennyson, clearly of Eliot's mind and against the opposite, upbeat April tradition from Geoffrey Chaucer through Robert Browning to Wallace Stevens,[35] knows that even April can be cruel. The second rhetorical question of section 83 (lines 7–8) demands an affirmative answer. Since Hallam lives no longer, "trouble" indeed lives with April days. "Sadness" indeed lives with "summer moons." This irony, this defamiliarization of conventionality, is the only ruffler, however, in a passage otherwise full of hope and otherwise based on the unalloyed beauty of nature. Writing of sections 83 and 86, in particular, Kincaid observes that "when the comedy falters" in "the second half of the poem," and when the "irony threatens to disappear," Tennyson "turns to images in nature to renew confidence and reform the [comic/ ironic] energies" of *In Memoriam*.[36]

The empirical method of *In Memoriam* yields even the poem's develop-

47

mental psychology, which is largely tender-minded. The Lockean as well as Wordsworthian doctrine that "the Child is Father of the Man" is a poetic formulation of the tabula rasa, and an especially well-observed datum in the discussion by Samuel F. Pickering, Jr., of Wordsworth's "Ode: Intimations of Immortality" (1802–4).[37] This datum is echoed in Tennyson's experientialist account of subject-object development in childhood:

> The baby new to earth and sky,
>   What time his tender palm is prest
>   Against the circle of the breast,
> Has never thought that "this is I";
>
> But as he grows he gathers much,
>   And learns the use of "I" and "me,"
>   And finds "I am not what I see,
> And other than the things I touch."
>
> So rounds he to a separate mind
>   From whence clear memory may begin,
>   As thro' the frame that binds him in
> His isolation grows defined.
>   (45.1–12)

This passage, referring like such Freudians as Ferenczi to subject/object differentiation in the child, emerges as pre-Freudian,[38] but its psychology is fundamentally post-Lockean, for Tennyson is interested not so much in the origins of repression and the subconscious as in such consciousness-related phenomena as subjectivity, memory, the mind's place in nature, the creative roles of the tactile and the ocular senses, and—clearly not least—the shaping power of experience in general. Although "isolation" is double-edged, this diction speaks of the discreteness of identity as much as of the subjective abyss.

Finally, the empirical method of *In Memoriam* yields the epistemologically robust perception theme of the poem. This theme can seem more Berkeleyan and ingenious than Lockean and robust, for the external world depicted in the scientific section 123 is so shifting and insubstantial as to be all but immaterial:

48

There rolls the deep where grew the tree.
　　O earth, what changes hast thou seen!
　　There where the long street roars hath been
The stillness of the central sea.

The hills are shadows, and they flow
　　From form to form, and nothing stands;
　　They melt like mist, the solid lands,
Like clouds they shape themselves and go.
　　　　　　　　　　　　(123.1–8)

This section, like *In Memoriam*, 7, is one we cannot do without. Compare it with Lyell's *The Principles of Geology*, which discusses the "interchange of sea and land" that has occurred "on the surface of our globe"; Lyell remarks that "in the Mediterranean alone, many flourishing inland towns and a still greater number of ports now stand where the sea rolled its waves since the era when civilized nations first grew in Europe."[39] This shifting scene achieves its reality only in the stable perceptions of the poet:

But in my spirit will I dwell,
　　And dream my dream, and hold it true;
　　For though my lips may breathe adieu,
I cannot think the thing farewell.
　　　　　　　　　　　　(123.9–12)

Although Tennyson writes that "our memory fades / From all the circle of the hills" (101.23–24), and although he thereby suggests that the hills are solidly objective realities independent of our perceptions of them, his allusion to the Book of Psalms (see Psalm 121.1: "I will lift up mine eyes unto the hills, from whence cometh my help") suggests to me that the hills themselves are accessible to if not partly determined by our perceptions, and thus, without our eyes upon the circle of the hills, it too may fade.

"To be is to be perceived" is not to Tennyson's taste, however, for being can hardly depend on perceivers who do not endure. Even more pertinent to my point of view than any transmutation of Berkeley by Tennyson, is Tennyson's appropriation of Locke's concept that things exist that are independent of, even while they correspond with, our ideas of them. Although the landscape would seem to derive significance only from association with

Hallam—"I find no place that does not breathe / Some gracious memory of my friend" (100.3–4)—and although the landscape will acquire new meaning from such aftercomers as "the laborer" and "the stranger's child" (101.20–21)—there is considerable consolation simply in the poet's present awareness that nature continues: the "garden bough shall sway," though "unwatched" (101.1); the "sunflower" shall shine "fair," though "unloved" (101.5); and things should not seem, but be. Since Hallam "seemed the thing he was" (111.13), Tennyson trusts empirical knowing, and despite the "shocks that flesh is heir to"[40] in the "world / Of all of us," he thus distinguishes, if not truth from falsehood and latency from patency, then reality from appearance.

The epilogue rejoices that "love is more / Than in the summers that are flown" (lines 17–18). Tennyson adds that "I myself with these have grown / To something greater than before" (lines 19–20). Thus assuming the simple efficacy of natural experience, he cultivates the reminiscentially Lockean (because relatively untroubled if not robust) faith that, even when time is tragic, brings not self-actualization but, if not spiritual progress, then the growth and development of character in "the world / Of all of us."

THREE

Evangelical Principles

The deeply inward yet outwardly directed and inquiring expression of faith that Tennyson features in the otherwise scientifically focused section 124 of *In Memoriam* is matched in other passages of the poem by the elegist's emphasis on spiritual experience as the complement to natural experience. Neither from the expatiating astronomy of section 124 nor from its incisive biology would any personally efficacious discovery of the divine appear to emerge, for Tennyson declares that "I found Him not in world or sun, / Or eagle's wing, or insect's eye" (124.5–6). These lines, after all, undercut the bumper-sticker mentality of "I found Him!" However, while thus giving vent to doubts worthy of Matthew Arnold's "Dover Beach" (1867), Tennyson's persona overcomes his doubt and, despite his grief over the death of Hallam, affirms his personal experience of religious discovery:

> If e'er when faith had fallen asleep,
>   I heard a voice, "believe no more,"
>   And heard an ever-breaking shore
> That tumbled in the Godless deep,
>
> A warmth within the breast would melt
>   The freezing reason's colder part,
>   And like a man in wrath the heart
> Stood up and answer'd, "I have felt."
>   (124.9–16)

These lines, echoing the experience of John Wesley in Aldersgate Street, London, where, "at a quarter to nine" on the evening of May 24, 1738, the founder of Methodism's "heart" was "strangely warmed,"[1] are more than a greeting-card version of Wesleyan conversion passages. The lines echo, too, Wesley's eight-year journey from skepticism to faith.[2] Thus the method of *In Memoriam* adds evangelical principles to empirical procedures. Tennyson's combination of dynamic skepticism with "postcritical naiveté"[3] is as much Methodistical as it is methodological, for section 124's deeply inward yet outwardly directed and inquiring expression of faith is matched in other passages of the poem by the spiritual-experience dimension that Tennyson adds to the natural-experience foundation of his experiential vision.

Although the "thoroughgoing subjectivism" of section 124 "does not meet the difficulties raised by science, but simply bypasses them," and although "the subjectivist attitude" in *In Memoriam* has accordingly received "the severest criticism," Graham Hough, for one, finds the attitude "both honest and extremely moving."[4] Christopher Ricks, too, admires Tennyson's subjective faith:

> Some believers might argue that Tennyson sells Christianity short in underrating the degree to which its beliefs are susceptible of substantiation by argument; or unbelievers might argue that it is bad for people to believe things which are not susceptible of argument. But it is possible to think that Tennyson's poem offers almost all that can hereabouts be honestly offered by the Christian, and that it is hearteningly free of the heartlessness which comes from the conviction that the problems of pain, death, and evil can be dealt with by arguments. . . . Indeed the *In Memoriam* stanza (*abba*) is especially suited to turning round rather than going forward. To speak personally for a moment: as an atheist, I should greatly prefer Tennyson to agree with me; but I find it hard to understand the view that somehow he is stuck there in a half-complacent, half-morbid tangle from which we know—know so uncomplacently—that we have escaped.[5]

The "subjectivism" of *In Memoriam*, however, is hardly so thoroughgoing as Hough and Ricks imply. This goes even for section 124. The faith that the elegist increasingly espouses takes into account the particulars of time, place, and circumstance, or of what Wordsworth, in a passage worth repeating here, calls "the world / Of all of us, the place in which, in the end, / We find our happiness, or not at all" (*The Prelude* [1850], 10.726–28). This faith even harks back to the "objectivist" patterns of conversion in particular and experiential faith in general. Laid beside if not superimposed on the empiricism of *In Memoriam*, then, is its "empirical" evangelicalism.

A variety of passages besides section 124 illustrate Tennyson's advance from struggle with self-absorption to what he clearly regards as the crowning touch of his "evangelical" theology, namely, the universal efficacy that he claims for the still "living" Hallam's Holy Spirit–like presence in the world. The most pertinent historical gloss on this theology, and hence the most powerful analogue to Tennyson's religious imagination, is the experiential, explicitly Lockean (as well as fully biblical) faith that Wesley and Edwards shared and notably promulgated throughout the Anglo-American world.[6] The effects of the transatlantic revivalism simultaneously begun by the founder of British and American Methodism and the leader of the Great Awakening were felt long after the time of Tennyson. Sections 108, 71, 82, 28, 33, 26, the prologue, sections 36, 31, 32, 52, 7, 103, 84, 50, 110, 87, and 113—when considered in this particular order and from this particular point of view—range from Tennyson's individualistic but respectful explorations of such Christian fundamentals as the sin of selfhood to his bold application to the here and now of a religious as well as poetic imagination that grows out of, and is indeed honed by, the native/binative, richly English-language, synthesizing, and far from unimaginative heritage of Wesleyan-Edwardsean evangelical faith.

Apropos of Tennyson's "subjectivity," consider, if you will, his warning against self-reflexivity or empty self-worship:

> What profit lies in barren faith,
>   And vacant yearning, though with might
>   To scale the heaven's highest height,
> Or dive below the wells of Death?
>
> What find I in the highest place,
>   But mine own phantom chanting hymns?
>   And on the depths of death there swims
> The reflex of a human face.
>   (108.5–12)

Keats's "Written upon the Top of Ben Nevis" (1818), similarly, looks both high and low for an object worthy of worship, but finding only "sullen mist" overhead and a "shroud / Vaporous" in the valley below, this sonnet discovers, too, only "mist" in "the world of thought and mental might!"

Keats presumably would be glad to discover even such "solid ground" as solipsism provides. To such a Keatsean mood of thoroughgoing doubt, Tennyson seems to prefer, if no more resounding an affirmation of faith, at least the nature reverence at which he has proved himself adept: "I'll rather take what fruit may be / Of sorrow under human skies" (108.13–14). Thus referring not just to his own sorrow but to sorrow as the general condition of humankind on earth, Tennyson works his way out of selfhood to a compassionate orientation toward objects and subjects in the world below. Section 108 thus divagates from the dead-end skepticism and the extreme subjectivity of Romanticism. Tennyson's milder Romantic stance is hardly orthodox, for Christianity emphasizes joy in a world elsewhere, but his nature reverence is experientially religious enough to be at least partially commensurate with the evangelical faith of Wesley and Edwards. Their combination of nature reverence and this-worldly compassion forms a legendary feature, after all, of their joint legacy to the nineteenth century.[7]

To natural religion, though, whether deistic, theistic, pantheistic, or chthonic, Tennyson clearly prefers an "evangelical" heart-religion, that is, an inward yet deeply engaged or experiential/other-directed faith. "Full fathom five thy father lies," writes Shakespeare in *The Tempest* (1.2.397); but far from being dead, "thy father" miraculously "doth suffer a sea change / Into something rich and strange" (*The Tempest*, 1.2.400–401). And Tennyson, while implying a rather different point, subtly alludes to these lines. Suggesting that the change is not so much from nature to another world as from natural to spiritual experience within "the world / Of all of us," Tennyson recalls that he and Hallam "talk'd / Of men and minds, the dust of *change*," reporting, significantly, that their days grew "to *something strange*" (71.9–11; my italics). Thus, even as their spirits transcended time, they remained in time. Where Tennyson affirms his faith in Hallam's afterlife—"Eternal process moving on, / From state to state the spirit walks" (82.5–6)—he means both that Hallam has passed from earth to heaven, where he continues to develop, and that amid the ceaseless activities of his life on earth, his spiritual progress occurred because of as well as despite those activities. During the first Christmas season after Hallam's death, Tennyson hears "the Christmas bells from hill to hill" (28.3), and despite their sing-song near monotony—his faith is ebbing at this point—they strike his ear the more forcefully for his lack of expectation that they would strike it at all: "The merry, merry bells of Yule" touch his sorrow "with joy" (28.19–20). The appeal of the bells, while not fundamental to doctrine, is evangelical enough, for their kerygmatic message of hope peals out to, connects with, and begins to heal even the lowest velleities of the poet's post-traumatic experience.

In Memoriam, at least insofar as section 33 brings up short the theological liberal who feels that his open-ended faith is superior to his sister's literal creed, is classically evangelical:

> O thou that after toil and storm
>> Mayst seem to have reach'd a purer air,
>> Whose faith has centre everywhere,
> Nor cares to fix itself to form,
>
> Leave thou thy sister when she prays
>> Her early heaven, her happy views;
>> Nor thou with shadow'd hint confuse
> A life that leads melodious days.
>
> Her faith thro' form is pure as thine,
>> Her hands are quicker unto good.
>> O, sacred be the flesh and blood
> To which she links a truth divine!
>
> See thou, that countest reason ripe
>> In holding by the law within,
>> Thou fail not in a world of sin,
> And even for want of such a type.
>
>> (33.1–16)

Timothy Peltason's comment acknowledges that the "dignity" of the sister's "religious position" is preferred over the position of both the brother and his "hazily defined group of fellow liberals."[8] A. C. Bradley, still the most thorough commentator on *In Memoriam*, rejects the possibility that "Tennyson is thinking of himself and his sister" Emily or Cecilia, but Bradley nonetheless calls the idea "plausible."[9] Tennyson may sometimes be more like the brother than like the sister, but his persona rejects the indefinite, unfixed, and indeterminate theology of the brother in favor of the sister's strong, definite, evangelical faith, which claims power as and because it values form. (Wesley, as I have pointed out, bases his influential emphasis

on power and form on such biblical passages as 1 Corinthians 2.1–6.[10])
Although Tennyson was intimately familiar with Liberal Anglicanism,[11]
these quatrains implicitly contrast Liberal Anglicanism with Evangelical
Anglicanism; the quatrains direct their satire against the former. The evangelical sister provides Tennyson with the standard by which he skewers the
brother's almost rationalistic-antinomian stance, which, besides forming
part of the brother's male pride, forms part of his "advanced" theology.
The sister's emphasis on "flesh and blood" (33.11) refers, by refreshing contrast, to the historical Jesus, the elements of communion, and all people
with whom her evangelical, practical charity comes in contact.

"How but in custom and in ceremony," asks William Butler Yeats, "are
innocence and beauty born?" (I refer to lines 78–79 of "A Prayer for My
Daughter" [1919].) Tennyson would agree with the experientially religious
implications of Yeats's rhetorical question. The sister's regulated but vital
experience excels by the richness of its spiritual form and content the mere
Sturm und Drang whereby, with more Continental-Romantic than British-
Romantic or British-evangelical warmheartedness, her Liberal Anglican
brother arrives at *his* truth.

What *In Memoriam* says about God can be so far from classically evangelical as to anticipate Thomas Hardy's "theology." Where Tennyson speaks of

> that eye which watches guilt
> And goodness, and hath power to see
> Within the green the moulder'd tree,
> And towers fallen as soon as built—
>
> (26.5–8)

he rivals the sarcasm with which Hardy apprehends a possibly omniscient
but clearly indifferent God. These lines emerge, too, as a satire against
the judgmental Calvinist God of sovereignty, especially since an additional detail—"if indeed that eye foresee / Or see—in Him is no before"
(26.9–10)—exposes the supersubtleties if not the superabsurdities of the
predestinarian position. In 1892 Roden Noel reported that "Lord Tennyson
believed in 'free will' ": "When I urged the argument of Jonathan Edwards,
and other more modern arguments against the popular conception of it,
he replied that free will, not being subject to the law of causation, was
a *miracle,* no doubt; but that consciousness testifies to the fact." [12] Tennyson's view is in line not only with Wesley's Arminian view but also with

the empiricist view of David Hume, for whom in all seriousness "free will" is a "miracle" of one's consciousness. Tennyson's dramatic monologue "St. Simeon Stylites" (1833) satirizes not just overzealous Catholics but, according to Roger S. Platizky, "the early nineteenth-century Evangelicals, whose dread of a punitive judgment and of the putridity of the flesh is similar to Simeon's." [13] Objection to Calvinist evangelicalism, however, leaves room for sympathy toward Arminian-Wesleyan and even toward experiential-Edwardsean (though not toward Calvinist-Edwardsean) evangelicalism. (See the warring paradigms in Edwards, and especially his Lockean middle phase. [14])

Fully evangelical because Christological and quite Arminian, is another of the conceptions of Godhead in *In Memoriam*. The opening phrase of the prologue, "*Strong* Son of God" (my italics), reflects an immediate historical context, namely, "muscular Christianity," a coinage of Charles Kingsley's. The vestiges of this Victorian form of Christianity, which led to the scouting movement for boys and girls, may still be found depicted in *Chariots of Fire*, a movie about the 1924 Olympics. Tennyson's Christ, however, is also the fundamental and therefore the decidedly evangelical Christ of traditional revelation:

> And so the Word had breath, and wrought
> With human hands the creed of creeds
> In loveliness of perfect deeds,
> More strong than all poetic thought;
>
> (36.9–12)

Tennyson said that "there were, of course, difficulties in the idea of a Trinity—the Three. 'But mind,' he said, 'Son of God is quite right—that he was.'" [15] Tennyson's Christ is consistent with the experiential, free-willist, Arminian evangelicalism that gained ascendancy over the foreknowing, predestinate, Calvinist evangelicalism in both England and America from the eighteenth century to the nineteenth. [16] Arminian evangelicalism bears on Tennyson's declaration that *In Memoriam* expresses "my conviction that fear, doubts, and suffering will find answer and relief only through Faith in a God of Love." [17]

Consider, in the light of the Arminian-evangelical emphasis on immediate versus traditional revelation, Tennyson's recasting of the Lazarus story (see John 11.1–44). "When Lazarus left his charnel-cave, / And home to Mary's house return'd," his sister asked him what anyone would ask: "Where wert thou, brother, those four days?" (*In Memoriam*, 31.1–2, 5). Bradley contrasts this question with the bland remark of Sir Thomas Browne: "I can read . . . that Lazarus was raised from the dead, yet not demand where, in the interim, his soul waited." [18] Tennyson, for his part, laments that "There lives no record of reply" (31.6); his disappointment is palpable: "telling what it is to die / Had surely added praise to praise" (31.7–8). Although Tennyson is greatly impressed with how much the original story of Lazarus discloses to anyone willing to read it with even a minimally Protestant attention to detail—"Behold a man raised up by Christ!" (31.13)—this miracle is not finally definitive for Tennyson's account. The proponent of spiritual theology, distinct from the Bible believer, grows dissatisfied:

> The rest remaineth unreveal'd;
> He told it not, or something seal'd
> The lips of that Evangelist.
> (31.14–16)

Without casting doubt on the account in traditional revelation, the poet suggests that there is room for and indeed a need for immediate revelation; since he does not yet know enough, he should be given to know more, and it is not as though there is nothing else to know. The more to know, while lending the appeal of mystery to what is already known, awakens his appetite for and his receptivity to further dispensations concerning not just the afterlife but, even more importantly here, other, more this-world-pertinent aspects of ultimate spiritual knowledge.

The version of the Lazarus story in *In Memoriam*, 31, is thus more ambitious than other Victorian versions of it (see, for example, A. Dwight Culler's discussion of Arnold's "Empedocles on Aetna" and Browning's "Epistle of Karshish" [19]). The theology in section 31 draws imaginatively and specifically on evangelical understanding, which, like the thinking of Tennyson's persona, insists on immediate revelation and, like the thinking of Tennyson's Mary, can be starker, more "fundamentally" clear than the Bible itself. It is almost as though Tennyson toys with a severely Protestant aesthetic whereby mediation of any kind is devalued as a most unfortunate, if necessary, distraction from the distinct, cohesive, point-blank meanings that he seeks. The poet's Mary knows three things: first that "[Lazarus] was dead"; second that "there he sits"; and third that "he that brought him back is there" (32.3–4). Thus she formulates, with a more than biblical clarity, her considerable and methodically acquired if not hard-won knowledge. Although Bradley observes that "in the mind of Lazarus's sister" curiosity as to the state beyond death was "absorbed in love and adoration," and although Bradley sees "a blessedness" in Tennyson's Mary,[20] this latter-day Mary shows such curiosity as to win her way through to a sufficiently astonishing set of religious discoveries. Not even Mary's and Lazarus's blunt, more down-to-earth than contemplative sister Martha, in Joan New's recasting of the Lazarus story (1986), shows any greater curiosity than Tennyson's Mary about what Lazarus learned on the other side. For despite deeply empathizing with Lazarus, who grieves over his sudden loss of heaven, New's Martha implores him to "Forgive me, . . . for I, / Knowing nothing else but life, choose life."[21] Carrying Tennyson's experiential fervor to such a narrow extreme that she leaves out Tennyson's rich-experiential desire for otherworldly knowledge, New's Martha chooses not even to inquire how the life she clings to might bear on, if not be made more abundant by, the "life" that lies ahead. Thus, even as New's poem shares in Tennyson's empirical "spirit," it skillfully and insightfully measures our distance from his spiritual "empiricism."

In view of the yearning for immediate revelation in section 31, to say nothing of the other evangelical idioms in *In Memoriam*, it may seem odd that nowhere does the elegy mention the Holy Spirit by name. Section 36, however, envisions Christ as acting in the present:

> Tho' truths in manhood darkly join,
> Deep-seated in our mystic frame,
> We yield all blessing to the name
> Of Him that made them *current* coin;
> (36.1–4; my italics)

Thus the evangelicals' blend of Christ and the Holy Spirit enables Tennyson's boldest theology to develop. The poet draws on spiritual theology as well as on Christology to depict the continuing influence of Hallam, from whom a spirit of forgiveness Christ-like in manner and pneumatological in immediacy emanates long after his death.

Tennyson worries that, as measured by his verses, his love for Hallam must be deemed imperfect: "I cannot love thee as I ought" (52.1). After creeping "like a guilty thing" to the door of Hallam's house on hearing of his death (7.7–8), the poet dreams that he is torn between maidens on the one hand and Hallam's statue on the other (see section 103), indicating that Tennyson may have in mind his homoerotic feelings for Hallam. Whatever the cause of his guilt, however, Hallam's still-active spirit is graciously Arminian, for Hallam is now "The Spirit of true love" (52.6), as though the Holy Spirit and he were one. Functioning as the Comforter, Hallam now speaks to Tennyson in explicitly Wesleyan terms of assurance:

> "Thou canst not move me from thy side,
> Nor human frailty do me wrong.
>
> "What keeps a spirit wholly true
>   To that ideal which he bears?
>   What record? not the sinless years
> That breathed beneath the Syrian blue;
>
> "So fret not like an idle girl,
>   That life is dash'd with flecks of sin.
>   Abide, thy wealth is gather'd in,
> When Time hath sunder'd shell from pearl."
>   (52.7–16)

(See the literary as well as theological importance of Wesley's doctrine of assurance.[22]) Whatever sins were committed are thus forgiven, and it is worth noting in this connection that the spiritual, distinct from any psychosexual, dimension of section 103 underlies the peculiar conclusion of the section, in which the statue of Hallam comes to life and, like the forgiving spirit of God, welcomes both Tennyson and the maidens into a full, a spiritual as well as physical, mutual fellowship.

Hallam's spirit as agent/manifestation/successor of the Third Person is not just far from dead but even perpetually efficacious in a world to which it constitutes further dispensations of faith/divinity. Tennyson's spiritual theology carries the evangelical emphasis on the Holy Spirit to a logical extreme (see my discussion of that emphasis [23]). Tennyson, speculating about the long life that he and Hallam might have had together, imagines that after "hovering o'er the dolorous strait / To the other shore," the two of them would have arrived at the "blessed goal" of heaven where "He that died in Holy Land" would have "reach[ed] us out the shining hand" and "take[n] us as a single soul" (84.39–44). Thus Tennyson makes a sharp distinction between Hallam and Christ; Tennyson next asks, however, as though any hope of Christ were a weak reed indeed (compared with hope of Hallam), "What reed was that on which I leant?" (84.45). In an even bolder passage, Hallam, by the same token of earthly spiritual experience, is a still more reliable because a still more present Christ than Christ himself. Section 50 ("Be near me when my light is low") is ultimately addressed to Hallam, type of the Christ-to-be, and while Gerard Manley Hopkins regrets that neither he nor any other priest—notwithstanding the utmost tenderness that priests regularly summon for extreme unction—can truly be "in at the end" for a dying person (I allude to Hopkins's "Felix Randall" [1880]), Tennyson, in this section, wants Hallam to perform that very godlike function for him, and thinks that he can. One is reminded here of Emily Dickinson's hope that, if Jesus cannot be "in at the end" of her life (I re-use Hopkins's phrase), then perhaps her good friend Susan Gilbert can (see Vivian Pollak's discussion of Dickinson's Poem 158[24]). Even as Tennyson contemplates his own life's final hour, Hallam's continuing pneumatological/parousial capacity puts the poet in the presence of whom he loves; Hallam as unnamed addressee of section 50 makes for an especially subtle sense of coalescence or interpenetration between Tennyson's persona and the more than human, as well as the fully human, subject of *In Memoriam*.

Hallam, then, is described evangelically. His probity, for example, proves especially infectious:

> On thee the loyal-hearted hung,
>> The proud was half disarm'd of pride,
>> Nor cared the serpent at thy side
> To flicker with his double tongue.
>> (110.5–8)

He is loved, moreover, for particular Christian reasons:

> While I, thy nearest, sat apart,
>> And felt thy triumph was as mine;
>> And loved them more, that they were thine,
> The graceful tact, the Christian art;
>> (110.13–16)

Although he does not preach, as did his fellow Cambridge Apostle F. D. Maurice, and even as does Tennyson in his more kerygmatic moods, the Hallam of *In Memoriam* seeks to bring about a third apostolic age, the second being that of Wesley and Edwards. Exemplifying Arminian free will, the fruits of the Spirit, enthusiasm as honorifically understood, and, not least, a spiritual sense of personal relationship with God, Hallam is quintessentially evangelical:

> A willing ear
> We lent him. Who but hung to hear
> The rapt oration flowing free
>
> From point to point, with power and grace
> And music in the bounds of law,
> To those conclusions when we saw
> The God within him light his face . . . ?
> (87.30–36)

(See my study of these particular congeries of evangelical traits.[25]) Tennyson believes that Hallam would have made his mark as a political leader, that is, as "A potent voice of Parliament" (113.11) or even as "A lever to uplift the earth / And roll it in another course" (113.15–16), but Tennyson's diction for the particular kind of social justice that Hallam would have represented is explicitly evangelical: "A life in civic *action warm,* / A *soul* on highest *mission sent*" (113.9–10; my italics).

What is commonly said about Tennyson, that he was to be "the awakener of a new Albion, the poet-prophet of the good society to come,"[26] could be said, too, of John Wesley and, with regard to America, of Jonathan Edwards. This parallel is hardly arbitrary. Entire dimensions of *In Memoriam*, and not just its portraiture of Hallam, emerge as derivations of and withdrawals from the evangelical legacy that the eighteenth century passed on to the nineteenth. "Whatever was the immediate prompting of *In Memoriam*, whatever the form under which the author represented his aim to himself," the deepest significance of the poem, according to George Eliot, is its "sanctification of human love as a religion."[27] It is a short step from her view to the argument of C. F. G. Masterman that Tennyson admired Christianity primarily for its consistency with humanism and morality.[28] Peltason concludes that "Tennyson's faith is not a religious faith" so much as "a faith in psychic integrity, in historical coherence, in the possibility of community."[29] These emphases on sanctification, love, good works, this-worldliness, and a balance between individualism and social consciousness, however, are especially consistent with the Arminian evangelicalism that I have sought to portray here as one of the most heady ingredients of Tennyson's vision at midcareer.

Other efforts than mine, of course, have historically grounded Tennyson's faith. Jerome H. Buckley, for example, describing an especially wide arc of Christianity, relates the faith of Tennyson to the faiths of Pascal, Newman, and Kierkegaard:

> [Tennyson's] faith, which . . . rests on the premise of feeling, resembles that of Pascal, who likewise trusted the reason of the heart which reason could not know. Its source, like the ground of Newman's assent, is psychological rather than logical, the will of the whole man rather than a postulate of the rational faculty. And in its development, it is frequently not far removed from Kierkegaardian "existentialism," which similarly balances the demands of the inner life against the claims of nineteenth-century "knowledge."[30]

Tennyson, however, is even more specifically indebted to the Broad Church theology of F. D. Maurice and others.[31] Notice, for example, these latitudinarian/tolerant/"relativist," yet still Christian lines from the prologue:

> Our little systems have their day;
>   They have their day and cease to be:
>   They are but broken lights of thee,
> And thou, O Lord, art more than they.
>   (lines 17–20)

Pointing to such Broad Church analogues to *In Memoriam* as John Keble's *The Christian Year* (1827), Julius and Augustus Hare's *Guesses at Truth* (1829), F. D. Maurice's *The Kingdom of Christ* (1838), and even Coleridge's *Aids to Reflection* (1825), Culler comments at helpful length:

> In *The Kingdom of Christ* Maurice distinguishes between *system* and *method,* two words which many people take to be synonymous but which seem to him "not only not synonymous, but the greatest contraries imaginable: the one indicating that which is most opposed to

life, freedom, variety; and the other that without which they cannot exist." "Method" is Coleridge's term, in *The Friend, Aids to Reflection*, and the *Essay on Method*; "system" might be predicated of his opposite, Bentham. The terms are, indeed, useful for making distinctions throughout the century. Arnold was interested in the "method and secret of Jesus" and was criticized by Frederic Harrison for not having "a philosophy with coherent, interdependent, subordinate, and derivative principles." Maurice himself might be distinguished from Herbert Spencer as a man of method rather than system. *In Memoriam* is certainly an unsystematic poem but it is not an unmethodical one.[32]

These comments are fully understandable along clear lines of my interest in evangelical method.

Tennyson, after all, considered entitling *In Memoriam* "The *Way* of the Soul" (my italics). This name, like the poem itself and, for that matter, like the Broad Church Movement, harks back to *Method*ism, broadly understood as the mainstream American as well as British—the mainstream experiential-Edwardsean as well as Arminian-Wesleyan—evangelicalism of the eighteenth century. Tennyson's "heat of inward evidence," his knowing beyond reason or intuition (I refer to Tennyson's "The Two Voices" [1833], line 248), informs his poetry as early as "Armageddon" (1824), in which, at the age of fifteen, he records his "dissociation and mystical communion."[33] His "religion," however, during the composition of *In Memoriam* from 1833 to 1850—that is, during the years of his greatest "soul-competency" (the term belongs to the late, but still-influential, Moderate of the Southern Baptist faith E. Y. Mullins)—became less subjective and more orthodox, because less mystical and more evangelical, than before. (See Harold Bloom's discussion of the post-Tennysonian, Late Romantic character of Mullins's Arminian-evangelical religious imagination.[34])

64

FOUR

Philosophical Theology

The tension/opposition of *In Memoriam*'s empirical-evangelical dialectic is perhaps best illustrated by the well-known rhetorical question of section 56 (the feminine pronoun refers to nature):

> And he, shall he,
>
> Man, her last work, who seem'd so fair,
>> Such splendid purpose in his eyes,
>> Who roll'd the psalm to wintry skies,
> Who built him fanes of fruitless prayer,
>
> Who trusted God was love indeed
>> And love Creation's final law—
>> Tho' Nature, red in tooth and claw
> With ravine, shriek'd against his creed—
>
> Who loved, who suffer'd countless ills,
>> Who battled for the True, the Just,
>> Be blown about the desert dust,
> Or seal'd within the iron hills?
>
> (56.8–20)

"Yes" is the implied answer, poignant as well as bitter. While the poet remembers religion with an idealistic, tender nostalgia, he grasps even more vividly the opposite truth of an empiricism tough-mindedly evolutionary in tone. Here Nature is essence, whereas religion seems merely part of shifting, insubstantial culture. However, that nature is apparently the only reality is so dissatisfying to the poet that, more intently than nostalgically, he reconsiders religion and makes it the possible leavening of and not just the antidote to such harsh vision.

The final sentence of section 35, for example, suggests that faith in an afterlife, however ill-founded, is nothing less than what one needs to support *this* life, that is, to make it civil:

> If Death were seen
>   At first as Death, Love had not been,
>   Or been in narrowest working shut,
>
> Mere fellowship of sluggish moods,
>   Or in his coarsest Satyr-shape
>   Had bruised the herb and crush'd the grape,
> And bask'd and batten'd in the woods.
>
> (35.18–24)

Without hope of immortality, our life is "as a beast's,"[1] or to paraphrase Tennyson's burst of poetry in another Shakespearean way, "love is not love"[2] which occurs in exclusively natural experience. A love devoid of spiritual hope, according to Tennyson as well as Shakespeare, is only lust, violence, indulgence, and an "expense of spirit in a waist of shame."[3] Thus Tennyson's sense-orientation is far from extending to decadence. In "The Two Voices," he doubts whether human effort can ever derive sufficient encouragement simply from the hope of empirical knowledge alone:

> " 'T were better not to breathe or speak
> Than cry for strength remaining weak,
> And seem to find, but still to seek.
>
> (lines 94–96)

This doubt haunts *In Memoriam*, especially in the implication of section 35 that the reality supplementary to evolutionary empiricism is faith.

Where the poem's faith is as real as its empiricism, the gulf between them can still seem yawning if not unbridgeable. In section 41 Tennyson does not doubt that Hallam enjoys an afterlife, but he worries that Hallam lies beyond any continuing contact with the living:

> Yet oft when sundown skirts the moor
>   An inner trouble I behold,

A spectral doubt which makes me cold,
That I shall be thy mate no more,

Though following with an upward mind
The wonders that have come to thee,
(41.17–22)

An air of defiance, like that of Tithonus, prefers earth to heaven despite Tennyson's admission of heaven's superiority (41.22). Hallam has not changed into something "rich and strange," as in Shakespeare's evocation of wonder and grace in the afterlife, but into something merely foreign or alien, of which Tennyson wants no part.

His tone extends to section 47, where Hallam himself prefers earth to heaven:

He seeks at least

Upon the last and sharpest height,
Before the spirits fade away,
Some landing-place, to clasp and say,
"Farewell! We lose ourselves in light."
(47.12–16)

Hallam's farewell to earth could be read as triumphant in that, as spirits fade from earthly sight into the light of heaven with no darkness of either doubt or partial knowledge, all becomes illumination. Seeking to prolong his last moments on earth, however, Hallam grasps at anything to keep him from the blazing, blinding, frightening unknown. In this connection one thinks of Robert Frost's similar emphasis on the tangible as the real in "To Earthward." One feels all the more sympathy for Hallam because, at the junction between his beloved familiar world and his as yet unloved destination, he disappears before one's very eyes. One thinks, too, of the similarly poignant disappearance of the baseball heroes of yesteryear in the recent movie *Field of Dreams*, where the heroes fade "unseen" into the "alien corn" of Iowa (*pace* Keats).[4]

The best of what is known on earth, then, should be replicated in heaven. In Kant's *Critique of Practical Reason* (1788), he "made immortality a postulate of the practical reason," and his "teleological argument" that "immortality is necessary for man to realize the full potentiality of his spiritual nature . . . became the standard argument in the nineteenth century."[5] Thus "it was not Eternity" that Tennyson desired "but an eternity of continual progress."[6] Perhaps the nearest analogue to Tennyson's view of heaven is that of Richard Whately in *A View of the Scripture Revelations concerning a Future State* (1829). Whately vehemently opposes the idea

> that the heavenly life will be one of *inactivity,* and perfectly *sta-tionary,*—that there will be nothing to be *done,*—nothing to be *learnt,*—no *advances* to be made;—nothing to be *hoped* for,—nothing to *look forward* to, except a continuance in the very state in which the blest will be placed at once. Now this also, is far from being an alluring view, to minds constituted as ours are. It is impossible for us to contemplate such a state . . . without an idea of tediousness and wearisomeness forcing itself upon them. The ideas of *change,*—*hope,*—*progress,*—*improvement,*—*acquirement,*—*action,*— are so intimately connected with all our conceptions of happiness . . . that it is next to impossible for us to separate them.[7]

Tennyson, accordingly, moves to the intriguing thought that the processes of the afterlife may not differ in kind from those of nature. Section 82 blames death, not for translating Hallam into something different but for keeping his still earth-like experience from intersecting with the still-earthly experience of Tennyson:

> For this alone on Death I wreak
> The wrath that garners in my heart:
> He put our lives so far apart
> We cannot hear each other speak.
>
> (82.13–16)

Section 82 states flatly that Hallam will continue to do as he has always done:

> Nor blame I Death, because he bare
> The use of virtue out of earth;
> I know transplanted human worth
> Will bloom to profit, otherwhere.
>
> (82.9–12)

This idea is thoroughly anticipated, thoroughly prepared for by section 64, which imagines that Hallam, from the heavenly perspective, reflects on what his earthly past could have been like:

> Dost thou look back on what hath been,
>   As some divinely gifted man,
>   Whose life in low estate began
> And on a simple village green;
>
> Who breaks his birth's invidious bar,
>   And grasps the skirts of happy chance,
>   And breasts the blows of circumstance,
> And grapples with his evil star;
>
> Who makes by force his merit known
>   And lives to clutch the golden keys,
>   To mould a mighty state's decrees,
> And shape the whisper of the throne;
>
> And moving up from high to higher,
>   Becomes on Fortune's crowning slope
>   The pillar of a people's hope,
> The centre of a world's desire; . . . ?
>
> (64. 1–16)

It is as though heavenly existence forms an analogue to, if not a continuum with, earthly existence. "*As* some divinely gifted man" is only a simile, but quatrains 2, 3, and 4 do more than analogize. They imply that the experience of the self-made man who proceeds from step to step toward the pinnacle or power of an almost charismatic leadership deeply resembles heavenly experience. Heavenly psychology remains essentially Lockean. The fifth quatrain speculates that Hallam

> Yet feels, as in a pensive dream,
>   When all his active powers are still,
>   A distant dearness in the hill,
> A secret sweetness in the stream,
>
> (64. 17–20)

Thus he still cherishes, still identifies with even the lowliest sense experience, for "yet" not only denotes his nostalgia for earthly existence but also connotes his heavenly reliving of it.

Section 117, where Tennyson thinks of joining Hallam, conceives of no better way to imagine heaven than through such temporal dimensions as astronomical science, the industrial revolution, and sense experience. "When we meet," declares the poet, "delight a hundredfold" will "accrue" for every "grain of sand that runs," every "span of shade that steals," every "kiss of toothed wheels," and "all the courses of the suns" (117.7–12). Thus abandoning simile altogether, he envisions a full-scale, heavenly "empiricism" in which even what Blake would call the "dark" or "Satanic" "mills" of the industrial revolution[8] are far from resembling the dehumanizing convolutions of "wheels within wheels" (see the imagery in the Book of Ezekiel). Friedrich von Schiller describes these convolutions in *Letters on the Aesthetic Education of Man*: "Everlastingly chained to a single little fragment of the whole, man himself develops into nothing but a fragment; everlastingly in his ear the monotonous sound of the wheel that he turns, he never develops the harmony of his being, and instead of putting the stamp of humanity upon his own nature, he becomes nothing more than the imprint of his occupation or of his specialized knowledge."[9] The toothed wheels of Tennyson's heavenly mills, in contrast, are celestial precisely because they constitute impressive, systematic products of his inductive imagination. Compare, for example, his honorific imagery with the similarly heavenly industrial imagery with which Wordsworth praises his wife, Mary, in "She Was a Phantom of Delight" (1804): "And now I see with eye serene / The very pulse of the machine" (lines 21–22). Thus in the context of *In Memoriam*, as well as in *In Memoriam* itself, mills are seen as symbols less of industrial squalor than of an experiential perfection as divine as earthly.

Earthly and heavenly experiences can be so conceivably similar as to intersect, or so, at least, section 38 implies:

> If any care for what is here
> Survive in spirits render'd free,
> Then are these songs I sing of thee
> Not all ungrateful to thine ear.
>
> (38.9–12)

Thus Hallam, along with Queen Victoria and many of her subjects (not to mention many Americans),[10] remains a sharp-eared auditor to *In Memoriam* in the first flush of its publishing success. A corresponding point emerges from section 65, which states flatly that, despite Hallam's death, the experiences of Tennyson and Hallam continue to be mutual or two-way:

> Since we deserved the name of friends,
>> And thine effect so lives in me,
>> A part of mine may live in thee
> And move thee on to noble ends.
>> (65.9–12)

With regard to his ongoing relationship with Hallam, Tennyson's emphasis lies ultimately on its more earthly than heavenly setting. Section 63, much as one might pray for the ministrations of the Holy Spirit, begs Hallam to condescend. Just as the poet's persona in 63.1–8 expresses his concern for horses and dogs (see Wesley's kindness to animals, which led him to entertain the idea of their afterlife[11]), so he implores Hallam to take pity on the poet himself:

> So mayst thou watch me where I weep,
>> As, unto vaster motions bound,
>> The circuits of thine orbit round
> A higher height, a deeper deep.
>> (63.9–12)

In this connection one might understand the ambiguity of two quatrains from section 42:

> And so may Place retain us still,
>> And he the much-beloved again,
>> A lord of large experience, train
> To riper growth the mind and will;

> And what delights can equal those
>> That stir the spirit's inner deeps,
>> When one that loves, but knows not, reaps
> A truth from one that loves and knows?
>> (42.5–12)

Place, capitalized, implies heaven. The quatrains may mean, therefore, that when Tennyson joins Hallam in heaven, the two will continue to change and develop as they did on earth. A more intriguing meaning, however, is that Hallam will reach down from the perspective of his "large experience" in heaven and increase from natural to spiritual the experience of Tennyson on earth. By this interpretation, *Place* refers to an earth transfused by heaven. Thus ambiguity allows for the congruency of nature with spirit. Tennyson's empiricism, his bias toward being in the presence of whom he loves, leads him to *will* Hallam's descent to earth. This marked determination contrasts with Shelley's determination in *Adonais* (1821) to place himself in the empyrean with Keats.

Tennyson's desire to bring Hallam back to earth, distinct from his desire to join him in heaven, helps explain one of the most beautiful lyrics of the poem. Lying in bed and meditating on the moonlight, Tennyson thinks, lugubriously enough, of Hallam in the tomb:

> When on my bed the moonlight falls,
>   I know that in thy place of rest
>   By that broad water of the west
> There comes a glory on the walls:
>
> Thy marble bright in dark appears,
>   As slowly steals a silver flame
>   Along the letters of thy name,
> And o'er the number of thy years.
>
> The mystic glory swims away,
>   From off my bed the moonlight dies;
>   And closing eaves of wearied eyes
> I sleep till dusk is dipt in gray;
>
> And then I know the mist is drawn
>   A lucid veil from coast to coast,
>   And in the dark church like a ghost
> Thy tablet glimmers to the dawn.
>   (67.1–16)

These lines, like the two quatrains from section 42, evince double meaning. They evoke, on the one hand, the natural course of the moon's movement, a natural night's sleep that "knits up the ravelled sleeve of care,"[12] the natural promise of the sun's rise, and the natural genres of epithalamium and aubade. By the same token of these experiential criteria, however—that is, despite or because of this suggestion of this natural idiom—the spiritual diction of *glory* and *ghost* creates the wonderful effect of the moon's light as a spiritual influence that would resurrect Hallam to the new day, the fresh start of a distinctly millennialist as opposed to simply heavenly expectation.

In Memoriam's view of earth and heaven, then, is that they are always related and sometimes intersecting. Tennyson's understanding of this relationship is especially distinctive and bold in its determinedly empirical language and meaning. Death, one might say, gives reason and resonance to life; one must "love that well" which one must "leave ere long."[13] The late twentieth-century reader may not fret or speculate about, nor even much need to believe in, an afterlife, for as long ago as 1902 the doctrine of immortality could seem so "secondary," in William James's term, that James did not include it in *The Varieties of Religious Experience*. Tennyson, though, finds such belief essential; he said to Edward Fitzgerald in the spring of 1842, "I would rather know I was to be damned eternally than not to know that I was to live eternally."[14] Early deciding that "life shall live for evermore" (*In Memoriam*, 34.2), Tennyson goes on to express his characteristic theme that without the hope of life everlasting, earthly life would not be worth living:

> 'Twere best at once to sink to peace,
>   Like birds the charming serpent draws,
>   To drop head-foremost in the jaws
> Of vacant darkness and to cease.
>
> (34.13–16)

The poet does not expend as much effort in proving the afterlife, which for him is simply a given, as in describing it. Thus he keeps to his empirical/ observational premises.

The "second birth of death" (45.16), moreover, produces a second-order experience recognizable from the perspective of and even accessible to natural experience. Although the light and shadow of sense experience will not be precisely duplicated in heaven—"no shade can last / In that deep dawn behind the tomb" (46.5–6)—"clear from marge to marge shall bloom /

The eternal landscape of the past" (46.7–8). What characterizes heavenly life is what characterizes earthly life too. Both kinds of living are understandable to Tennyson from the full Lockean perspective of a sweeping picture of all that has happened.

Heaven would not be worthwhile without an earthly love itself "heavenly" in nature, or so Tennyson's focus on such love implies. The five years shared by him and Hallam suggest that earthly existence contains the promise of at once a paradise within and a paradise without, that is, of a spiritual paradise regained in the world of nature:

> A lifelong tract of time reveal'd,
>   The fruitful hours of still increase;
>   Days order'd in a wealthy peace,
> And those five years its richest field.
>
> (46.9–12)

This "paradise" writ large—that is, for all practical purposes heavenly indeed—is all one needs to know of heaven itself. Love, "a brooding star, / A rosy warmth from marge to marge" (46.15–16), is transcendental. In taking on finite form—"O Love, thy province were not large, / A bounded field, nor stretching far" (46.13–14)—love suffers no reduction, no lessening. Not for Tennyson, therefore, is any notion of the afterlife as "Remerging in the general Soul," for such faith is "as vague as all unsweet" (47.4–5). Rather, the poet "shall know" Hallam "when we meet," and "we shall sit at endless feast, / Enjoying each the other's good" (47.8–10).

Thus the afterlife revivifies the separate, corporeal identities who have engaged in and will continue to engage in intersubjective communion, or subject-object interaction. In this sense, intercourse occurs in heaven. "It has been asserted by some," observes Whately, "that in heavenly society, there will be no mutual knowledge between those who had been friends on earth; nor even any such thing as *friendship* towards one person more than another." [15] This idea, too, Whately finds "not very alluring." Tennyson, for his own empirical-experiential reasons, would wholeheartedly agree.

One infers a more detailed conception of the afterlife from *In Memoriam*, then, than from any other Western work, with the possible exception of Dante's *Paradiso*. This trait is all the more remarkable in that such rarefied tones of the nineteenth century as act 4 of Shelley's *Prometheus Unbound*

(1820) are generally sustained more through utopian means than through millennial-paradisal ones.

Empirical-evangelical methodology informs not only the relation between heaven and earth but also the emphasis on earthly experience alone in *In Memoriam.* "Among the Apostles," writes Buckley, Tennyson found "a reflection of his own religious doubts, his distrust of dogma, and at the same time a confirmation of his reliance upon direct intuitions of meaning, the rediscovery of spiritual values through the sort of personal experience that ultimately would give him both as man and artist his only real certainty." [16] Accordingly, much of what is commonly said about Tennyson can be understood as getting at his particular combination of skeptical method with spiritual quest. Boyd-Carpenter's comments about Tennyson's almost science-oriented religious views are a case in point: "He distrusted narrow views from whatever side they were advanced. The same spirit which led him to see the danger of the dogmatic temper in so-called orthodox circles led him to distrust it when it came from other quarters. There was a wholesome balance about his mind." [17] For Tennyson, as for Wesley and Edwards and even as for Locke in his more religious moods, skepticism is not a static state of unbelief but a method or process of knowing that allows one to keep the data of one's empirical experience and at the same time to keep open, however barely, one's access to faith.

"When I remarked that God did not take away men till their work was done," Boyd-Carpenter continues, "[Tennyson] said, 'He does; look at the promising young fellows cut off.'" Tennyson's skepticism, though dynamic, never quite lets this particular empirical datum go. *In Memoriam* never underestimates, and even directly confronts, what Wordsworth calls "the worst pang that sorrow ever bore," [18] namely, deep personal bereavement. Here, from Tennyson's account of his initial desolation, are undoubtedly more courage and vitality than mere morbid self-indulgence:

> Let Love clasp Grief lest both be drowned,
>   Let darkness keep her raven gloss;
>   Ah, sweeter to be drunk with loss,
> To dance with Death, to beat the ground,
>
> Than that the victor Hours should scorn
>   The long result of love, and boast,

> "Behold the man that loved and lost,
> But all he was is overthrown."
>
> (1.9–16)

If these lines should sound like the early stages of psychological grief as "scientifically" understood by Elizabeth Kübler-Ross, who focuses on grief over one's own mortality, they finally sound even more like Job's initial response to his sorrow. Job's tough-minded resilience, what Byron would have called his "vitality of poison,"[19] leads Job inexorably, albeit by fits and starts, to a faith all the deeper for his having taken account of and included his harrowing experience. The persona here seems reduced to nothing, seems to have nothing but the love on which the poem is based and which deepens and grows as the poem progresses, and is preserved by passing through rather than skirting the valley of the shadow of death. Tennyson's love soon causes him to ask, " 'Is this the end of all my care?' / . . . / 'Is this the end? Is this the end?' " (12.14–16); and although these repeated questions find no quick answers, they imply by their insistence that death is not and cannot be the end (see Job 14 and 19). These questions, though unglib, remain intently open as well as persistently searching.

An especially illuminating epitome of Tennyson's skeptical stance is to be found in the kinetic first two quatrains of section 23:

> Now, sometimes in my sorrow shut,
> Or breaking into song by fits,
> Alone, alone, to where he sits,
> The Shadow cloaked from head to foot,
>
> Who keeps the keys of all the creeds,
> I wander, often falling lame,
> And looking back to whence I came,
> Or on to where the pathway leads;
>
> (23.1–8)

Although the persona does not know the secrets of the creeds, he is far from denying that such creeds exist, or even that they may be true. Although he alternates between the highs and lows of his search for truth, he never stops pursuing truth. In the present, as in the past and future, he remains open to whatever he might learn, even from the place of death. He seems more hopeful than Browning's persona in "Childe Roland to the Dark Tower Came" (1855), for Browning's poem never "breaks into song" and, unlike these lines from *In Memoriam*, seems almost cocksure that there are no secrets to learn either from the shadow of death or from the shades of the departed.

Another instance of Tennyson's dynamic skepticism is to be found in section 29, where, "With such compelling cause to grieve / As daily vexes household peace," the persona intriguingly "keep[s] our Christmas-eve" (29. 1–2, 4) despite his disinclination to do so:

> Yet go, and while the holly boughs
>> Entwine the cold baptismal font,
>> Make one wreath more for Use and Wont,
> That guard the portals of the house;
>
> Old sisters of a day gone by,
>> Gray nurses, loving nothing new—
>> Why should they miss their yearly due,
> Before their time? They too will die.
>> (29.9–16)

The poet, putting up the wreath once more, harbors no illusion of much longer perpetuating an empty form of faith. His skepticism here is unremitting, relentless. However, although he evinces no apparent fear of the dangers of ritual such as are outlined, for example, in "The Lottery" (1948) by Shirley Jackson, and although at the other extreme he hardly believes with Yeats that "innocence and beauty" are born *only* "in custom and in ceremony," [20] he takes a compromise view of custom, that is, the Humean view of it as the great rule or determiner of life. Despite the frequent mindlessness of habit and despite the poet's yearning for a revelation that will free him from mere formularies of faith, custom and habit provide him with his short-term strategy for managing spiritual crisis. Even going through the motions of faith serves, if not to support his quest for it, then simply to pass the time as he awaits its return. Recall, in this connection, Habakkuk 2 and Milton's "They Also Serve Who Only Stand and Wait" (ca. 1652). Tennyson, in short, reflects a healthy complacency with regard to custom, which, as Hume points out, is better than no action at all.

The open quality of Tennyson's skepticism lends special integrity to his expressions of faith. A famous utterance from section 55 impressively combines his religious observances with the nervous energy of his questioning:

> And falling with my weight of cares
> Upon the great world's altar-stairs
> That slope through darkness up to God,
>
> I stretch lame hands of faith, and grope,
> And gather dust and chaff, and call
> To what I feel is Lord of all,
> And faintly trust the larger hope.
>
> (55.14–20)

Another of his strategies for conflating the empirical with the religious, while equally skeptical in methodology, is more positive, less doubting in tone. The first quatrain of the prologue, the last part of *In Memoriam* to be written, declares authoritatively that "Believing where we cannot prove" we embrace Christ "By faith, and faith alone" (lines 3–4). Such phrasing is opposed, say, to "always believing rather than ever proving." The phrasing suggests a harmonious, or at any rate unproblematic, relationship between science on the one hand and experiential faith on the other. Although "By faith, and faith alone" evokes the Calvinist/Arminian controversy over faith versus works, and although this phrase is thus unmistakably evangelical in tone and in import, it is not finally antinomian so much as subtly indicative of the poet's more Arminian than Calvinist view that, in the sphere of life and thought, experiential faith takes up where science leaves off.

What enables Tennyson to interrelate scientific evidence on the one hand and religious conviction on the other is his broad view that experience is both natural and spiritual. Thus he keeps his empirical knowledge, but adds to it. He has his cake and eats it too. Consider his exquisite summary of Lyellian geology:

> The hills are shadows, and they flow
> From form to form, and nothing stands;
> They melt like mist, the solid lands,
> Like clouds they shape themselves and go.
>
> (123.5–8)

Langbaum rightly calls this "perhaps the most beautiful rendition in English poetry of a modern scientific theory."[21] The hills to which one looks for strength and permanence are, as Psalm 121.1 recognizes, themselves temporary: "solid" (line 7) is poignantly ironic.

Juxtaposed to this harsh truth, however, is an equally powerful though infinitely tender truth:

> But in my spirit will I dwell,
>   And dream my dream, and hold it true;
>   For though my lips may breathe adieu,
> I cannot think the thing farewell.
>   (123.9–12)

The transition between these quatrains is not so abrupt as it may seem. The second quatrain, by including the internal in the catalogue of experience, is as experiential as the first. Thus Tennyson, even as he lives, is convinced of the afterlife. Aware, from one point of view, of the absurdity of thinking that a single voice can add significant truth to what Wordsworth calls "this mighty sum / Of things forever speaking" (see Psalm 19),[22] Tennyson gives pride of place to his spiritual voice, which he thinks of as adding to the mighty sum of a speaking and hence essentially personal if not divine reality.

Where Tennyson is first persuaded that "life shall live for evermore" (34.2), he finds the perennial embodiment of eternal life in a nature independent of but correlative to humankind:

> This round of green, this orb of flame,
>   Fantastic beauty; such as lurks
>   In some wild poet, when he works
> Without a conscience or an aim.
>   (34.5–8)

Toward the end of the poem, at the apex of a composition-experience that has gradually restored his faith, Tennyson announces that he apprehends the truth without quite comprehending it: "And what I am beheld again / What is, and no man understands" (124.21–22). Ascribing this advance to an external, objective force—"And out of darkness came the hands / That reach through nature, moulding men" (124.23–24)—the poet refers to a pantheistic force, if, that is, one reads "through" to mean "throughout and confined to" rather than "by means of." (Compare this meaning to Dylan Thomas's "force that through the green fuse drives the flower / Drives my green age.") Tennyson makes clear in *In Memoriam*, 116, however, that the force is both within and other than nature, for the "songs" of birds, the "stirring air," and "the life re-orient out of dust" (116.5–6) are all spring-time signs of theistical agency. They "Cry thro' the sense to hearten trust / In that which made the world so fair" (116.7–8).

Such cooperation of nature and spirit if not of empiricism and evangeli-calism informs a range of characteristic effects in *In Memoriam* from puns to loco description. Although nature's indifferent boast that "A thousand types are gone" (56.3) refers to species impermanence, the word *types*, at least, includes religious as well as scientific meaning, and the Evangelical Anglican sister is a "type," too, a foreshadowing of imminent/immanent millennium (33.16). Hallam himself is a "noble type" of the millennial as well as the evolutionary progress of the human race (epilogue, line 138). Finally, Tennyson never thinks that poetry should be so otherworldly, so broadly expatiating as to exclude loco description:

> Take wings of fancy, and ascend,
>   And in a moment set thy face
>   Where all the starry heavens of space
> Are sharpened to a needle's end;
>
> Take wings of foresight; lighten through
>   The secular abyss to come,
>   And lo, thy deepest lays are dumb
> Before the mouldering of a yew;
>   (76.1–8)

Although art, as the first six lines suggest, should be general, ideal, ambi-tious, and visionary, the eight lines taken together mean that even properly spiritual, properly prophetic poetry should attempt to include within its ken the objects of nature.

Tennyson, by implying that the cosmic must take account of flux, and that even a dying yew tree partakes of mystery, implies too that no art which fails to explain decay, or which fails to value what decays, suffices for the truth, no matter how supreme the fiction of that art. In this connection one thinks of *The Book of Thel* (1789–91) by Blake: "Does the Eagle know what is in the pit, / Or wilt thou go ask the Mole?" Truth lies, for Blake, in a combination of Mole- and Eagle-knowledge.[23] No more than Blake, accordingly, would Tennyson confine his apperceptions to the spiritual side of the natural-spiritual dialectic.

Tennyson devotes an especially lovely passage to a pleasing mix of the chthonic and the sacred, as though the mix, despite his doubting mood at this early point in the poem, were indicative of the synthesis toward which he will strive. "Thee" refers to the ship that bears Hallam's body home from Vienna for burial:

> O, to us,
> The fools of habit, sweeter seems
>
> To rest beneath the clover sod,
>   That takes the sunshine and the rains,
>   Or where the kneeling hamlet drains
> The chalice of the grapes of God;
>
> Than if with thee the roaring wells
>   Should gulf him fathom-deep in brine,
>   And hands so often clasped in mine,
> Should toss with tangle and with shells.
>   (10.11–20)

This tentative mix of nature description with the bare beginnings of experiential-sacramental faith becomes a confident blend in two later passages, sections 86 and 121. The former is pneumatological, the latter Christological. Each is triumphant. Both passages secure the empirical-evangelical synthesis of *In Memoriam*.

As for 121, Christ is associated with the morning star, and Tennyson builds on this symbolism throughout his awareness of the identity between morning and evening star.

> Sad Hesper o'er the buried sun
>   And ready, thou, to die with him,
>   Thou watchest all things ever dim
> And dimmer, and a glory done.

The team is loosened from the wain,
    The boat is drawn upon the shore;
    Thou listenest to the closing door,
And life is darkened in the brain.

Bright Phosphor, fresher for the night,
    By thee the world's great work is heard
    Beginning, and the wakeful bird;
Behind thee comes the greater light:

The market boat is on the stream,
    And voices hail it from the brink;
    Thou hear'st the village hammer clink,
And see'st the moving of the team.

Sweet Hesper-Phosphor, double name
    For what is one, the first, the last,
    Thou, like my present and my past,
Thy place is changed; thou art the same.

                (121.1–20)

In 1864 Hopkins wrote that "surely your maturest judgment will never be fooled out of saying that [this section] is divine, terribly beautiful."[24]

In one sense, to be sure, the lyric operates on an exclusively natural plane. The contrast between the evening and the morning manifestations of a single star need signify no more than death/birth, winter/summer, and decay/regeneration. The star, as is indicated by the penultimate line of the section, may represent Tennyson. He presides over the tragic death of his friend, but he comes to accept death as natural, and he even takes legitimate comfort in the fresh day's hope of recurring life.

Just as the natural contrasts with the supernatural, however, so Hesper contrasts with Phosphor; the morning star, an accordingly strong copresence in the lyric, may signify Christ's gift of resurrection. The fifth quatrain's reminder that the evening and morning star are the same suggests the identity of nature with spirit. Thus, in Alistair W. Thomson's phrase, section 121 reassures us of "a singleness which was always there" in the poem.[25] Hopkins would have especially appreciated Tennyson's implication that Christ's Alpha and Omega (see Revelation 22.13) encompass earth and heaven, time and eternity. Tennyson's "Alpha-Omega," his Hesper-

Phosphor, seems to guarantee not only identity in time but also the survival of identity from time to eternity. Finally, the "greater light" may signify Hallam's more than evangelical supplanting of Christ.

The pneumatological 86, like the Christological 121, should be quoted in full.

> Sweet after showers, ambrosial air,
>   That rollest from the gorgeous gloom
>   Of evening over brake and bloom
> And meadow, slowly breathing bare
>
> The round of space, and rapt below
>   Through all the dewy tasselled wood,
>   And shadowing down the horned flood
> In ripples, fan my brows and blow
>
> The fever from my cheek, and sigh
>   The full new life that feeds thy breath
>   Throughout my frame, till Doubt and Death,
> Ill brethren, let the fancy fly
>
> From belt to belt of crimson seas
>   On leagues of odor streaming far,
>   To where in yonder orient star
> A hundred spirits whisper "Peace."
>   (86.1–16)

This single sentence, an almost flamboyant display of enjambment, underscores the wholeness, the seamlessness, of natural-spiritual experience. One cannot but salute again the ability first remarked by John Stuart Mill: Tennyson described landscapes in accordance with languorous, receptive states of mind.[26] Thus, object impinges on subject in this rich imagining; auditory, visual, and tactile images abound, creating the synthesis of matter with mind. Embedded, too, in this romance is the spiritual nuance of such diction as *sweet, ambrosial, rapt,* and *shadowing.* The metaphor of *ruah* in "slowly breathing," "sigh," and "feeds thy breath / Throughout my frame," augurs identity among the atmosphere, the speaker, and the influx of the Holy Spirit.

Thus the spiritual nuance of 86 is even more pronounced, more transcendent, than Kincaid recognizes. "Especially in 86," Kincaid writes, but also in 83 and 88 (which I will discuss), "nature's deep rhythms catch [Tennyson] up and he feels the elemental breath of life that provides a 'peace' that is alive and vibrant, contrasting with the dead and awful 'calm' of 11."[27] The final two lines of 86 predict Hopkins's lambent-sacramental view of nature, his joyous imperative to "Look at the stars! look, look up at the skies! / O look at all the fire-folk sitting in the air."[28] Tennyson's "sigh / The full new life" operates on the finally religious and even evangelical plane of conversion idiom. Although "ill brethren" represent a distinct theological problem ("the wages of sin is death" [Romans 6.23a]), the problem is solved, at least momentarily, by the speaker's transmigration to and his transfiguration among a fellowship of saints ("the gift of God is eternal life through Jesus Christ our Lord" [Romans 6.23b]). Thus Hopkins's favorable response to *In Memoriam* is quite understandable; although Tennyson is empirical-evangelical and not Catholic, he has progressed from his doubts about everlasting life to his new-faithful configurationing of Phosphor-Christ with *ruah*-Spirit. Such immediacy is perhaps as consistent with empirical-evangelical sensibility as, say, with the transubstantiating dimension of Hopkins's Catholicism.

Returning now to the portrait of Hallam, I conclude my overview of the philosophical theology in *In Memoriam*. Tennyson asks his brother Charles not to be vexed by the fact that Hallam is "More than my brothers are to me" (79.1). Tennyson knows, to be sure, "what force" Charles possesses "To hold the costliest love in fee" (79.3–4). The natural experiences shared by the two brothers, moreover, emphasized Lockean nurture: "And hill and wood and field did print / The same sweet forms in either mind" (79.7–8). Similarly, their shared spiritual experiences emphasized their mother's evangelical transmission of traditional revelation:

> At one dear knee we proffered vows,
>> One lesson from one book we learned,
>> Ere childhood's flaxen ringlet turned
> To black and brown on kindred brows.
>
> (79.13–16)

("Mrs Tennyson," writes Robert Bernard Martin, "was probably more genuinely religious than her melancholy clergyman husband, and she passed on to Alfred her spirit of reverence."[29] Martin's addition, "although [Alfred] early deserted her strict Evangelical beliefs," is tempered by my approach.) Although nothing can take away what Alfred and Charles shared, however, *In Memoriam* asks Charles to indulge its tribute to one with whom Alfred continues to share an even more intense and a fuller experience.

While the experience with Charles is only alternately natural and spiritual, the experience with Hallam, like empirical-evangelical experience in general, is simultaneously so. Tennyson's best wish for the world is that it will grow more like Hallam:

> I would the great world grew like thee,
>> Who grewest not alone in power
>> And knowledge, but by year and hour
> In reverence and in charity.
>
> (114.25–28)

Thus Hallam's character is formed by equal parts of empirical-evangelical heart and empirical-evangelical mind. Charles Wesley, though not as conscious of Locke's importance as his brother John was, regarded Locke's *Essay concerning Human Understanding* as solid, substantial truth.[30] Apropos of Hallam's character are these pertinent lines from a hymn sung "at the opening of a School in Kingswood," where the Wesley brothers put Locke's *Essay* on their required reading list:

> Learning's redundant part and vain
>> Be here cut off, and cast aside:
> But let them, Lord, the substance gain,
>> In every solid truth abide,
> Swiftly acquire, and ne'er forego
> The knowledge fit for man to know.
>
> Unite the pair so long disjoin'd,
>> Knowledge and vital piety.

When Tennyson proposes to "keep the day" of Hallam's birth, namely, February 1, winter makes it difficult to do so, for winter "admits not flowers or leaves / To deck the banquet" (107.5–7). Despite "The blast of North and East" (107.7), however, section 107 goes on to bid the friends of Hallam "Be cheerful-minded, talk and treat / Of all things even as he were by" (107.19–20). This, surely, is one of the most abrupt transitions, one of the largest leaps of faith in this or any other poem; but the transition is made more graspable if not less mysterious by the peculiar simultaneity of natural and spiritual in Tennyson's portrait of Hallam.

Because empirical knowledge of Hallam now proves almost out of reach, section 122 (still on experiential grounds) strains for a spiritual knowledge of him. Tennyson implores, commands Hallam to be present, so that, like Coleridge's "one Life within us and abroad," [31] but also like the Holy Spirit whom Coleridge too might have had in mind, Hallam transfigures, yet still relates to Tennyson's spirit-body and the natural-spiritual world. "Be with me now" (122.10), Tennyson pleads with Hallam,

> And enter in at breast and brow,
> Till all my blood, a fuller wave,
>
> Be quicken'd with a livelier breath,
> And like an inconsiderate boy,
> As in the former flash of joy,
> I slip the thoughts of life and death;
>
> And all the breeze of Fancy blows,
> And every dewdrop paints a bow,
> The wizard lightnings deeply glow,
> And every thought breaks out a rose.
>
> (122.11–20)

With similar world-altering, world-begun effects, Milton enters Blake's foot.[32] Peltason finds no spiritual dimension in section 122: "The spiritual claims of earlier lyrics have given way entirely to the imaginative claims of Romantic landscape." [33] (The occasion referred to, "the former flash of joy," is unknown.[34]) But the section joins the world of object-subject to the world of nature-spirit, with no attenuations of "as if."

In Memoriam's synthesis of empirical thesis with evangelical antithesis culminates, perhaps, in section 130, which suggests that Hallam is resurrected not just in heaven (see Shelley's *Adonais*) but even in all that is heard, seen, felt, and touched on earth:

> Thy voice is on the rolling air;
> I hear thee where the waters run;

> Thou standest in the rising sun,
> And in the setting thou art fair.

> .   .   .   .

> My love involves the love before;
>   My love is vaster passion now;
>   Though mixed with God and Nature thou,
> I seem to love thee more and more.

> Far off thou art, but ever nigh;
>   I have thee still, and I rejoice;
>   I prosper, circled with thy voice;
> I shall not lose thee though I die.
>   (130. 1–4, 9–16)

I disagree with Peltason's description of this section's single mention of God (line 11) as "unintegrated" and therefore unimportant.[35] Peltason says 130 is "a dream of mingling that is once again private and fantastic," but Ricks, I think more pertinently, points to the allusion in line 3 to Revelation 19. 17: "And I saw an angel standing in the sun; and he cried in a loud voice."[36] I suggest, at any rate, that section 130's bold claim to natural-spiritual knowledge prepares the reader for the one quatrain of the entire poem in which the poet allows himself to "conjecture"—notice the modest skepticism of this diction—that Hallam is literally back:

> Nor count me all to blame if I
>   Conjecture of a stiller guest,
>   Perchance, perchance, among the rest,
> And, though in silence, wishing joy.
>   (epilogue, lines 85–88)

Thus Tennyson speculates that Hallam is among the company at the wedding of Tennyson's sister Emily to Edmund Lushington, professor of Greek at Glasgow. The all but empirical as well as decidedly spiritual presence of Hallam at this particular occasion raises the possibility that Tennyson's portrait of the experientially faithful, Evangelical Anglican sister in section 33 is inspired by Emily Tennyson.

Be that as it may, the low-key effectiveness of a vision in section 91

almost persuades the reader that, in the full light of the best days nature
has to offer, in her two gladder seasons, the poet is back in the presence of
whom he loves:

> When rosy plumelets tuft the larch,
>   And rarely pipes the mounted thrush,
>   Or underneath the barren bush
> Flits by the sea-blue bird of March;
>
> Come, wear the form by which I know
>   Thy spirit in time among thy peers;
>   The hope of unaccomplished years
> Be large and lucid round thy brow.
>
> When summer's hourly-mellowing change
>   May breathe, with many roses sweet,
>   Upon the thousand waves of wheat
> That ripple round the lowly grange,
>
> Come; not in watches of the night,
>   But where the sunbeam broodeth warm,
>   Come, beauteous in thine after form,
> And like a finer light in light.
>
>   (91.1–16)

These quatrains, indeed, reveal the philosophically theological reasons, if
such reasons were needed, for agreeing with Edmund Gosse's fair estimate
of Tennyson's achievement:

> Where then has his greatness lain? It has lain in the various per-
> fections of his writing. He has written, on the whole, with more
> constant, unwearied, and unwearying excellence than any of his con-
> temporaries. . . . He has expended the treasures of his native talent
> on broadening and deepening his own hold upon the English lan-
> guage, until that has become an instrument upon which he is able to
> play a greater variety of melodies to perfection than any other man.[37]

Tennyson's perfection, though, is more than aesthetic. Even his aesthetic
perfection shows forth the excellence of his content. These quatrains, for

88

their part in the overall perfection of *In Memoriam*, combine floral, aviary, and granular delicacies with the even rarer, even more rarefied delicacy by which, without losing any of his famous feeling for the earth, Tennyson announces his organic and all but evolutionary heaven on earth, his millennial and mythic as well as dawn-inspired expectation of Hallam-come-again.

FIVE

Spiritual Sense

A crucial criterion of *In Memoriam* is the status of the senses in the quest for faith. Consider, in this regard, his account of Lazarus's sister Mary:

> Her eyes are homes of silent prayer,
>   Nor other thought her mind admits
>   But, he was dead, and there he sits,
> And he that brought him back is there.
>
> (32.1–4)

In concert with Mary's reason, her eyes put her in the presence of her brother and Jesus, the ground of her knowing. Although her senses take on spiritual power, and although the "doors" of her "perception" are thus "cleansed,"[1] her spiritual vision retains natural sight. According to John Dixon Hunt, the symbolism of *In Memoriam* is as much this-worldly as otherworldly,[2] and the poem's as much empirical as evangelical religious methodology resembles the spiritual sense shared by Wesley and Edwards.[3] Tennyson is far from regarding the physical senses as merely analogous to spiritual vision; he also conceives of them as underlying it.

The only "sensationalist" methodology to which the poet at first lays any claim is not so much the *spiritual* sense as the "*awful* sense / Of one mute Shadow watching all" (30.7–8; my italics). Death can fill and dominate all perception, as though it were the only reality. Tennyson's depiction of even the first Christmas after Hallam's death, however, entertains the possibility that the physical senses are fully, albeit subtly, efficacious. Tennyson's hearing tends to validate both the faith of his father and his own spiritual experience in youth, for the bells that "controll'd" him "when a boy" continue, in this Christmas season, to "rule" his "troubled spirit" (28.17–18). Insofar as these bells touch his "sorrow" with "joy" (28.19), they leaven his suffering and manifest grace. Winds blow, hymns waft, Christmas dawns, and this kinetic, tactile, aural, and visual experience accompanies and is indispensable to an insight that comforts Tennyson like an epiphany: "a gentler feeling crept / Upon us: surely rest is meet" (30.17–18). This revelation, although slight, suggests that the nothing new of custom shades over into the something new of grace. Tennyson's reticence, his skeptical refusal to be glib, is a better religious strategy than the emptiness of formula; his sense experience, however numbed by grief, keeps his persona open to such comforts as there are, whether or not these comforts constitute immediate revelation from the Comforter.

The highlighting of *sense* in section 44, significantly, marks an important step in Tennyson's development of the spiritual sense ("thee" refers to Hallam):

> How fares it with the happy dead?
>> For here the man is more and more;
>> But he forgets the days before
> God shut the doorways of his head.
>
> The days have vanished, tone and tint,
>> And yet perhaps the hoarding *sense*
>> Gives out at times—he knows not whence—
> A little flash, a mystic hint;
>
> And in the long harmonious years—
>> If Death so taste Lethean springs—
>> May some dim touch of earthly things
> Surprise thee ranging with thy peers.
>
> If such a dreamy touch should fall,
>> O, turn thee round, resolve the doubt;
>> My guardian angel will speak out
> In that high place, and tell thee all.
>> (44.1–16; my italics)

These lines pose a challenge but constitute a crux. "If 'man' (line 2) refers to the dead," writes George H. Ford, "the passage means that in our living world the dead man is more and more remembered, but that he, in the afterworld, is shut off through death from remembering past experiences on earth." "Alternatively," Ford continues, "if 'man' refers to living mankind rather than to the 'happy dead,' the passage means that as man grows up (line 2) he forgets his earliest infancy, especially the two-year period before the sutures of his skull are closed." This ambiguity augurs the simultaneity of earthly and heavenly perspectives.[4]

The heavenly perspective works so clearly in all four quatrains as to be primary, for although Hallam continues to grow in heaven, his "hoarding sense," his memory, reminds him of Tennyson on earth. That same sense may even put him in touch with Tennyson, who "joins" Hallam in heaven. The secondary perspective of earth, though, is at least as intriguing if not quite as thoroughly applicable. Although humankind, in the midst of sense experience, gradually forgets divine preexistence, such "earthly things" as a familiar haunt and an object that belonged to a dead loved one may give fresh access to divine existence. Thus the "hoarding sense," whether memory or simply the collective senses still gathering experience, is more than merely natural in function. From whichever perspective one chooses to read the passage, the senses in it constitute validators, manifesters, accompaniments, and harbingers of spiritual truth. One should read it, perhaps, from both perspectives at once.

Tennyson's "*awful* sense" of death in the first Christmas lyric (section 30) gives way in the second such lyric (section 78) to "The *quiet* sense of something lost" (line 8; my italics). Although the third Christmas lyric (section 85) does not quite win its way through to a *spiritual* sense of something *present,* such as one finds most notably in section 130 (previously discussed), nevertheless, one finds a significant advance toward just such a sense of presence.

What Tennyson calls his "imaginative woe" (85.53), I call his sensationalist "epistemology" of grief; his "passion" for Hallam

> hath not swerved
> To works of weakness, but I find
> An *Image* comforting the mind,
> And in my grief a strength reserved.
>
> Likewise the *imaginative* woe,
> That loved to *handle* spiritual strife,

> Diffused the shock through all my life,
> But *in the present* broke the blow.
>> (85.49–56; my italics)

Through this sensationalist-empirical language, Tennyson visualizes Hallam so assiduously and with such method that the poet's eyes are schooled to "see" his other dead friends as well: "My pulses therefore beat again / For other friends that once I met" (85.57–58). It is not enough that Hallam is "sacred essence," "other form," "solemn ghost," and "crowned soul" (85.35–36). Tennyson's empirical temperament clings to and insists on the worlds of action and sense experience, too:

> Yet none could better know than I,
> How much of act at human hands
> The sense of human will demands
> By which we dare to live or die.
>> (85.37–40)

Logically, then, Tennyson testifies to a continued experience with Hallam, as intent and intimate as ever:

> Whatever way my days decline,
> I felt and feel, though left alone,
> His being working in mine own,
> The footsteps of his life in mine;
>> (85.41–44)

Tennyson is not speaking entirely figuratively; notice, for example, that nature all but embodies Hallam:

> But Summer on the steaming floods,
> And Spring that swells the narrow brooks,
> And Autumn, with a noise of rooks,
> That gather in the waning woods,
>
> And every pulse of wind and wave
> Recalls, in change of light or gloom,
> My old affection of the tomb,
> And my prime passion in the grave.
>> (85.69–76)

The last two lines return, jarringly, to the reality of death. These quatrains, however, assume that the presence of Hallam remains perceivable; *recalls* means not just *reminds me of,* but *brings before me once again* as well.

Section 92 is based on the comprehensive methodology of 85, the longest numbered section of *In Memoriam* (the epilogue is somewhat longer); 92 also boldly entertains the idea of literally seeing Hallam:

> If any vision should reveal
>   Thy likeness, I might count it vain
>   As but the canker of the brain;
> Yea, tho' it spake and made appeal
>
> To chances where our lots were cast
>   Together in the days behind,
>   I might but say, I hear a wind
> Of memory murmuring the past.
>
> Yea, tho' it spake and bared to view
>   A fact within the coming year;
>   And tho' the months, revolving near,
> Should prove the phantom-warning true,
>
> They might not seem thy prophecies,
>   But spiritual presentiments,
>   And such refraction of events
> As often rises ere they rise.
>   (92.1–16)

This passage, of course, depends on an especially tentative "if" clause. The "yea, though" pattern subverts the rhetoric of Psalm 23, for "Yea, though I walk through the valley of the shadow of death, I will fear no evil; . . . thy rod and thy staff they comfort me" yields, in effect, to "yea, though you should come back from death, I would not believe my eyes nor readily accept either natural or spiritual proofs that you are you." (Hallam would naturally know details of their past friendship, and as a spirit would possess the gift of prophecy.) At just the point where Tennyson's faith grows boldest and most speculative, he holds most tightly to his skeptical method, thus keeping the data of his empirical experience. He does so, however, almost as the precondition for further spiritual progress; section 92 finally constitutes a thorough exposition of the spiritual sense.

Whether "vision" (line 1) means "a mode of apprehending merely analogous to the physical senses" or "the physical senses themselves," the spiritual sense at which Tennyson hints revalidates Hallam's life, remanifests him. Although the persona distinguishes between "*spiritual* presentiments" and such *natural* "refraction of events / As often rises ere they rise," Tennyson speaks between these lines to suggest that since the physical senses can function spiritually as harbingers, the spiritual sense can be one with the natural senses. Although seeing Hallam in natural objects is one thing, seeing Hallam himself is quite another. This latter "seeing," however, is what section 92 entails. This passage poeticizes the continuum that joins scientific method and rational empiricism to natural and revealed religion; thus the empirical-evangelical way of looking at the section emerges as perhaps even more fully explanatory than the admittedly more immediate context of Tennyson's occasional interest in seances and spiritualism.[5]

Section 93 completes Tennyson's elucidation of the spiritual sense:

> I shall not see thee. Dare I say
>   No spirit ever brake the band
>   That stays him from the native land
> Where first he walked when claspt in clay?
>
> No visual shade of some one lost,
>   But he, the Spirit himself, may come
>   Where all the nerve of sense is numb,
> Spirit to Spirit, Ghost to Ghost.
>
> O, therefore from thy sightless range
>   With gods in unconjectured bliss,
>   O, from the distance of the abyss
> Of tenfold-complicated change,
>
> Descend, and touch, and enter; hear
>   The wish too strong for words to name,
>   That in this blindness of the frame
> My Ghost may feel that thine is near.
>   (93.1–16)

The focus here is on immediate revelation. Although "the Spirit" (line 6) is Hallam, the word also denotes the Holy Spirit (Hopkins would say "ghost guessed"[6]). The passage begins with an apparently complete rejection of

95

sensationalist epistemology: "I shall *not* see thee." The Holy Spirit's implied identification with Hallam, however, constitutes a decidedly sense-like impression of Hallam, a wondrous delivery of him up to Tennyson. Even where the poet's spiritual sense bears no relation to his physical eye, his "sense" indeed sees, that is, perceives in a way understandable only with reference to point-blank ocular powers.

While "Dare I say . . .?" (line 1) conveys the speaker's extreme reluctance to think that he will never see Hallam again on earth, the question also suggests that natural-spiritual, spiritual-natural vision recurs. Insofar as the spirits of both Tennyson and Hallam continue to mix with nature, the variables of their natural experience remain especially and wonderfully unpredictable. This mixture, this blend, is assumed by *In Memoriam*. The "touch" of "Descend, and touch, and enter" (line 13) suggests, in particular, an incarnation especially graspable by, and even fully commensurate with, the empirical understanding.

SIX

Theodiceal Impulse

Tennyson's theodicy ranks with such other comprehensive, profound corollaries of his philosophical theology as his spiritual sense. He, like Milton and the author of the Book of Job, attempts to vindicate the justice of God, especially God's ordaining or permitting natural and moral evil. Ricks, in finding "affinities" between *In Memoriam* and John Berryman's *Dream Songs*, points out that both are "theodicies."[1] Culler finds fault, however, with the theodicy of *In Memoriam*: "Tennyson is not attempting a complete theodicy. . . . Rather he offers . . . mere guesses at truth, which dimple the surface of his pool of tears but do not penetrate to the depths."[2] I argue, to the contrary, that among the most successful characteristics of *In Memoriam* is its impulse toward theodicy.

Boyd-Carpenter tells an anecdote fraught with implications for the poem's theodiceal aspect:

> [Tennyson] never shirked the hard and dismaying facts of life. Once he made me take to my room Winwood Reade's *Martyrdom of Man*. There never was such a passionate philippic against Nature as this book contained. The universe was one vast scene of murder; the deep aspirations and noble visions of men were the follies of flies buzzing for a brief moment in the presence of inexorable destruction. Life was bottled sunshine; death the silent-footed butler who withdrew the cork. The book, with its fierce invective, had a strange rhapsodical charm. It put with irate and verbose extravagance the fact that sometimes
>
> > Nature, red in tooth and claw
> > With ravine, shrieked against [man's] creed

but it failed to see any but one side of the question. The writer saw clearly enough what Tennyson saw, but Tennyson saw much more.[3]

William Winwood Reade (1838–75) was a novelist, traveler, and polemicist; with classic understatement, *The Dictionary of National Biography* observes of Reade's *Martyrdom of Man* (1872) that "the author does not attempt to conceal his atheistical opinions."[4] Boyd-Carpenter's story points up Tennyson's "evangelical" fervor in "sharing" with Boyd-Carpenter even the most pessimistic of Darwin-inspired philosophy; on May 9, 1863, moreover, Tennyson declared to Queen Victoria that "if there is no immortality of the soul, one does not see why there should be any God."[5] This comment to the sovereign who appointed him laureate goes on in an especially pointed, boldly theodiceal way: "You cannot love a Father who strangled you."

Hallam, significantly, had written *Theodicaea Novissima* (1831), which, at Tennyson's request, was included in Hallam's *Remains* (1834). *Theodicaea Novissima*, according to Philip Flynn, is "an amalgam of the Coleridgean philosophy of Christian experience encountered at Cambridge with Optimistic rationalism"; Flynn also points to the importance of "Hallam's private readings in Plato, Dante, and medieval philosophy."[6] Flynn studies the influence of *Theodicaea Novissima* on *In Memoriam*, concluding that the latter is even "more consistent in epistemology," and even more "comprehensive of human aspiration." Tennyson's theodiceal combination of epistemology and aspiration is clearly understandable along lines of his empirical-evangelical method. Eschewing rationalism, his method arrives at theodicy through a "philosophy of Christian experience" as much Wesleyan-Edwardsean as Coleridgean (Coleridge's "philosophy of Christian experience" is itself arguably empirical-evangelical[7]). *In Memoriam*, like *Paradise Lost* and the Book of Job, acknowledges that on theological grounds the problem of suffering is far from easily solvable, but on the basis of the philosophical as well as theological epistemology of experience the elegy makes its unique contribution to the emotional-intellectual theodiceal tradition.

The prologue, written last, emphasizes the orthodox result of Tennyson's quest for explanation. Even his opening announcement that Christ kills death, however, introduces theodiceal inquiry. Addressing Christ, the poet bluntly declares, "Thou madest Death" (prologue, line 7). Death, however, though solved as a problem—"and lo, thy foot / Is on the skull which thou hast made" (prologue, lines 7–8)—remains a disturbing mystery to the theodicean Tennyson, who is still unsatisfied, still uncomplacent, and still worried about good and evil. It is no full comfort yet that he can retain faith in the monotheistic God as somehow the source of "evil" as well as "good." The haunting assertion of the prologue that "Thou wilt not leave us in the dust" (line 9) sounds more like whistling in the dark than like resonant affirmation of faith. Thus the speaker, even where he first articulates faith, and even where he first claims victory over intellectual crisis as well as personal grief, is no Pangloss. Tennyson retains an insistent/persistent theodiceal impulse not only in the less serene moments of his emotional-intellectual inquiry but also in his overarching prologue.

Section 1 reports that the poet once believed, with Goethe, "That men may rise on stepping-stones / Of their dead selves to higher things" (1.3–4). Thus he once held that "suffering builds character," that "adversity marks the earnest of one's better self." Now, however, Tennyson regards this theodicy as unsatisfactory. Without exactly refuting it, he no longer even mouths it. He recognizes how it gives rise to further difficult questions:

> who shall so forecast the years
> And find in loss a gain to match?
> Or reach a hand thro' time to catch
> The far-off interest of tears?
> (1.5–8)

Tennyson, for one, would not be so presumptuous. He refuses even to predict that Hallam's death will produce a better Tennyson, for Hallam is so far preferable to any "better" Tennyson as to make the very idea of such a substitution a worse than contemptible insult to theodiceal intelligence. Some "better" Tennyson as a held-out compensation for the intensity of the poet's present grief is too calculating a concept to measure up to the worthiest standards of theodicy.

The emphasis in section 54 on natural and moral evil, on "pangs of nature, sins of will, / Defects of doubt, and taints of blood" (54.3–4), is as sweeping and unflinching a theodiceal formulation as one can find in *In Memoriam*. The section also offers, however, a full synthesis of doubt and faith—that is, a resoundingly theodiceal breakthrough. Tennyson, to be sure, cannot yet intellectually account for evil: "Behold, we know not anything" (54.13). For that matter, he cannot poetically account for evil either, since language is inadequate:

> what am I?
> An infant crying in the night;
> An infant crying for the light,
> And with no language but a cry.
> (54.17–20)

(Ricks points to the echo of Jeremiah 1.6: "Then said I, Ah, Lord God! behold, I cannot speak: for I am a child."[8]) Under the circumstances, the only thing for the poet to do is to take the leap of faith: "O, yet we trust that somehow good / Will be the final goal of ill" (54.1–2). Although this "leap" is not as intellectual as theodicy usually tries to be, it is at least rigorously honest: "I can but trust that good shall fall / At last—far off—at last, to all" (54.14–15). This awkward and repetitious groping for faith is deliberate, for it is intellectually respectable precisely because it is tentative.

In thus stuttering and stumbling his way to "all," Tennyson finally gives witness to Arminian aspiration to universal salvation. As an intellectual resource, Arminian-evangelical theology should accompany and can naturally leaven the rigorous empiricism that also informs and gives substance to the theodiceal ambitions of section 54. (Recall my previous discussion of this section's empirical procedures.) "Nothing walks with aimless feet" (54.5) can signify predestination. This line can also mean, however, that one enjoys free will. In accordance with the latter possibility, section 54 resolves Calvinist-Arminian ambiguity on the Arminian side of possible redemption for all. Such joyful affirmations as "not one life shall be destroyed," "not a worm is cloven in vain," "not a moth with vain desire / Is shrivelled in a fruitless fire," and "every winter [will] change to spring" (54.6, 54.9–11, 16) lend touches of Arminian triumph to the growing optimism of *In Memoriam*'s theodiceal designs.

Compare my view of section 54 with the sharply parallel, if only implicitly theodiceal, view of it put forward by Peltason: "Here, at the grim center of *In Memoriam*, we are characteristically given no single moment of greatest despair, but a pattern of related moments, a virtuosity and variety of despair. And this despair, like the charged and changing grief of earlier lyrics, is both the evidence and the cause of imaginative activity, an

incitement to us to rechart the poet's course."[9] Peltason's otherwise helpful statement gives perhaps insufficient weight to the section's charged
variety of theodiceal imagination. The section, after all, is finally affirmative.

Another theodiceal hypothesis, besides "suffering builds character," is
"the existence of good and evil indicates dualistic reality," but Tennyson's
fidelity to ethical monotheism, among the stances that he holds in common with Job, obviates any need for him to adopt the escapist, relatively
intellectually shallow argument of theodiceal dualism. Consider, for example, his or Hallam's struggle with doubt, which, regardless of whom
"he" refers to, is signal theodicy indeed:

> He fought his doubts and gathered strength,
>   He would not make his judgment blind,
>   He faced the spectres of the mind
> And laid them; thus he came at length
>
> To find a stronger faith his own,
>   And Power was with him in the night,
>   Which makes the darkness and the light,
> And dwells not in the light alone,
>
> But in the darkness and the cloud,
>   As over Sinai's peaks of old,
>   While Israel made their gods of gold,
> Although the trumpet blew so loud.
>   (96.13–24)

These quatrains allude to Exodus 19.6, which suggests that the existence
of moral evil indicates how divine anger may be ethically justifiable. The
quatrains are paraphrasable as follows: questions about the origin of evil
cause religious doubts, which are calmed, in turn, by a threefold realization: first that God does not ask us to endure more than it is possible to
endure; second that God will be with us amidst pain; and third that God,
being one, must be the source of suffering as well as of everything else.

Thus, while not exactly pessimistic, the passage offers an Old Testament
image of a God of wrath and judgment, a jealous God who tolerates no
other gods before him (see Exodus 19 and 32), and a Calvinistic God whose
sovereignty leaves no doubt about who transcends, and could explain or

even synthesize, good and evil. Clearly, Tennyson did not wholly escape the influence of his Calvinist aunt Mary Bourne of Dalby; Martin's colorful account deserves full quotation:

> It was not much fun to stay there, for a curtain of depressing religiosity hung over the house; the Bournes attended a Dissenting chapel and expected the "Servants to do the same, & also to be in attendance every morning & evening at Family prayers."
>
> Alfred managed to find some relief in tight-lipped amusement at the rigidity of his aunt's beliefs. Once when she had taken him with her to chapel, she began to weep while listening to a sermon on Hell. He asked her with concern whether it was for pity of the poor creatures in torment, but she said, no, it was because she alone, miserable woman, had been picked out by Providence for salvation. Perhaps it was his amusement that caused her to begin looking hard at the state of Alfred's soul. On another occasion she saw him across the street and called, "This reminds me of 'A great gulf shall divide the cursed & blessed.' " It was perhaps harder to laugh when she said directly to him, "Alfred, Alfred, whenever I look at you I think of the words, 'Depart from me, ye cursed, into everlasting fire.' " "Which didn't make a boy of fourteen feel very comfortable," Tennyson added when telling the story as an adult. Mrs Bourne's excesses may have contributed to his extreme dislike of the doctrine of eternal damnation the rest of his life.[10]

Those same excesses have to do with the fear of God in section 96, which accepts the challenge of and does not shrink from the problem of evil as heightened by ethically monotheistic premises. Consequently, section 96 shows an exceptional strength, for it goes so far as to draw a flattering portrait of being "perplext in faith": "There lives more faith in honest doubt, / Believe me, than in half the creeds" (96.9, 11–12).

Section 118, penultimate among the poem's meditations of theodicy, attempts to incorporate empiricism into the deepening theodicy of *In Memoriam*:

> They say,
> The solid earth whereon we tread
>
> In tracts of fluent heat began,
>   And grew to seeming-random forms,

The seeming prey of cyclic storms,
Till at the last arose the man;

Who throve and branched from clime to clime,
    The herald of a higher race,
    And of himself in higher place,
If so he type this work of time

Within himself, from more to more;
    Or, crowned with attributes of woe
    Like glories, move his course, and show
That life is not as idle ore,

But iron dug from central gloom,
    And heated hot with burning fears,
    And dipt in baths of hissing tears,
And battered with the shocks of doom

To shape and use.
    (118.7–25)

To the extent that geology constitutes reality, Tennyson finds some cause for optimism. Extreme tough-mindedness, however, receives pride of place in this geological concept. Tennyson seems to think that nineteenth-century empiricism is more adept at posing the problem of evil than at solving it. This section's vision of the climb by humankind up the geological ladder is one of the most horrifying of all Victorian evolutionary imaginings. (Ricks's annotations are helpful in their quotations of analogues from the tender-minded Chambers and the tough-minded Lyell.[11]) Evolution, according to the just-quoted passage, achieves its ends, but far from emphasizing the hope that science will confirm Victorian notions of progress, Tennyson recoils at the violent means employed by evolutionary reality. He sees as much reason to wonder whether humankind will endure as to celebrate the emergence of the most advanced species on earth.

Section 118 is sometimes obscure, for by no means clear is the subject of *move* and *show* (line 19), but achieving an adventurous spirit of experimentation, the section also achieves probing theodicy. According to Peltason, 118 "is the self-conscious laureate at his best, forging a scientifically precise and poetically powerful account of the earth's creation, and then relating that account, through argument and metaphor, to the particular and human

THE METHOD OF *IN MEMORIAM*

story his poem has recorded." [12] This section's concluding imperatives to
"Move upward, working out the beast," and to "let the ape and tiger die"
(lines 27–28), analogize fully proportionally to its opening imperative:

> trust that those we call the dead
> Are breathers of an ampler day
> For ever nobler ends.
>
> (118.5–7)

"Suffering builds character," then, while inadequate theodicy for the individual is adequate and even intriguing theodicy for the species as a whole.
To have said anything more explicit about religion in this section would
have been out of keeping with its focus on empiricism. By bringing a
measure of orthodoxy to bear on natural philosophy, however, Tennyson
finds even here a measure of relief for and even the foretaste of a solution
to his especially acute, because almost scientific, awareness of evil. Thus,
theodiceally, he cherishes the hope of everlasting life.

Dominated by theodicy, finally, is section 128. Aware that "throned
races may degrade" or decompose (128.7), the speaker knows that civiliza-
tions decline and fall, that species fade and disappear, that the future, far
from being gloriously Victorian, brings no progress but only change. "To
draw, to sheathe a useless sword," to perpetuate the futility of war; "To
fool the crowd with glorious lies," to impose tyranny through propaganda
(notwithstanding the precedent of Napoléon, this anticipation of the Big
Lie is uncanny); "To cleave a creed in sects and cries," to suffer the abuses
of literal or figurative religious warfare; and "To cramp the student at his
desk," at once to neglect the need for education and to deny academic freedom (see Dickens's *Hard Times*)—are all acts amounting to "old results
that look like new" (128.11, 13–15, 18). Suddenly juxtaposed to such folly,
however, are the efficacious epistemology and the splendid teleology of the
spiritual sense:

> I see in part
> That all, as in some piece of art,
> Is toil coöperant to an end.
>
> (128.22–24)

Peltason, intriguingly, goes against the prevailing view of these lines as
"evidence and illustration of Tennyson's vision of order"; "the closing asser-

tion of this lyric," he insists, "is, in fact, abrupt and unsponsored" (Peltason's *unsponsored* alludes to line 112 of Wallace Stevens's "Sunday Morning"
[1915]).[13] The abrupt assertion of Tennyson's open-ended quest, however,
is sponsored by the experiential mystery of his empirical-evangelical world;
at the beginning of section 128 purposiveness operates on the spiritual as
well as natural plane:

> The love that rose on stronger wings,
>   Unpalsied when he met with Death,
>   Is comrade of the lesser faith
> That sees the course of human things.
>
> (128.1–4)

The doubt that insists on taking all things into account and on questioning them at whatever risk to faith coexists with, and is indeed the ally
of, otherworldly assurances. Tennyson's theodicy gives the rich but strange
impression that good and evil, joy and sorrow, are undeniably copresent,
paradoxically interactive, and even conclusively progressive elements in
the natural-spiritual, individual-collective life of humankind.

The defining tough-mindedness of *In Memoriam*'s theodiceal designs lingers even in the hopefully affecting thesis of section 127: "[A]ll is well,
though faith and form / Be sundered in the night of fear" (127.1–2). If,
despite the possibility and even despite the fact of sundered faith and form,
"all is well," then surely the mind and heart of Tennyson have successfully
joined in the all-out effort of the ages to effect complete theodicy.

SEVEN

Set Pieces

Tennyson's belief in "the reality of the unseen world" does not necessarily entail, as Culler thinks it does, the poet's belief in "the unreality of the material universe."[1] The continuing importance of sense-imagery in *In Memoriam*, 95, for example, assures that an empirical as well as evangelical, a hardly partial because not exclusively mystic, experientialism makes for the climactic quality of this important section.

"This lyric," according to Kincaid, "climaxes the comic movement" of *In Memoriam* with "a vision of absolute assurance, a full realization of a new self, and a concurrent realization of the unity of all creation in love." Here, at last, "irony's tenuous mixture becomes comedy's pure and triumphant assertion of continuity."[2] Peltason, calling the section the poet's "fullest vision of the sum of things and the most celebrated account of the experience of transcendence in all of Tennyson's poetry," argues that "the mystical experiences of Tennyson's youth were its model."[3]

"A kind of waking trance I have frequently had quite up from boyhood," declares Tennyson, "when I have been all alone"; here is Hallam Tennyson's further account of his father's testimony to such mystical experience:

> This has generally come upon me thro' repeating my own name two or three times to myself silently, till all at once, as it were out of the intensity of the consciousness of individuality, the individuality itself seemed to dissolve and fade away into boundless being, and this not a confused state; but the clearest of the clearest, the surest of the surest, the weirdest of the weirdest, utterly beyond words, where death was an almost laughable impossibility, the loss of personality (if so it were) seeming no extinction but the only true life.[4]

Similar experiences are recounted in such early poems as "The Mystic," "Armageddon," and "Timbuctoo," and in such later ones as "The Ancient Sage" and "De Profundis"; in these, as in 95, "the intense experience of self-hood carries the poet beyond selfhood, just as language carries him beyond language."[5] Buckley finds "literary precedent" for the mysticism of 95: "In the Confessions of St. Augustine—to cite but one striking example—[Tennyson] might have found a remarkably similar passage recounting the ascent of the mind by degrees from the physical and transitory to the un-changeable until 'with the flash of a trembling glance, it arrived at *that which is*.'"[6] Augustine continues: "But I was not able to sustain my gaze. My weakness was dashed back, and I lapsed again into my accustomed ways." This, too, is characteristic of Tennyson's section for, almost by definition, the mystic moment is fleeting.

"The mystical vision," according to Buckley, is "assuredly the sanction of [Tennyson's] faith";[7] such sanction, however, does not necessarily re-dound to his credit as a poet. Although Tennyson's mysticism bolsters his belief in "the reality of the unseen world," which Culler calls "one of his most deeply held convictions,"[8] this same mysticism gives rise to what Daniel Albright calls the "strange desire for contentlessness that comes upon Tennyson at his peak moments."[9] Albright's statement concerning 95 is well worth quoting in full:

> The passage is perhaps as impressive as the high moments in Milton's work or Wordsworth's spots of time, but its confidence in its ability to sustain its imaginative vigor is far lower, and those prosaic forces antagonistic to vision have gained in power. Also, while the sublime has always been expressed by vague billowy abstractions, this imagery here is unusually evacuated; Hallam and Tennyson and the landscape all whirl out into a condition of imagelessness. In this extreme con-fusion the content of the poetry refines itself almost to nothing; and what replaces the content, after this delirium of deletion, is pure rhythm, naked rhythm and heavy, inorganic, extenuated by no vari-ance in beat or syncopation. It is as if Tennyson had stopped writing words and simply transcribed a pattern of macrons and breves onto the page, plain marks of emphasis, steps, shocks, blows. At the mo-ment of greatest intensity the metrical ictus becomes the subject of the poem; but the landscape that has turned into letters, stressed

iambs, is, disturbingly, no longer a landscape in any ordinary sense, and must cool from this state of superheated meaningfulness if the moths and the trees, the teapot, are to be visible at all. Doubt had better enter the poem, or the poem would be unable to continue. Here music is the enemy of grace, and wit, and design, and even thought; and the sublime is a hammer likely to destroy what it hits.[10]

The reentry of sense imagery into the final third of the section may be more deliberate and better integrated than Albright implies. While Culler sees this "gradualist" section as "not well adapted" to the "one apocalyptic moment" of *In Memoriam*,[11] I find the very "gradualism" of 95 especially well adapted both to the section and to the character of the poem, which is more sense-millennial than mystical or apocalyptic. Section 95 is the climax of *In Memoriam* in that its empirical-evangelical synthesis is complete.

The twilight setting of the section, a garden formerly frequented by Tennyson and Hallam together, is now visited only by Tennyson and some unnamed companions; these, like the disciples in Gethsemane, do not watch with Tennyson long, but soon retire, leaving him to reread old letters from Hallam:

> So word by word, and line by line,
>> The dead man touched me from the past,
>> And all at once it seemed at last
> The living soul was flashed on mine,
>
> And mine in this was wound, and whirled
>> About empyreal heights of thought,
>> And came on that which is, and caught
> The deep pulsations of the world,
>
> Æonian music measuring out
>> The steps of Time—the shocks of Chance—
> The blows of Death.
>
>> (95.33–43)

This central passage of the central section of *In Memoriam* can be read empirically to mean that for the first time Tennyson understands, however briefly, his scientific studies. Whether on the macroscientific level of vast ages, as indicated by Lyell (the coinage *AEonian* derives from Tennyson's reading of specific geological texts [12]), or on the microscientific and even anthropocentric level of the evolutionary fate of individual species, these studies reveal that sense-based hypotheses turn out to be true. The passage, however, can also be read spiritually to mean that Tennyson's inner experience provides access both to a reality beyond appearances and to hints of the divine in appearances. "Empyreal heights of thought" and "that which is" function together as the subject-object spiritual thesis to the natural antithesis of the rest of the passage, which is nearly exclusively objective. A natural-spiritual if not empirical-evangelical synthesis forms a single though hardly univocal interpretation of these lines.

The credibility of the section is heightened by its careful, exemplary skepticism: "[I]t *seemed* . . . / The living soul was flashed on mine." The context of these lines, both before and after, foreshadows and develops this skeptical "seemed," for the epiphany emerges despite, or because of, the fact that the letters are "bold to dwell / On doubts that drive the coward back" (95.29–30). The poet's revelation, because of his doubts, proves fugacious at best: "At length my trance / Was cancelled, stricken through with doubt" (95.43–44).

Skeptical method, of course, formed such a recurring part of Wesley's experience as to help define it; the evangelical diction of section 95, accordingly, is precise. After singing "old songs" (hymns?) "that pealed / From knoll to knoll," Tennyson feels that in an atmosphere of "genial *warmth*" his "*heart*" is seized by a spiritual hunger (lines 3, 13–14); under these auspicious circumstances,

> *strangely* on the silence broke
> The silent-speaking words, and *strange*
> Was love's dumb cry defying change
> To test his worth; and *strangely* spoke
>
> The faith, the vigor, . . .
> (95.25–29; my italics)

This testimony is more than merely reminiscent of Wesley's "heart . . . strangely warmed." The suddenness of Tennyson's epiphany—it occurs "all at once" (95.35)—parallels the precision with which Wesley dated his experience at "a quarter to nine" in the evening. Even the month of May is the same! And although Aldersgate Street, London, where Wesley's conversion takes place, is hardly pastoral, the year of Tennyson's experience, 1837, falls short by only one year of being a century after Wesley's. The section's progress from the written word to the immediate, unmediated "flashing" of Hallam's soul on the soul of Tennyson is more than merely reminiscent of the evangelical progress from traditional to immediate revelation—especially since Tennyson's phrasing, "*The* living soul was flashed on mine, / And mine in *this* was wound," refers ambiguously both to Hallam's soul in particular and to an active spiritual force in general. For "this," Tennyson originally wrote "his," [13] and this change, besides avoiding homoerotic associations, admits of the rich ambiguity of an inclusive interpretation.

These central lines of section 95 are framed at the beginning and the end by seemingly exclusively natural descriptions of the garden. The opening description, however, anticipates even the spiritual dimension of the central lines; in addition, the closing description is finally spiritual, for the end of the section confirms the central spiritual vision. Brief readings of these two descriptions can round off my empirical-evangelical approach to section 95; each description employs natural-spiritual means to unify the section. The spiritual component of these means is especially heightened in the second description, which follows the similarly natural-spiritual (but finally more spiritual than natural) central encounter with Hallam.

The opening description includes some striking observations:

> And bats went round in fragrant skies,
> And wheeled or lit the filmy shapes
> That haunt the dusk, with ermine capes
> And woolly breasts and beaded eyes;
>
> (95.9–12)

But ermine moths and bats eerily and ominously suggest the transitoriness of the natural state. One might even read into the "*fluttering* urn" on the "board" (line 8; my italics) the suggestion that natural life is fleeting and threatened. By *haunting* the dusk, moreover, the moths can seem spirit-like, as though their implication of transitoriness were itself embedded in an other than natural context. Although "tapers burn" (line 5) and life is thus implicitly consumed by time, they burn "unwavering" (line 6) as though spirit-based identity persists through change. The enjambment of lines 5 and 6—"tapers burn / Unwavering"—reinforces and calls attention to this natural-spiritual paradox. These details prepare the reader for Hallam's strangely simultaneous presence/absence at the center of the section: recall "The dead man touch'd me from the past" (95.34).

The section's closing description sharply parallels its opening one in that Tennyson repeats the distinctive pastoral coloring in lines 15–17:

> couched at ease,
> The white kine glimmered, and the trees
> Laid their dark arms about the field;
> (95.50–52)

These words, however faintly, are tinged with suggestions of tender nostalgia and dark, exquisite melancholy; but while the opening garden scene is simply observed, the closing one is "revealed" (line 49). Tennyson's closing perspective, then, is more than naturally enriched by the lingering effects of his spiritual as well as almost natural encounter with Hallam. The world of the closing perspective accordingly looks quite different, for the inauspiciousness of almost mute calm in the first description, for example, "The brook alone far-off was heard" (line 7), gives way in the second to sustained, dynamic promise:

> And sucked from out the distant gloom
> A breeze began to tremble o'er
> The large leaves of the sycamore,
> And fluctuate all the still perfume,
>
> And gathering freshlier overhead,
> Rocked the full-foliaged elms, and swung
> The heavy-folded rose, and flung
> The lilies to and fro, and said,
>
> "The dawn, the dawn," and died away;
> (95.53–61)

Although this promise fades at last, it makes a lasting impression even on the physical senses; witness the auditory, olfactory, visual, and kinesthetic imagery. The promise, too, shapes a spiritual sense that, even while including the physical senses, goes beyond them; thus the promise achieves the mystic as well as natural-spiritual power of apprehension. The effect of these remarkable lines is of a synesthetic and as much spiritual as natural message of hope that never dies, a message that lingers even where it does not inspire complete confidence (recall the skepticism of the lines).

The first quatrain of the just-quoted lines (95.53–56) may seem only a fairly straightforward nature description, but the diction carries religious-literary as well as particularly Protestant and even immediately evangelical connotations. *Gathering* recalls the "gathered church" of British Noncon-formist (to say nothing of American Puritan) ecclesiology.[14] *Rocked* fore-shadows, in a softened manner, Hopkins's apocalyptic question, "But ah, but O thou terrible, why wouldst thou rude on me / Thy wring-world right foot rock?"[15] *Swung* recalls the "chain-swung censer teeming" of Keats's priestly poetic function.[16] *Rose* makes one think of rose windows. *Lilies* makes one think of Jesus, if one may proleptically read "the lily of the valley" from the Song of Songs. Finally, *dawn,* besides its biblical/secular associations with aubade/epithalamium, brings to mind more millennial than apocalyptic prophecy that Christ will come "in the morning" (see Mark 13.26, 35).

The lines immediately following the just-quoted passage unmistakably bring forward the religious connotations of the section's second description.

> And East and West, without a breath,
> Mixt their dim lights, like life and death,
> To broaden into boundless day.
> (95.62–64)

In this scene-painting one senses intimations of God's new day of mil-lennium rather than apocalypse, or resurrection rather than immortality. Bradley long ago noticed the simultaneously natural-spiritual meanings of this passage and, indeed, of the entire closing description:

> The last four stanzas [of section 95] form surely, if taken alone, one of the most wonderful descriptive passages in all poetry; but in their context they have an indescribable effect, the breeze seeming to re-call the coming and passing of the wind of the Spirit in the trance, and the mingling of the dim lights of East and West being seen as that meeting of life and death which has just been experienced as the precursor of an endless union to come.[17]

These words hold up. Section 95, to use an empirical-evangelical concept that parallels Bradley's aperçu, is the high watermark of *In Memoriam*'s argument that experience is so far from falling into the compartments of inner and outer that it blends natural with spiritual life.

The method of *In Memoriam*, its expression of "the way of the soul," is punctuated by the three Christmas poems of 1833, 1834, and 1837; having already discussed sections 30 and 78, I focus here on section 105, in order to mark off another strain of the speaker's empirical-evangelical progress through his grief. "Sadly fell our Christmas-eve" (30.4) becomes "calmly fell our Christmas-eve" (78.4), which, in turn, becomes "strangely falls our Christmas-eve" (105.4). "Strangely" denotes "in an alien manner," and the Tennysons, in 1833, had just removed from Somersby to High Beech, Epping Forest. It was undoubtedly disconcerting, if not deeply disturbing, for Tennyson to "celebrate" Christmas in an unfamiliar place; disoriented, even as late as Christmas 1837, he finds the Christmas ritual empty: "To-night ungathered let us leave / This laurel, let this holly stand" (105.1–2). Or again: "For who would keep an ancient form / Through which the spirit breathes no more?" (105.19–20). The Reverend George Tennyson had died, and since the family circle is now broken, the family seems all the more rootless and death all the more dominant: "Our father's dust is left alone / And silent under other snows" (105.5–6). Section 105, however, does not contain much dwelling on the past, for the verb *to fall* in 30.4, 78.4, and 105.4 changes from the past tense in 30 and 78 to the present in 105, and where "the spirit," in effect, "breathes" on the poet (105.20), he finds at last a grace, an intimation of immortality in "What lightens in the lucid East / Of rising worlds by yonder wood" (105.24–25). Thus in the strangeness of 105 is not just the foreign but even the uncanny, a new dispensation, and a something at once about to be and here already; thus, too, the Christmas season of 1837 is not only strange but also rich.

Section 106, confirming Tennyson's arrival at consolation, epitomizes the "normal science" of my paradigm; by combining empirical knowledge with experiential faith, the section visualizes and hence makes credible a better world. "Normal science" does not quite do justice to the rapture of the section, which, like Leonard Bernstein's Berlin performance of Beethoven/Schiller's "Ode to Joy" in December 1989, would surely move even the most brittle art consumer. Constituting more than just the "glib abstractions" that Kincaid finds in it,[18] this exquisitely beautiful as well as measurably straightforward section is the high watermark of the empirical-evangelical continuum in British if not Anglo-American literature. "Ring out the old, ring in the new" (106.5) hails Victorian social progress: "[T]he feud of rich and poor" (line 11), the "slowly dying cause" (line 13), "ancient forms of party strife" (line 14), "false pride in place and blood" (line 21), "the civic slander and the spite" (line 22), and "the thousand wars of old" (line 27), will all yield both to "the valiant man and free" (line 29) and to "the nobler modes of life, / With sweeter manners, purer laws" (lines 15–16). "The new" denotes as well, however, especially beneficial scientific discovery: "Ring out old shapes of foul disease" (line 25). Especially significant is "the new"'s denotation of Arminian-evangelical programs of practical charity and social justice: "[T]he grief that saps the mind" (line 9), "the false" (line 8), "the want, the care, the sin, / The faithless coldness of the times" (lines 17–18), "the narrowing lust of gold" (line 26), and "the darkness of the land" (line 31), will all yield to "the true" (line 8), to "redress to all mankind" (line 12), to "the love of truth and right" (line 23), to "the common love of good" (line 24), to "the thousand years of peace" (line 28), and, clearly not least, to "the Christ that is to be" (line 32). Line 32, bold indeed, is especially evangelical, for even the idea of a Christ as present as Parousia would not faze the Christ-centered faith of evangelicals. Thus the bells of the New Year's season of 1837–38, in contrast with the not so much heard as overheard Christmas bells of 1833 and 1834, are overt and proclamatory, for, by kerygmatically activating the physical sense of hearing, they augur millennium.

EIGHT

Language Method

It is hard to imagine that readers will ever perceive much aesthetic value in some of *In Memoriam*; "readers," as Dorothy Mermin points out, "often find in Tennyson's poems a mannered formality and slick artfulness of surface that seem to close off access to any depths below." [1] One need only think of the historical range of opinion from Christopher North and J. W. Croker through Edward Bulwer and Samuel Butler to W. H. Auden to see the truth of her remark. [2] She concludes that "there is still no firm consensus about the aesthetic value of even those poems that are most often taught and written about"; she has in mind, among other poems, *In Memoriam*.

"There is much in *In Memoriam*," observes Ricks, "that does not carry conviction":

> Its language falters or coarsens whenever Tennyson pretends that his life until the death of Hallam had been a happy one; whenever he swings into politics . . .; whenever he refuses to admit that he cannot imagine heaven, let alone activity and energy in heaven; whenever he remembers his father; whenever he tries to feel that his love must daunt time, whereas it is time which does the daunting; whenever he makes any lordly claim about his attitude to death; whenever he has patent recourse to allegory . . .; most of all, whenever he offers hopes which deep down he knows are hopeless. [3]

Kincaid objects that *In Memoriam* moves too often "into the realm of melodrama or genre painting," [4] and Thomson laments the poem's "tendency to hide behind large utterance." [5]

Section 40's gratuitous image of a maiden's departure from home at the time of her marriage can only strike the modern reader as kitschy Victorian bathos or kitschy Victorian sexism:

> Crowned with blessing she doth rise
>> To take her latest leave of home,
>> And hopes and light regrets that come
> Make April of her tender eyes;
>
> And doubtful joys the father move,
>> And tears are on the mother's face,
>> As parting with a long embrace
> She enters other realms of love;
>
> Her office there to rear, to teach,
>> Becoming as is meet and fit
>> A link among the days, to knit
> The generations each with each;
>> (40.5–16)

Few, moreover, could stomach either the offhand theology or the dubious cosmology of section 85's depiction of Hallam's entry into heaven:

> The great intelligences fair
>> That range above our mortal state,
>> In circle round the blessed gate,
> Received and gave him welcome there;
>> (85.21–24)

But perhaps we grow too brittle. "A link among the days" remains modestly effective, and the sincerity of Tennyson's timeless lyric cry remains powerful:

> Ah, dear, but come thou back to me!
>> Whatever change the years have wrought,
>> I find not yet one lonely thought
> That cries against my wish for thee.
>> (90.21–24)

Sincerity characterizes the best of Tennyson's art, for however unfortunately this trait sometimes strays from its point-blank beginnings in his life to its tepid fallings-off in the more conventional and religiously straitened passages of his verse, his stance is never quite separated from his experience. Just as dead metaphors are former metaphors, so also bad verse (or in his case the combination of conventionality with religious conformity) is included in the catalogue of experience.

Tennyson considered calling his poem *Fragments of an Elegy*, and the fragment, of course, is consistent not just with the idea of empirical bits and pieces[6] but also with the idea of isolated, discrete epiphanies.[7] Hence the fragment is also consistent with the notion of natural-spiritual experiences in the here and now. A philosophical discourse with which *In Memoriam* has been associated is *Roland Barthes by Roland Barthes*, but although "this volume of autobiographical reminiscences and reflections, composed of brief sections," is indeed "like Tennyson's poem," and although Tennyson's "relationship to his writing was much more like Barthes' than nineteenth-century assumptions about well-shaped poems enabled him to acknowledge," it is too much to conclude with Alan Sinfield that "Tennyson's inability to discover a unifying principle for his writing" is finally like Barthes's inability.[8] "Barthes' aim," according to Sinfield, is "to prevent a structure from forming," for "if that happened, it would appear that Barthes had represented a coherent self," but Tennyson's structure in the abba stanza, to say nothing of his structured set of Christmas lyrics, is more than sufficiently uniform and regular to imply a coherent self. "Empirical" genres with which the poem has been associated are the commonplace book, the diary, the epistolary novel, and the sonnet sequence.[9] Religious genres with which it has been associated include the confession and the "dark night of the soul" account.[10] Tennyson himself said that *In Memoriam* "was meant to be a kind of *Divina Commedia*," and Gordon D. Hirsch argues that the poem embodies "the Dantean theories of Arthur Hallam."[11]

Charles Kingsley's comment on Tennyson's abba stanzas suggests how they are appropriate to his empirical-evangelical theme: "Their metre [is] so exquisitely chosen, that while the major rhyme in the second and third lines of each stanza gives the solidity and self-restraint required by such deep themes, the mournful minor rhyme of each first and fourth line always leads the ear to expect something beyond."[12] The meter and the rhyme embed the spiritual sense, which might be defined in Kingsley's formalistic-thematic terms as the combination of the physical ear's access to thick *dinglich* substance with the spiritual ear's grasp of "something beyond" (recall Keats's "Pipe to the spirit ditties of no tone" [13]).

Ricks observes of Tennyson's abba stanza that it can

> "circle moaning in the air," returning to its setting out, and with fertile circularity staving off its deepest terror of arrival at desolation and indifference. . . . The very reasons which make the stanza so utterly unsuitable for sustained argument . . . its continual receding from its affirmations, from what it momentarily clinches, so unlike the disputatious sequences of the heroic couplet: these very reasons make it the emblem as well as the instrument for poems in which moods ebb and flow. [14]

Ricks's experiential-religious insight into abba's alternation of skepticism with open-ended affirmation suggests that *In Memoriam* is self-consciously empirical-evangelical in its passages about the nature of language as well as in its verse form. The empirical-evangelical tenor of these passages, taking its rise and footing from the modest and more humbly referential than endlessly deferring linguistic temper of the poet himself, constitutes the language *method* of the poem, distinct from any *theory* of language it might adumbrate.

Vita brevis, ars longa gives way in *In Memoriam* to the "empirical," hardly hopeful nostrum, *vita brevis, ars brevis*. Poems do not last even as long as many life-forms do. Before the oak has clothed its "branchy bowers / With fifty Mays," the works of poets "are vain" (76.13–14). Tennyson, not excepting his own works, claims neither poetic immortality nor, for that matter, poetic longevity. His self-deprecation in this regard is marked by a welcome if uncharacteristic humor:

> These mortal lullabies of pain
> May bind a book, may line a box,
> May serve to curl a maiden's locks;
>
> (77.5–7)

Like Locke, then, Tennyson perceives the finitude of language, for he, too, regards experience as prior to language, and hence as always more than verbal and often non- or extra-verbal. Among the Apostles when Hallam was still alive, "Thought leapt out to wed with thought / Ere Thought could wed itself with Speech" (23.15–16). Thus an ineffable sympathy informs but also precedes language, which may even hinder and is certainly after the fact of the primary, immediate, and all but spiritual experience of fellowship and communion in days gone by.

Nothing could be more intensely experiential, and hence more real, than Tennyson's relation to Hallam; yet even Hallam, if not especially he, remains, for all that (or because of that), utterly, frustratingly ineffable:

> What practice howsoe'er expert
> In fitting aptest words to things,
> Or voice the richest-toned that sings,
> Hath power to give thee as thou wert?
>
> (75.5–8)

Although Tennyson excels at linguistic opulence, and although he subscribes here to the Lockean view that language is at least potentially referential, neither rich words nor words carefully calibrated to externality will ever suffice to fit the only subject he cares to render truly well. His verses may soothe him (see especially section 5). They may even trigger his hopeful speculation with regard to the essential existence of Hallam. Even *Tennyson's* art, however, leaves Hallam finally untouched, finally distant from, and finally irrelevant to the very verses that would pay him faithful, thorough tribute:

> I leave thy praises unexpressed
> In verse that brings myself relief,
> And by the measure of my grief
> I leave thy greatness to be guessed.
>
> (75.1–4)

Words, indeed—and this is hard news for Late as much as High Romantics—are not even reliably *self*-expressive. Being unable to express one's grief aright, they cannot express one's deepest experience: "[T]hat large grief [of mine] which these [words] enfold / Is given in outline and no more" (5.11–12). Silence, then, is logical:

> The Wye is hushed nor moved along,
> And hushed my deepest grief of all,

> When filled with tears that cannot fall,
> I brim with sorrow drowning song.
> (19.9–12)

"The lesser griefs that may be said" (20.1) may not be said *well*. Although "servants in a house / Where lies the master newly dead" grieve sincerely (they "speak their feeling as it is"), they say such banal things as to seem fatuous at best, and unintentionally self-centered at worst: "It will be hard . . . to find / Another service such as this" (20.3–5). "The degree of fluency in these biting lines," writes Kincaid, "is made directly proportionate to the absence of real feeling," and he adds that "it is often said that death proves the hopeless inadequacy of language, forcing us into the formulated meaninglessness of clichés."[15] When Tennyson's friends try to comfort him for Hallam's death, the poet strikes out at the inadequacy of their shibboleths; when they say such trite things as "other friends remain" and "loss is common to the race," Tennyson responds: "And common is the commonplace, / And vacant chaff well meant for grain" (6.1–4). These lines are worth repeating in the present context of arguing for Tennyson's awareness of the limitations of language.

Tennyson implies, nevertheless—consistent with Kincaid's observation concerning section 20 that "death acts to confirm the value of clichés and of the domestic simplicity supporting them"—that even shallow language has a place and serves a function in the experience of grief. His own poem, though inadequate, is never less than therapeutic:

> But, for the unquiet heart and brain,
> A use in measured language lies,
> The sad mechanic exercise,
> Like dull narcotics, numbing pain.
> (5.5–8)

The poem demonstrates ultimate distance from the logic of silence. Just as the Wye is heard whenever the tide is in, so Tennyson can and regularly does voice his grief:

> The tide flows down, the wave again
> Is vocal in its wooded walls;

My deeper anguish also falls,
And I can speak a little then.
(19.13–16)

To the extent that Tennyson specifically believes experience to be preverbal, he also believes that experience gives rise to and relates to words.
With regard to spiritual experience especially, he makes it clear that Christ
takes precedence over and gives meaning to poetry. Christ

               wrought
With human hands the creed of creeds
In loveliness of perfect deeds,
More strong than all poetic thought;
(36.9–12)

Section 37, accordingly, suggests that the deeds of Christ give meaning
to Hallam's deeds and words and, albeit at a remove from the originating
reality of Christ's deeds, the words of Tennyson.

Melpomene, Tennyson's muse of tragedy and elegy, holds "dear . . . as
sacred wine / To dying lips" all that Hallam ever said "of things divine";
and although Melpomene is but "earthly," Tennyson broods on the divinity
of Hallam and his words and murmurs "Of comfort clasped in truth revealed" (37.13, 18–20, 22). At the end of 37 Melpomene admits to having
"*darkened* sanctities with song" (line 24; my italics). Although poetry is
thus not only different from but also less than the prevailing but ineffable
mysteries of both Hallam and Christ, however, there is no better thing
for Melpomene to do, and indeed no other thing for her to do, than to
loiter "in the master's field" (line 23), that is, to make the attempt, no
matter how remote her chances of succeeding, and no matter how indirect
or glancing her expression, to tell the truth in words.

Tennyson's desire to get words right with experience, including his view
that words form part of experience, are consistent with and grow out of
the experiential sensibility of his empirical-evangelical worldview. Consider, from this perspective, section 95, where Tennyson at first admits the
deficiencies of his attempt to describe his now faded trance:

Vague words! but ah, how hard to frame
In matter-moulded forms of speech,

Or even for intellect to reach
Through memory that which I became;
(95.45–48)

Bradley offers this paraphrase: "The forms of speech, being moulded by and meant to express our sensible experience, are inadequate to describe a higher experience." [16] Sense-language, the only language available to the poet, applies to matter alone, not to soul, and can hardly describe a trance. An empirical-evangelical paraphrase of the lines, however, is that it would be difficult ("how hard to frame") but not impossible for empirical language to describe spiritual experience. Just as not yet verbalized, sense-based memory qualifies as being closer to natural reality than words are, so also does that memory come closer than any words do to spiritual reality. But words say this. And Tennyson's words strongly imply as much.

The reader of *In Memoriam*, like its author, works from language back to referent. As Tennyson says with regard to Hallam as reader, Hallam's "faith" was "keen through wordy snares to track / Suggestion to her inmost cell" (95.31–32). Although words fail to trap the referent, meaning is not simply confined to words as though language were a prison house. The referent both comes to words and leaves behind a scent so fresh that the reader who reads with faith, or with what Paul Ricoeur calls the "second naiveté" of "postcritical faith," [17] hunts down the extra-verbal (as well as coverbal) meaning. Such a reader is able to apprehend the fullest, that is, the empirical-evangelical, import of the poem.

Donald S. Hair's *Tennyson's Language* (1992) is intent on aligning Tennyson's views of language with two major early nineteenth-century language theories.[18] The empiricist view, deriving from the 1820s Cambridge curriculum, held, with Locke, that a word is merely "attached to a sensation." The idealist view, deriving from Kant and favored by the "Germano-Coleridgean" Apostles with whom Tennyson is associated, held that "a word is not essentially a sign which points to some phenomenon . . . in the world outside . . . but is the sign, rather, of shaping powers in the mind: the powers of . . . ordering our experiences in ways that realize our human concerns. These ways . . . are born in us . . . they are God-given." Tennyson, Hair argues, favors the idealist perspective; "words, like Nature, half reveal / And half conceal the Soul within," writes Tennyson in *In Memoriam* (5.3–4), and insofar as this passage emphasizes "the Soul within," it is indeed idealist. Insofar as the passage emphasizes "Nature," however, it suggests the dual, inner-and-outer/subject-object reality within which language mediates; words, though they reveal the soul and are therefore akin to it, also conceal the soul and are therefore alien to it, and thus they resemble nature, which is also other than as well as similar to the soul. Words, nature, and the soul, all mysterious as well as familiar and accessible, are all susceptible to empirical as well as evangelical understanding. Thus just as Wesley's language method is Lockean and Coleridge's is empirical-evangelical (as well as "Germanic"),[19] so too is Tennyson's language method Lockean-"Wesleyan" as well as Kantian; for Tennyson, in his exploration of nature and the soul in relation to language, remains flexible enough in his linguistic attitudes as to be (like Locke, Wesley, and Coleridge) more open-ended or methodological than rigid or theoretical.

Between my argument and my conclusion concerning *In Memoriam*'s empirical-evangelical language method falls the shadow of Postmodernist critics who find in the poem only the wan theology of a proto-late-twentieth-century language theory. Albright, reflecting poststructuralist challenges to the stability of the self, argues that " 'Tennyson,' the ostensible speaker" of *In Memoriam*, is "far from being an incisive, confident character" and is "only a nervous locus of conflicting and unresolved feelings" who "embodies his shapelessness in the piecemeal construction of the poem."[20] Terry Eagleton similarly concludes that Hallam is "nothing less than the empty space congregated by a whole set of ideological anxieties concerned with science, religion, the class-struggle, in short with the 'revolutionary' decentering of 'man' from his 'imaginary' relation of unity with his world."[21] Sinfield, administering new historicism and feminist criticism, suggests that Tennyson entertains the hypothesis that sexuality is "not a given" but is "constructed in determinate historical conditions," but if such "margins" as homosexuals and women "bid for centrality" in Tennyson's poetry, they lose the bid, for although *In Memoriam* "seems to have served the function for Tennyson of *My Secret Life* and the sexual diaries of J. A. Symonds and A. J. Munby," Tennyson drew back from experimentation and restored to Hallam "a masculine identity as the statesman who will control the lower classes."[22] Although Tennyson envisages "a convergence of (supposed) male and female attributes," he finally "reinstates the gender distinctions" he "purports to criticize."[23]

If Eagleton and Albright seem somewhat wide of the mark, Sinfield is closer to it, for in pointing to section 59—

> My centred passion cannot move,
>   Nor will it lessen from to-day;
>   But I'll have leave at times to play
> As with the creature of my love;
>
> (59.9–12)

—Sinfield observes that Tennyson "does not, like the post-structuralist Barthes, acknowledge that the waywardness of writing points to the instability of the self, but he does detach his claim for stability from his writing, offering that writing as a space in which subjectivity moves rather than a representation of its coherence."[24] Thus Sinfield appears to recognize that Tennyson is finally conservative and even somewhat naive concerning the problematic of semiotic reference. Sinfield, a Postmodernist critic, is perhaps more willing to see Tennyson as he is than the more old-fashioned critic Gerhard Joseph, who, taking "The Lady of Shalott" (1832) as Tennyson's most characteristic poem, cannot seem to decide between the 1950s reading of it "as an allegory of the artist who must remain detached from the world in order to create" and "poststructuralist notions that the poem is about the impossibility for human beings of gaining pure, unmediated access to reality."[25] Between Joseph's two readings of Tennyson as the "autonomous agent" who "weaves" his material into his "existence," and of Tennyson as the artisan "written into being" by the "representational systems" of his "culture," I am partial, I guess, to the former, but there is room for both interpretations in my synthesizing concept of Tennyson as an empirical-evangelical artist who is interactive, that is, at once autonomous and receptive to natural-spiritual influx.

Tennyson indeed preserves a representational role for language, which, tentatively and deferentially but subtly and precisely, he believes refers—whether as criticism or as belles lettres—to thought that points to image that points to thing. Sinfield argues that Tennyson's language is "the product of a desperate need for order in the absence of any clear and agreed means of establishing it."[26] Meanings, accordingly, are sufficiently multiple for Tennyson, who, when asked whether the three ladies with King Arthur represent Faith, Hope, and Charity, replied, "They do and they do not. They are those graces, but they are much more than those. I hate to be tied down to say, 'This means that,' because the thought in the image is much more than the definition suggested or any specific interpretation advanced."[27] Tennyson knows, however, that words derive "from nature" (49.1), that is, that they mimetically both reflect and participate in noumenal as well as phenomenal externality.

With his "both/and" logic, he also knows that words derive from other words, that is, "from art" and "from the schools" (49.1). He is even sensible of the ludic dimension of language, what deconstructionists call the endless play of signifiers; Melpomene "sports with words" (48.9). She is no formalist, however, and no forerunner of deconstructionist art; she

> serves a wholesome law,
> And holds it sin and shame to draw
> The deepest measure from the chords;
> (48.10–12)

("The meanest flower that blows," as Wordsworth puts it, "can give / Thoughts that do often lie too deep for tears."[28]) Although Tennyson does not elaborate on "wholesome law," he clearly prefers didacticism to wallowing in however rich a medium. Far from calling undue attention to form by milking the subject, far from indulging in a fermata of verbal complexity, and far from muddying polysemy with gratuitous layeredness and endless resonance, he remains content with melodic lines of words distinct from chordal structures of them. Even melody, of course, battens on accompaniment, for Tennyson's expression of personal experience is moderately playful and hardly univocal, but his expression is also relatively simple, that is, never overingenious or convoluted:

> Nor dare [Melpomene] trust a larger lay,
> But rather loosens from the lip
> Short swallow-flights of song, that dip
> Their wings in tears, and skim away.
> (48.13–16)

The words of Tennyson's poetic art relate lightly, but so surely, to the extra-linguistic as to alter if not transform it: "The slightest air of song shall breathe / To make the sullen surface crisp" (49.7–8). Contrast, if you will, Tennyson's principle with Pope's, which teaches that art decorates the extra-linguistic, but does not alter or transform it:

> But true expression, like th' unchanging sun,
> Clears and improves whate'er it shines upon,
> It gilds all objects, but it alters none.[29]

To summarize, the language method of *In Memoriam* is more fully articulated than any language theory in it. This method reimagines the poet's relation to an empirical-evangelical and hence bipolar if not unitary world of science and religion. The method seeks to accomplish what Ford, in describing the poem's form, calls its "ordering" of Tennyson's "own most intimate experience,"[30] that is, his spiritual as well as natural life. Although, as Ford adds, the "unvarying tetrameter quatrains taxed Tennyson's ingenuity in achieving variety," they nevertheless constitute "one of several means by which the diverse parts of the poem are knitted together." Not only may *In Memoriam* be thus thought of as more song cycle than set of individual lyrics, but the cycle may also be thought of as hymnic, that is, as deep-evangelical in structure and mode. T. S. Eliot called *In Memoriam* "the concentrated diary of a man confessing himself,"[31] and indeed it bears striking resemblance to evangelical spiritual autobiography. It also resembles empirically philosophical discourse; like the Lockean structure and mode of Wesleyan-Edwardsean religious methodology, the language method of *In Memoriam* is subsumed under, marked, and distinguished by the experiential category as most broadly defined. The central paradox of the poem, its abiding "self-consciousness" about medium, is its tough and tender "awareness" that language is alternately, or even at once, flawed and mysterious.

NINE

Intra-Romantic
Relationships

From as much a philosophical as a theological vantage point, I swerve from Harold Bloom's comment (in his "Emerson: The American Religion"): "But what if poetry as such is always a counter-theology, or Gentile Mythus, as Vico believed? [M. H.] Abrams, not unlike Matthew Arnold, reads religion as abiding in poetry, as though the poem were a saving remnant. But perhaps the saving remnant *of poetry* is the only force of what we call theology?"[1] The Romanticism of Tennyson's *In Memoriam* is not so much an English-speaking world's only abiding place of religion alone as a whole remaining force of that world's philosophical theology, which I define as the experiential common denominator between empiricism and evangelicalism.[2] While I do not share Bloom's puzzlement "that *In Memoriam*, an outrageously personal poem of Romantic apotheosis, a poem indeed of vastly eccentric mythmaking, should have been accepted as a work of consolation and moral resolution in the tradition of Christian humanism," I agree with Bloom's general comment that "the Tennyson who counts for most" is "certainly a Romantic poet, and not a Victorian anti-Romantic resembling the Arnold of *Merope* or the straining Hopkins of *The Wreck of the Deutschland*."[3] Tennyson, Bloom adds, "is a major Romantic poet," and what makes him so, I argue, is the force of his philosophical theology. The empirical-evangelical perspective of *In Memoriam* is at once sufficiently "counter" (that is, sufficiently rigorous and open-ended in method) and sufficiently salvific (that is, sufficiently conserving of religious tradition) to contribute to an English-language Romanticism even broader and even more complex than the satisfying/composite but attenuatedly religious, and coaxial rather than triangular, Romanticism envisioned by Arnold, Abrams, and Bloom together.

Robert Langbaum, for his part in defining Romanticism, identifies "the essential idea of Romanticism" as

> the doctrine of experience—the doctrine that the imaginative appre-
> hension gained through immediate experience is primary and certain,
> whereas the analytic reflection that follows is secondary and problem-
> atical. The poetry of the nineteenth and twentieth centuries can thus
> be seen in connection as a poetry of experience—a poetry constructed
> upon the deliberate disequilibrium between experience and idea, a
> poetry which makes its statement not as an idea but as an experi-
> ence from which one or more ideas can be extracted as problematical
> rationalizations.[4]

Langbaum argues, moreover, that "one of the most distinctive features of modern culture (beginning with Enlightenment philosophy but enter-ing literature with romanticism)" is that "we now look downward for the Word—downward to the origins of the earth and the cosmos, to our own origins in single-cell organisms hardly distinguishable from inanimate mat-ter, to the unconscious motives that are the real origins of our 'noble' endeavors."[5] This thesis is worth repeating here, but I would add that one does not so much find "the word" as "the preverbal" at such points of origin. Langbaum thinks (and this also is worth repeating) that "in literature" the "imagery of regression" has had the effect of "renewing spirituality through intensification rather than elevation—a way convincing to modern sensi-bilities."[6] His "Epiphanic Mode in Wordsworth and Modern Literature," in particular, concludes that "modern epiphany differs from traditional vision in that epiphany always derives from physical sensations and often from trivial details out of proportion to the sublime epiphanic moment."[7] This conclusion is analogous to my view of the empirical-evangelical mix in Anglo-American literature from the Romantic to the Late Romantic or Victorian period.

Langbaum's broad view of Romanticism as an experiential art that crosses national boundaries and extends even into the twentieth century continues to exert an enormous influence. "Langbaum's formulation," ac-knowledges Peltason in his discussion of *In Memoriam*, "helps to bring into clearer relationship a great deal of obviously but obscurely connected material, from the first expressions of Romantic intuitionism and the quest for an 'unmediated vision,' to the prestige of 'the objective correlative,' to the latest assertion in poetry workshop or composition text of the superiority of 'showing' to 'telling.' "[8] My view, however, entails not so much "disequilibrium" as "continuity" between experience and idea. The Romantic work, in Wordsworth's phrase, is "emotion recollected in tranquillity,"[9] which means, I think, "natural and spiritual experience connected to natural and spiritual idea." Even Langbaum, in his associations of *Romanticism* with *idea* and *experience* with *doctrine,* also associates the literature of experience not only with immediacy and cosmic/inanimate/unconscious origins but also with idea/doctrine/reflection/analysis and hence with all manner of problematical abstraction.

The Romanticism of Great Britain, according to L. J. Swingle (in Langbaum's mold), is grounded in the rigorous yet constructive methodology of the British skeptical tradition, which Swingle defines as the "propensity" to see "polarities as differing so fundamentally at the axiomatic level that each becomes not merely a viable system unto itself but also a nearly unsolvable mystery to systems beyond itself."[10] Thus Swingle's model follows Hume more than Berkeley or Locke, and one even catches a whiff of Derrida's skepticism from Swingle's otherwise refreshing interest in immediate historical contexts. Swingle's notion of skepticism, however, remains dynamic rather than static, and sense-oriented rather than rationalistic. While he declares that "the specter of enthrallment to single-minded perception haunts [British] Romantic literary art" (49), he adds that "the [British Romantic] literary artifact is designed to move the reader, in company with the artist, toward a free mental space beyond or between enthrallments through simultaneous invocations of competing enthrallments" (52).

Swingle knows, too, that British Romantic skepticism is consistent with the "mild faith" (Shelley's concept)[11] of British Romanticism, for Swingle argues that, despite the "nagging uneasiness or suspicion" and the "obstinate questionings of sense and outward things"[12] that abound everywhere in British Romantic art, the British Romantics are nonetheless "cautiously supportive of many of our most traditional, fundamental human values" and "inclined to grant or at least explore sympathetically various clusters of provisional truths" (72). Swingle concludes that British Romanticism lets "spirit and inward things emerge" (72), or, as he further paraphrases what may be the greatest discovery by the British Romantics, "It is only by touching the abyss that the soul comes to recognize its power" (77).

I seek to explore the widest ramifications of Swingle's view,[13] for to pair representative works by Blake, Wordsworth, Coleridge, Shelley, and Keats with Tennyson's *In Memoriam* is to link Romantic skepticism with Romantic faith and—recalling the Romantic *Emerson's* skeptical faith[14]—British with American Romanticism. The actual/ideal tension in Tennyson's Late Romanticism is not only fully understandable but also partially reconcilable along clear lines of the empirical-evangelical vision of British High Romanticism. The high quality of that Romanticism matches the high quality of *In Memoriam* in that these five major poets (as I have previously argued)[15] and Tennyson are creatively grounded in the twin experiential traditions of empiricism and evangelicalism.

Although Tennyson was hardly familiar with works by Blake, Bloom points to a broadly mythic parallel between Blake's *The Vision of the Daughters of Albion* (1793) and Tennyson's *The Hesperides* (1833),[16] and three experiential parallels between Blake's works and *In Memoriam* seem well worth mentioning as part of my argument for Tennysonian Romanticism's empirical-evangelical propensity. The experiential wisdom of the clod of clay in Blake's *The Book of Thel* (1789–91)—"I ponder, and I cannot ponder; yet I live and love" (plate 5, line 6)—is strikingly similar to Tennyson's experiential formula, "I cannot understand; I love" (97.36). Blake's doctrine of Higher Innocence, that is, his goal of "spiritual blessedness amidst pain"[17]—and not just Goethe's doctrine, as Tennyson claimed in later life—anticipates Tennyson's experiential formula that "men may rise on stepping-stones / Of their dead selves to higher things" (1.3–4). In Blake's evangelically experiential "The Divine Image" (1789)—

> For Mercy has a human heart,
> Pity a human face,
> And love, the human form divine;
> And Peace, the human dress
> (lines 9–12)

—is a concept of the divine in the everyday[18] that one also finds in Tennyson's portrait of the Evangelical Anglican sister: "O, sacred be the flesh and blood / To which she links a truth divine!" (33.11–12).

Yeats is surely wrong to say that Wordsworth and Tennyson do not belong to the same "school."[19] Although Peltason emphasizes differences between *The Prelude* (1850) and *In Memoriam*,[20] and although Patricia Ball argues that—explicitly unlike *The Prelude*—*In Memoriam* fears that "the lone self" is "without meaningful identity in the universe,"[21] Buckley draws persuasive parallels between the other long poem that appeared in the England of 1850 and *In Memoriam*. "Like *The Prelude*," writes Buckley, *In Memoriam* "describes the loss of hope and the recovery of assent, the reassertion of the dedicated spirit; it grounds a new faith on the persistence of the remembered past; and it freely reorders literal facts to achieve its psychological pattern, to illustrate 'the growth of a poet's mind' or, as Tennyson called it, 'the way of the soul.'"[22] "I believe," declares Tennyson, "that everything which happens to us we remember; it is all stored up somewhere to come forth again upon occasion, though it may seem to be forgotten—even this movement to the window we shall remember."[23] Although he adds, "perhaps not this, so trivial a circumstance!" Roden Noel concludes, "And now how that very utterance has impressed this circumstance upon me." Noel's account is worth repeating in this context, for Wordsworth's "spots of time" in *The Prelude*, not to mention Proust's *A La Recherche du Temps Perdu*, provide a clear parallel. Critics, Ball and Peltason included, notice many individual echoes of Wordsworth in Tennyson's poetry;[24] *In Memoriam*, in particular, works almost explicitly with the broadly experiential range of Wordsworth's phrases and ideas. Wordsworth's nostalgia for "old, unhappy, far-off things, / And battles long ago,"[25] for example, prepares not only for Tennyson's famous "tears, idle tears" in "thinking of the days that are no more,"[26] but also for his conviction in *In Memoriam* that "the past will always win / A glory from its being far" (24.13–14). Wordsworth's rhetorical question in "Expostulation and Reply" (1798)—

> "Think you, 'mid all this mighty sum
> Of things for ever speaking,
> That nothing of itself will come,
> But we must still be seeking?"
> (lines 25–28)

—all but prophesies the "wise passiveness" ("Expostulation and Reply," line 24) with which Tennyson's art also awaits, with however modest a hope of success, the capture or recapture of "The glory of the sum of things" (*In Memoriam*, 88.11). Wordsworth's tribute to his sister, Dorothy, as one so tender-hearted that she "feared to brush / The dust from off" the wings of a butterfly[27] prefigures Tennyson's similarly delicate portrait of his sister Cecilia (or possibly his sister Emily) as one "whose light-blue eyes / Are tender over drowning flies" (96.2–3). Just as Dorothy instructs Wordsworth's spiritual vision—

> She gave me eyes, she gave me ears;
> And humble cares, and delicate fears;
> A heart, the fountain of sweet tears;
> And love, and thought, and joy[28]

—so Cecilia, or Emily, teaches Tennyson something about faith (review section 33).

Wordsworth's broadly experiential portraits of himself and others remind me especially of *In Memoriam*'s broadly experiential portrait of Hallam. Just as Wordsworth's depiction of the hypothetical ideal leader emphasizes a "master-bias" that "leans to homefelt pleasures and to gentle scenes; / . . . / More brave for this, that he hath much to love,"[29] so Tennyson's enumeration of Hallam's virtues highlights both Hallam's "love of freedom rarely felt" (109.13) and Hallam's "manhood fused with female grace" (109.17). (The delicacy shared by Wordsworth and Tennyson will degenerate into the mawkish sentimentality of Edgar A. Guest, for whom "lilacs by a little porch," "the row of tulips red," and "the grass plot" where "children play" are "the things that make a soldier great and send him out to die": these "homefelt pleasures," to use Wordsworth's phrase, are diminutive and cute.[30]) *The Prelude*, to be sure, could not have influenced *In Memoriam*, but just as Wordsworth commemorates the dreamlike splendor of his youthful sojourn with Robert Jones in France—"Bliss was it in that dawn to be alive, / But to be young was very Heaven!" (*The Prelude*, 11.108–9)—so Tennyson, through his recounting of a dream, perpetuates a "past" in which he and Hallam "went through summer France" (71.3–4).

Wordsworth's deep understanding of grief readily glosses the central theme of *In Memoriam*. The intensely rhetorical question that arises out of Wordsworth's anguish over the death of his daughter Catherine—

> Through what power,
> Even for the least division of an hour,

> Have I been so beguiled as to be blind
> To my most grievous loss![31]

—matches both Tennyson's "last regret," namely, that "regret can die," and his rhetorical questions, "O sorrow, then can sorrow wane? / O grief, can grief be changed to less?" (78.15–17). Tennyson's grief is sometimes expressed in crying, as when the "muffled motions" of his sorrow "blindly drown / The bases of [his] life in tears" (49.15–16); at other times, there are "griefs within, / And tears that at their fountain freeze" (20.11–12). Although "with long use" grief's "tears are dry," then, "her deep relations are the same" (78.19–20), and in this connection one is put in mind of Wordsworth's "Thoughts that do often lie too deep for tears" ("Ode: Intimations of Immortality," 11.17).

Such thoughts seldom lie too deep for words. Although Wordsworth denounces the "sad incompetence of human speech,"[32] and although Tennyson is fully aware of the limitations of language, they both utter their grief and thereby discover the muted, exclusively natural means of their consolation. Wordsworth's Lucy and Tennyson's Hallam preserve—after their deaths—their at least organic identity; for just as "trees," along with "rocks, and stones," are "rolled round" with and tend to activate Lucy,[33] so the "fibres" of an "old yew" lend their humous vitality to the dry-bones posthumous, and "net the dreamless head" of Hallam (2.3). Just as Wordsworth's "Yew-tree, pride of Lorton Vale," is "a living thing / Produced too slowly ever to decay,"[34] so, too, is Tennyson's yew tree a powerful image of natural "immortality."

Wordsworth, moreover, aids Tennyson's search for images of spiritual experience. Although *Lucy/light* suggests spiritual illumination or immediate revelation, Wordsworth tends to ironize her name, for the only "revelation" in "A Slumber Did My Spirit Seal" (1800) is tragedy. Tennyson, for his part, does not give up on the possibility that even the "dead" Hallam is a continuing, positive source of spiritual illumination, for the poet pleads with Hallam, "beauteous in [his] after form, / And like a finer light in light," to come "where the sunbeam broodeth warm" (91.14–16).

Tennyson, indeed, himself maintains the sort of spiritual experience that Wordsworth too is capable of maintaining. Compare, for example, the central epiphany of Wordsworth's "Lines: Composed a Few Miles Above

Tintern Abbey" (1798) with the triumphant first quatrain of *In Memoriam*, 130. Here are Wordsworth's lines:

> And I have felt
> A presence that disturbs me with the joy
> Of elevated thoughts; a sense sublime
> Of something far more deeply interfused,
> Whose dwelling is the light of setting suns,
> And the round ocean and the living air,
>
> (lines 93–98)

And here is Tennyson's quatrain, addressed to the living presence of Hallam:

> Thy voice is on the rolling air;
> I hear thee where the waters run;
> Thou standest in the rising sun,
> And in the setting thou art fair.
>
> (130.1–4)

Just as Wordsworth's "Ode: Intimations of Immortality" (1802–4) uses preexistence—

> Not in entire forgetfulness,
> And not in utter nakedness,
> But trailing clouds of glory do we come
> From God, who is our home;
>
> (5.5–8)

—so Hallam in heaven remembers "at times—he knows not whence—/ A little flash, a mystic hint" of "the days before" (44.3, 7–8).

Wordsworth, however, does not go as far as Tennyson does in reaching for a concept of a spiritual realm. In this respect, *In Memoriam*, 44–47 takes up where "Ode: Intimations of Immortality" leaves off. If preexistence helps explain what Wordsworth calls the "visionary gleam" of childhood ("Ode," 4.21), then, quite beyond Wordsworth's speculation about the matter, it occurs to Tennyson that natural experience may similarly correspond to and may similarly serve as guide to the character of the afterlife:

This use may lie in blood and breath,
  Which else were fruitless of their due,
  Had man to learn himself anew
Beyond the second birth of death.
                    (45.13–16)

The meaning here, though somewhat obscure, is surely that human development after death is after the manner of changes wrought in humankind by sense experience on earth.

Finally, Wordsworth's "Ode: Intimations of Immortality" lends its natural-spiritual, empirical-evangelical oscillations[35] to the alternating moods of *In Memoriam*. In the ode's plea to the child not to speed toward adulthood—

Full soon thy Soul shall have her earthly freight,
And custom lie upon thee with a weight,
Heavy as frost, and deep almost as life!"
                    (8.19–21)

—lies much of the bitterness to be found also in *In Memoriam*'s worth-repeating personification of "Use and Wont" as "Gray nurses, loving nothing new" (29.11, 14). If Yeats sees something innocent in custom,[36] and if Shirley Jackson sees something horrifying,[37] then Wordsworth and Tennyson find a middle ground, for in custom they see something inevitable. Just as Wordsworth traces human development from the time when "the sun shines warm, / And the Babe leaps up on his Mother's arm," to the time when "the Man perceives" this vision "die away, / And fade into the light of common day" ("Ode," 4.13–14, 5.18–19), so Tennyson combines empiricism with pre-Freudian psychology to bring "The baby new to earth and sky" from oneness with its mother to the "separate mind" and "isolation" of subject/object differentiation (45.1, 9, 12). "In the faith that looks through death," however, Wordsworth recaptures some "joy" of his boyhood ("Ode," 9.31, 10.18), and Tennyson, similarly, calls on Hallam to "be with me" till

                    like an inconsiderate boy,
    As in the former flash of joy,
    I slip the thoughts of life and death;
                    (122.10, 14–16)

135

The relation between Coleridge and *In Memoriam* plays a give-and-take role in the empirical-evangelical dialectic of Tennyson's Romanticism. While Coleridge's speaker in "Kubla Khan" (1798), for example, closes his vision by imagining that he has "drunk the milk of Paradise" (line 54), the speaker of *In Memoriam* closes one of his visions by hearing "behind the woodbine veil / The milk that bubbled in the pail" (89.50–51), and although both of these rich imaginings are spiritual in their probings of the unseen and both personae employ especially memorable sense-language, Tennyson's language is more real, or less figurative, than the words by which Coleridge emphasizes the otherworldly, as distinct from the merely pastoral, ideal. The milk images, though superficially similar, evoke strangely different associations along the Coleridgean-Tennysonian continuum that joins nature to spirit.

Although Coleridge and Tennyson are both interested in the subject of friendship, they differ as to its durability. While Coleridge's narrator in "Christabel" (1797–1801) laments that "constancy lives in realms above" (line 410) and that such earthly friendships as the one between Sir Leoline and Lord Roland are doomed to dissolution, the persona of *In Memoriam* deems his friendship for Hallam still strong, even after Hallam's death. The poet's sustained "piping" will suffice, despite Hallam's absence from earth, to "gain / The praise that comes to constancy" (21.11–12), for constancy, by implication, and by contrast with Coleridge's implication, lies on the earthly side.

The differences between Coleridge and Tennyson would at first seem dominant. Tennyson, indeed, by contrast with his relation to Wordsworth, would seem to range nearer than Coleridge to the natural end of the natural-spiritual spectrum. While Coleridge responds to his wife Sara's "mild reproof" of his unorthodoxy by ceasing his "dim and unhallow'd" line of questioning,[38] Tennyson responds to his sister's "sweet-hearted" reminder that "doubt is Devil-born" with his own (worth repeating) insistence that "There lives more faith in honest doubt, / Believe me, than in half the creeds" (96.2, 4, 11–12).

Tennyson's other echoes of Coleridge's experiential themes, however, are more consistently in line with them. Dwight Culler points to parallels between *In Memoriam* and such proto–Broad Church theology as Coleridge's *Aids to Reflection*,[39] but I confine my interest here to Coleridge's poetry. Coleridge even joins Tennyson on the natural end of the spectrum, for just as Coleridge's "grief without a pang, void, dark, and drear" causes him to "see, not feel" how beautiful the moon and stars are,[40] so Tennyson's grief makes him numb and leads him to contrast the "fantastic beauty" of the earth and sun—"This round of green, this orb of flame"—with his state of mind, which, at this juncture of *In Memoriam*, can seem to have no purpose whatsoever: "What then were God to such as I?" (34.5–6, 9).

Perhaps the most fully mutual aspect of their give-and-take is found in the equal proportion of nature to spirit in Coleridge's "The Nightingale" (1798) and in Tennyson's lines on the nightingale (*In Memoriam*, 88). Coleridge's nightingale is not finally "melancholy" so much as "full of love and joyance!" (lines 14, 42–43); his emphasis on the "comic" possibilities of even tragedy-conditioned bird song surely encouraged and enabled Tennyson's own contribution of his spiritually synesthetic sense-language, his abrupt "evangelical" rapture, to nightingale art:

> Wild bird, whose warble, liquid sweet,
>   Rings Eden through the budded quicks,
>   O, tell me where the senses mix,
> O, tell me where the passions meet,
>
> Whence radiate: fierce extremes employ
>   Thy spirits in the darkening leaf,
>   And in the midmost heart of grief
> Thy passion clasps a secret joy;
>
> And I—my harp would prelude woe—
>   I cannot all command the strings;
>   The glory of the sum of things
> Will flash along the chords and go.
>   (88.1–12)

Tennyson's nightingale is not finally akin to Arnold's; while Arnold's "Philomela" (1853) stresses tragic myth—"Eternal passion! / Eternal pain!" (lines 31–32)—the "secret joy" of Tennyson's "wild bird," despite his own premonition of "woe," outweighs the bird's awareness of and nearness to grief. Nor is Tennyson's bird fully akin to Keats's nightingale, which is more transcendent. Like Coleridge's bird, Tennyson's alloys the gravity of Philomela's story with a comic overlay, and so *In Memoriam* anticipates Yeats's tragicomic "Lapis Lazuli" (1938), which, albeit without reference to any nightingale, bespeaks the "gaiety" that transfigures "all that dread" (line 17). Although Tennyson himself fails in section 88 to duplicate either the glory or the joy of his nightingale's message of a paradise regained, his all but miraculous stanzas, nevertheless, constitute a noble attempt to do so, and they in fact do so momentarily. Although Coleridge's "The Nightingale" is not itself as joyful as its bird's envisioned message, Coleridge, in full anticipation of Tennyson's section, takes from that message his very cue as poet: the nightingale's message to both poets is at once tragic-"empirical" in grounding and comic-"evangelical" in tone.

In a review of Tennyson's *Poems, Chiefly Lyrical* (1830), Hallam wrote of Shelley and Keats: "So vivid was the delight attending the simple exertions of eye and ear, that it became mingled more and more with trains of active thought, and tended to absorb their whole being into the energy of sense."[41] Tennyson always kept at hand one of the review's admonitions to him: "That delicate sense of fitness which grows with the growth of artist feelings, and strengthens with their strength, until it acquires a celerity and weight of decision hardly inferior to the correspondent judgments of conscience, is weakened by every indulgence of heterogeneous aspirations, however pure they may be, however lofty, however suitable to human nature."[42] Thus Hallam recognized the signal importance of the Shelleyan-Keatsian background to Tennyson's poetry. Thus, too, Hallam uses his one-sided, empiricist view of Shelley and Keats not only to identify Tennyson's sense and feeling but also to attempt to check Tennyson's natural-spiritual desire to be in the world yet not of it.

Yeats took his own personal cue from Hallam's review of Tennyson— "when I began to write I avowed for my principles those of Arthur Hallam in his essay upon Tennyson"—and reported as Hallam did that "Tennyson, who had written but his early poems when Hallam wrote, was an example of the school of Keats and Shelley, and Keats and Shelley, unlike Wordsworth, intermixed into their poetry no elements from the general thought, but wrote out of the impression made by the world upon their delicate senses."[43] With all due respect to this view of Tennyson (made popular by Bloom),[44] I suggest that it does some disservice to Tennyson's reputation, for his "delicate senses" are not finally inimical to his "general thought," and his "heterogeneous aspirations," by the same experiential token, are not finally dissimilar to his familiar life of every day. His "artist feelings," indeed, correspond to his "judgments of conscience," and his "delights" of "eye and ear" indeed operate along a continuum that includes his "active trains of thought," so that his world orientation is of a piece with his spirituality. The empirical-evangelical vision shared by Shelley and Keats[45] is shared also by Tennyson, so that my view of the two of them offers an especially comprehensive means of comparing them with him. Shelley and Keats, like Tennyson, not only delight in eye and ear but also follow trains of active thought and make judgments of conscience, "indulging" pure and lofty aspirations that suit human nature just as much as human nature suits them.

Tennyson espouses what Buckley calls the "Shelleyan moral-aesthetic" of the Cambridge Apostles,[46] and Shelley's androgynous ideal[47] helps explain such Tennysonian gender concepts as Hallam's "manhood fused with female grace" (109.17). Shelley's *Adonais* (1821), like *In Memoriam*, is a pastoral elegy,[48] and both poems, as Bloom points out, address "the ultimates of human existence."[49] Shelley's empirical-transcendental and even empirical-evangelical skeptical subtlety[50] finds a precise, and more than merely reminiscential, parallel in the skeptical subtlety with which *In Memoriam* oscillates from empiricism to evangelicalism. Just as Shelley writes that "from secret springs / The source of human thought its tribute brings / Of waters,"[51] so Tennyson remembers when "all the secret of the Spring / Moved in the chambers of the blood" (23.19–20). Thus, although ultimate reality remains unknown to both poets, each aspires to knowledge, for each cultivates not only subject-object participation in the world but also apprehension, however dim, of the indeterminate, ineffable world.

Consider, in this connection, these lines from Shelley's "With a Guitar, To Jane" (1822):

> The artist wrought this loved Guitar,
> And taught it justly to reply,
> To all who question skilfully.
> (lines 58–60)

Consider, too, *In Memoriam*, 96, which refers to an unnamed poet who espouses skepticism that leads to faith:

> One indeed I knew
> In many a subtle question versed,
> Who touched a jarring lyre at first,
> But ever strove to make it true;
>
> Perplext in faith, but pure in deeds,
> At last he beat his music out.
> (96.5–10)

The mysterious poet is variously identified as Tennyson or Hallam,[52] but Hallam's talents were perhaps more political than poetical, and although much characteristic Tennysonian method infuses these lines, my candidate for whom they refer to is Shelley. Both these lines and the just-quoted passage by Shelley, at any rate, closely identify art with skeptical inquiry, and just as Shelley's mature art enhances his quest for faith—

> For [the guitar] had learned all harmonies
> Of the plains and of the skies . . .
>
> . . . .
>
> All this it knows, but will not tell
> To those who cannot question well
> The Spirit that inhabits it;
> ("With a Guitar, To Jane," lines 64–65, 79–81)

—so Tennyson's poet, whether Shelley or not, grows in faith because he experiments in art.

Shelley and Tennyson hold on to the empirical while allowing for the transcendental. Just as *Power* is both Hume's skeptically vague name for unknowable causation and Shelley's most frequent name for the divine principle of the world,[53] so "Power" is the sufficiently indeterminate yet explicitly present reality within and outside the poet figure in section 96. Shelley empirically distances himself from and yet pursues transcendental speculation:

> *Some* say that gleams of a remoter world
> Visit the soul in sleep,—that death is slumber,
> And that its shapes the busy thoughts outnumber
> Of those who wake and live.—*I look* on high;
> Has some unknown omnipotence unfurled
> The veil of life and death? or do I lie
> In dream, and does the mightier world of sleep
> Spread far around and inaccessibly
> Its circles?
> ("Mont Blanc," lines 49–57; my italics)

Precisely, if only because he is skeptical enough to remain open-minded about most possibilities, Tennyson similarly keeps his speculations about the afterlife:

> So hold I commerce with the dead;
>   Or so methinks the dead would say;
>   Or so shall grief with symbols play
> And pining life be fancy-fed.
>   (85.93–96)

Just as Shelley observes with "both/and" logic that the late Keats "wakes or sleeps with the enduring dead" (*Adonais*, line 336), so Tennyson's address to Hallam's pallbearers includes both the empirical line that Hallam is nothing but dead and the spiritual implication that he only seems that way: "Come then, pure hands, and bear the head / That sleeps or wears the mask of sleep" (18.9–10).

Shelley and Tennyson at times give priority to the transcendental alone. Just as Shelley, in the most famous stanza of *Adonais*, concludes that "Life, like a dome of many-coloured glass, / Stains the white radiance of Eternity" (lines 462–63), so Tennyson implies that "clouds of nature" would "stain / The starry clearness of the free" (85.85–86), that is, the heaven of Hallam. At other times, Shelley and Tennyson give priority to empiricism alone. Just as Shelley abandons inspired Platonism for a sense-experience all but scientific in its modesty—"Clasp with thy panting soul the pendulous Earth" (he advises the reader in *Adonais*, line 417)—so Tennyson is not so much interested in "the starry heavens of space," or even in "the secular abyss to come," as in the humble "mouldering of a yew" (76.3, 6, 8).

In the thoroughness of their shared skepticism both poets are prepared to abandon each term of their shared dialectic. There is neither any empiricism at all nor any ringing transcendentalism, for example, in Shelley's central tenet that "the deep truth is imageless,"[54] nor is there anything but the bleakest empiricism and the most attenuated transcendentalism in the moving quatrain where Tennyson arrives at the deep, ineffable truth of grief:

> Beneath all fancied hopes and fears
>   Ay me, the sorrow deepens down,
>   Whose muffled motions blindly drown
> The bases of my life in tears.
>   (49.13–16)

Thus, like Locke from one point of view and like Wesley/Edwards from another, Shelley and Tennyson refuse to be glib about bringing empiricism and transcendentalism together; where they do so, they succeed all the more credibly for having doubted the permutations and combinations of their own shared terminology.

Keats, for his part, lies in the most immediate background of Tennyson's Late Romantic/Romantic, empirical-evangelical dialectic. Since, in Jack Stillinger's view, Keats's "poetry of earth" values "process" as "[Keats's] own and man's chief good," and since Keats came to regard the "lure" of the transcendental as "false" (Stillinger's terms),[55] I first focus on the empirical phase of the empirical-evangelical dialectic that, in my view, Keats and Tennyson share.

Tennyson's attitude toward nature undeniably builds on Keats's "poetry of earth."[56] In "Ode to a Nightingale" (1819), Keats attempts to merge with the visionary world of the bird by means of "the viewless wings of Poesy" (line 33), but failing in this attempt, he acquires instead a resigned and contented perspective on natural fruition and decay. His sequence of thought compares strikingly with the stages of progress in *In Memoriam*, 41, where, after emphasizing the distance between himself "here upon the ground" and Hallam in heaven, Tennyson first entertains the wild surmise

> that this could be—
> That I could wing my will with might
> To leap the grades of life and light,
> And flash at once, my friend, to thee!
> (41.7, 9–12)

and then, unable to sustain the speculation, and even less able to "leap the grades," reemphasizes the gulf between himself and Hallam, albeit with a softening measure of continued aspiration:

> Yet oft when sundown skirts the moor
> An inner trouble I behold,
> A spectral doubt which makes me cold,
> That I shall be thy mate no more,
>
> Though following with an upward mind
> The wonders that have come to thee,
> (41.17–22)

Keats considers opiates and wine as his means of escape into the world of the nightingale, and one thinks, again, of the ode when one reads Tennyson's comparison of the "measured language" of poetry to "dull narcotics, numbing pain" (5.6, 8). While Keats rejects literal narcotics in favor of the superior, though finally ineffectual, "narcotic" of poetry, Tennyson, at this point, escapes any way he can and includes even poetry among his desperate remedies for achieving not translation but oblivion.

In "Ode on a Grecian Urn" (1819), Keats finally recoils from the urn's depiction of a priest's leading a heifer to the sacrifice, and he turns his attention instead to human life "by river and seashore" (lines 31–40). Tennyson, similarly, turns away from any purely transcendental religion to share the common lot of humankind, namely, mortality:

> What profit lies in barren faith,
>   And vacant yearning, though with might
>   To scale the heaven's highest height,
> Or dive below the wells of death?
>
> . . . .
>
> I'll rather take what fruit may be
> Of sorrow under human skies:
>   (108.5–8, 13–14)

In "Ode to a Nightingale" and "To Autumn" (1820), Keats sees in the purely natural life a grace that idealizes life without supernaturalizing it. "By a cider-press, with patient look," Autumn watches "the last oozings, hours by hours" ("To Autumn," lines 21–22). And just as Keats evokes earthly beauty merely by calling for "a draft of vintage! that hath been / Cool'd a long age in the deep-delvéd earth" ("Ode to a Nightingale," lines 11–12), so, in Tennyson's completely happy memory of Hallam's visits to Somersby, Tennyson recalls a pastoral moment suspended but not eternalized both by "buzzings of the honeyed hours" (see the imagery of "To Autumn," lines 21–22) and by "the wine-flask lying couched in moss, / Or cooled within the glooming wave" (89.44–45, 52). In the sonnet "Ben Nevis" (1817), Keats seems to doubt both matter and mind: "mist is spread / Before the earth, beneath me,—even such / Even so vague is man's sight of himself!" (lines 7–9). He does not finally doubt, however, his mind's lordship over at least his immediate sphere of influence, as symbolized by the rocks beneath his feet: "I tread on them" (line 12). Since at certain especially low moments Tennyson finds no "ground" whatsoever—

"I falter where I firmly trod" (55.13)—his skepticism can be even more thoroughgoing than Keats's.

Keats ultimately shares with Tennyson a spiritual sense.[57] Just as Keats's "Ode to Psyche" (1820) charts new poetic territory "in some untrodden region of the mind" (line 51), so *In Memoriam*, 70, explores the "shadowy thoroughfares of thought" (line 8). Just as Keats's new kind of poetry celebrates the possibility of the mind's access to unearthly love, for example, just as "Ode to Psyche" promises "a casement ope at night, / To let the warm Love in!" (lines 66–67), so even Tennyson's closed world of mind finds sudden, all but miraculous access to Hallam:

> all at once beyond the will
> I hear a wizard music roll,
> And through a lattice on the soul
> Looks thy fair face and makes it still.
>
> (70.13–16)

Line 190 of Keats's "I Stood Tip-toe" (1816)—"Ah! surely he had burst our mortal bars"—initiates a central idea of his poetry from *Endymion* (1818), through *Hyperion: A Fragment* (1819), and *The Fall of Hyperion: A Dream* (1819), namely, that the coming poet will be neo-transcendentalist. Yet Keats's development of this myth in *Hyperion* includes such process-oriented, sense-based values as Hyperion's advice to his sons:

> "Be thou therefore in the van
> Of circumstance; yea, seize the arrow's barb
> Before the tense string murmur.—To the earth!"
>
> (1.343–45)

Compare this Keatsian dialectic of ideal with actual, this implicit spiritual sense, with *In Memoriam*, 64, where Tennyson explicitly imagines that Hallam misses his earthly life, even though he is in heaven. Tennyson, comparing the state to which Hallam has attained with the struggles and attainments of the self-made man on earth, asks, through an especially Keatsian language of actual-aspiring-to-ideal,

> Dost thou look back on what hath been,
> As some divinely gifted man,
> Whose life in low estate began
> And on a simple village green;

> Who breaks his birth's invidious bar,
>   And grasps the skirts of happy chance,
>   And breasts the blows of circumstance, . . . ?
>
> (64. 1–7)

Although this extended simile refers to earthly existence, it also refers to both the nature and the quality of Hallam's afterlife.

Experience, then, whether natural or spiritual, earthly or heavenly, is at once deeply engaged and aspiring. Thus Keats's new kind of person on earth, the person who perceives at once naturally and spiritually, foreshadows Tennyson's Hallam in heaven. In a letter written to Benjamin Bailey on November 22, 1817, Keats speaks of a "favorite Speculation of mine, that we shall enjoy ourselves here after by having what we called happiness on Earth repeated in a finer tone and so repeated—And yet such a fate can only befall those who delight in sensation rather than hunger as you do after Truth."[58] Bloom paraphrases the passage thus: "A recurrent idea in Keats's poems is that through certain intense experiences of pleasure man might achieve a kind of divinity, an unconditioned existence which in *Endymion*, 1.779, he speaks of as 'a fellowship with essence.' It is this that he suggests by the 'finer tone.'"[59] I would add that the empiricism of Keats's "Speculation" is at once so thoroughgoing and so optimistic as to insist on sense experience even in heaven.

Tennyson, too, far from abandoning empiricism when he speaks of heaven, uses empiricism to give intimations of the life to come.[60] Section 3, most notably, while contemplating the possibility of embracing as "man's chief good" both "Sorrow" and "Sorrow"'s exclusively naturalistic view of "Nature" (lines 1, 9), finally resists the temptation to do so, despite the intensity of Tennyson's grief at this point. Denouncing "Sorrow"'s view as "blind," the poet vows, instead, to "crush" sorrow "like a vice of blood, / Upon the threshold of the mind" (3.15–16). Not for him, even early in the poem, is the slightest suggestion of actual without ideal. He cannot finally embrace, as Stillinger says that Keats does, a nature unrelated to spirit. Neither, however, can Tennyson finally force or contrive the elevation of subject over object; the poem regards matter and mind as equal parts of natural and spiritual experience here, if not hereafter. Keats and Tennyson, then, frame issues and answers in much the same way, namely, the broadly experiential way of science-cum-religion.

The experiential range of Tennyson's Romanticism emerges most fully, perhaps, from one of his greatest lyrics, namely, *In Memoriam*, 95. The seemingly inauspicious but experientially portentous beginning of the section is reminiscent of the similarly low-key but also similarly experiential-suggestive opening lines of "The Nightingale" by Coleridge. Here is "The Nightingale":

> No cloud, no relique of the sunken day
> Distinguishes the West, no long thin slip
> Of sullen light, no obscure trembling hues.
> Come, we will rest on this old mossy bridge!
> You see the glimmer of the stream beneath,
> But hear no murmuring; it flows silently,
> O'er its soft bed of verdure. All is still.
>
> (lines 1–7)

And here is 95:

> By night we lingered on the lawn,
>   For underfoot the herb was dry;
>   And genial warmth; and o'er the sky
> The silvery haze of summer drawn;
>
> And calm that let the tapers burn
>   Unwavering: not a cricket chirred;
>   The brook alone far-off was heard,
> And on the board the fluttering urn.
>
> (95.1–8)

Thus nature, so muted for Coleridge and Tennyson as to require their close attention, conduces to their rich experience.

Two passages from *The Prelude* in which Wordsworth is first in company and then alone is fully predictive, moreover, of the combination of nature with spirit in 95. In both the Esthwaite skating scene (*Prelude*, 1.426–63) and the call to poetic vocation (*Prelude*, 4.309–38), specifically, the speaker first absents himself, for example, "Not seldom from the uproar I retired / Into a silent bay" (1.447–48), and then feels receptive to, encounters, a nature suffused with spiritual signification, for example, "Magnificent / The morning rose, in memorable pomp, / Glorious as e'er I had beheld" (4.323–25).[61] Compare this natural process of spiritual preparation with Tennyson's prelude to epiphany:

> But when those others, one by one,
>   Withdrew themselves from me and night,
>   And in the house light after light
> Went out, and I was all alone,
>
> A hunger seized my heart;
>   (95.17–21)

Although Tennyson does not initiate, as Wordsworth does, his separation from people, his natural setting seems as indispensable to his spiritual energies as Wordsworth's does to his.

The wording of Wordsworth's emphasis on sudden spiritual insight, moreover—"*all at once* I saw a crowd, / A *host,* of golden daffodils" ("I Wandered Lonely as a Cloud," lines 3–4; my italics)—matches Tennyson's revelation in 95, "*all at once* it seemed at last / The living soul was flashed on mine" (lines 35–36; my italics). The first line of *The Prelude,* "O there is blessing in this gentle breeze," resonates, if only coincidentally, with Tennyson's "breeze" that "tremble[s] o'er / The large leaves of the sycamore" (95.54–55). Both breezes are harbingers of natural-spiritual experience.

Finally, there is a more millennial than apocalyptic imminence in both the "gathering swallows" of Keats's "To Autumn" (line 33) and the "gathering" breeze that "rocked the full-foliaged elms" in Tennyson's central epiphany (95.57–58). Both images evoke the paradoxical calmness prelusive to, and even attendant on, change. Just as a "chain-*swung* censer" teems in the "*rosy* sanctuary" of Keats's newly inspired poetry ("Ode to Psyche," lines 33, 59; my italics), so Tennyson's breeze "*swung* / The heavy-folded *rose*" (95.58–59; my italics). For both poets, then, one a High Romantic and the other a Late Romantic, the poetry of natural-spiritual experience highlights and appeals to the spiritual sense.

Soon after *In Memoriam* made him famous, and on the eve of being named poet laureate, Tennyson dreamed, apropos of my interest in his relation to national character, that Prince Albert gave him a kiss on the cheek, to which the still-dreaming poet responded, "Very kind, but very German."[62] His skittishness of things foreign extended to the French. His French Revolution–inspired apocalyptic fears correlate with his implicit interpretation of that event as the ominous beginning of uncontrolled violence in the West. His shocked, disapproving observation that "thrice," that is, in 1789, in 1830, and in 1848, "the red fool-fury of the Seine / . . .

pile[d] her barricades with dead" (127.6–8) contrasts sharply with his praise for Hallam's "love of freedom rarely felt, / Of freedom in her regal seat / Of England" (109.13–15). It is true that "the agrarian and Reform Bill disturbances of 1830–32 had been followed in England by Chartism, which had presented petitions for universal male suffrage to Parliament in 1839, 1842, and 1848,"[63] but Tennyson especially feared the other than English effects of the French Revolution, for in 1848 alone there were uprisings not only in France but also in Germany, Italy, Hungary, and Ireland. Thus nothing if not quintessentially British in politics and sensibility, or at most quintessentially Anglo-American,[64] Tennyson was also nothing if not quintessentially British or Anglo-American in literary connection.

In *In Memoriam* the Romantic apotheosis of humankind becomes the apotheosis of Arthur Hallam by "Anglo-American" (more empirical-evangelical than apocalyptically revolutionary) means. Hallam the natural man is the very type of the spiritual person to come in that "one far-off divine event, / To which the whole creation moves" (epilogue, lines 142–43).[65] *In Memoriam* makes the evangelical as well as empirical context of this new dispensation clear, for "rapt," "free," "power," "grace," "heavenly-wise," and "ethereal" are all the code words by which Tennyson describes "the God within" his friend (87.32–39).

In sum, then, *In Memoriam* does not so much repudiate as recast its Romantic heritage. Herbert Tucker argues that in order to explore "the fluctuating, reciprocally definitive relation between circumstance and volition, history and originality, opportunity and genius," Tennyson deliberately rejects his Romantic precursors who, by implication, have to do only with "genius," "originality," and "volition," never with "circumstance," "history," and "opportunity."[66] Many, however, have delineated among the English Romantics, at least, that very "fluctuating, reciprocally definitive relation."[67] Tucker hears in a scornful phrase of Tennyson's "Ulysses" (1842), namely, "As though to breathe were life!" (line 24), Tennyson's rejection of the Romantic equation of "literal respiration and spiritual inspiration"; "when read aloud," Tucker observes, the lines that follow the phrase "so exhaust the breath as to bring home the limitations of any merely respiratory or Aeolian conception of life."[68] Tennyson himself, however, makes the equation, for while recognizing distinctions between natural and spiritual experience, he equates empirical with evangelical experience.

Tucker's ingenious study (as Mermin pointed out) is perhaps insufficiently so with regard to the word *doom* in his title. *Tennyson and the Doom of Romanticism* suggests not only that Tennyson confronted the end of Romanticism but also that he was fated to be one of the last Romantics. The kind of Romanticism he exemplified, as his intra-Romantic relationships show, is an efficacious combination of tough mind and tender heart. This combination, if I may speak personally, characterizes both the Romanticism taught by my quondam mentor, Edwin G. Wilson, and the outlook represented by this legendary teacher himself.

Although he grew up during the Great Depression, Wilson notes the bittersweet nature and even the joys of that time. "I've always been a rather hopeful and optimistic person," he says. "That is not to say that the Romantic poets were naive or without pain or anguish. But it is to say that there is something idealistic and something very heroic and compassionate about Romanticism." His view of Romanticism, that it emphasizes optimism without either oversimplifying intellectual problems or underestimating spiritual dilemmas, permeates my work. Without implying that he agrees with what I have written, I continue to profit from his masterly exploration of British High Romanticism. His pedagogy remains impeccable, but his teaching as long ago as the fall semester of 1965 continues to inspire my placement of *In Memoriam* within the empirical-evangelical, the Anglo-American as well as British, precincts of Romanticism.

Exposition the Second

THE METHOD OF EMERSON'S PROSE

TEN

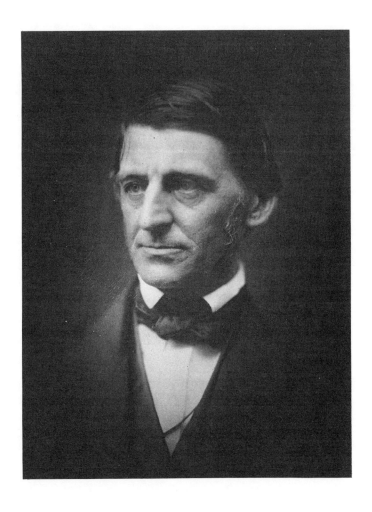

Introit

Although Emerson's perspective deepens over time and although his tones vary, his ideas/ideals of sensation tend to unify his works. Stephen E. Whicher, it is true, traces changes from Emerson the rhapsodist (1841–43), through Emerson the reformer (1844–45), to Emerson the preacher of the "sacredness of private integrity" (1846–52).[1] Whicher notes, accordingly, Emerson's tonal modulations from the prophetic, through the dramatic, to the "coolly professional." David Van Leer, however, by focusing on Emerson's ideas about Kantian epistemology and German idealism, resists, as I do, the notion of distinct stages in Emerson's life of writing: "Although Emerson clearly comes to understand more fully the [epistemological] question with which he began his philosophical career, the issues themselves remain sufficiently constant that it may be unwise to speak of this refinement as 'growth' or 'change.'"[2] "At the very least," Van Leer adds, "it seems unfair to see the tonal progression from *Circles* through *Experience* to *Fate* as the characteristic shift: each of these pessimistic essays is published in a collection whose predominant tone is optimistic." Rather than echoing Van Leer's influence studies through German idealism, I call attention to Emerson's British as well as American reflection of Lockean epistemology and empirical-evangelical philosophical theology. Consistent with the method I see in *In Memoriam* and throughout my exposition of Emerson's prose method, I argue that the empirical-evangelical dialectic he forges in *Nature* (1836)[3] methodically and faithfully synthesizes the aesthetic as well as intellectual-emotional effects he creates in seven other characteristic essays. *The American Scholar, The Divinity School Address, Self-Reliance, The Over-Soul,* and *The Poet* (1837–42), first, complete the formative phase of his empirical-evangelical art, and even *Experience* and *Fate* (1842, 1852), despite the so-called "pessimism" of these fully mature works, contribute signally to the complex coherence of his empirical-evangelical vision.

Van Leer, in an especially theoretical mood, observes that "an idea" is "unlike history" in that "an idea is true not because it 'really happened' but because it is 'really believed.'"[4] He adds:

> By this definition a "history of ideas" is not merely a debased kind of history: it is a literal oxymoron, inherently self-contradictory. For the methods by which we believe ideas are so independent of those by which we prove events that the coupling of the two seems counterproductive. One might almost say that we study as history only what we have first failed to believe as truth: that only the idea that seems intellectually unjustifiable on its own terms requires the further justification offered by historical contextualization.

Does the relatively unchanging nature of a given set of ideas mean, however, that it cannot "happen" in a broad historical context? Are "happening" and "belief" necessarily mutually exclusive? According to Locke, Wesley, and Edwards (whatever Kant and the German idealists thought), they are not. While it may be (as Nietzsche says) that "terms that have histories cannot be defined,"[5] I do not go as far as Van Leer does toward separating Emerson's ideas from the stories that underlie them. If I do not fully succeed in defining the influence of empiricism and evangelicalism as they operate on the heart, mind, and language of this prophet, nevertheless, I fully establish their spatiotemporal configuration with him.

Van Leer finds fault with Whicher for focusing on Emerson's "shifting tone" rather than his "ideas,"[6] but shifts in tone are surely consistent with the notion of a unified career. While Emerson's ideas are indeed sufficiently persistent to make his vision cohesive, his work remains intact under the scrutiny of tone-sensitive intellectual/historical criticism. A sociology of knowledge arising from the relation between Emerson and his empirical-evangelical roots is no less unified for being dynamic.

Whicher's approach to Emerson, despite Whicher's belief that three discordant periods disrupt the career, is united, in effect, by his concern with religious issues. Whicher argues that the Emerson of the 1820s was a "natural believer" troubled by "skepticism and self-doubt"; the Emerson of the 1830s and the 1840s, in turn, found relief from skepticism through the "nearly miraculous" discovery of the "moral law within him"; and the Emerson of the 1840s began to waver in his secular religion called self-reliance.[7] Whicher concludes that beneath the public Emerson there grew "a finite consciousness troubled with a tragic sense of contingency and loss."

This conclusion, though anticipated by Ralph Rusk and elaborated by Jonathan Bishop and Joel Porte,[8] is not finally convincing to me. I resist the notion that over the course of time Emerson fell from "freedom" into "fate," from the "infinite aspirations" of his early work into his later acceptance of the "fated limitations of human power."[9] Whicher himself admits, albeit only of the years 1844 and 1845, that Emerson's "settled aim as an author" was "to marry faith and skepticism."[10] Thus acknowledging that Emerson strives to consolidate his career, Whicher somewhat militates against his larger argument. His admission implies that the themes spanning the career are not so much discordant as either prefiguring or following from the defining "moment" of the career, namely, *Nature*. At any rate, Whicher's view of 1844 and 1845 accurately describes the career's larger arc. From the beginning to the end of Emerson's prime his specific aim if not his accomplishment was to "unite" empiricism with evangelicalism.

Although Leonard Neufeldt calls for more attention to the "rigorously descriptive, systematic, analytical, and philosophical" side of Emerson's works and less to the "moral, appreciative, and privately aesthetic side" of them,[11] one's emphasis need not be thus "either/or." Newton Arvin, with "both/and" logic, argues that since any given point of Emerson's prime synthesizes freedom with fate, "the best of Emerson lies on the other side" of tragedy.[12]

Stanley Cavell, similarly, sees Emerson as neither a philosopher nor a theologian, but as something of both, that is, as a moral philosopher who, like Nietzsche, Wittgenstein, and Heidegger, succeeds in substituting for philosophy and theology as separately understood a unitary (because philosophical-theological) language that interprets "thinking as the receiving or letting be of something."[13] Thus Emerson avoids philosophical and moral nihilism. While I agree that Emerson's ideas/ideals of sensation foreshadow Nietzsche, Wittgenstein, and Heidegger, and while these ideas/ideals of Emerson's prime certainly derive in part from Hume and Kant,[14] I argue here that the ideas/ideals of Emerson's prime relate even more directly to, even as they transmogrify, the Anglo-American trinity of Locke, Wesley, and Edwards. "Why did it take me [so long]," asks Cavell, "to begin to look actively at [Emerson's] work, to demand explicitly my inheritance of him?" I, too, regret having come to Emerson so late. The line of descent from Emerson to the fashionable master figures of Nietzsche, Wittgenstein, and Heidegger, however, is primarily Continental, and another legacy bequeathed by Emerson to the twentieth century is the inheritance he received from domestic/binational precursors. Like Cavell, too, I comprehend Emerson by means of the "both/and" logic of a particular dialectic. "Both/and," however, is especially the logic of the English-language dialectic in which I am interested. The empirical-evangelical dialectic is not only spatiotemporally pertinent to but also comprehensively explanatory concerning the experientially broad form of Emerson's philosophical-theological unity.

Thus I am far from finding Emerson lacking in the standard of unity, nor would I celebrate such lack. His essays, to be sure, can seem as fragmented as the "forms of ruin" found by Thomas McFarland among the works of Wordsworth and Coleridge.[15] According to Neufeldt and John Michael, the essays break down into "disharmonious personae," the "rhetoric of contradiction," and the only partially "managed" "theater of conflict." [16] While acknowledging that Emerson's trope of drama is strong enough to constitute his "identity," Neufeldt and Michael do not admire the dramaturgical integrity of the essays so much as they delight in the dramatic iconoclasm, the strangely prescient energy, by which their centers of form and meaning, prelusive to Yeats's "The Second Coming" (1919), do not hold. The "central interpretive problem" for readers of Emerson, according to Julie Ellison, is not so much "change" from one phase of his career to another as the "constant tension between freedom and fate, convention and rebellion *within* each essay" (Ellison's italics); but neither "change" nor "tension" is so much a "problem" for Ellison as each is the exhilarating occasion for her to problematize Emerson's essays, that is, to render them consistent with the most gleefully ruining Postmodernism or most ideologically correct but finally disbelieving *fröhliche Wissenschaft*.[17] Herschel Parker agrees that "even within a single work, Emerson's point of view may shift from one pole of a subject to the other" and that Emerson's "mind moved like that of a dramatist who embodies felt or imagined moods in various characters," but Parker parts company from the strictly Modernizing/Postmodernizing critical tendency that would make Emerson's essays

"diasparactive" (McFarland's term) or disjointed. Parker remarks, in contrast to the fragmenting views of Ellison, Neufeldt, and Michael, that "the
subject remains Emersonian," that is, that not only within a given essay
but also over the course of Emerson's career his ideas remain the same.[18] I
seek to enlarge the space opened up by Parker's observation.

His observation tacitly invokes the "blessed rage for order" that Wallace
Stevens somewhat uncharacteristically opposes to the "modalities of fragmentation" (McFarland's phrase) rampant among Stevens's fellow Modern-
ists.[19] One might oppose a similar rage to the even more normative disjunc-
tions indulged in by Postmodernist critics. Consistent with the formalistic
as well as thematic implication of Parker's insight, I reaffirm in specifically empirical-evangelical language the coherence of Emerson's thought
and feeling. As arguments and as belles lettres, his essays are all the more
mainstream for their empirically and evangelically synthesizing unity. Notwithstanding some critics' views of "dead authors" as impersonal sites of
cultural/semiotic transactions,[20] Emerson's experiential vision carries its
own full measure of credible authority. His intellectual-emotional art, no
more univocal than illustrative of aporia, is sufficiently uniform, nevertheless, in that it is both cumulatively intense and holistically effective. On
grounds of content and form, his essays more than sufficiently justify (if
justification were needed) their canonized status. I defend this status by
means other than the usual readings-back into nineteenth-century literature of a Modernist fragment-shoring against personal ruins; far from being
"disjointed but obliquely relevant scraps" that both "render" Emerson's
"unrelieved situation" and "support him in his isolation and loneliness,"[21]
his essays break out of solipsism yet do not surrender "self-reliance," for by
blending the empirical thesis with the evangelical antithesis they join the
problematical but graspable classically Anglo-American issues of social-
intellectual cohesion and philosophical-religious experience.

Thus, although the essays can appear to constitute the American counterpart to McFarland's British High Romantic "modalities of fragmentation,"
Emerson's authenticating vision—his synthesis of empirical philosophy
with evangelical faith—exemplifies a Late but not belated Romanticism
that, without fudging differences or papering them over, remains at such
a considerable if respectful distance from Modernism as to be primarily
an independent, irreducible phenomenon, and only secondarily a proto-
Modernist symptom.[22] Notwithstanding Modernist and Postmodernist re-

jections of aesthetic integrity,[23] the Romantic/Late Romantic as well as perennial criterion of unity undergirds canonical essays that, since they complete Emerson's empirical-evangelical dialectic, fulfill his hope for a complex, imaginative whole. The method of his prose, like the method of *In Memoriam*, exemplifies a more process-intensive than transumptive Romanticism that, besides being sufficiently sublime, is experience-validated, that is, endowed with the religion- and world-making imagination of the Anglo-American world. (In "The Religion-Making Imagination of Joseph Smith," chapter five of Harold Bloom's *The American Religion: The Emergence of the Post-Christian Nation*, Bloom argues that "the religion-making genius of Joseph Smith, profoundly American, uniquely restored the Bible's sense of the theomorphic, a restoration that inevitably led the prophet into his most audacious restoration, patriarchal plural marriage." "To apply a strictly rhetorical and literary term to the prophet's religion-making career," Bloom adds, "we can say that Smith accomplished a transumption, by joining his Latter-Day Saints to the ever earliness of the great patriarchs, and to Enoch in particular. In a transumption, earliness and lateness change places, while everything that comes in between is voided." [24] Emerson, acutely aware of earliness and lateness, is far from leaving out the in-between.) Thus I will test my historical-critical, philosophical-theological overview of Emerson's career.

Whether one approaches *The American Scholar, The Divinity School Address, Self-Reliance, The Over-Soul*, and *The Poet* empirically or evangelically, or in both ways at once, all five essays succeed in recasting *Nature*'s reconciliation of the internal with the external, God with nature, and God with humankind. Although *The American Scholar, The Divinity School Address*, and *Self-Reliance* shift focus continually and do not observe much unity of antipodal perspective between the actual and the ideal, and although the philosophical-theological thrusts and parries of these three essays do not quite sustain the extended empirical-evangelical synthesis to be found in *Nature*, they drive, nevertheless, at that synthesis. *The Over-Soul*, despite an emphasis on the ideal, exercises a paradoxical logic by which idealism meets actuality on the ground of experience, and this experiential interrelation recurs, too, in *The Poet*, which applies the case to literature. Thus *The Over-Soul* and *The Poet* demonstrate the dialectic more than the disjointedness and paradox more than dualism, and the concept of experience in all five essays, perhaps more dramatically than in any other essays by

Emerson, forms the ground of his at least alternately empirical and evangelical sensibility. While *The American Scholar, The Divinity School Address*, and *Self-Reliance* collectively constitute the most definitive elaboration of each term in the dialectic by which Emerson builds his literary universe, a unity of opposing perspectives forms the overriding motif of *The Over-Soul* and *The Poet*; if not overtly in *The American Scholar, The Divinity School Address*, and *Self-Reliance*, however, the empirical-evangelical imagination is clear in the relation between them and such even more fully developed, even more characteristically inclusive representatives of the canon as *The Over-Soul, The Poet*, and *Nature*. Thus, despite the shifting perspectives of Emerson's midcareer, it is of a piece not only in itself but also in relation to the formative essay of his career, for the experiential emphases of *Nature*— its permutations and combinations of empiricism and evangelicalism—find especially full reworkings in the five most canonized essays of Emerson's prime. Finally, my empirical-evangelical approach to *Experience* and *Fate* reassesses the crucial issue in Emerson criticism whether his optimism is foolish or earned.

ELEVEN

Perspective-by-Perspective Understanding

Although *The American Scholar* has received little critical attention,[1] and although even the interpretation of Emerson as quintessentially American gives this "American," if not "Anglo-American," essay short shrift,[2] it is nonetheless firmly canonized.[3] It certainly rewards careful reading. Although not entirely without the full unity of Emerson's broadly experiential vision, the essay excels at delineating each component of this vision separately, as though unity depends, after all, on perspective-by-perspective understanding. Nowhere else in all his works does one find a clearer, more succinct focus on empiricism per se and evangelicalism per se, for the writing of *The American Scholar* overlapped with the writing of *Nature*, and *The American Scholar* also stakes out and breaks ground for Emerson's complex, yet single, world picture.

The essay's portrait of the scholar, first, is anything but solipsistic; "the deeper he dives into his privatest secretest presentiment," declares Emerson, "to his wonder he finds, this is the most acceptable, most public, and universally true."[4] (Emerson's scholar, incidentally, is male, and so is his audience. Let it be admitted at the outset that his language is peculiarly if not risibly sexist even by the standards of his day; Wesley, for example, uses "people" and "men and women."[5] Underlying many of Emerson's passages is what Parker calls "the defensiveness of a man who has chosen to be a thinker rather than taking what his contemporaries would have seen as an active role in affairs, a defensiveness, in the sexist terminology which he regularly employed, against the charge of effeminacy."[6] This defensiveness, which we cannot correct and which we may not even want to forgive, is especially explicit in *The American Scholar*: "The so called 'practical men' sneer at speculative men, as if, because they speculate or *see*, they could do nothing. I have heard it said that the clergy . . . are addressed as women: that the rough, spontaneous conversation of men they do not hear, but only a mincing and diluted speech. They are often virtually disfranchised; and, indeed, there are advocates for their celibacy" [864]. Thus Emerson, even though part of the growing alliance between clergymen and women in the nineteenth century,[7] remains ambivalent about that alliance; David Leverenz argues that "male rivalry" is a much more basic source of Emerson's defensiveness than "maternal scapegoating," and given Leverenz's view of Emerson as "struggling with what it means to be a man," it is logical for him to register impatience with "Emerson's idealism" as a subject of Emerson studies. While I, too, am impatient with "Emerson's idealism" when seen instead of, or to the exclusion of, his "actualism," I cannot agree with Leverenz's implication that "gender pressures" bury all other interdisciplinary-historical considerations of his works whatsoever.[8]) By thus affirming the inward in terms of the outward, Emerson follows a peculiarly Lockean mode of prefiguring their identity.

Neither is the scholar at all rationalistic, and this trait, albeit negative, is a full indication of the essay's empiricism. The scholar admires geometry as "a pure abstraction of the human mind" (861), but the essay makes it clear that even mathematics comes down to sense-based reason. Even mathematics constitutes a mirror held up to but not superior to or independent of nature: "The geometer discovers that geometry" is "the measure of planetary motion" (861). Mathematical diction figures in the scholar's definition of science as "nothing but the finding of *analogy, identity* in the most remote parts" of matter (861; my italics). Thus even the most purely mental realm of mathematics functions like a sense to reveal the world outside, for the curious apposition of mathematical terms, "analogy, identity," refers not only to the Emersonian continuum that joins nature to Man— that is, the human-driven relation between nature and humankind—but also to Nature alone. Proportionalities and samenesses among objects not only overlap with but also simply parallel subjects. The scholar, then, is both separate from and intimate with the objects of his or her analysis; the essay highlights a formulation that takes full empiricist account of the stubborn otherness of things, even as this same formulation assimilates all things: "The ambitious soul sits down before each refractory fact; one after another, reduces all strange constitutions, all new powers, to their class and their law, and goes on forever to animate the last fibre of organization, the outskirts of nature, by insight" (861).

Consider, accordingly, the essay's Lockean cast; regretting that "meek young men grow up in libraries, believing it their duty to accept the views which Cicero, which Locke, which Bacon have given, forgetful that Cicero, Locke and Bacon were only young men in libraries when they wrote those books" (862), Emerson makes an only seemingly anti-Lockean point, for this very feature, in its assumption that one's views should arise from experience, is finally Lockean. "Out of unhandselled," that is, seemingly unpromising, "savage nature," out of "terrible Druids and Berserkirs," come at last "Alfred and Shakespeare" (867), for just as nature thus precedes culture and earlier culture thus precedes later culture, so, by Emerson's implication, experience is precisely as Locke says it is, namely, utterly formative in ordinary as well as extraordinary lives. "A strange process, too, this, by which experience is converted into thought, as a mulberry leaf is converted into satin" (865), but the process, as the essay's elaboration on experience implies, is increasingly Lockean. "The first in time and the first in importance of the influence upon the mind," Emerson teaches, "is that of nature" (860), and this clear assumption of the tabula rasa entails an equally clear, equally Lockean corollary, namely, apprehension of nature's shaping power: "Every day, the sun; and, after sunset, night and her stars. Ever the winds blow; ever the grass grows. Every day, men and women, conversing, beholding and beholden. The scholar must needs stand wistful and admiring before this great spectacle" (860). Just as Locke argues that sense experience gives rise to ideas, so too does *The American Scholar* hold that "the new deed . . . detaches itself from the life like a ripe fruit, to become a thought of the mind" (865). "The office of the scholar," accordingly, is "to cheer, to raise, and to guide men by showing them facts amidst appearances" (867). This twofold implication, first that things exist which correspond to our ideas of them, and second that our means of knowing them can save us from illusion, reveals a distinctly Lockean, because robust and untroubled, mindset.

Somewhat in line with one's preconception of Emerson as an idealist, next witness how the generally evangelical and even the particularly Wesleyan-Edwardsean cast of *The American Scholar* comes into play. "Colleges," Emerson asserts, "can only highly serve us when they gather from far every ray of various genius to their hospitable halls, and, by the concentrated fires, *set the hearts of their youth on flame*" (64; my italics). This warmheartedness, this quasi-revivalistic fervor, carries over into Emerson's portrait of the scholar, whose "work" is "the *conversion* of the world," whose quasi-evangelical task is to make the principles of scholarship "prevalent" (874; my italics). Although such honorifically evangelical diction may simply lend authority to the only indirectly evangelical goal of spreading the gospel of education, Emerson elsewhere in the essay directly assumes for his own persona, as well as for the "American scholar" generally, the leading role of scholar-converter. Where he laments, for example, that "man has become of no account" and "has almost lost the light that can lead him back to his prerogatives," Emerson intends a spiritual meaning (870). He would "wake" humankind from the "sleep-walking" of the unregenerate, and all too natural, inclination to "money or power" or "sensual indulgence" (874), and thus he sounds a certain, a more than quasi-evangelical, trumpet.

Emerson's conception of the scholar, and of himself as a scholar, resembles my conception of the evangelical preacher.[9] "The clergy," observes Emerson, are "more universally than any other class, the scholars of their day" (864). It may be said of scholars and clergy alike that they do not so much belong to the "studious class" as share the ideal or common goal, if not the sometimes accomplished fact, of "action" (864). "Action," though "with the scholar subordinate," is nonetheless "essential" (864–65). The scholar, like the evangelical clergy and, by extension, the evangelical laity, lives by faith in the kind of experience through which significant, natural-spiritual things happen to and because of him or her. "Only so much do I know," concludes the clergyman-scholar Emerson, "as I have lived" (865).

"Man Thinking," declares Emerson in especially perpendicular masculinist mood, "must not be subdued by his instruments" (863). "When he can read God directly," he adds, "the hour is too precious to be wasted in other men's transcripts of *their* readings," and "Books," therefore, are only for the scholar's "idle times" (863; my italics). (See Wordsworth's "The Tables Turned" [1798].) Books merely mediate a spiritual truth better acquired not so much through a wisely passive receptivity to the Bible or the book of nature as through a wisely active questing for spiritual communion, perhaps with the Holy Spirit, through the all but millennial phenomenon of intersubjectivity: "I grasp the hands of those next me, and take my place in the ring to suffer and to work, taught by an instinct that so shall the dumb abyss be vocal with speech" (865). In such an effusion lies something of the Arminian and even the consciously anti-Calvinist spirit of universal freedom, for something of a Wesleyan and hence Arminian cast lies in Emerson's announcement that "the soul is free, sovereign, active" (863). *Sovereign,* of course, is Calvinist diction, but this soul is sovereign not so much in divine as in human authority, and Emerson goes so far in an anti-Calvinist direction as all but explicitly to oppose the doctrine of election. His Arminian-like freedom-doctrine entails "not the privilege of here and there a favorite, but the sound estate of every man" (863); "every man," then, is as likely to be the free-spirited, "Arminian-evangelical" scholar in particular as the spiritual person in general.

In sum, then, *The American Scholar* is now empirical and now evangelical. Emerson specifically gives credit for the subject-object paradox to "one man of genius who has done much for this philosophy of life" and "whose literary value has never yet been rightly estimated;—I mean Emanuel Swedenborg" (872). What Swedenborg "saw and showed," however, is "the connection between nature and the affections of the soul" (872). This connection is seen and shown, too, by Wesley and Edwards, for Wesley uses Lockean philosophy as his principle for abridging Edwards's *Religious Affections*.[10] With thanks to Locke, Wesley, and Edwards as well as in acknowledgment of Swedenborg, then, "the connection between nature and the affections of the soul" entails subject-object playfulness. Thus bringing together, however briefly, discrete emphases on empiricism and evangelicalism, *The American Scholar* refers to the empirical-evangelical continuum that joins man and nature to God.

The spiritual sense continuum lies near even the essay's most Swedenborgian flight. Emerson asks "What would we really know the meaning of?" He answers along lines not only Swiss but also native, and indeed more native than Swiss. After cataloguing several experiential particulars—"The meal in the firkin; the milk in the pan; the ballad in the street; the news of the boat; the glance of the eye; the form and gait of the body"—he derives a triple-imperative conclusion at once from experience-philosophy and from experience-theology: "Show me the ultimate reason of these matters;—show me the sublime presence of the highest spiritual cause lurking, as always it does lurk in these suburbs and extremities of nature; let me see every trifle bristling with the *polarity* that *ranges it* instantly on an eternal law" (872–73; my italics). Submerged in the diction of the last clause, significantly, is the natural-spiritual, empirical-evangelical metaphor of continuum.

TWELVE

Religious Methodology

The Divinity School Address builds on Emerson's Unitarianism by means of his empirical-evangelical epistemology. While the address grows out of his Unitarian sense of "self-culture,"[1] it implies "not that Unitarianism is right, but that, though irrelevant, [Unitarianism] will not interfere with the real project," identified by Van Leer as the development and advancement of Kantian method.[2] The address, however, is neither exclusively neo-idealistically epistemological nor exclusively Unitarian; in addition, it employs a Lockean as well as Wesleyan-Edwardsean perspective to bolster its hearer's/reader's resources of religious methodology. Thus, although its unlabored style makes for an especially pleasurable reading experience, it remains substantial; it alternates between, and even seeks to blend, neo-actualistic epistemology and experimental faith.

The address out-Lockes Locke, first, precisely in its religious views. Not even divine truth can be "received at second hand," for "what [another soul] announces, I must find true in me, or wholly reject; and on his word, or as his second, be he who he may, I can accept nothing" (878). This declaration compares with Wesley's obviously identical, philosophically as well as theologically experiential search for "that faith which none can have without knowing that he hath it."[3] Thus, while Locke is merely *wary* about accepting religious testimony,[4] Emerson refuses even to *listen* to any such testimony that his own spiritual experience does not corroborate.

Since his testimonial language typically confines itself to the report of his senses, he often shows the courage of Locke's convictions about direct experience of whatever truths may be. Notice the robust, untroubled turn of a passage that concerns the correspondence of inner and outer: "Speak the truth, and all things alive or brute are vouchers, and the very roots of the grass underground there, do seem to stir and move to bear you witness" (876). Consider the following even greater sustainment of subject-object balance:

> One is constrained to respect the perfection of this world, in which our senses converse. How wide; how rich; what invitation from every property it gives to every faculty of man! In its fruitful soils; in its navigable sea; in its mountains of metal and stone; in its forests of all woods; in its animals; in its chemical ingredients; in the powers and path of light, heat, attraction, and life, it is well worth the pith and heart of great men to subdue and enjoy it. The planters, the mechanics, the inventors, the astronomers, the builders of cities, and the captains, history delights to honor. (875)

Such cataloguing of Lockean legacy reflects in full measure the harmony between nature per se and all natural manifestations of the human subject from simple exertion of common muscular force to Newtonian-scientific imagination. From one perspective, *The Divinity School Address* establishes the primacy of mind over matter: "But the moment the mind opens, and reveals the laws which traverse the universe, and make things what they are, then shrinks the great world at once into a mere illustration and fable of this great mind" (875). The address is also capable of respecting the autonomy of the objective to the point of subordinating mind to it: "The mystery of nature was never displayed so happily. The corn and the wine have been freely dealt to all creatures, and the never-broken silence with which the old bounty goes forward, has not yielded yet one word of explanation" (874–75). Thus the essay's grasp of empirical philosophy is especially tight; despite (or perhaps because of) its theological occasion, the essay features Locke's main tenets. The experience-philosophy of the eighteenth century was far from over in the nineteenth-century world of Emerson and his works.

The address, though delivered to the senior class of Harvard's Divinity College, can seem anything but religious; the announcement that "the Christian Church is gone or going" (865), for example, attacks both church and clergy (see Philip Larkin's "Church Going" [1955].) The essay laments that empty ritualists abound among ministers: "Whenever the pulpit is usurped by a formalist, then is the worshipper defrauded and disconsolate"

(882). In Emerson's age, as in Milton's, "the hungry sheep look up, and are not fed."[5] Emerson puts the point even more bluntly: he reports that "I have heard a devout person, who prized the Sabbath, say in bitterness of heart, 'On Sundays, it seems wicked to go to church' " (885). He may well have had in mind his devout but independent aunt Mary Moody Emerson, who wrote of the Malden minister that "I could not be reverent tonight with poor Mr. G.'s preaching."[6] No Harvard audience invited Emerson back for more than thirty years, when Harvard had become more secular and Emerson more famous.

Andrews Norton's denunciation of the address as "the latest form of infidelity"[7] is wide of the mark, for Emerson envisions a church restored along experiential lines. Notice, first, the standard by which Emerson judges and finds wanting a preacher "I once heard . . . who sorely tempted me to say, I would go to church no more":

> He had no one word intimating that he had laughed or wept, was married or in love, had been commended, or cheated, or chagrined. If he had ever lived and acted, we were none the wiser for it. . . . Not one fact in all his experience, had he yet imported into his doctrine. This man had ploughed, and planted, and talked, and bought, and sold; he had read books; he had eaten and drunken; his head aches; his heart throbs; he smiles and suffers; yet was there not a surmise, a hint, in all the discourse, that he had ever lived at all. Not a line did he draw out of real history. . . . [I]t could not be told out of his sermon, what age of the world he fell in; whether he had a father or a child; whether he was a freeholder or a pauper; whether he was a citizen or a countryman; or any other fact of his biography. (882–83)

The hapless original of this scathing account is likely the Reverend Barzillai Frost, minister of the Unitarian church at Lexington during the years following Emerson's resignation from Boston's Second Church;[8] but Emerson is not attacking all Unitarian preaching; for the great Unitarian minister W. E. Channing writes that "we ought to speak of religion as something which we ourselves know."[9] David Robinson sums up Channing's preaching this way: "Establishing a middle ground between hellfire ranting and scornful intellectualism, Channing . . . placed the emphasis on a deeply felt religious experience communicable to the hearers." The slogan of not only Unitarian but also evangelical homiletics could be "experience into words,"[10] for by recasting their lives as spiritual autobiographies[11] evangelical preachers provided their flocks with the nearest and most pertinent exemplar of how to live. In Emerson's twofold byword that "the capital secret" of the ministerial "profession" should be "to convert life into truth" and that the "true preacher can always be known by this, that he deals out to the people his life,—life passed through the fire of thought" (883) he appeals as much to the evangelical as to the Unitarian tradition. In appealing to the Unitarian tradition, indeed, he appeals in part to the evangelical tradition that inspired it. Even Harvard Unitarians, as Daniel Walker Howe has shown, "were more than participants in the Second Great Awakening; they were among its pioneers."[12]

Thus Emerson's twofold principle that the near influence is always telling and that value lies in the here and now clearly derives from the experiential, almost Lockean criterion by which Wesley's preachers attended to their lives. Thus, too, the address attempts to make the divinity student over into that most faithful type of Christian minister, the evangelical preacher. The address does not attack ministers or churches so much as it argues that "evangelical" ministers can reform the church. "What," asks Emerson, "shall we do?" (888). His answer does not lie in destroying the church: "I confess, all attempts to project and establish a Cultus with new rites and forms, seem to me vain" (888). His answer lies in the hope that the young men of his audience will work diligently within the church: "Let the breath of new life be breathed by you through the forms already existing" (888). The prototype of such "breathing" is the revivalism of Wesley and Edwards, who lived by an injunction reaffirmed, and especially memorably expressed, by Emerson: "Faith makes us, and not we it, and faith makes its own forms" (888). Especially evangelical is the advice given by Emerson to future ministers that they "speak the very truth" "in lecture rooms, in houses, in *fields,* wherever the invitation of men or your own occasions lead you" (888; my italics). Field-preaching is the hallmark of Wesley's ministry and revivalism in general, but Emerson is careful, even where he thus implies itinerancy, to append the sort of advice that Wesley also gave and followed, namely, that ministers should speak above all "in *pulpits*" (888; my italics).

It is no more Emerson's fault than Wesley's that these two preachers are taken as more iconoclastic than they are. Where Emerson speaks of "a decaying church and a wasting unbelief, which are casting malignant influences around us" (885), he does not so much attack the church as grieve on its behalf. He even offers the evangelical antidote of belief or spiritual renewal. He declares that "God incarnates himself in man, and evermore goes forth anew to take possession of his world" (878). He even declares that God incarnates himself explicitly in the "one man . . . true to what is in you and me," namely, "Jesus Christ" (878). Thus God will incarnate himself again in the renewed ministry and the revitalized church.

Evangelicalism, of course, pertains to the Great Commission to preach the gospel to all the world (see Matthew 28.19–20), and the address's portrait of the ideal preacher is evangelical in precisely this strict sense of the word. Emerson opposes any missionary effort on the part of a congregation whose spiritual state falls short of good repair, for he hopes that any minister who does "*not* give bread of life," any slothful minister, would be ashamed "to propose to his parish, that they should send money a hundred or a thousand miles, to furnish such poor fare as they have at home" (884; Emerson's italics). The proper minister, however, whose "hope and commission it is to preach the faith of Christ," will develop "a desire and need to impart to others the same knowledge and love" of Christ that he himself enjoys (881–82). "If utterance is denied[,] the thought lies like a burden on the man" (881–82; see Coleridge's "The Rime of the Ancient Mariner"). "I wish," exclaims Emerson to would-be ministers, that "you may feel your call in throbs of desire and hope" (881); what he calls on them to preach, specifically, is "the life and dialogues of Christ" as they "befell, alive and warm, part of human life, and of the landscape, and of the cheerful day" (881).

The address's portrait of preacher-as-evangelical matches its affinities with evangelicalism in general. Emerson teaches that "the doctrine of divine nature being forgotten, a sickness infects and dwarfs the constitution" (878), and nothing could be more broadly evangelical than this statement's assumption that to forget God amounts to the sickness of sin (see the discussion in Wesley's "On Living Without God" [1790]).[13] The assumption of a personal God, though, is at least equally broadly evangelical, as Blake's relation to the Wesleyan tradition demonstrates.[14] Emerson objects, accordingly, to the "manner in which [Christ's] name is surrounded with expressions, which were once sallies of admiration and love, but are now petrified into official titles" (879). This manner, by "kill[ing] all generous sympathy and liking" for Christ (879), destroys one's sense of Christ as personal savior, and if such a sense borders on enthusiasm, then Emerson does not shrink from it. In another context he defiantly adopts the most enthusiastic though still most biblical metaphor he can think of, namely, glossolalia: "Courage, piety, love, wisdom, can teach; and every man can open his door to these angels, and they shall bring him *the gift of tongues.* But the man who aims to speak as books enable, as synods use, as the fashion guides, and as interest commands, babbles. Let him hush" (881; my italics; see Acts 10.46). Thus Emerson conveys his conviction that the opportunities for spiritual growth offered by the nearest influences on one's daily life far outweigh the spiritual experiences that one acquires indirectly from creeds and rote observances. Love, after all, if not courage, piety, and wisdom, is a fruit of the Spirit.[15]

The address's evangelical theology is assuredly not so general as to include that theology's Calvinist strain. Emerson admires "stern, high, stoical, Christian discipline" (884); such discipline smacks more of his Puritan/ Edwardsean heritage than of his less stern, more accessible, and less stoical heritage of Wesleyan Methodism. He shows his vehement antipathy, however, to specific formulations of Calvinism; hear, for example, what he says of election: "that the divine nature is attributed to one or two persons, and denied to the rest, and denied with fury," is "perversion" (878). Emerson thinks that the generality of preachers leans too much to the Calvinist side of theological discourse. He laments that "the preachers do not see that they make [Christ's] gospel not glad" (881).

Thus revealing his preference for joy, Emerson also reveals the Arminian strain of his evangelical theology. His theology, to be sure, does not lapse into fuzzy-minded sentimentality, for he bluntly acknowledges that "souls proceed into heaven, into hell" (876), but by emphasizing that souls do so "of their own volition" (876), he bases his tough-mindedness on free-willism rather than predestinarianism. "Evil," he argues, "is merely privative, not absolute," whereas "benevolence is absolute and real" and "good is positive" (876). This view of evil is not inconsistent with the latter-day Calvinism of Karl Barth, for whom "evil," for all its "terrifying effect in the world," is essentially unreal.[16] As "the shadow-side of God's good creation," Barth argues, it tyrannizes humanity but has no sovereignty over God. Emerson's view of evil, however, resonates with Arminianism more than with the conservative Calvinism of his day. Subscribing to the doctrine of the "indwelling Supreme Spirit" who resides, at least potentially, in every heart (878), he subscribes to a democratic/Arminian doctrine, and nothing could be more explicitly Arminian than his crystalline declaration that "the gift of God to the soul is not a vaunting, overpowering, excluding sanctity, but a sweet natural goodness" (880). Although "natural goodness" may sound vaguely Latitudinarian or even Rousseauistic, it occurs in the context of Emerson's rejection of Calvinist sanctification, and thus the phrase connotes the natural opposite of exclusionary sanctification, namely, the doctrine of spiritual perfection best embodied by John Fletcher of Madeley, Wesley's chief Arminian lieutenant (George Whitefield was his chief Calvinist lieutenant; Madeley was arguably the most sweet-tempered Arminian of all eighteenth-century British or American culture).[17]

By searching for what makes "a true conversion, a true Christ," and by concluding that "only by coming again to themselves, or to God in themselves, can [men] grow forevermore" (880), Emerson uses a language decidedly Arminian, because decidedly open-ended in tone. His emphasis on "God in themselves," indeed, is bold, and such virtual apotheosis of self recurs throughout *The Divinity School Address*. Witness, for example, its proverb, "that which shows God in me, fortifies me" (880). The address adds, however, a proverb with un-Rousseauistic, albeit sufficiently Latitudinarian, implications of ethics and morality: "That which shows God out of me, makes me a wart and a wen" (880). Emerson's formulations of apotheosis are, theologically speaking, not so much iconoclastic as reflective of Arminian belief in the individual's power to choose the right: "If a man is at heart just, then in so far is he God; . . . If a man dissemble, deceive, he deceives himself, and goes out of acquaintance with his own being" (876). Sin, at least in that Emerson defines it as a self not God, most definitely exists.

The address's version of Emerson's evangelical theology, then, evinces the subthemes of church renewal, proclamatory preaching, lostness without God, personal relation to God, moral action, Christological presence, conversion, Arminian optimism, and Arminian astringency. These make up Emerson's master evangelical theme of experiential faith. "Thank God," he exclaims, "for the Wesleys of this world," that is, for the "Saints and Prophets" who have loved God "without mediator or veil" (886). (He mentions, too, the evangelical Oberlins of Ohio.) He adds, with marked Arminian diction, that "*all* men have sublime thoughts" and "*all* men do value the few real hours of life" (886; my italics). Thus hailing everyone as his or her own Wesley, Emerson teaches the universality of direct spiritual experience. Such experience can take the form of theistical natural religion: "The religious sentiment makes the sky and the hills sublime" and "the universe safe and habitable" (877). More importantly, though, such experience takes the form of evangelical practical charity: "Low as he now lies in evil and wickedness," man is born "to the good" and "to the perfect" through "the sentiment of virtue" (875), that is, through emotionally driven, but voluntaristic, "acts / Of kindness and of love" (to use Wordsworth's phrase for the same phenomenon).[18]

Just as many phrases of Wesley, if not of Edwards, say such things,[19] so Emerson's language—building perhaps on Wordsworth's as well as the evangelicals'—amounts to positive proof that this-worldly Arminian theology, complete with its goal of spiritual perfection through good works, triumphed in the nineteenth century.[20] The "religious sentiment" is not only "divine"—that is, otherworldly—but also "deifying"—that is, of avail or available to the soul-making process (877). Experience, as an ongoing present, makes humankind "illimitable" (877).

The well-shaped crown of the address's experiential theology, perhaps, is its doctrine of immediate revelation. This doctrine, without being merely derivative from, is virtually interchangeable with the evangelicals' conviction that the Holy Spirit continues to operate in the present. Like Wesley and Edwards, Emerson bases the doctrine on a careful but adventurous interpretation of the Bible. He argues that although Jesus "felt respect for Moses and the prophets," Jesus emphasized "the hour and the man that now is" (879). This evangelical-Emersonian Jesus not only commands "Would you see God, see me," but also advises, at once more carefully and more boldly, "or, see thee, when thou also thinkest as I now think" (879). Compare this "Jesus" with Blake's similarly adventurous yet also similarly "evangelical" interpretation of John 17.33.[21] Emerson, as though anticipating God-is-dead theology yet also heading it off,[22] regrets that "men have come to speak of the revelation as somewhat long ago given and done, as if God were dead" (881). He adds a sentiment with which Wesley and Edwards would have concurred, namely, that "the stationariness of religion" caused by "the assumption that the age of inspiration is past, that the Bible is closed," indicates with "sufficient clearness" the "falsehood" of our theology (885).

Emerson, for his part, reminds the budding preachers of the same sort of thing that Wesley was wont to remind such preachers of,[23] namely, in Emerson's words, that they are "open to the influx of the all-knowing Spirit" (887). Accordingly, he calls on them to "cheer the waiting, fainting hearts of men with new hope and new revelation" (888). He announces in no uncertain terms that "the need was never greater of new revelation than now" (882). This, in the context of the address as a whole, is confident expectation of revelation rather than concern about its infrequency. Thus Emerson assumes a role in the third apostolic age (the nineteenth century), the second being the eighteenth century of Wesley and Edwards.[24]

Nowhere else among Emerson's works, then, does one find a clearer, more fully sustained exposition of evangelical faith than here in the address; perhaps the most precisely comprehensive of all of Emerson's characteristically evangelical pronouncements, indeed, is his imperative in the address's conclusion: "Yourself a newborn bard of the Holy Ghost, cast behind you all conformity, and acquaint men at first hand with Deity" (886). The experiential emphases of this imperative may be seen in its peculiarly Protestant flavor, for the young men are expected to be *non*conformists (Nonconformity is the proper historical name for British Protestant Dissent). The imperative not only explicitly names the particular Third Personhood of immediate revelation but also calls on the hearer to be born again, that is, converted to new life in God. The imperative occurs, significantly, in a paragraph affirming that to be a "newborn bard" is to "live with the privilege of the immeasurable *mind*" (886; my italics); to be most fundamentally evangelical, in other words, is also to be most fundamentally intellectual. The evangelical faith delineated by the address specifically emerges as especially intellectual; recall, for example, its grasp of empirical philosophy.

The address is empirical-evangelical, indeed, in the experiential sense in which empiricism is consistent with evangelical faith. By way of further affirming the philosophical aspect of faith simultaneously with its all but enthusiastical property, the same paragraph appeals to the chief feature of both the faith of, say, Sir Thomas Browne, and the "faith" of the Cartesian-Lockean tradition, that is, the method of radical skepticism whereby all is called into doubt precisely, if only, for the sake of establishing new grounds of spiritual as well as natural knowledge. After posing the question of what preachers should say to their congregations, Emerson answers his own question thus: "Let their doubts know that you have doubted" (886). The concept of sensation, which brings together more memorably if not more fully than anywhere else in his works the experiential biases of both empiricism and evangelicalism, is the address's particularly recommended means of acquiring natural and spiritual knowledge. In theology as well as philosophy lies the address's general, all-consuming interest in the status of the senses, for "Man," declares Emerson, should be "made sensible that he is an infinite Soul" (882), and "made sensible" is in every way emphatic. Emerson declares that "the earth and heavens," that is, narrowly terrene reality and earth's common sky or atmosphere, "are passing into [man's] mind" (882). He implies, growing more specific, that the physical senses are avenues to religious knowledge, for although the physical senses can seem at best mere analogues to the spiritual sense, the two conditions of anyone's perception—"that the earth and heavens are passing into his mind; [and] that he is drinking forever the soul of God"—are so strictly appositional (note the need to add the coordinate conjunction) as to be the same thing. The natural senses perceive spiritually even as the spiritual sense perceives naturally, and all perceiving forms one continuous operation or activity.

Where Emerson laments that "life is comic or pitiful, as soon as the high ends of being fade out of sight, and man becomes near-sighted, and can only attend to what addresses the senses" (878), he denigrates the natural senses and he implicitly embraces the far-sighted spiritual sense only because it differs from them completely. But in the context of the essay as a whole, with its accurate, though concise, understanding of empirical philosophy *and* its incorporation of the physical senses into an argument for the possibility of religious knowledge, the spiritual sense of Emerson, like that of both Wesley and Edwards, embraces not only analogistic worlds elsewhere but also immediate revelation here and now, theistical natural religion, and, *mirabile dictu*, scientific method.

In conclusion, I quote the last paragraph of the address, where Emerson describes the best ministers as both spiritual and natural seers whose collective vision includes not only heart-religion but also Newtonian science; although the paragraph acknowledges that "the Hebrew and Greek Scriptures contain immortal sentences, that have been the bread of life to millions," it adds the rather harsh judgment that "they have no special integrity; are fragmentary; are not shown in their order to the intellect"

(888–89). Emerson couches his hopes for *immediate* revelation, therefore, in his portrait of the new kind of minister for whom he calls: "I look for the new Teacher, that . . . shall see the world to be the mirror of the soul; shall see the identity of the law of gravitation with purity of heart; and shall show that the Ought, that Duty, is one thing with Science, with Beauty, and with Joy" (889). The informing experiential concept here is broad indeed, that is, empirical as well as evangelical. The new kind of preacher should import into his doctrine the *facts* of his experience.

The Divinity School Address, according to Bloom, is "the greatest document" of "an American religious criticism."[25] Its "vision of Christ" is "extraordinarily American." Bloom's identification of the address's "key sentence" is sufficiently correct: "The idioms of [Christ's] language and the figures of his rhetoric have usurped the place of his truth; and churches are not built on his principles, but on his tropes." This sentence and its context, however, constitute more of a search for truth and principles than a proliferation of idioms, figures, and tropes, for just as Emerson's vision is broad enough to include natural as well as spiritual experience, so is it broad enough to include traditional as well as immediate revelation. Unlike Southern Baptist fundamentalists, or what Bloom calls "Freudian Fundamentalists of the Ego Psychology sect," but very much like such indigenous American groups as Moderate Southern Baptists and Mormons, Emerson (according to Bloom's interpretation of his address) emphasizes that "religion is imagined, and always must be reimagined," that is, that the Bible does not somehow inerrantly interpret itself but is a renewable source for poetic tales from which to choose new forms of worship (see Blake's *The Marriage of Heaven and Hell*). For Bloom the practical consequence of the address is a nation of 250 million sects with each individual embarked on a gnostic journey back to the uncreated, unfallen world. Although Emerson indeed bequeaths to Americans a highly experiential religion, however, the Emersonian version of American religion is compatible with the experiential foundation of Anglo-American religion. The address includes not only individuals but also groups within its experiential-religious, empirical-evangelical purview.

THIRTEEN

Suspenseful Subjectivity

Self-Reliance, although seemingly lacking clear structure, boasts a dual, empirical-evangelical argument; indeed, despite William K. Bottorff's view that the essay lacks a single, unifying argument,[1] it hints at least at a synthesized, empirical-evangelical one. Emerson's skepticism, according to Michael, "inevitably links the identity of the self to the other's recognition," and since I hold that subjectivity in *Self-Reliance* leaves room for the other, I agree with Michael's view that "identity for Emerson is first and foremost a social creation."[2] Nowhere, however, does Michael include *Self-Reliance* among his close readings of Emerson's prose. Thomas P. Joswick uses Kenneth Burke's *The Rhetoric of Religion: Studies in Logology* to demonstrate the "rich paradox" of the "notion of conversion" in *Self-Reliance*; "time," writes Joswick, is "transcended" in the essay "by an aggressive beginning in time."[3] Similarly, my own approach translates this paradoxical notion into terms less Burkean, perhaps, but no less "aggressive" for being historical-evangelical, for the conversion motif in *Self-Reliance*, like all the essay's other idioms of spiritual experience, appropriates the "being in the world, but not of it" motif of the Bible. Evaluation of the essay, of course, can depend on one's judgment of its tone: while Whicher sees it as nonironic and disapproves of it,[4] Barbara Packer and Van Leer see it as ironic and approve of it,[5] but I see it as nonironic and approve of it. *Self-Reliance*, like *The American Scholar* and *The Divinity School Address*, emphasizes empirical thesis and evangelical antithesis over empirical-evangelical synthesis. As indicated by the title, moreover, the essay focuses on subjectivity so forcefully as to make the essayist's shifts to short, sharp presentations of the objective on the one hand and actual-ideal hints on the other essentially suspenseful; these hints and presentations are all the more satisfying, therefore, when they occur.

The philosophical focus of the essay, distinct from its theological and philosophical-theological emphases, can be so far from the empirical, so subjective, as to seem exclusively idealistic. Where Emerson speaks of "the resolution of all into the ever blessed ONE" (900), for example, he speaks Platonically, and where he declares that "it was in his own mind that the artist sought his model"—where, that is, he asks that since "it was an application of his own thought to the thing to be done and the conditions to be observed," "why need we copy the Doric or the Gothic mode?" (906)— he explores an idealism that approaches truth through the mind first, as though truth cannot primarily be found in a world in which the mind exists uneasily at best. Where he calls a person "timid and apologetic" because "he does not say 'I think,' 'I am,' but quotes some saint or sage" (899), and where he insists, for his part, that "few and mean as my gifts may be, I actually am, and do not need for my own assurance or the assurance of my fellows any secondary testimony" or any account of truth from any source other than himself (893), he explores a Cartesian idealism that grounds knowledge on the cogito rather than in a world from which the cogito is fully independent. "The great genius," concludes Emerson, "returns to essential man" (908); by this he means that subjectivity is all. Just as Galileo, who possessed only "an opera-glass," depended not so much on scientific observation as on his own inner resources, so Emerson thrives the more impressively for his small reliance on anything outside himself (908). Just as Napoléon, who developed only the bivouac, conquered Europe not through an elaborate technological warfare but through his own "naked valor," so the Emersonian genius encamps with little or no shelter and spends the night in the open (908).

This "philosophy" is so very ideal, indeed, as to border on antiempiricism. Emerson's "aboriginal Self," coequivalent with his "Spontaneity of Instinct," is that "Intuition" to which "all later teachings," including British experience-philosophy, are mere "tuitions" (898). Even such impressive dimensions of empirical experience as "vast spaces of nature," the Atlantic Ocean, the South Sea, and "vast intervals of time, years, centuries," are "of no account" (900). In comparison with the "Tranquillity" of a "soul raised over passion" (900) and hence translated out of space and time, these dimensions are mere fluxes and vicissitudes. There is no more fundamental a Lockean tenet, perhaps, than that identity arises from day to day; in Lockean mood, for example, Tennyson's Ulysses announces that "I am a part of all that I have met."[6] Emerson's statement that "a foolish consistency is the hobgoblin of little minds" (895), and his all-purpose command to "speak what you think to-day in words as hard as cannon-balls, and to-morrow speak what to-morrow thinks in hard words again, though it contradict every thing you said to-day" (895), assume the quite opposite notion that identity bears no relation to story-in-time, that is, to the quotidian thread of empirical data. By Emerson's implication, iden-tity derives from the unanchored self, that is, a core of his being that, by forming no part of what it has met, is not dependent on where it has been or even on what it feels. His famous utterances also imply how his self-reliance differs from what Jacques Lacan calls "le sujet," and even from what Norman Holland calls "the I"; the "I" in much of *Self-Reliance* is spe-cifically less experience-grounded than either the concept of Lacan, whose "sujet" is always "subject to," or the concept of Holland, whose "I" is also shaped by influences from without.[7]

The "I" in most of *Self-Reliance*, however, is quite experience-grounded. Michael, finding common ground between Lacan and Emerson, argues that the Möbius strip—

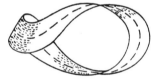

—serves to model not only Lacan's but also Emerson's concept of the self-and-other. The strip, according to Michael, is

> a structure that faces an exterior that is interior to it at the same moment that it exposes its interior to the exterior around it. None-theless, it must preserve a distinct boundary between inner and outer since that boundary gives it whatever shape and identity it has. . . . [T]he Möbius strip originates in and is characterized by a singular doubleness. It twists and folds back on itself. It faces inside and out-side at the same time and with the same face. . . . The Möbius strip defines a space that merges inside and outside, self and other, identity and alterity.[8]

179

Thus Michael uses this "simplest of topological puzzles" both to paraphrase Lacan and to introduce Emerson. While the "I," or "sujet," in Emerson's prose is more or less consistent with that of Lacan, however, the experiential ground of Emerson's "sujet" is even closer to the narrow Humean skepticism in which Michael is primarily interested.

That ground is closer still to Lockean epistemology. Michael, acknowledging Locke's importance, associates his view of identity with the sphere: "If one were to draw a picture representing the exclusivity of identity as Locke, for example, describes it, the problem would be simple. A sphere would serve admirably to suggest a self that is at once integral, simple, and isolated from the world in which it lives. The sphere conceals what it contains." At least one of the images for the self in *Self-Reliance* is explicitly the sphere: "All the sallies of [the aboriginal man's] will are rounded in by the law of his being as the inequalities of Andes and Himmaleh are insignificant in the curve of the sphere" (895). This especially idealistic strain of the Emersonian self bears an only negative relation to the external world; there can seem to be little or no relation between self and world in that "a character is like an acrostic or Alexandrian stanza;—read it forward, backward, or across, it still spells the same thing" (895). One may read a character backward and forward, but one may not read him/her either from character outward or from the world inward to character, for a character, like a palindrome, evinces a remarkable self-consistency, a mantra-like self-resonance. No matter what "happens" to this version of the Emersonian self, it remains the same; thus Emersonian self-sufficiency can seem immune to experience. The acrostic stanza and the sphere, however, while intrinsic to the most subjective if not the most solipsistic passages of the essay, are not as fully explanatory for Emerson's concept of self-reliance as is the Möbius strip. The essay mixes the subjective with the objective, and this blend is fully consistent with a Lockean identity that, as I have previously argued, is by no means "exclusive."[9]

Having pointed to the essay's philosophical idealism, then, and despite the power of the essay's subjectivity, I emphasize now its philosophical empiricism. That this significant element of Emerson's philosophy should exist alongside other significant elements in an essay renowned primarily for subjectivity proves, if proof were needed, the importance of reading each essay in the light of some others, for in the present context of my argument concerning *The American Scholar* and *The Divinity School Address*, the philosophical empiricism of *Self-Reliance* emerges as less surprising than it would be if it were encountered only in the context of the essay's prior reputation. *Self-Reliance* should not be considered in complete isolation from works that tend to disprove the view of Emerson as exclusively idealistic.

His general interest in empiricism is evident in a passage that stakes out the common ground between the ideal and the actual: "For the sense of being which in calm hours rises, we know not how, in the soul, is not diverse from things, from space, from light, from time, from man, but one with them, and proceedeth obviously from the same source whence their life and being also proceedeth" (898). Although this catalogue of experience includes transcendental idealism, the idealism of the passage unmistakably shades over into transcendental realism. The broad view of experience that thus allows for both empiricism and idealism follows, moreover, from the essay's broad interpretation of Locke as "a *mind* of uncommon activity and power" (904; my italics). The mind, after all, is included in the catalogue of experience, and Locke's mind, like the minds of such inheritors of his empiricism as the chemist Antoine Lavoisier, the geologist James Hutton, the utilitarian philosopher Jeremy Bentham, and the physician Johann Spurzheim, "imposes its classification on other men, and lo! a new system" (904–5). Thus preserving an active role for the mind, Emerson's interpretation of Locke also preserves an "empirical" form of idealism, for Locke's philosophy, while emphasizing objective truth, retains the stamp of Locke himself, and so it offers a mentally powerful as well as commandingly intersubjective-objective appeal.

The epistemology of *Self-Reliance* is sufficiently Lockean even where schematizable *Subject-object*. Subjectivity, to be sure, can be so "uppercase" as to seem prior to all other criteria: "Character, reality, reminds you of nothing else. It takes place of the whole creation. The man must be so much that he must make all circumstances indifferent,—put all means into the shade" (896). Even this Subject, however, while master/organizer and not simple participant, is not so much detached from as involved in experience: "There is a great responsible Thinker and Actor moving wherever moves a man" (896); or again: "A true man belongs to no other time or place, but is the centre of things" (896). Emerson writes, moreover, that "though the wide universe is full of good, no kernel of nourishing corn can come to [any man] but through his toil bestowed on that plot of ground which is given to [him] to till" (890). Thus the very concept of subjective importance seems dependent on the laborious shaping of and the humbly relating to, as well as the simple control of, things. "Not for nothing one face, one character, one fact," declares Emerson, "makes such an impression on him, and another none" (890); here the undifferentiated impingement of sense-impressions relents, but the mind is sufficiently "lord and master"—the words are Wordsworth's [10]—to choose what to work with in the world around. Never, however, does the impingement quite abate, nor does it ever quite fall into abeyance.

Indeed, and again surprisingly, in view of the essay's touted subjectivity, *Self-Reliance* implicitly but finally includes a narrower, more usual interpretation of Locke, that is, one whereby the mind is so enmeshed in the world as to be overwhelmed by it, where not simply influenced by it. The formulation, in this case, could be *s-o,* or even *s-O.* Emerson writes that "the swallow over my window should interweave that thread or straw he carries in his bill into my web also" (895). This mood makes him so big a part of what he has met that he is all but defined by what has happened to him. "History," he writes, "is an impertinence and an injury, if it be anything more than a cheerful apologue or parable of my being or becoming" (899); even if "being" is only analogous to history, "becoming" operates in as well as like history. "Every man" knows that "a perfect respect" is due to his "involuntary perceptions," for "he may err in the expression of them, but he knows that these things are so, like day and night, not to be disputed. . . . [M]y perception . . . is as much a fact as the sun" (898). One "cannot be happy and strong" until one "lives with nature in the present, above time" (899), and this conclusion, à la Joswick, involves the paradox of transcending time by means of time. This floating "sense" of release, although it is almost a spiritual perspective, depends on a moment by moment or at least a momentary involvement with or sense perception of the world.

The most inclusively yet concisely Lockean formulation of *Self-Reliance* lies, perhaps, in its blunt statement that "every man discerns *between* the voluntary acts of his mind, and his involuntary perceptions" (898; my italics). Compare this, if you will, with Wallace Stevens's "poem of the act of the mind," which may be of a "man skating" or a "woman combing," that is, of the mediating act between and hence the uniting of mind and matter, subject and object. [11] In Emerson's exquisite prose expression of the particularly Lockean, apart from the generally Kantian, blend of subject and object, all distinctions between inner and outer fall into abeyance, not only as but also because the emphasis falls not so much on either mind or matter and not even so much on both mind and matter as on the border between mind and matter and hence on neither-yet-both. The empirical strain of *Self-Reliance* thus defines the self or subject as "subject to" others in particular and otherness in general, and, therefore, no philosophical passage of the essay allows any complacent assumption that selfhood entails solipsism.

The philosophical strain of the essay lines up with, even if it does not quite overlap or merge with, the essay's religious strain. Emerson's continuum of actual and ideal represents self-reliance by means of "Copernicus, and Galileo, and Newton" at one end and "Socrates, and Jesus, and Luther" at the other (895). The latter trinity is certainly "in the world, but not of it," and the former, though divagating from the churchly, is religious at least in the awe of its collective, inquiring spirit. Emerson, accordingly, holds self-reliance to be not so much an isolating quality as a trust in the ability of selfhood to interact with either natural or spiritual things, and even with both kinds of things at once.

Postponing, for now, my discussion of philosophically theological overtones in the essay, I take up the essay's exclusively theological implications. Since it proceeded from the journal entries of 1832, when Emerson resigned his pulpit, and 1838–40, when his self-trust was sorely tried by the hostile reaction to *The Divinity School Address, Self-Reliance* can seem archly, fanatically antireligious. Consider, for example, the following rank antinomianism: "On my saying, What have I to do with the sacredness of traditions, if I live wholly from within? my friend suggested—'But these impulses may be from below, not from above.' I replied, 'They do not seem to me to be such; but if I am the devil's child, I will live then from the devil.' No law can be sacred to me but that of my nature" (892). One can hardly scan these words without thinking of, without shuddering at, the excesses worked by the apotheosis of the self in, say, modern Western history, but the passage must have seemed frightening even in Emerson's day. The exasperated outburst of Oliver Cromwell to his followers, "I beseech you, in the bowels of Christ, think it possible you may be mistaken," [12] indicates how fanaticism, of whatever stripe, has always been the "devil's workshop." Emerson's injunction to "do your thing" (893), regardless of whether it was Charles Manson's inspiration to do *his* thing, is an especially disturbing phrase of *Self-Reliance*.

To the extent that Emerson's presentation of the subjective is at best only iconoclastically religious, moreover, it can seem dangerously so. "The Puritans," observes Sacvan Bercovitch, "banished Anne Hutchinson because she set her private revelation above the public errand," [13] and Emerson, too, might have been banished in Hutchinson's time. His antinomian tendency was more like hers than his conscious public errand would let him realize. In his journals he reminded himself to "beware of Antinomianism" and conceived of his public role as a battle against "mere antinomianism." [14] The "habits of thought" that led him to resign his pulpit, moreover, "owe less to Antinomian antiformalism than to orthodox Puritan concepts of the Spirit," for "the sermons and their legacy" reveal that Emerson's place in the Puritan tradition is "even more central than has been supposed." [15] Sermon 160 (1832), most notably, clearly states that "it is not our soul that is God, but God is in our soul." [16] If Emerson is not finally an antinomian, however, he may fairly be said to be strongly and repeatedly tempted in that direction. Although Bloom emphasizes Emerson's "psychological honesty and individualism" and praises as "antinomian and strong" what Yvor Winters rejects as "unreasonable and obscurantist," [17] such antinomian passages as the ones just quoted (892, 893) remain disturbing.

Even where the Emerson of *Self-Reliance* gestures toward the canons of traditional morality by extending his sympathy to others, he can come across as willfully unbiblical and comically unattractive. Job's "comforters," of course, preach (see Job 3ff.); they do not silently empathize with the afflicted (see Job 2). Similarly, the Emerson of *Self-Reliance* is much too preachy to be a genuine comforter; he even indicts behavior that characterizes genuine comfort. Too often "we come to them who weep foolishly, and sit down and cry for company," instead of "imparting to them truth and health in rough electric shocks, putting them once more in communication with the soul" (904). The reader of *Self-Reliance* may well wish to do without the "comfort" of such electric truth telling, of such lobotomizing tough love. The reader may shy away, too, from the sheer egotism of Emerson's surely unintentionally humorous marriage of himself to himself: "There is a time in every man's education when he arrives at the conviction that . . . he must take himself for better, for worse, as his portion" (890). *This* self-reliance reaches the point of autoeroticism.

Even this most subjective essay, however, is by no means always so nonreligious, so nontraditional, or so unattractive, for it is often attractively, traditionally religious, and this is my emphasis. Although Emerson calls "creeds" a "disease of the intellect," they are not so much false as simply remote from experience: "everywhere I am bereaved of meeting God in my brother, because he has shut his own temple doors, and recites fables merely of his brother's, or his brother's brother's God" (904). "When my genius calls me," he modestly confesses, "I shun father and mother and wife and brother" (892), but although this confession may seem cruel, it alludes to Matthew 10.34–37, and so it suggests that genius, after all, is a divine and hence not solely self-originated commander. The essay's confident authority derives in part from its homiletical verve, and from Emerson's evident remembrance of proper prophetic naysaying: "We are afraid of truth, afraid of fortune, afraid of death, and afraid of each other. Our age yields no great and perfect persons. . . . Our housekeeping is mendicant, our arts, our occupations, our marriages, our religion we have not chosen, but society has chosen for us" (903). This particular subjectivity's religious quality is not far from creeds, that is, the tenets of specific theologies. Neither is it far from at least the more countercultural than culturally determined sort of organized religion. Emerson's twofold conviction, first that "whoso would be a man must be a nonconformist," and second that "the integrity of our own mind" is the only "sacred" thing (891), is generally Protestant if not precisely evangelical; for *Protestants* and *Nonconformists* overlap; and even evangelical Protestants, if not especially them, were as bent on intellectual as on spiritual integrity.

Much of Emerson's emphasis in *Self-Reliance* lies on his search for self-justification, which parallels the preoccupation among all stripes of evangelicals, Arminian and Calvinist alike, with the question of faith versus works.[18] In one sense, he clearly distrusts works: "I do not wish to expiate, but to live. My life is not an apology, but a life. It is for itself and not for a spectacle. . . . I ask primary evidence that you are a man, and refuse this appeal from the man to his actions. . . . Men imagine that they communicate their virtue or vice only by overt actions and do not see that virtue or vice emit a breath every moment" (893, 895). Some of the most dubious, most curmudgeonly passages of *Self-Reliance*, indeed, range themselves against various forms of practical charity: Emerson hopes, for example, to "have the manhood to withhold" his dollar "by-and-by" from "your miscellaneous popular charities; the education at college of fools; the building of meeting-houses to the vain end to which many now stand; alms to sots; and the thousandfold Relief Societies" (892); and he expostulates, in addition, both that "at times the whole world seems to be in conspiracy to importune you with emphatic trifles" (892) and that "friend, client, child, sickness, fear, want, charity, all knock at once at thy closet door and say, 'Come out unto us'" (901). Here is the solution: "Do not spill thy soul; do not all descend; keep thy state; stay at home in thine own heaven; come not for a moment into their facts, into their hubbub of conflicting appearances" (901). Rather at odds with this solution, though, is the conclusion that "[you should] let in the light of thy law on their confusion," for "isolation must not be mechanical, but spiritual" (901). Thus guarding one's spiritual independence, one nevertheless remains physically present to the needs of the world, for Emerson, after all, is not averse to action and the practical in matters of religion: "hardship, husbandry, hunting, whaling, war, eloquence, personal weight, are somewhat, and engage my respect as examples of the soul's presence and impure action" (893). This emphasis reflects, albeit at a distance, the joint emphasis of Wesley and Edwards on the religious life as "running, warring, wrestling." [19] "Act singly," declares Emerson, "and what you have already done singly, will justify you now" (895).

Emerson's seeming lack of charity, perhaps, is simply his conviction that charity begins at home. One's proper self-regard emanates in love, especially in one's sphere of influence. He gladly acknowledges that "there is a class of persons to whom by all spiritual affinity I am bought and sold"; "for them I will go to prison, if need be" (892). Like Charles Dickens's portrait of Mrs. Jellyby, who, in *Bleak House*, cares more for African missions than for her own children, Emerson's satire exposes, in particular, the hypocrisy of love in the abstract:

> If malice and vanity wear the coat of philanthropy, shall that pass? If an angry bigot assumes this bountiful cause of Abolition, and comes to me with his last news from Barbadoes, why should I not say to him, "Go love thy infant; love thy woodchopper: be good-natured and modest: have that grace; and never varnish your hard, uncharitable ambition with this incredible tenderness for black folks a thousand miles off. Thy love afar is spite at home." (892)

The evangelicalism of *Self-Reliance*, although the essay's subjectivity necessarily implies that its persona belongs among the elect and although this implication is sufficiently Edwardsean if not sufficiently Wesleyan, lies at a great distance from the Calvinist emphasis on original sin. For although "all men have my blood, and I have all men's" (901), Emerson sets himself apart—as Wesley does through his doctrine of spiritual perfection[20]—from the general sinfulness of humankind: "Not for that will I adopt their petulance or folly, even to the extent of being ashamed of it" (901). Thus the evangelicalism of the essay is more Wesleyan-Arminian than Edwardsean-Calvinist in tone. "Abolition," the particular Arminian-evangelical practical charity of attempting to end the slave trade that disgraced England, is the "lengthened shadow" (897) of the evangelical Anglican reformer, Thomas Clarkson,[21] whom Emerson explicitly praises (897). Emerson's desire to be in the world but not of it, and his belief that "the great man is he who *in the midst of the crowd* keeps with *perfect* sweetness the independence of solitude" (893; my italics), smack of the Wesleyan-Arminian understanding of Christianity as a delicate balance between faith and works, that is, a balance leading in the best of circumstances to the crowning of spiritual experience by spiritual perfection. Elsewhere in the essay Emerson echoes a proof text for Wesley's doctrine of perfection: compare Emerson's "there is simply the rose; it is *perfect* in every moment of its existence" (899; my italics) with Matthew 6.28–29. Although, like Milton's Abdiel, Emerson is more of a sect of one than a follower of Wesleyan Methodism, and although he himself founds no sect—notwithstanding that there are Emersonians—he respects Wesley's sect-founding ability. He explicitly admires Methodism as Wesley's "lengthened shadow" (897). "He who is really of [the] class of great men," Emerson intones, "will not be called by the name of a sect," but instead will "be the founder of a sect" (908). Thus may Emerson be said to acknowledge in Wesley a soul brother, for by Emerson's own concept of greatness, namely, self-reliance, Wesley, who is more than sufficiently self-reliant to be a sect founder extraordinaire, is the very type thereof.

Another evangelical example of self-reliance, however, is Emerson's aunt, Mary Moody Emerson (1774–1863). Although the essay should but does not give as much credit to her as it gives to Wesley, I credit her for informing the religious atmosphere in which Emerson conceives of self-reliance. His much-loved aunt was a more Arminian than Calvinist evangelical, for whose individualistic, subjective traits the leader of British and American Methodism was even more of a precursor than Jonathan Edwards was. "The symbolically and numerically representative Awakening convert," observes Phyllis Cole, "was a woman," and Cole adds that "a majority of New England church members had been female at least since the late seventeenth century, and the revivals of both eighteenth and nineteenth centuries tipped the balance toward women more and more." [22] Accordingly, and especially intriguingly, Mary Moody Emerson prays to her empowering God that "to individuate myself in thy presence, is all." [23] Her singularity constituted "a major deflection" of her piety "precisely in the direction of transcendental self-reliance," but this singularity, this "autonomous solitude," was "enabled," ironically enough, by what Cole calls "affective evangelical religion." [24]

Mary Moody Emerson's self-reliance, to be sure, could be the corollary of her Calvinist doctrine of election; "the indefinable combinations of genius," she writes in her "Almanacks," "will never be the portion of vulgar souls (it seems) even in ages of blessedness!" [25] Although she acknowledges that the features of the soul are "indelibly stamped for eternity at its formation," she adds insights concerning the soul's progress that are so broadly experiential as to be Arminian-evangelical and, for that matter, Lockean. Notice, for just two examples, her reference to the doctrine of spiritual perfection and her emphasis on the importance of education: "Education forms—marrs {sic}—or perfects [the features of the Soul]—and informal influence directs and sanctifys {sic} them. We anticipate new powers in eternity—true, but they will be in unison perhaps to those we exercise now." [26] Thus the experiential-experimental if not empirical-evangelical antiphony of Emerson's fond aunt forms a union of earth and heaven. Significantly, her brand of antiphon foretastes not only Emerson's quotidian as well as sublime self-reliance but also, not coincidentally, Tennyson's finely speculative interrelations of earth and heaven in *In Memoriam*.

Cole supposes that Emerson "does not acknowledge" the debt that *Self-Reliance* owes to his aunt because he does not "perhaps see" the debt. [27] The debt is clear enough, however, from an 1837 journal entry in which he pays tribute to Mary Moody Emerson for being "a saving counterforce" (Cole's phrase) against Harvard's "levitical education" (Emerson's phrase):

> I cannot hear the young men whose theological education is exclusively owed to Cambridge and to public institutions without feeling how much happier was my star which rained on me influences of ancestral religion. The depth of the religious sentiment which I knew in my Aunt Mary imbuing all her genius & derived to her from such hoarded family traditions, from so many godly lives & godly deaths

of sainted kindred at Concord, Malden, and York, was itself a culture, an education. . . . In my childhood Aunt Mary herself wrote the prayers which first my brother William & when he went to college I read aloud morning & evening at the family devotions, & they still sound in my ears with their prophetic & apocalyptic ejaculations. Religion was her occupation, and when years after, I came to write sermons for my own church I could not find any examples or treasuries of piety so high-toned, so profound, or promising such rich influences as my remembrances of her conversations and letters.[28]

(See Wallace Stevens's "High-Toned Christian Woman.") It would be hard to overemphasize the importance of this passage as justification for the view that the evangelical roots of Emerson's self-reliance are at least as important as the Unitarian roots, but the passage is important too for understanding his attitude toward women.

Had he not feared seeming effeminate, and had he been able to include such passages in his essays, he might well have shown his better side, and relieved the unfruitful tension in his prose between affirmation and power on the one hand and anxiety and sex on the other.[29] It might be argued, indeed, that Mary Moody Emerson did, on occasion, bring out a fruitful, that is, an interesting and not restrictingly sexist, tension in his prose. Notice, for example, the sexually loaded but finally expansive language of his letter to her in 1823. He pays psychologically intriguing tribute to his great precursor David Hume:

Next comes the Scotch Goliath, David Hume; but where is the accomplished stripling who can cut off his most metaphysical head? Who is he that can stand up before him & prove the existence of the Universe, & of its Founder? He hath an adroiter wit than all his forefathers in philosophy if he will confound this Uncircumcised. The long & dull procession of Reasoners that have followed since, have challenged the awful shade to duel, & struck the air with their puissant arguments. But as each new comer blazons "Mr. Hume's objections" on his pages, it is plain they are not satisfied the victory is gained.[30]

Emerson's easy and natural awareness of debt to his aunt combines with his anxiety of influence here to produce puns more playful than either darkly portentous or overweeningly sententious. There would have been less "anxiety," perhaps, with regard to the comfortable empiricism of Locke, distinct from the perhaps overingenious empiricism of Hume.

Even the most inward expression of the specifically Methodistical strain of *Self-Reliance* retains an other-directed, almost empiricist bias. The prose, to be sure, can still sound as disturbingly self-indulgent as Frank Sinatra's lyric does in his surely unintentionally bathetic "I Did It My Way." "I must be myself," declares Emerson, adding that "I cannot break myself any longer for you, or you. . . . I must be myself. I will not hide my tastes or aversions" (902). Emerson's "way," however, makes heavy ethical demands on him: "I will still seek to deserve" to be loved and will "endeavor to nourish my parents, to support my family, to be the chaste husband of one wife" (902). This is hardly the *pietas* of an Aeneas, but it does rise considerably above the 1970s, me-generation oversimplifiers of Emersonian subjectivity. What is "deep" or inward for him is "holy" or manifestly sacred to him too (902). "Whatever inly rejoices" him, therefore, is what "the heart appoints" for him to "do strongly before the sun and moon" (902). There is something more than Methodistical, and indeed something Puritan, in this strain of other-directedness; notice the combination of joy and holiness in the implicit heart-religion, and notice too the at least quasi-empirical impulse to active, participatory observation.

Emerson, like Wesley and Edwards in their Lockean modes, finally develops a notion of the self in sense-like contact with the divine. Not only does God "deign to enter and inhabit" the individual soul (909), but God's entry or self-revelation is also cast in the language if not in the fact of natural experience: "it must be that when God speaketh, he should communicate not one thing, but all things; should fill the world with his voice; should scatter forth light, nature, time, souls, from the centre of the present thought; and new date and new create the whole" (898–99). Emerson's advice to the reader, accordingly, arises from his blend of natural religion with spiritual theology: "Accept the place the divine Providence has found for you; the society of your contemporaries, the connexion of events. Great men have always done so and confided themselves childlike to the genius of their age, betraying their perception that the Eternal was stirring at their heart, working through their hands, predominating in all their being" (890). A passage so empirically evangelical as to be evangelically empirical suggests that even the physical senses perceive divine nature directly: "Trust your emotion. In your metaphysics you have denied personality to the Deity; yet when the devout motions of the soul come, yield to them heart and life, *though they should clothe God with shape and color*" (894–95; my italics).

Thus, "when we have a new perception" (900), that is, when we see the world anew not only with the spiritual sense but also with the natural senses, self-reliance arrives. Through the implicit interaction of both kinds of sensation, specifically, "we shall gladly disburthen the memory of its hoarded treasures as old rubbish" (900). While this prophecy evinces anti-Lockean antipathy to the conditioning dimension of experience, it also evinces pro-Lockean faith in the promise of experience. "Light unsystematic, indomitable," writes Emerson, "will break into any cabin" (905). Thus he implies that what can be learned through natural-spiritual experience will arrive in just the natural way Locke thought experience enters the cabinet of the mind. In view of such memorable, albeit scantly sustained blending of the empirical with the evangelical sensibility, the twofold conclusion in the last paragraph of *Self-Reliance* is especially apt. First, "the Will work[s]," "acquires," and finally "chain[s] the wheel of Chance," thereby "always drag[ging] her after" (909). And second, since "Cause and Effect" are the "Chancellors of God," self *finds* religious truth (909).

To summarize, then, I proffer a broadly experiential basis for redefining Emersonian self-reliance, which is too often defined nowadays in terms of narrow inner experience alone. Recent concentrations on "civic virtue" and "community" in Emerson criticism, for example, explicitly encourage the view of him as the advocate of an "isolating preoccupation with the self," as Robert Bellah puts it.[31] Communitarians object, specifically, to Emerson's "expressive individualism," which they think is "limited to a language of radical individual autonomy," and which, they also think, provides an "inadequate counterweight to the acquisitive or 'utilitarian' individualism that governs American culture."[32] Emerson's promise of an "inner refuge," argues David Marr, leads only to an "ideological assault upon politics and the political."[33] Yet Carolyn Porter reminds us of Emerson's defining interest in social questions.[34] I conclude that the underpinning of his two-way reliance on self and other is at once philosophical and religious.

Bloom's exclusively quasi-gnostic emphasis on Emerson's "knowledge of what in the self . . . is Godlike" and Barbara Packer's gnosticizing study of *Emerson's Fall* (1982) both rest primarily on only partial quotation,[35] but through frequent quoting I have tried to indicate that the concept of knowledge in *Self-Reliance* grows out of and depends on the epistemological concepts of natural as well as spiritual experience. The essay lays claim to knowledge of the Godlike in both self and not-self. Thus I agree with Christopher Lasch's view that Emerson favored "common experience" over "experience shared only by a self-selected spiritual elite."[36] "The gnostic cult of mysteries accessible only to a few initiates," Lasch adds, "was deeply at odds with the general tendency of Emersonian spirituality." While I reserve a place for knowledge among the goals of *Self-Reliance*, I identify with Lasch's conclusion that Emerson was "so little disposed to regard religious knowledge as a closely guarded body of secrets" that he regarded "faith, not knowledge, as the heart of religious experience."

In Bloom's view, Emerson's religion was so timeless and universal as to transcend experience; in Bercovitch's view, Emersonian spirituality is so "highly parochial," so "completely bound up with the American sense of mission," that it "lost sight of any higher truths";[37] and in my view, the at once transcendent and immanent experientialism of the empirical-evangelical sensibility in *Self-Reliance* allows Emerson to be this-worldly without lapsing into "self-congratulatory illusion" (Bercovitch's phrase) concerning America as the morally superior savior of humankind. "The migration to America," according to Bercovitch, "displaces conversion as the crucial event," but I point out, by contrast, that both migration to America and a continuing identification with "Anglo-America" are consistent with a countercultural as well as cultural concept of conversion. Bercovitch is "surely right," says Lasch, "to place Emerson in the Puritan succession," but Lasch is also right to point out that the Puritan tradition "has to be understood as a continuing attempt to negotiate treacherous ground between Arminianism and antinomianism," and he reminds us that "a deep strain of Anglophilia—often associated with Arminianism— early appeared alongside the ritual denunciation of old-world corruption." I would only add, regarding Emerson's revitalization of complex tradition in *Self-Reliance*, that his Anglo-American vision is empirical as well as evangelical.

FOURTEEN

Experience and Faith

Experience and faith in *The Over-Soul*, in that the Over-Soul "contradicts all experience" and "abolishes time and space" (912), appear antipodal if not mutually exclusive, and the transcendentalism can be Platonic, for Emerson writes that "I desire, even by profane words, if sacred I may not use, to indicate the heaven of this deity," namely, the Over-Soul, "and to report what hints I have collected of the transcendent simplicity and energy of the Highest Law" (911). His belief that "the spirit of prophecy" is "innate in every man" (911) keeps far from the twofold view shared among Locke, Wesley, and Edwards that knowledge of God is no more a priori than any other kind of knowledge and that nothing is innate. Perhaps the most fundamental assumption of evangelical faith is its precisely experiential efficacy, and surely no evangelical would approve of the rhapsodic tone of apotheosis, whereby Emerson goes so far as to imply an equation between one's aspiring to and one's attaining to Godhead: "For, in ascending to this primary and aboriginal sentiment [of moral beatitude], we have come from one remote station on the circumference instantaneously to the centre of the world, where, as in the closet of God, we see causes, and anticipate the universe, which is but a slow effect" (914). Thus *The Over-Soul* can seem as far as possible from empirical actuality and from evangelical idealism. Of all the critics whom I cite, only Richard Poirier analyzes *The Over-Soul* in terms resembling mine; in understanding the Over-Soul according to its "secularized versions" in both the genetic codes of today's science and the evolutionary theory of Emerson's day, Poirier compares it to William James's "primordial units of mind-stuff or mind-dust," which James represents as "summing themselves together in successive stages

193

of compounding and re-compounding, and thus engendering our higher and more complex states of mind." [1] Viewing the Over-Soul as a quasi-scientific personification of the collective mind-stuff, Poirier comes near the empirical component of my approach, but missing from his scheme is an element sufficiently ideal to account for or parallel the essay's evangelical component. Not only does *The Over-Soul* feature empiricism per se and evangelicalism per se but, much more fully than any of the three essays studied thus far, and indeed as fully as any essay Emerson ever wrote, this essay also brings them together.

Much philosophy in *The Over-Soul* relates to and borrows authority from Lockean terms. Where Emerson distinguishes between "Spinoza, Kant, and Coleridge," who "speak *from within,* or from experience," and "Locke, Paley, Mackintosh, and Stewart," who speak *"from without,* as spectators merely," he adopts a view of Locke both narrow and dim (919; Emerson's italics). Where Emerson defines the Over-Soul as "that overpowering reality which confutes our tricks and talents, and constrains every one to pass for what he is, and to speak from his character and not from his tongue; and which evermore tends and aims to pass into our thought and hand, and become wisdom, and virtue, and power, and beauty" (910–11), he seems antiempirical, for rather than assuming the Lockean formula of "nature yields idea yields word yields action," he assumes, instead, that the Over-Soul is both different from and prior to natural experience. Even here, however, centrality is accorded to "thought and hand," as though natural experience were both result and manifestation of reality. Emerson declares, moreover, that "the blindness of the intellect begins when it would be something of itself" (911). Although what makes the intellect "something" is the Over-Soul ("when it breathes through the intellect, it is genius; when it breathes through his will, it is virtue; when it flows through his affection, it is love" [911]), the intellect is grounded, like Lockean reason, in something outside. Locke would applaud Emerson's tendency to temper Cartesian assumptions concerning the mind's self-sufficiency and superiority; where Emerson denominates the Over-Soul "the vast back-ground of our being" (911), he rejects the cogito as ground. Thus Lockean assumptions are latent in the only apparently exclusively ideal doctrine of the Over-Soul.

If the essay seems to return to an antiempirical strain—"Before the immense possibilities of man, all mere experience, all past biography, however spotless and sainted, shrinks away" (923)—it does not really do so, for this statement does not mean an assumed mutual exclusivity of experience and faith; rather, it means that spirituality occurs within experience. All future biography, distinct from the afterlife, will contain even sense-experientially dependent potential for infinitely more saintliness than has ever been known or conceived of before.

"In ev'ry work regard the writer's end," advises Alexander Pope, "since none can compass more than they intend."[2] Paul Ricoeur, focusing on Marx, Nietzsche, and Freud as forerunners of Postmodern critical theory, delineates, without fully subscribing to, a "hermeneutics of suspicion" in which consciousness, as masker of dialectical materialism, power, and sex, is "false."[3] Although Pope's dictum may seem naive to late twentieth-century critics, the dictum partakes of the first flush of Lockean faith in the conscious mind.[4] Even such a far-flung child of Locke as Emerson is not immune to this faith's appeal. "We know the truth when we see it," he writes in *The Over-Soul*, "as we know when we are awake that we are awake" (915). Or again: "We know truth when we see it, let sceptic and scoffer say what they choose" (915). Despite Locke's use of Descartes's radical skepticism, Locke, unlike Descartes, never doubts that things exist which correspond to point-blank, univocal ideas of them. If Locke and Pope are thus naive, then so too is Emerson, more than a century later, and for the same reason of faith in consciousness. The empiricism of *The Over-Soul* is closer to Locke's than to Hume's. There is a decidedly pre-Humean tenor in Emerson's belief that "the soul will not have us read any other cipher but that of cause and effect" (918), for Hume seeks to refute causation. A more Lockean than Humean skepticism informs Emerson's conclusion that questions arising out of the natural world are answerable: "The only mode of obtaining an answer to these questions of the senses, is, to forego all low curiosity, and, accepting the tide of being which floats us into the secret of nature, work and live, work and live, and all unawares, the advancing soul has built and forged for itself a new condition, and the question and the answer are one" (918). Emerson, according to such natural-experiential assumptions, observes that the "acts and words" of our friends point to and indeed go to make up their "character" (918). With similarly Lockean assumptions about child psychology, he instructs "the children of men to live in to-day" (918).

Such oneness with nature is matched if not exceeded by *The Over-Soul*'s sense of oneness with Spirit, that is, its evangelical mode of knowing and believing. "And so, always," announces Emerson, "the soul's scale is one; the scale of the senses and the understanding is another" (913). Thus he knows that natural and spiritual experiences are from one perspective mutually exclusive, but just as he knows too that sense-based reason or the method of John Locke provides the means of developing one's character from the lowest data base of life, so he knows that one's "Methodist" experiences form the building blocks of a "Methodist" ideality, for an at least quasi-evangelical affinity for the here and now characterizes *The Over-Soul*. "See," he commands, "how the deep, divine thought . . . makes itself present through all ages" (912). The heightened subjectivity of the following passage is similarly in line with evangelical sensibility, and it stops so far short of solipsism as to participate in intersubjectivity, if not in spiritual communion: "In all conversation between two persons, tacit reference is made as to a third party" (914). Emerson adds the explicitly religious note that "that third party or common nature is not social; is impersonal; is God. . . . I feel the same truth how often in my trivial conversation with my neighbors, that somewhat higher in each of us overlooks this byplay, and Jove nods to Jove behind each of us" (914–15).

This mundane operation of God, despite being "impersonal," represents what may well have led Herschel Parker to conclude that *The Over-Soul* "is Emerson's most comprehensive and sensitive analysis of the varieties of religious experience."[5] Parker's allusion to William James strikes me as an especially apt gloss on the evangelical quality of idealism in the essay. The Over-Soul, first, belongs to the realm not so much of ideal forms as of all the religions that have ever thrived on earth. "Had Emerson used the word *God*," observes Parker, "his readers would have interpreted him as meaning merely the Jehovah of Judaism and Christianity, not the power which lies behind all religions," but the Over-Soul includes and features the Jehovah of Judaism and Christianity. Although "the trances of Socrates," "the 'union' of Plotinus," and "the vision of Porphyry" constitute non-Christian items in Emerson's catalogue of humankind's experience with the Over-Soul, most of his examples lie either well within or very near the Christian tradition: "the conversion of Paul," "the aurora of Behmen," "the convulsions of George Fox and his Quakers," "the illumination of Swedenborg," "the rapture of the Moravian and Quietist," "the opening of the internal sense of the Word, in the language of the New Jerusalem Church," and, clearly not least, "the revival of the Calvinistic Churches" and "the experiences of the Methodists" (916–17). Experience and faith, whatever the terminology of the Over-Soul that underlies all faiths, are so far from being mutually exclusive as to be intimately interinvolved. The last two examples in Emerson's list are the most significant for my purposes; his culminating sequencing of "the revival of the Calvinistic Churches" and "the experiences of the Methodists" gives pride of place to two such important varieties of religious experience that they constitute the gamut of evangelical theology in the America and England of Emerson's day and yesterday.

His sequencing also suggests that Calvinism, though important, is less important than Methodism to Emerson's characteristic concept if not his personal experience of the Over-Soul. His conclusion that an experience of the Over-Soul will make one "cease from what is base and frivolous in his own life" (923) resonates Calvinistically enough. One overhears perhaps the distinguishing Calvinist doctrine in his assumption that "the growths of genius" belong to "the elect individual" who "expands there where he works, passing, at each pulsation, classes, populations of men" (913). Even in this passage, though, election is not so much the Calvinist matter of having been chosen before time as the Arminian—because potentially universal—matter of emergence within, in part because of time. Emerson, at this stage of his career, simply lacks both a sufficient idea of sin and a sufficient sense of evil to qualify as in any way finally Calvinist. The following, for example, is as close as *The Over-Soul* ever gets to the sort of tough-minded theodicy at which the Calvinist Milton excelled: "How dear, how soothing to man, arises the idea of God, peopling the lonely place, effacing the scars of our mistakes and disappointments!" (921). At one point, Emerson goes so far as to reject, albeit gently, the idea of John Calvin as an authority: "When I rest in perfect humility, when I burn with pure love,—what can Calvin or Swedenborg say?" (923). Thus his attitudes toward Calvinism, though perhaps more tolerant in *The Over-Soul* than in any other single work of his, tilt here as elsewhere toward the negative; but I reiterate the relative importance of Calvin among *The Over-Soul*'s exemplars of religious experience. Emerson's experience of the Over-Soul is so inclusively evangelical as to be somewhat Calvinist as well as Arminian.

What makes the evangelicalism of *The Over-Soul* more Arminian, or

Methodist, than Calvinist is that it is first and foremost experiential. The Over-Soul, significantly, is misnamed in that it is not above us at all; rather, it is "this *deep* power *in which we exist,* and whose beatitude is *all accessible* to us, . . . self-sufficing and perfect *in every hour*" (911; my italics). Ultimate reality for Emerson as for the experiential evangelicals is distributed in time and space; Acts 17.28 affirms that in Christ "we live, and move, and have our being," and Emerson's allusion to this verse keeps the Over-Soul from being pantheistic. The Over-Soul, however, decidedly indwells, for it is described in the biblical language for the third person of the Trinity to whom evangelicals accorded unprecedented attention.[6] Just as the Holy Spirit "bloweth where it listeth" (John 3.8), so, too, does the Over-Soul "inspire whom it will" (911). Emerson, Parker observes, "felt no impulse" to account for religious emotion "according to the tenets of a particular church,"[7] but even Parker acknowledges that "undogmatic about Christianity as he became," Emerson seems to have "undergone an intense religious experience around . . . 1830 or 1831," and although this conversion was comparable to what Parker calls Edwards's "sweet inward burning," it resembled even more closely the "heart . . . strangely warmed" of Wesley, who described his experience as delightful, that is, as more Arminian-joyful than any inwardly burning or corrosive Calvinism, however "sweet" (or bittersweet), could be.

Emerson, similarly, feels an impulse to account for his experience according to the tenets of a particularly experiential, particularly Arminian strain of thought and practice, namely, evangelical spiritual theology.[8] Consider the essay's opening words: "There is a difference between one and another hour of life, in their authority and subsequent effect. Our faith comes in moments; our vice is habitual. Yet is there a depth in those brief moments, which constrains us to ascribe more reality to them than to all other experiences" (910). This passage is by no means so far as a century's distance would suggest from the Wesleyan emphasis on such moments as "a quarter to nine" on the evening of May 24, 1738. Just as "the love of God . . . shed abroad in our hearts" (Romans 5.5) is a phrase that helped create infinite moments for the evangelicals,[9] so too Emerson's "man in whom [inspiration] is shed abroad" finds it impossible to "wander from the present" (918). If Emerson's view of spiritual influx is not precisely cognizant of those particular tenets whereby evangelicalism understands conversion, his view is close enough to them to seem congruent with them, for without shrinking from the fact that "a certain enthusiasm attends the individual's consciousness of . . . divine presence" (916), Emerson, like the evangelicals, distinguishes between extraordinary and ordinary encounters with God. Here, in the words of Isaac Watts, is the distinction as made by the evangelicals:

> The ordinary witness maintains the soul in such a degree of peace, comfort, and well-grounded hope, as carries the christian onward through the difficulties and duties of life, though without such raptures of inward joy. . . . It is certain . . . that wise, and judicious, and holy men, have had very extraordinary impressions . . . made on their souls, so that they were almost constrained to believe that they were divine; and the effects of these impressions have been holy and glorious: We should set a guard therefore on our hearts and our tongues, lest we cast a reproach and scandal on such sacred appearances, which the Spirit of God will hereafter acknowledge to have been his own work.[10]

Here is Emerson's similar distinction: "The character and duration of this enthusiasm varies with the state of the individual, from an extasy {*sic*} and trance and prophetic inspiration,—which is its rarer appearance, to the faintest glow of virtuous emotion, in which form it warms, like our household fires, all the families and associations of men, and makes society possible" (916). It is noteworthy that Emerson, despite his antinomian sublimities of the "God within," and despite his antisocial moods, here stresses a much less enthusiastic, an almost didactic, form of spiritual experience.

Emerson hopes, in particular, to avoid the charge of fanaticism and at the same time to preserve the warmest possible manifestations of spiritual experience; he fulfills this hope by making especially fine and careful distinctions among the gradations of immediate revelation. Like Wesley, who preaches that any emotional outbursts will indicate genuine spiritual experience if and only if they are attended by good works,[11] Emerson applies the test of an externally observable behavior to the claims of inner-experiential access to the divine: "If [a man] have not found his home in God," he writes, "his manners, his forms of speech, the turn of his sentences, the build, shall I say, of all his opinions will involuntarily confess it, let him brave it out how he will" (919). He adds that "if he have found his centre, the Deity will shine through him, through all the disguises of ignorance, of ungenial temperament, of unfavorable circumstance," for "the tone of seeking, is one, and the tone of having is another" (919). Equally carefully, however, Emerson insists on the frequency and the intensity as well as simply the validity of even the warmest religious experience. The varieties of such experience can employ an almost sexual tone in their bold claims to the coalescence of humankind with God: "Ineffable is the union of man and God in every act of the soul. The simplest person, who in his integrity worships God becomes God; yet forever and ever the influx of this better and universal self is new and unsearchable" (921). The most sexual of all Methodist hymns, "Love Divine, All Loves Excelling, / Joy from Heaven to Earth Come Down," [12] glosses the passage from *The Over-Soul* in which Emerson praises "the experiences of the Methodists" (917), which, as he observes with more than merely spiritual frisson, exemplify "that *shudder* of awe and *delight* with which the individual *always mingles* with the universal soul" (917; my italics). In the expression of religious immediacy, the sexual metaphor proves as useful to Emerson and the evangelicals as, say, to Donne and Herbert.

The Over-Soul brings empirical philosophy and evangelical faith together emphatically, methodically, and at length. "The philosophy of six thousand years," writes Emerson, "has not searched the chambers and magazines of the soul," for "in its experiments there has always remained, in the last analysis, a residuum it could not resolve" (910). Skepticism, forming the method of philosophies as otherwise different as empiricism and rationalism, would seem to have no part in the soul's experience of revelation, for revelations "do not answer the questions which the understanding asks" (917). Those questions, however, are "solutions of the soul's own questions" (917), and while Emerson precisely and accurately maintains the distinction between philosophy and religion, he intriguingly envisions how philosophy can be helpful to faith.

Lockean content, specifically, forms part of his "evangelical" faith, for not just Locke's language of sense—but also his tenet that an analogy of proportionality constitutes our best help in religious inquiry—makes up a large, sufficiently Wesleyan-Edwardsean component of what turns out, after all, to be *The Over-Soul*'s capacious philosophical theology. Although sense-like, two-way avenues to something rich and strange differ from the physical senses, the creative as well as receptive spiritual sense in the essay remains proportional to the essay's depiction of physical-sense mystery in subject-object interpenetration. In such repeated if not near-repetitious formulations as "the soul is the perceiver and revealer of truth" (915), "thus is the soul the perceiver and revealer of truth" (918), and "we are all discerners of spirits" (918), Emerson captures the twofold function of his spiritual vision, namely, contributory power in combination with wise passivity. As for the latter, he believes in the proverb that "God comes to see us without bell" (912), for just as the physical senses put one in the presence and in point-blank recognition of the thing one knows, so too is "every man" "at some time *sensible*" and receptive to the overtness of "*pure nature*" (912; my italics). "There is no bar or wall in the soul where man, the effect, ceases, and where God, the cause, begins" (912). "The walls are taken away," and "we lie open on one side to the deeps of spiritual nature, to all the attributes of God" (912). "Justice," as a result, "we see and know, Love, Freedom, Power" (912).

Emerson's name for the soul's perceiving faculty, that is, "the religious sense" (916), is also the evangelicals' name for it. His most extensive, most sustained description of this sense does not emphasize passivity, but mixes or blends objective with subjective language. Emerson, indeed, intimates the subject-object interaction of empirical-evangelical spiritual experience. While objective language is in my italics, subjective language is in my small capital letters:

> We distinguish the announcements of the soul, its manifestations of its own nature, by the term *Revelation* [Emerson's italics]. These are always attended by the EMOTION OF THE SUBLIME. For this communication is *an influx of the Divine Mind into our mind*. It is an ebb of the individual rivulet before the flowing surges of the sea of life. Every distinct *apprehension* of this central commandment AGITATES MEN WITH AWE AND DELIGHT. *A thrill passes through all men at the reception of new truth*, OR AT THE PERFORMANCE OF A GREAT ACTION. . . . In these communications, the *power to see*, is not separated from the WILL TO DO, but the *insight* [INSIGHT?] proceeds from OBEDIENCE [*obedience?*], and the *obedience* [/OBEDIENCE] proceeds from a JOYFUL perception. Every moment when the individual feels himself invaded by it, is MEMORABLE. (916)

Thus the heart-religion of *The Over-Soul*, like that of the evangelicals, is variously, infinitely perceptive. "When we have broken our god of tradition, and ceased from our God of rhetoric," that is, when we can sincerely aspire to a personal relation to God, "then may God fire the heart with his presence" (921). If God does so, then the result will surely be "the doubling of the heart itself, nay, the infinite enlargement of the heart with a power of growth to a new infinity on every side" (921–22).

Spiritual experience in *The Over-Soul* is finally more than merely sense-like. This is my main emphasis. However proportionally analogous to natural experience, Emerson's spiritual experience is more than merely analogous to it. "All history," Emerson declares, "is sacred" (923). By this he means that spiritual experience occurs within and is enmeshed in the secular. "The world," he declares, "is the perennial miracle which the soul worketh" (923). Here, to be sure, is an implicit distinction between the soul and the world, but this declaration also affirms the dependence of the world on the power of the soul to perceive creatively. Both the natural and the spiritual are again included within the catalogue of experience.

Natural experience does not so much parallel or come athwart spiritual experience as intersect and unite with it. In the following, for example, the timeless and time, however different, are only describable as interlinked: "Always our being is descending into us from we know not whence. The most exact calculator has no prescience that somewhat incalculable may not baulk the very next moment. I am constrained every moment to acknowledge a higher origin for events than the will I call mine" (910). Emerson believes that "the soul's advances are not made by gradation, such as can be represented by motion in a straight line; but rather by ascension of state, such as can be represented by metamorphosis,—from the egg to the worm, from the worm to the fly" (913). Thus Emerson's view differs from Locke's emphasis on external influences on the self. Although Emerson's view of the soul's relation to experience differs from Locke's where Locke is in a mood to say that we are a part of all that we have *met,* Emerson is more than sufficiently Lockean at least in his insistence that what happens either externally or internally changes us in space and time and is therefore crucial to the nurturing of our souls and selfhoods.

Perhaps the most inclusive, most sense-filled as well as sense-related statement of Emerson's philosophical theology comes toward the end of *The Over-Soul,* where an especially prayerful, particularly resounding credo occurs: "Let man then learn the revelation of all nature, and all thought to his heart; this, namely; that the Highest dwells with him" (922). The evangelical quality of this combination of heart-religion with spiritual theology hardly needs pointing out. *Of all nature,* however, implies the part that immediate revelation takes in *sense* experience. Thesis-like statements typically come at the ends of Emerson's essays, and such inductive procedure is consistent with the experiential bias of his empirical-evangelical frame of mind. Another phrase from the conclusion, namely, "the sure revelation of time" (922), implies that revelation not only takes place in and tells something about time but also—more importantly—belongs to, originates in, and emanates from time.

The status of the physical senses, not just the role of the spiritual sense, is an appropriate issue for the essay's concluding epistemology of faith: "O believe, as thou livest, that every sound that is spoken over the round world, which thou oughtest to hear, will vibrate on thine ear" (922). This article of faith, about which Emerson grows so evangelical as to want to share it with his reader, does not simply speak of some vaguely ear-like soul function that "hears" the figurative "still, small voice," but rather, this article of faith unmistakably ordains the auditory sense itself as a door wide open to what God says both through and in creation. In yet another concluding passage Emerson brings together natural and spiritual experience so intimately as to indicate their interchangeability or even their potentiality for being coterminous. He explicitly includes both the kinesthetic sense and the sense of taste: "But the soul that ascendeth to worship the great God . . . dwells in the hour that now is, in the earnest experience of the common day,—by reason of the present moment, and the mere trifle having become porous to thought, and bibulous of the sea of light" (920–21). A soul so much in the world, indeed, that its very spirituality is grounded, has not merely "the conviction" but "the sight" that "the best is the true" (922). Not less than the evangelicals and not less than Locke does Emerson hold to the view that, as Wesley and Edwards put it in their shared Lockean mood, "men will trust their God no further than they know him, and they cannot know him one ace further than they have a sight of his fulness and faithfulness in exercise." [13] A less masculinist and even more directly pertinent, empirical-evangelical context for *The Over-Soul* comes from Emerson's female model of self-reliance, his aunt Mary Moody Emerson, who, as I have shown from her "Almanacks," embodies the varieties of not only religious but also religious-philosophical, experience. *The Over-Soul*, like its author's aunt, keeps sight of and sounds the empirical-evangelical antiphon.

FIFTEEN

Roots of Theory

The fullness of vision in *The Over-Soul* parallels, and may indeed enable, the inclusiveness of *The Poet*. Although the empirical context of *The Poet* has received no attention, Lawrence Buell comes close to acknowledging the evangelical context of the essay, for he argues that Emerson's idea of the poet-priest culminates the Unitarian development of a bond between aesthetic experience and revivalistic emotions.[1] In 1831 Emerson reviewed F. W. P. Greenwood's *Collection of Psalms and Hymns for Christian Worship* (1830); demonstrating the hymnic foundation of his taste for bardic poetry, Emerson's review reveals the rudiments of his poetic theory.[2] The bardic dimension of Emersonian aesthetics, however, is also understandable in the larger historical context of evangelicalism, which, after all, stresses the hymnic. Thus the dogma of Matthew Arnold, that literature replaces a Christianity threatened by science, is not as much in the nineteenth-century mainstream as one might think, for Emerson views the poet as the gardener of "imaginary gardens with real toads in them,"[3] that is, as the priest of a far from attenuated, because almost scientifically concrete, religion. I argue that Emerson's empirical-evangelical method, and hence his radically immanent Christianity, inform his aesthetics. While Van Leer and David Porter emphasize the essay's "weaknesses"—they describe it as "troubled"[4]—and while Packer hears in *The Poet*'s "ironies" only the muted "affirmation" of a "second best" writer,[5] Joel Porte praises *The Poet* as "the culmination of the energy of the first series."[6] I agree; the essay's energy is fully empirical-evangelical.

Emerson's poet, first, can be more of a scientist than scientists themselves. "The poet alone," he declares, "knows astronomy, chemistry, vegetation, and animation, for he does not stop at these facts, but employs them as signs" (932). Undaunted by any negative implications of even the Industrial Revolution, the Emersonian poet extends unqualified scientific praise to the Revolution, which is nothing less than the richest dividend, the most creative by-product of subject-object interaction:

> Readers of poetry see the factory-village, and the railway, and fancy that the poetry of landscape is broken up by these; for these works of art are not yet consecrated in their reading; but the poet sees them fall within the great Order not less than the bee-hive, or the spider's geometrical web. Nature adopts them very fast into her vital circles, and the gliding train of cars she loves like her own. (931)

(See Wordsworth's "Steamboats, Viaducts, and Railways" [1835].)

The empirical concept of what the poet knows is matched by the empirical concept of poets as products of natural experience, for Emerson's account of literature as essentially autobiographical draws on such tenets of experience-philosophy as "experience yields idea yields word." Emerson's famous definition of poetry, namely, "it is not metres, but a metre-making argument, that makes a poem" (927), essentially duplicates the Lockean subtenet "idea yields word" (927). Emerson adds that while "the thought and the form are equal in the order of time," "in the order of genesis" the thought is "prior to the form" (927). His elaboration of this point assumes the even more Lockean subtenet that "experience yields idea," for "the poet," writes Emerson, "has a new thought: he has a whole new experience to unfold; he will tell us how it was with him, and all men will be the richer in his fortune" (927).

Seemingly contrary to Locke's focus on the conscious mind, Emerson's antidote for writer's block anticipates Freud's exploration of the subconscious mind:

> Doubt not, O poet, but persist. Say, 'It is in me, and shall out.' Stand there, baulked and dumb, stuttering and stammering, hissed and hooted, stand and strive, until, at last, rage draw out of thee that *dream*-power which every night shows thee is thine own; a power transcending all limit and privacy, and by virtue of which a man is the conductor of the whole river of electricity. (940; Emerson's italics)

Consciousness, however, informs this very process of dream-exploration, for Emerson, like Freud, knows that dreams originate from the mind's involvement with sense experience.[7]

Empiricism, much more than Aristotelianism, accounts for the high degree and almost realistic extension of mimeticism in Emerson's poetics. Since "the iterated nodes of a sea-shell, or the resembling difference of a group of flowers," should be "pleasing" in the same way as and even "pleasing" *more* than "a rhyme in one of our sonnets," and since "poems are a corrupt version of some text in nature, with which they ought to be made to tally," the sciences of botany and biology illuminate Emerson's latter-day mimeticism, his view of the poem's proper "abandonment to the nature of things" (934). Aristotle's view, by contrast, is more selective, more general; it does not, as Samuel Johnson puts it, "number the streaks of the tulip," nor, as Emerson puts it, iterate the "nodes of a sea-shell." Thus Emerson, though farther along than Wordsworth toward, say, the sordid detail of Dreiser's realism, is closer to the Romantic mimeticism of Wordsworth, who, without being "culpably particular,"[8] keeps his eye on the object.

There is something empirical, too, as well as enthusiastical in Emerson's memorable comment that not only the poet but also the reader accomplishes "the ravishment of the intellect *by coming nearer to the fact*" (935; my italics). In other words, from poetry the reader, to say nothing of the poet, learns to speak sincerely of all things that are and thus to become, if not more empirically poet-like, then ever more experientially proto-poetical. The people are "all poets," though they "fancy they hate poetry" (930).

Emerson seems to think that their poetical state is due not only to the richness of even the most commonplace experiences but also to the tendency for each experience to take on its own most appropriate form of expression: "The poorest experience is rich enough for all the purposes of expressing thought. Day and night, home and garden, a few books, a few actions, serve us as well as would all trades and spectacles" (930). Notice the inclusion of books in this catalogue of experience. Emerson is as far as possible from implying that books are only self-referential, or even only intertextual, for he assumes that books and nature are interreferential. Nature, depicted by such diction as *day, night, garden,* and *spectacles,* if not by *trades, books,* and *home,* remains as preeminent in Emerson's art as it is, say, in empirical philosophy, and even more preeminent than in Aristotelian poetics, where its outlines are less sharp. Although nature's "rays or appulses have sufficient force to arrive at the senses," they do not usually have "enough [force] to reach the quick, and compel the reproduction of themselves in [poetic] speech" (925), for "the impressions of nature" fall too feebly on us "to make us artists" very often (925). One of the most famous sentences of *The Poet*, however, concludes that "every man should be so much an artist, that he could report in conversation what had befallen him" (925); although too few Americans, at least in this Emersonian sense of poetic reporting, have ever been able to report what befalls them,[9] many Americans, as recently as the turn of the century and in part because of the Methodist as well as empirical tradition of experientialism,[10] retained a certain natural eloquence whereby they fashioned from experience such lively metaphors as "making the grade" (from the railroad industry) and "panning out" (from the gold rush). Nineteenth-century readers of Emerson's essay could no doubt still hear his empirical if not Methodistical call for every citizen to be a poet, to express his or her sense-based ideas/ideals carefully enough to usher in, if not the millennium, then a more beautiful world. Walt Whitman, if not Emily Dickinson, heeded Emerson's call.

Emerson's aesthetics are as Methodistical as empirical. "The birth of a poet," he declares, "is the principal event in chronology," for by that event the reader is "invited into the science of the real" (928), a "science" not only empirical but also metaphysical or theological in tone. Both the tone and the content of *The Poet*, specifically, are experientially religious as well as generally empirical; "poetry," writes Emerson, "was all written before time was" (926), and while this announcement sounds like the ploy that Plato uses for demoting poets to vatic vessels,[11] it also sounds like the biblical principle that "in the [historical] beginning was the word" (John 1.1). "I think nothing is of any value in books," declares Emerson, "except the transcendental and extraordinary" (937), but *extraordinary* operates in a more evangelical than philosophical context, for Emerson adds, by way of reinforcing the religious as well as philosophical implications of such phraseology and as though poets were possessed by godhead, that "a man is inflamed and carried away by his thought" (937), that is, that an almost religious enthusiasm is desirable for poets to cultivate.

Emerson declares too, for reasons of similar reinforcement, that "to that degree he forgets the authors and the public, and heeds only this one dream, which holds him like an insanity, let me read his paper, and you may have all the arguments and histories and criticism" (937). This attitude also resembles Plato's argument in the *Ion* that the poet is "out of his senses," but there is a difference, for while Plato keeps poets out of his ideal republic, Emerson regards them as both truly sane and sufficiently religious/establishmentarian. Seeking honorific signification for what some would regard as religious fanaticism, he uses the evangelical criterion of enthusiasm as his own best measure for genuine poetic inspiration.

One source by which poetry of the nineteenth century might find a new "carnival" of the gods lies in the "Calvinism" that followed the Middle Ages (939), but the Methodist-Arminian content of evangelicalism is what specifically informs Emerson's concepts of poets and poetry, for "Methodism and Unitarianism," though "flat and dull" to "dull people," are more likely than Calvinism to be inspirations for the literary renaissance that he envisions (939). Writers willing to draw on these two "liberal" manifestations of religion in Emerson's day become even more "Methodist" than "Unitarian" in their visionary imaginations. Alluding to a more Methodist-Arminian than Unitarian-Arminian proof text for free will, that is, "And ye shall know the truth, and the truth shall make you free" (John 8.32),[12] he declares that since poets "are free, and make free," they are "liberating gods" (937). Any book written by such an artist is a "new witness" (937); this is what evangelicals would call an "extraordinary witness." Such a book, indicating the uniqueness and intensity of the artist's spiritual experience, carries his or her ordinary but still evangelical message to people who, "on the brink of the waters of life and truth," are "miserably dying," and who therefore seem in need of salvation from some fallen state (937).

The reader's response is accordingly far from impressionistic or individual, for invariably it evinces a second birth. "The birth of a poet" is the "principal event in chronology" precisely, if not only, in that it leads to the rebirth of the reader who "became an animal" on his or her "birthday" but who, through the instruction as well as the delight of poetry, is now "invited into the science of the real" indeed, that is, into the all but empirical knowledge of the evangelically true (928). Poetry is thus "God's wine" (935). Emerson's theory of the reader's response, of course, would seem to anticipate "reader response criticism," which emphasizes how interpretation functions according to one's membership in particular groups.[13] His emphasis on second-birth patterns seems especially intended for evangelical readers whose reality is as much to be found, however, in the non- or preverbal circumstances of their times and places as in their interpretive community's verbal constructs.

Both the poet and the audience thus experientially harmonize philosophy with faith. This merger is especially well indicated by the most concise of all *The Poet*'s expressions of the relation between science and religion; by concluding that "science always goes abreast with the just elevation of the man, keeping step with religion and metaphysics; or, the state of science is an index of our self-knowledge" (929), Emerson discerns no conflict between science and faith and he all but asserts the identity of them. He comes to this bold conclusion, despite the evolutionary clouds gathering at the time of writing *The Poet*. Not only "the spirit of the world" but also "the great calm presence of the creator" (notice the apposition, the imaginative synonymity, between these otherwise arguably antipodal phrases: the former is pantheistic, the latter theistic) comes forth "from every dry knoll of sere grass, from every pine-stump, and half-imbedded stone, on which the dull March sun shines," to the "quiet hearts" of both the "epic poet" and all other people "of simple taste" (935). "Every man so far a poet as to be susceptible" to the "enchantments of nature" will sincerely as well as coarsely worship "nature the symbol" (929–30); Emerson intends by this the only seemingly contradictory meanings of "body overflowed by life" and "nature certifying the supernatural" (930), for *Nature the symbol* signifies the paradoxical unity of an uneasy relation, not so much between pantheism and neo-Platonist tradition as between theistical natural religion and Lockean-evangelical tradition.

Finally, the fact that the poet "will tell us how it was with him" (927) evokes the empirically evangelical basis of spiritual autobiography as well as of literature as self-expression. "Poets," Emerson believes, should never write "at a safe distance from their own experience" (924). He adds that "the highest minds of the world" should "explore the double meaning, or, shall I say, the quadruple, or the centuple, or much more manifold meaning, of every sensuous fact" (924). Although this concept harks back to the fourfold exegesis of Thomas Aquinas's methodology,[14] a Lockean-evangelical and hence nearer paraphrase of the concept would be (1) that every sensuous fact includes a spiritual dimension, and (2) that every poet perceives naturally in the same way as spiritually and spiritually in the same way as naturally.

Not just poets themselves but even readers of poetry share the spiritual sense. "Men have really got a *new sense*," and have "found within their world, another world" (936; my italics). The variety of ways to speak of this sense, for example, the "intellect . . . suffered to take its direction from its celestial life" or "the intellect inebriated by nectar" (934), speaks of the mind yielding, as well as yielded up to, spirit in nature. "As the traveller who has lost his way, throws his reins on his horse's neck, and trusts to the instinct of the animal to find his road, so must we do with the divine animal who carries us through this world" (934). This analogy of proportionality, appropriate to both empiricism and itinerant evangelicalism, would appeal to the sensibility fostered by Wesley, who was in the world but not of it and whose horse knew the circuit by heart. Emerson, then, defines the poet at the beginning of the essay as one who "traverses the whole scale of experience" (925); at the end he predicts that "the ideal shall be real to thee," that is, to the poet of the future, "and the impressions of the actual world shall fall like summer rain, copious, but not troublesome, to thy invulnerable essence" (941). The philosophical theology of Emerson's poet, as of Emerson himself, finds not only an analogy of proportionality but also identity between "the Father, the Spirit, and the Son" on the one hand, and "cause, operation, and effect" on the other (925). Thus, in a combination reminiscent of Locke as well as of Wesley and Edwards, the "whole scale of experience" includes not only the actual as well as the ideal but also the empirical as well as the evangelical; thus, too, throughout both Emerson's practice in essays besides *The Poet* and his aesthetic method or roots of theory in *The Poet*, his empirical-evangelical antiphon is effective.

SIXTEEN

The Play of Skepticism

I will test now the applicability of my argument to two essays in which it might not be expected to obtain, namely, *Experience* (1844) and *Fate* (1852). (Emerson's tough-minded, "pre-Modern" essays also include *Compensation* [1841], *Prudence* [1841], *Circles* [1841], and *Montaigne* [1850].) Critics see *Experience* and *Fate* as emphasizing for the first time in Emerson's career the ordinary over the ideal; with regard to *Experience*, for example, Van Leer points out that "by so naming his essay, Emerson makes explicit what is implicit throughout the second series: that bracketing questions of noumenality, even of existence—the transcendentality of epistemology— he now wishes to speak solely for our experience as empirically real."[1] *Experience*, moreover, is seen as advocating an especially tough-minded empiricism, for Whicher associates the essay's usage of *experience* with empirical experiment,[2] and Packer associates this same usage with Humean empiricism.[3] Michael, for his part, associates Humean empiricism with both *Experience* and *Fate*,[4] but Gayle L. Smith, on the other hand, reading *Experience* in the light of the famous Transparent Eyeball image in *Nature*, finds that *Experience* reflects the optimistic, "ideal" empiricism of Emerson's early career.[5] And even Van Leer argues that the "source" of *Experience* "lies less in the empirical tradition, where the more representative term is 'impression,'" than in the optimistic German idealism of Kant, for whom "'experience' is almost literally the first word of the first *Critique*."[6] I, of course, am especially intrigued by Gertrude Hughes's view that experience functions throughout the essays as it does for Paul in Romans 5.3–5: "We glory in tribulations also: knowing that tribulation worketh patience; and patience, experience; and experience, hope; and hope maketh

211

not ashamed."[7] "In *Experience* and other [such] essays," observes Herschel Parker, "Emerson resolutely faced the conflict between idealism and ordinary life,"[8] but even on the basis of *Experience* and *Fate*, Emerson resolves the conflict not as Parker says he does—that is, by placing the "ordinary" over the "ideal"—and certainly not by omitting one or the other of these two exhaustive categories of human existence, but by reconciling them instead through what Abrams calls "the sustained tension, without victory or suppression, of co-present opposites" (Abrams has in mind Blake's *The Marriage of Heaven and Hell* [1793][9]). Such tension is the specific means by which these two essays not only confront the harshest truth but also grasp the fullest truth, for the empirical-evangelical synthesis that Emerson finally reaffirms resonates the more strongly for his determined effort to *use* his doubts and fears—precisely by bringing them into play with his continuing faith.

Thus, although a mix of Humean skepticism, evolutionary science, and Calvinist thought in *Experience* and *Fate* would appear to undermine the predominantly tender-minded Late Romanticism of the five essays thus far considered,[10] the empirical- and Arminian-evangelical viewpoint of even these later two essays emerges, once again, from Emerson's late-prime struggle with the challenges posed to philosophy and faith by the increasingly tough-minded midcentury sensibility of the Anglo-American world.

Experience, at first, is so tough-minded as to assume a Humean-empirical pessimism. The essayist laments at the outset that "in the great society wide lying around us, a critical analysis would find very few spontaneous actions" (943). He adds, with particularly Humean diction, that "it is almost all custom and gross sense" (943). While Locke had said that "all those sublime Thoughts, which towre above the Clouds, . . . take their Rise and Footing here,"[11] Hume pursued this view of mankind as conditioned to its logical conclusion. He emphasized that we can no more help thinking than we can help eating, and his characteristic emphasis on the conditioning tendency of repeated experience [12] helps account for the more Humean than Lockean, more attenuated than robust tone with which *Experience* demystifies the so-called "special talent" of individual "men" (947). "The mastery of successful men," Emerson explains, "consists in keeping themselves where and when that turn [of special talent] shall be oftenest to be practised" (947), and in even more Humean mode he adds that "we do what we must, and call it by the best names we can, and would fain have the praise of having intended the result which ensues" (948).

Experience can out-Hume Hume. The form of empiricism in *Experience*, unlike Hume's preservation of liberty as well as necessity,[13] is at first so severely deterministic as to preclude even the barest possibility of free will: "temperament is the iron wire on which the beads are strung" (945). "Men," Emerson adds, "resist the conclusion in the morning, but adopt it as the evening wears on, that temper prevails over everything of time, place, and condition, and is inconsumable in the flames of religion" (945). He concludes that "some modifications the moral sentiment avails to impose, but the individual texture holds its dominion, if not to bias the moral judgments, yet to fix the measure of activity and of enjoyment" (945). His deceptively simple but actually sophisticated and suggestive philosophical principle that "nature does not like to be observed" (944) reflects not only his Humean awareness of limitations in empiricism but also his doubts about any other kind of empirical method, for he laments that we are nature's "fools and playmates" and that while "we may have the sphere for our cricket-ball," we may not have "a berry for our philosophy" (944).

Thus, inasmuch as Emerson would like to observe nature, his fear of being unable to do so disturbs him greatly. While deconstructionists may found philosophy on the ludic aspect of reality,[14] Emerson the philosopher is not satisfied by even the most serious idea of play. He grieves that "direct strokes [nature] never gave us power to make; all our blows glance, all our hits are accidents" (944).

His emphasis on chance as reality, in particular, applies to the personal realm. "Our relations to each other," he perceives, "are oblique and casual" (944). This emphasis carries all the horror and all the forlorn apprehension of randomness to be found in Wallace Stevens's "casual flocks of pigeons" or in Thomas Hardy's "Crass Casualty."[15] The pain caused by the search for a "lasting relation" between "intellect" and "thing" equals "the plaint of tragedy which murmurs" from the vain search "in regard to persons, to friendship and love" (947).

Under the circumstances, then, the only affirmation or "distinguished thing"[16] is death. "Nothing is left us now," Emerson writes, "but death," and "we look to that with a grim satisfaction, saying, there at least is reality that will not dodge us" (944).

Thus his fruitless search for the *ding an sich* and for intersubjectivity suggests that, even at its most basic level of sense perception, empiricism is tragically flawed. At the beginning of the essay a crisis of perception recasts Dante's feeling of spiritual bewilderment. Here are the opening lines of *The Inferno*:

> Midway in our life's journey, I went astray
>   from the straight road and woke to find myself
>   alone in a dark wood. How shall I say
>
> What wood that was! I never saw so drear,
>   so rank, so arduous a wilderness!
>   Its very memory gives a shape to fear.[17]

And here is the opening passage of *Experience*: "We wake and find ourselves on a stair; there are stairs below us, which we seem to have ascended; there are stairs above us, many a one, which go upward and out of sight. . . . All things swim and glitter. Our life is not so much threatened as our perception" (942). "We" remain within the empiricist universe; "we" are still conscious. But not even the philosophy of Hume calls all into doubt so relentlessly as does this passage. It derives from Emerson's melancholy apperception that sense perception works no more. His description of stairs (related to the mysterious ladder in *Circles?*) lies nearer to Piranesi's visually confusing stairways leading nowhere, than, say, to Yeats's gyres leading to purposive though frightening shifts of history. Even toward the end of *Experience,* where Emerson has well begun to win his way through to the other side of his despair, he does not forget that we rightly "suspect our instruments": "we do not see directly, but mediately," and "have no means of correcting these colored and distorting lenses which we are, or of computing the amount of their errors" (955).

The very essence of unproblematic empiricism, as one might say, is security in the presence of what one knows, and, in the exact proportion as the Emerson of *Experience* finds himself unable to sustain such empiricism, he reaches the inescapable (if preliminary) conclusion that mind is alienated from a nature in which one neither plays a role nor discovers one's abiding place. Not even the keener senses of the lower animals, their especially empirical avenues, suffice to make nature their home; for although "we fancy that we are strangers, and not so intimately domesticated in the planet as

214

THE PLAY OF SKEPTICISM

the wild man, and the wild beast and bird," "the exclusion reaches them also; reaches the climbing, flying, gliding, feathered and four-footed man" (950). "Fox and woodchuck, hawk and snipe, and bittern," as Emerson's commiserating mode concludes, "when nearly seen, have no more root in the deep world than many, and are just such superficial tenants of the globe" as we (950).

Empiricism, then, would seem to have nothing whatsoever to tell the Emerson of *Experience*. He asks with particularly bitter pointedness whether chemistry, with its "astronomical interspaces betwixt atom and atom," is only insubstantial emptiness, "all outside" and "no inside" (942). Not even to such a manifestation of empirical practicality as the Industrial Revolution does the essay allude with any of Emerson's wonted confidence or hope. Unlike earlier essays, this essay can refer to that Revolution only by means of a wasteland tone of desolation and depletion: "We are like millers on the lower levels of a stream, when the factories above them have exhausted the water" (942).

Emerson's perception crisis, moreover, is matched by the essay's dim view of experience in general. Far from relying on experience as the best means of knowing what is true whether naturally or supernaturally, he announces that " 'tis the trick of nature . . . to degrade today" (943). Experience is thus unimportant and ineffectual. Far from writing autobiography as the genre most consistent with experiential expectations, he offers, instead, this precisely antiexperiential reason for not doing so: "Our life looks trivial, and we shun to record it" (943). Thus the texture of experience seems drained of meaning. Although the experiences that show off the mind's role in nature remain significant, even *they* are relatively negligible: "The pith of each man's genius contracts itself to a very few hours" (943).

Experience, however, remains empirically positive at least in that, by making such a strong case against experiential certainty, the skeptical method of the essay keeps Emerson from succumbing to the specious truth claims of anyone else. His resistance to the intellectual tyranny of "physicians" and "phrenologists," who impose their ill-considered conclusions, is especially memorable: "Theoretic kidnappers and slave-drivers, they esteem each man the victim of another, who winds him round his finger by knowing the law of his being, and by such cheap signboards as the color of his beard, or the slope of his occiput, reads the inventory of his fortunes and character. The grossest ignorance does not disgust like this impudent knowingness" (946). These dogmatists are not true empiricists. Since economists are more theoretical than scientific, they too, despite pretending to scientific method, receive the Emersonian barb: "What help from thought? Life is not dialectics. We, I think, in these times, have had lessons enough of the futility of criticism. Our young people have thought and written much on labor and reform, and for all that they have written, neither the world nor themselves have got on a step" (948). In this mood Emerson would be no more receptive to dialectical materialism than to empirical-evangelical dialectics.

Shelley's "awful doubt" repeals "large codes of fraud and woe." [18] Thus Shelley ironically contrasts the enlightened Code Napoléon with Napoléon's code/mode of exporting tyranny. Similarly, the Emerson of this part of *Experience* espouses a skepticism that protects both him and the reader from any particular system or combination of systems. Although the empiricism of *Experience* makes only such modest claims to knowledge as to represent almost no gain in knowledge, the skepticism in this part of *Experience*, like the skepticism to be found in other, more "positive" essays, [19] is not so much a static state of unbelief as it is a method or process which assumes discovery to be the realistic, though obstinately questioned, goal of intellectual if not spiritual life.

At the beginning of the essay, to be sure, Emerson is out of tune not simply with the consolation of philosophy but with that of theology as well. Truth in the essay can be downright antitheological. Consider the horrific possibility, the likelihood, that so fundamental a religious concept as religious affections, notwithstanding the lavish attention paid to it by Wesley as well as Edwards, derives from merely naturalistic origins: "What cheer can the religious sentiment yield, when that is suspected to be secretly dependent on the seasons of the year, and the state of the blood?" (945). "I knew a witty physician," Emerson witticizes, "who found theology in the biliary duct, and used to affirm that if there was disease in the liver, the man became a Calvinist, and if that organ was sound, he became a Unitarian" (945). Such antitheological reductionism is expressed at one point in terms seemingly consistent with a biblical point of view; Emerson's proverb, mournful in rhythm as in message, that "dream delivers us to dream, and there is no end to illusion" (944), reflects the tone of futility for which the books of Ecclesiastes and Job (despite being canonized) are famous. Emerson acknowledges that the problem of good may be more difficult for the pessimist than the problem of evil for the optimist, for he states at the outset that "there are always sunsets, and there is always genius" (944), but, according to another of the essay's emphases, life is so hectic that we can scarcely enjoy what good there is: there are "only a few hours so serene that we can relish nature or criticism" (945).

The essay can seem so pessimistic, then, so at odds with Emerson's characteristic impulse of theological optimism, that it militates against even the most tough-minded theological tradition, namely, that of theodicy. (Wendy Farley, in an especially tough theodicy, draws on such thinkers as Emmanuel Levinas, Emile Fackenheim, Sharon Welch, John Calvin, and Julian of Norwich.[20]) The problem of evil in respect to the justice and holiness of God can pale beside Emerson's inability even to ask, much less to know, what grief can tell him of God's ways.

"Broodings over the death [in January 1842] of his young son Waldo" gave rise to *Experience*.[21] Although some "darker passages" were first drafted before 1842, while some "more optimistic passages" derive from journal entries made after that date, and although "no simple autobiographical reading," therefore, is "tenable,"[22] Waldo's death brings about a "new and ruthless determination to tell the truth as [Emerson] saw it."[23] Although David Robinson argues that the "seeds" of Emerson's later rigor in truth telling were sown "in the intellectual task he set for himself as an apostle of [Unitarian] self-culture," even Robinson acknowledges that Waldo's death "added to [Emerson's] later skepticism."[24] Because *Experience* is "perhaps Emerson's most self-allusive essay," and because the self alluded to is, without doubt, a severely dislocated one, the logical method of the essay, according to Van Leer, is "to shore up the pieces" with fragments from his earlier works.[25]

Even the theodiceal urgency of pain, sorrow, and suffering is lost to Emerson the father, who, with honesty and courage to be sure but also with hollowness and numbness, reacts to the death of his son in a completely nontheodiceal, completely godless and shocking way:

People grieve and bemoan themselves, but it is not half so bad with them as they say. There are moods in which we court suffering, in the hope that here, at least, we shall find reality, sharp peaks and edges of truth. But it turns out to be scene-painting and counterfeit. The only thing grief has taught me, is to know how shallow it is. That, like all the rest, plays about the surface, and never introduces me into the reality, for contact with which, we would even pay the costly price of sons and lovers. Was it Boscovich who found out that bodies never come in contact? Well, souls never touch their objects. An innavigable sea washes with silent waves between us and the things we aim at and converse with. . . . In the death of my son, now more than two years ago, I seem to have lost a beautiful estate,—no more. . . . [I]t does not touch me: some thing which I fancied was a part of me, which could not be torn away without tearing me, nor enlarged without enriching me, falls off from me, and leaves no scar. It was caducous. I grieve that grief can teach me nothing, nor carry me one step into real nature. (944)

Packer, in order to understand this intriguingly crucial passage, draws on Jonathan Bishop's concept of Emerson's "tonal puns." [26] The tone, here, is perhaps both "self-lacerating" and filled with "casual brutality," for "we *can* imagine a voice that says all of these things with bitter irony," but we can also imagine "a voice as toneless and detached as that of a witness giving evidence in a war crimes trial." An additional analogy to the latter voice, according to her, is the "wasted and suffering" discharged soldier whom Wordsworth questions in Book IV of *The Prelude*:

> In all he said
> There was a strange half-absence, as of one
> Knowing too well the importance of his theme
> But feeling it no longer.

Packer observes that "the casual brutality of the sentence in which Emerson introduces the death of his son *as an illustration* is unmatched by anything I know of in literature, unless it is the parenthetical remark in which Virginia Woolf reports the death of Mrs. Ramsay in the 'Time Passes' section of *To the Lighthouse*." Packer thinks, too, of Emily Dickinson's "After great pain, a formal feeling comes," and of Sir Thomas Browne's *Hydriotaphia*: "There is no antidote," writes Browne, "against the *Opium* of time."

Ben Jonson and Charles Wesley, despite their accesses to religious consolation, grieve over the losses of their children. [27] The philosopher in chapter 18 of Samuel Johnson's *Rasselas* (1759), despite his expertise in Stoicism, grieves over the loss of his daughter. Wordsworth, in "Surprised by Joy" (1817), mourns so intensely over his daughter Catherine's death at age five that he does not permit even time to assuage his grief. Emerson, however, does not lament his child's passing at all. Though willing, like Wordsworth, to do so, he is finally even more stoical than Johnson's philosopher. He is either beyond the need for religious consolation or chillingly indifferent to whether such consolation betokens divine concern. Thus the emotional-theodiceal responses of Jonson and Charles Wesley to the conditions of their bereavements are so far removed from Emerson's extra-theodiceally tough-minded response to the condition of *his* bereavement that their responses form especially good indications of just how far Emerson is, at this point in *Experience*, from availing himself of even the cold or merely intellectual consolation that theodicy provides (see the theodicy of *In Memoriam*).

A strange paradox, however, is my emphasis here, namely, that despite or because of the extremely skeptical procedures of both the "philosophy" and the "theology" in *Experience*, this essay contains some of the purest statements of Emerson's evangelical procedures and values. Consider his experientially spiritual theme. He injects the idiom of immediate revelation as early as the third of eight sections: "Like a bird which alights nowhere, but hops perpetually from bough to bough, is the Power which abides in no man and in no woman, but for a moment speaks from this one, and for another moment from that one" (948). Visitations are few and far between, and the vessel is disjoined, in the main, from its spiritual content. As the tree "waits" for the restless bird, moreover, so man—and woman (as Emerson's sympathy for all humankind grows, his gender bias decreases)—can do nothing but abide the unpredictable influx. But when the influx comes, an intersection of spirit with experience occurs. One thinks, in this connection, of Hardy's "The Darkling Thrush" (1901), in which, although "every spirit upon earth / Seemed fervourless as I,"

> At once a voice arose among
> The bleak twigs overhead
> In a full-hearted evensong
> Of joy illimited;
> (lines 15–20)

As with conversion, and even as with the ordinary witness of the Spirit,[28] nothing is ever the same again. The inclusion of women bespeaks the

Arminian-evangelical and democratic intensity of Emerson's deepening theology of spiritual experience. His momentous moment, so utterly pivotal that both before and after fade into subordination, transfigures the even tenor of life: "But ah! presently comes a day, or is it only a half-hour, with its angel-whispering,—which discomfits the conclusions of nations and of years! . . . Life is a series of surprises, and would not be worth taking or keeping, if it were not. God delights to isolate us every day, and hide from us the past and future" (952). *Experience*, 6, accordingly speaks emphatically of *"the universal impulse to believe"* (955; Emerson's italics). Although Emerson concludes here that "the spirit is not helpless or needful of mediate organs; it has plentiful powers and direct effects" (955), his "impulse to believe" is like that of Locke, Wesley, and Edwards,[29] for his impulse, like theirs, derives from without as well as from within. It is thus a full access to religious knowledge in the here and now.

After all, much of Emerson's spiritual experience in *Experience* has the ring of his former ebullient outlook. Although the Emerson of *Experience* does not forget that "temperament is the veto or limitation-power in the constitution" (947), temperamental limitation merely conditions his newfound affirmation that temperament "very justly . . . restrain[s] . . . excess in the constitution" (947) and is no "bar" to "original equity" (946). "When virtue is in presence, all subordinate powers sleep" (946). This discovery, hinting at experiential open-endedness, more than merely recalls the experiential theology of the evangelicals.[30] Emerson's declarations that "nothing is of us or our works," that "all is of God," and the corollary that "all writing" and "all doing and having" come "by the grace of God" (952–53) draw on the Calvinist distinction between faith and experience, but his principle that "life itself is a mixture of power and form" (949) and its implication that we should eschew mere "form" without "the power" (see 2 Timothy 3.5) reflect Arminian evangelicalism, for Emerson alludes to a Wesleyan proof text for spiritual experience.[31]

The skepticism of *Experience* saves Emerson from intellectual pride. The quasi-moral aspect of his skepticism—for example, "our young people have thought and written much on labor and reform, and for all that they have written, neither the world nor themselves have got on a step"—suggests his continuing closeness to religion; and indeed, despite his virtual denial of dialectical materialism, he reaffirms the dialectic between skepticism and faith to be found, for example, in *Nature*;[32] for not only does he mention them in the same breath but he also implies that we purposefully go from one to the other: "So it is with us, now skeptical, or without unity, because immersed in forms and effects all seeming to be of equal yet hostile value, and now religious, whilst in the reception of spiritual law" (953). Spiritual experience, to be sure, can be so unconscious as to adumbrate Freudian precepts: "that which is co-existent, or ejaculated from a deeper cause, as yet far from being conscious, knows not its own tendency" (953). Empirical experience, however, belongs to the conscious mind: "that which proceeds in succession might be remembered" (953). The radically skeptical stance of Emerson at last enables the conscious synthesis of philosophy with faith in what he calls a "*new* philosophy" (955; my italics) and what I, remembering his overall practice, call his philosophical theology.

"No man ever came to an experience which was satiating," writes Emerson, "but his good is tidings of a better" (955), and this formula, bespeaking the intersection of natural with spiritual experience, entails the belief that skepticism leads to fresh perfections of faith. He adds that

> the elements already exist in many minds around you, of a doctrine of life which shall transcend any written record we have. The new statement will comprise the skepticisms, as well as the faiths of society, and out of unbeliefs a creed shall be formed. For, skepticisms are not gratuitous or lawless, but are limitations of the affirmative statement, and the new philosophy must take them in, and make affirmation outside of them, just as much as it must include the oldest beliefs. (955)

Skepticism, far from threatening the epistemological status of experience, tends, then, to assimilate old-experiential tenets into the doctrines that arise from new-experiential data bases. Thus, ironically enough, belief is fuller, more resonant, than before. In a remarkable passage that shows Emerson's spiritual receptivity to time, place, and character as well as his obedience to the biblical reminder that at any time and place we may entertain if not Christ himself then "angels unawares" (see Hebrews 13.2), *Experience* highlights the exact point of synthesis between an unsoured skepticism and the wide-eyed acknowledgment of religious encounter in the here and now: "I never know, in addressing myself to a new individual, what may befall me. I carry the keys of my castle in my hand, ready to throw them at the feet of my lord, whenever and in what disguise so ever, he shall appear. I know he is in the neighborhood hidden among vagabonds" (946). The certitude of the final sentence is not so much dogmatic as indicative of Christological-pneumatological reality (see Tennyson's awareness of that same reality). The passage reflects the theological as well as philosophical quest-motivation of the properly receptive, properly unprepossessing mind-spirit.

The spiritual sense in *Experience*, above all, as in Wesley's abridgment of Edwards's *Religious Affections*,[33] seeks to apprehend point-blank, natural-spiritual truths. *Experience, 5*, to be sure, emphasizes a clause from Luke 17.20, namely, "the kingdom that cometh without observation" (952), which would seem to exclude the physical senses from any role in, and even from any analogy to, spiritual revelation; for the kingdom of God, even if broadly experiential, distinct from simply otherworldly, does not necessarily cooperate with the understandable human desire to equate believing with seeing. The proverbial commonplace that "the watched pot never boils," moreover, finds its counterpart in Emerson's less theological than psychological anticipation of Freud's reality as unseen reality: "Power keeps quite another road than the turnpikes of choice and will, namely, the subterranean and invisible tunnels and channels of life" (952). Finally, spiritual experience has admittedly little to do with either the "habitual standards" of a Humean empiricism or the "real and angular" appearance of every day, when "[natural] experience is hands and feet to every enterprise" (952). But the same paragraph implies that the subterranean passages of spiritual power originate, make manifest, and are even manifested in the waking life: "all good conversation, manners, and action," declares Emerson, "come from a spontaneity which forgets usages, and makes the moment great" (952). Following his immediate admission that "our chief experiences have been casual," he establishes an optimistic, because potentially spiritual as well as overtly natural, meaning for *casual:* "We *thrive* by casualties" (952; my italics). Now that Emerson once again regards natural and spiritual experience as intersected, *casual* can signify not so much the purblind world's crass accident as the grace that intercedes "where it listeth" in the natural world. The physical senses participate in spiritual perception, at least in that one's practical charity engages the here and now: "Five minutes of today are worth as much to me, as five minutes in the next millennium. . . . Let us treat the men and women well: treat them as if they were real: perhaps they are" (949).

The Gospel of Mark (13.6) foretells that Christ will come in the morning. This prophecy contrasts with *Experience*'s association of morning not so much with apocalypse as with the millennium in which sense and spirit coexist and coinhere: "In the morning I awake, and find the old world, wife, babes, and mother, Concord and Boston, the dear old spiritual world, and even the dear old devil not far off" (950). The chummy, even precious reference to the devil risks trivializing evil. The emphasis, however, lies on experiential grace and the grace of experience: "If we will take the good we find, asking no questions, we shall have heaping measures. The great gifts are not got by analysis. Everything good is on the highway" (950). Thus, like the teaching of Johnson in chapter twenty-nine of *Rasselas* that "*nature* sets her *gifts* on the right hand and on the left" (my italics), *Experience* mixes natural with spiritual diction, in order to suggest that experience is both one and inclusive: "The middle region of our being is the temperate zone. We may climb into the thin and cold realm of pure geometry and lifeless science, or sink into that of sensation. Between these extremes is the equator of life, of thought, of spirit, of poetry,—a narrow belt" (950). One recognizes here Emerson's precisely stated and inclusive, even encyclopedic, philosophical theology. Although the "narrow belt" excludes both rationalism above it and the pure sensationalistic below it, the "belt" remains an ample and even sufficiently exhaustive band made up of sense-based reason, spirituality, and imagination. The "belt" emerges, accordingly, as the empirical-evangelical continuum found elsewhere in Emerson's works, and elsewhere in this particular essay.

As early as *Experience*, 3, first, where skepticism threatens to be total, his practicality seems reminiscent of the not too ingenious, not too intellectual empiricism of Locke: "Do not craze yourself with thinking, but go about your business anywhere. Life is not intellectual or critical, but sturdy. . . . We live amid surfaces, and the true art of life is to skate well on them" (948–49). Like "Fortune, Minerva, Muse," writes Emerson, the "Holy Ghost" is a "quaint" name "too narrow to cover" the "ineffable cause" symbolized by Thales as water, Anaximenes as air, Anaxagoras as thought, Zoroaster as fire, and Jesus as love (954). Emerson's thought is itself broader than any or all of these labels. Both his thought and his methodology, however, are often describable as and often understandable in accordance with the spiritual theology of the evangelicals.[34] As early as *Experience*, 1, he defines the spiritual in empirical terms: "the definition of *spiritual* should be" not "matter reduced to an extreme thinness: O *so* thin!" but, rather, *"that which is its own evidence"* (946; Emerson's italics). "That which is its own evidence" might well include *thick* matter, which would not be the less spiritual for that.

"The Ideal journeying always with us," "the heaven without rent or seam" (953), is both an implicit continuum that joins ideal to actual and a belief in experience as broadly defined. This heaven, this ideal, underlies the final definition given in *Experience*, namely, that of consciousness. Since "the consciousness in man is a sliding scale, which identifies him now with the First Cause, and now with the flesh of his body" (954), consciousness is, rightly understood, both an empirical phenomenon and a religious location. Notice the appropriateness of "sliding *scale*"—one thinks of glissando—to my similarly musical notion of the *antiphony* of Emerson's empiricism with his evangelicalism.

"The bulk of mankind," writes Emerson in *Fate*, "believe in two gods."[35] "They are under one dominion here in the house, as friend and parent, in social circles, in letters, in art, in love, in religion; but in mechanics, in dealing with steam and climate, in trade, in politics, they think they come under another" (343). One god appeals to the tough-minded sensibility, and the other to the tender-minded imagination. Emerson adds that "the bulk of mankind" think it would be difficult, "a practical blunder," to transfer "the method and way of working of one sphere into the other" (343). The posing of this problem near the center of *Fate*, however, suggests that the essay explores the blending of the two methods. Despite or because of Emerson's awareness that even evangelicalism can be tough-minded, the philosophical theology of the essay, its religion of empiricism as well as evangelicalism, not only includes but also harmonizes bright, bracing versions of these two complementary systems of experience.

Whicher thinks that *Fate* derives exclusively from Emerson's newfound interest in Orientalism.[36] Cavell uses the essay to place Emerson between Kant and Heidegger in relation to Nietzsche.[37] From my point of view, however, and despite the philosophical/religious interests of Whicher and Cavell, the sparse critical commentary on this undeservedly neglected essay is unnecessarily far afield. *Fate*, like *Experience*, confronts and overcomes dark, disturbing versions of empiricism and evangelicalism, for, like *Experience, Fate* reconciles a severe, that is, evolutionary, understanding of

empiricism on the one hand, with a severe, that is, Calvinistic, understanding of evangelicalism on the other. He does so, in particular, by
once more working his way through to the less severe—because the similarly human-scale or common-experiential—versions of each, and on this
broadly experiential basis he finds, by the skin of his teeth and therefore
to his great relief as well as satisfaction, that reason- as well as sense-based
empiricism on the one hand and Arminian evangelicalism on the other are
antipodal, complementary modes of existence.

Evolution, first, is as unsettling to the Emerson of *Fate* as to his counterparts in 1850s Britain. "When a race has lived its term, it comes no more
again" (336). Thus this Emerson implies that humankind is so far from
secure as to be doomed to extinction, and he concludes, with considerable
courage, that "no picture of life can have any veracity that does not admit
the odious facts" (338). His "Darwinian" science finally places humankind
in no very exalted position: "[Man] betrays his relation to what is below
him,—thick-skulled, small-brained, fishy, quadrumanous, quadruped ill-
disguised, hardly escaped into bi-ped,—and has paid for the new powers
by loss of some of the old ones" (339). For humankind is both illustration
and victim of the Darwinian principle that "Nature," in Tennyson's words,
is "red in tooth and claw / With ravine" (*In Memoriam*, 56.15–16):

> But Nature is no sentimentalist,—does not cosset or pamper us. We
> must see that the world is rough and surly, and will not mind drown-
> ing a man or a woman, but swallows your ship like a grain of dust. . . .
> The habit of snake and spider, the snap of the tiger and other leapers
> and bloody jumpers, the crackle of the bones of his prey in the coil
> of the anaconda,—those are in the system, and our habits are like
> theirs. . . . [T]he forms of the shark, the *labrus,* the jaw of the sea-
> wolf paved with crushing teeth, the weapons of the grampus, and
> other warriors hidden in the sea, are hints of ferocity in the interiors
> of nature. (332–33)

The empiricism of *Fate*, however, like the empiricism of *Experience*, is
finally tender-minded, for Emerson's summary of Lyellian science trium-
phantly secures humankind at the top of the evolutionary scale:

> The book of Nature is the book of Fate. She turns the gigantic
> pages,—leaf after leaf,—never re-turning one. One leaf she lays

down, a floor of granite; then a thousand ages, and a bed of slate; a thousand ages, and a measure of coal; a thousand ages, and a layer of marl and mud: vegetable forms appear; her first misshapen animals, zoophyte, trilobium, fish; then, saurians,—rude forms, in which she has only blocked her future statue, concealing under these unwieldy monsters the fine type of her coming king. The face of the planet cools and dries, the races meliorate, and man is born. (336)

Ascendant subjectivity is found even in the essay's hardest science, which grows as epistemologically adventurous as it has been ontologically dour. Where the Emerson of *Fate* assumes that nature exists for humankind, indeed, he can sound as optimistic and as naive as the Emerson of *Nature*: "Adjustments exist for man. His food is cooked when he arrives; his coal is in the pit; the house ventilated; the mud of the deluge dried; his companions arrived at the same hour, and awaiting for him with love, concert, laughter and tears" (346).

In the world of the 1850s, I suppose, one found justification for such human-centered empiricism; Emerson, at any rate, draws on his world for his celebration of sense-based reason. Here, at some length, is his especially optimistic yet finally not so naive account of medical, technological, and scientific mastery:

The annual slaughter from typhus far exceeds that of war; but right drainage destroys typhus. The plague in the sea-service from scurvy is healed by lemon juice and other diets portable or procurable; the depopulation by cholera and small-pox is ended by drainage and vaccination; and every other pest is not less in the chain of cause and effect, and may be fought off. . . . The mischievous torrent is taught to drudge for man; the wild beasts he makes useful for food, or dress, or labor; the chemic explosions are controlled like his watch. . . . Man moves in all modes, by legs of horses, by wings of wind, by steam, by gas of balloon, by electricity, and stands on tiptoe threatening to hunt the eagle in his own element. (344)

This account, telling of the many years of patient observation that it takes to make a breakthrough, tells also of the slow genius of humankind. Tennyson, prophesying in "Locksley Hall" (1842) the technological advance of airplanes, is hardly more predictive than Emerson in *Fate*.

The tender-minded versions of subject-object interaction in *Fate*, for example, "matter and mind are in perpetual tilt and balance, so," or, "every solid in the universe is ready to become fluid on the approach of the mind" (349), inform even the toughest-minded, most rigorously accurate as well as most resonant understanding of evolution in the essay, namely, "Eyes are found in light; ears in auricular air; feet on land; fins in water; wings in air; and each creature where it was meant to be, with a mutual fitness. Every zone has its own *Fauna*" (346). In the final analysis of *Fate*, then, evolution is cause for rhapsody, not recoil:

> The first and worst races are dead. The second and imperfect races are dying out, or remain for the maturing of higher. In the latest race, in man, every generosity, every new perception, the love and praise he extorts from his fellows, are certificates of advance out of fate into freedom. . . . The whole circle of animal life—tooth against tooth, devouring war, war for food, a yelp of pain and a grunt of triumph, until at last the whole menagerie, the whole chemical mass is mellowed and refined for higher use—pleases at a sufficient perspective. (346)

The third sentence is alone sufficient to call into question such an interpretation based on chronology as Whicher's, for Emerson, if *Experience* as well as *Fate* is any indication, is so far from always proceeding from freedom into fate that he advances, even in his later period, from fate into freedom.

Especially ascendant in *Fate*, especially tender-minded, is Emerson's subjective diction for natural experience: "Some people are made up of rhyme, coincidence, omen, periodicity, and presage: they meet the person they seek; what their companion prepares to say to them, they first say to him; and a hundred signs apprise them of what is about to befall" (351). "A man," as he earlier puts the point, "will see his character emitted in the events that seem to meet, but which exude from and accompany him" (349). The very localities of the world take on the characters of certain subjectivities: "We know in Massachusetts who built . . . Lynn, Lowell, Lawrence" (349). "The reading of history," in line with such ebullience, need not "make us fatalists," for "what courage does not the opposite opinion show! A little whim of will to be free gallantly contending against the universe of chemistry" (343).

The approach to theology in *Fate* can be as unflinchingly unsentimental as its approach to science. Emerson's notion of fate can be redolent of

THE METHOD OF EMERSON'S PROSE

Calvin's dourness, for Emerson's flat statement that "we trace Fate" not only in "matter" and "mind" but also in "morals" (339) is so explicitly Calvinistic that it is especially intriguingly uncharacteristic of Emerson's usually Arminian-evangelical tone. "Great men, great nations," says he, "have not been boasters and buffoons, but perceivers of the terror of life, and have manned themselves to face it" (321). He adds that "our Calvinists in the last generation had something of the same dignity. They felt that the weight of the Universe held them down to their place. What could *they* do?" (331). Thus, as though Calvinism were both sufficiently explanatory and plausible enough, Emerson draws on the part of his evangelical heritage with which he has been in less than complete sympathy; his latter-day trial of all possibilities finds even Calvinist dissonance a potentially bracing means of facing up to "the terror of life."

Where he realizes, moreover, that "even thought itself is not above Fate," he discovers that "the freedom of the will" is among fate's "obedient members" (339), and what comes to mind here, distinct from Edwards's Arminian as well as Lockean *Religious Affections* (1746), is Edwards's more characteristically Calvinist *Freedom of the Will* (1754). Toward the end of *Fate*, in a divagation on the "defects" of nature, Emerson applies to humankind a description so relentlessly unflattering, so Calvinistic, as to parallel if not to overlap with the notions of natural depravity and original sin:

> A crudity in the blood will appear in the argument; a hump in the shoulder will appear in the speech and handiwork. If his mind could be seen, the hump would be seen. If a man has a seesaw in his voice, it will run into his sentences, into his poem, into the structure of his fable, into his speculation, into his charity. And as every man is hunted by his own daemon, vexed by his own disease, this checks all his activity. (350)

Finally, early in the essay Emerson imagines a human condition so Calvinistic, so doomed, cursed, and solitary as to put one in mind of William Cowper's especially horrific, especially Calvinistic "The Castaway" (1798). Here is "The Castaway":

> No voice divine the storm allayed,
> No light propitious shone,

> When, snatched from all effectual aid,
> We perished, each alone;
> (lines 61–64)

And here is *Fate*:

> The force with which we resist these torrents of tendency looks so
> ridiculously inadequate that it amounts to little more than a criticism
> or protest made by a minority of one under compulsion of millions.
> I seemed in the height of a tempest to see men overboard struggling
> in the waves, and driven about here and there. They glanced intel-
> ligently at each other, but 'twas little they could do for one another;
> 'twas much if each could keep afloat alone. Well, they had a right to
> their eye-beams, and all the rest was Fate. (338)

This mood of Emerson's career is about as far as he or anyone else could
ever get from the democratic grace to be found specifically in Arminian-
evangelical theology. In a final instance of the mood are the bitter ironies
and the almost Job-like sarcasm with which *Fate* mocks the idea of universal benevolence: "Providence has a wild, rough, incalculable road to its
end, and it is of no use to try to whitewash its huge, mixed instrumentali-
ties, or to dress up that terrific benefactor in a clean white shirt and white
neckcloth of a student in divinity" (333). This, while said in sorrow, is also
said in anger, for "terrific benefactor," surely, is about as sarcastic as one
can be.

Despite its title and despite Emerson's courageous and thorough treatment of this subject, *Fate* leans, finally, toward the Arminian freedom
emphasized by earlier essays. Even in *Fate*'s most empiricist passages, freedom is a decided emphasis. Recall, for example, what Whicher's approach
to Emerson would perhaps regard as an inclusive statement of his early and
middle thought, but which turns out in *Fate* to be a vital element of his
later thought too, namely, "In the latest race, in man, every generosity,
every new perception, the love and praise he extorts from his fellows, are
certificates of advance out of fate into freedom" (346). *Fate* subsumes this
empirical sense of freedom under its theological sense of freedom. As early
as the fifth paragraph, where Emerson complains that "the broad ethics of
Jesus were quickly narrowed to village theologies, which preach an election

229

of favoritism" (332), he signals his finally anti-Calvinist, antielectionist stance. He implies, thereby, that both he and Jesus believe in the possibility of universal participation in ethical behavior and divine fellowship. As early as the third paragraph he declares that "if we must accept Fate, we are not less compelled to affirm liberty, the significance of the individual, the grandeur of duty, the power of character" (331). If there are shades/ foreshadowings of Schopenhauer or Nietzsche in *Fate*'s later declaration that "there can be no driving force except through the conversion of the man into his will, making him the will, and the will him" (343), then there are also vestiges or recastings of both the Wesley and the Edwards of Wesley's abridgment of Edwards's *Religious Affections* in this very combination of free will with the concept of conversion.[38]

In the last sentence of *Fate*, where Emerson acknowledges an ultimate "Law," he concludes that although this "Law" is "impersonal," it nonetheless "solicits the pure in heart to draw on all its omnipotence" (352). Thus the "Law" behaves like the Holy Spirit in early modern heart-religion. Such watershed functions of spiritual experience as immediate revelation, freedom of the will, and conversion come together with special clarity in the especially Wesleyan-evangelical idiom of a passage that, not coincidentally, occupies the exact center of *Fate*: "The revelation of Thought takes man out of servitude into freedom. We rightly say of ourselves, we were born and afterward we were born again, and many times. We have successive experiences so important that the new forgets the old, and hence the mythology of the seven or the nine heavens" (341). Whether the phrase "the revelation of Thought" means God's disclosures of himself to the mind or merely the mind's own remarkable self-disclosures, in either case the phrase speaks to the ascendant subjectivity found throughout the spiritual as well as natural vision of experience in *Fate*. Emerson boldly claims that "what we seek we shall find" (351). Thus alluding to such especially experiential verses of the Bible as Matthew 7.7 and Luke 11.9, he adds, appropriately (if somewhat too beamingly), that "since we are sure of having what we wish, we [must] beware to ask only for high things" (351). Even where he says that we pray not to God but to ourselves, even where his subjective diction is so extreme as to constitute the apotheosis of the self, his language of experience is honorifically as well as exultantly spiritual: "But the *soul* contains the event that shall befall it; for the event is only the actualization of its thoughts, and what we pray to ourselves for is always granted" (348; my italics).

The largest question explicitly, if haltingly, asked by *Fate* is, "Now whether, seeing these two things, fate and power, we are permitted to believe in unity?" (343). Emerson's answer, far from halting, rings with affirmation. It suffers no loss of subtlety: "One key, one solution to the mysteries of human condition, one solution to the old knots of fate, freedom, and foreknowledge, exists; the propounding, namely, of the double consciousness" (351). Emerson's entertainment of fate and power simultaneously, his "double consciousness," finds analogues, perhaps, in the New Critics' theory of literature as paradox, in Freud's "primal sense of the antithetical,"[39] in Blake's multivocal strategies against "Single vision & Newtons sleep,"[40] and in F. Scott Fitzgerald's "test of a first-rate intelligence" as "the ability to hold two opposed ideas in the mind at the same time, and still retain the ability to function."[41] Emerson's "double consciousness is also distinctive, however, for it follows a "both/and" logic that, without loss of meaning to either pole of fate-power understanding, not only sustains but also interinvolves both poles. "If Fate follows and limits Power," then Emerson equally confidently declares, "Power attends and antagonizes Fate" (339). Or again: "We must respect Fate as natural history, but there is more than natural history. For who and what is this criticism that pries into the matter? Man is not order of nature . . . but a stupendous antagonism" (339). By the principle that for every action is an equal and opposite reaction, fate relates definitively to power: "we should be crushed by the atmosphere, but for the reaction of the air within the body," and "a tube made of a film of glass can resist the shock of the ocean if filled with the same water" (341).

Power, in sum, always holds its own with fate because mind, according to *Fate*, is spiritual and partakes of divinity. The mind "is of the maker, not of what is made" (341). This triumphant subjectivity anticipates a Romantic mood of Wallace Stevens:

> And when she sang, the sea,
> Whatever self it had, became the self
> That was her song, for she was the maker. Then we,
> As we beheld her striding there alone,

THE METHOD OF EMERSON'S PROSE

Knew that there never was a world for her
Except the one she sang and, singing, made.
("The Idea of Order at Key West" [1935]; lines 37–42)

Clearly, Stevens echoes *Fate*. In the long run, according to Emerson, power is even greater than fate: "we stand against Fate, as children stand up against the wall in their father's house and notch their height from year to year. But when the boy grows to man, and is master of the house, he pulls down that wall and builds a new and bigger" (343). Thus Emerson's relation of fate to power elevates, however slightly, power over fate. Since a complex unity is indicated by the oxymoron "fateful power," he permits himself to believe in unity.

The most historically pertinent analogue to his "double consciousness," perhaps, is the oxymoron "philosophical theology," for the empirical-evangelical continuum also employs the "both/and" logic by which, with religion slightly elevated over science and with both clearly positioned under the experiential banner, science and religion come together in *Fate*. "Why," asks Emerson, "should we be afraid of Nature, which is none other than 'philosophy and theology embodied'?" (352). Thus he indicates the larger context in which he brings fate and power together—the dialectic of experience-philosophy with religious experience that informs his career from the beginning. Near the center of *Fate* he offers one of his fullest statements of the spiritual sense: "The day of days, the great day of the feast of life, is that in which the *inward eye* opens to the Unity in things, to the omnipresence of law:—sees that what is must be and ought to be, or is the best. This beatitude dips from on high down on us and we see. . . . We are as lawgivers; we speak from Nature; we prophesy and divine" (341; my italics). One finds here all of the essentially empirical-evangelical ingredients of this "sense," namely, passivity at first, activity at last, the physical senses as analogies to spiritual insight, and, most intriguingly perhaps, the physical senses as both harbingers and accompaniments of at once transcendent and immanent truth.

"The desire that [truth] shall prevail" is just as important, declares Emerson, as "the perception of truth" (342). Thus his spiritual sense is evangelical in that he wishes to spread the word about what he discovers through it. Toward the end of *Fate* he issues an evangelical invitation to revere the dialectical synthesis of world with spirit: "Let us build altars to the Blessed Unity which holds nature and souls in perfect solution" (351). He implies, thereby, the continuum that joins the visible to the invisible, for "Man" is not even "possible," he argues, "until the invisible things are right for him, as well as the visible" (347). Then, and only then, "some Dante or Columbus" of the spiritual sense appears, and "what changes" in "sky and earth, and in finer skies and earths!" (347).

A fitting conclusion to my discussion of *Experience* as well as *Fate* is to examine *Fate*'s address to theodicy. "The Marquis of Worcester, Watt, and Fulton," writes Emerson in *Fate*, "bethought themselves that where was power was not devil, but was God" (345); while they thus readily blink away the pain caused by the release of destructive energy, Emerson himself is so finely attuned to theodicy that he acknowledges the potential for evil in power, even as he seeks to reconcile that potential with power: "Steam," he points out, "was till the other day the devil which we dreaded" (344). While it is true that "the cold . . . freezes a man like a dewdrop," it is also true that we can "learn to skate" and that "the ice will give you a graceful, sweet, and poetic motion" (344). (Emerson possibly borrows this image from the Esthwaite skating scene of *The Prelude*;[42] the injunction to skate well is the corollary of his important concept of surface.[43]) Fate is "*unpenetrated* causes" (344; my italics), for suffering, though unfathomable now, is for that very reason eschatologically consistent with a purposive universe,[44] and here is *Fate*'s most searching, best sustained, most full-bodied, and perhaps even most empirical-evangelical attempt to extricate bliss from its neighbor pain:

> A man must thank his defects, and stand in some terror of his talents. A transcendent talent draws so largely on his forces as to lame him; a defect pays him revenues on the other side. The sufferance which is the badge of the Jew, has made him, in these days, the ruler of the rulers of the earth. If Fate is ore and quarry, if evil is good in the making, if limitation is power that shall be, if calamities, oppositions, and weights are wings and means,—we are reconciled. (345)

Although these are big "ifs" (Emerson's "answer" to Jewish suffering seems insensitive, since the Jew was by no means "the ruler of the rulers of the earth"), the statement anticipates some of the central insights of twentieth-century theodicy: the problem of suffering does not yield if the problem of Jewish suffering does not yield,[45] and Emerson's treatment of that suffering, though glancing, is prescient with regard to post–World War II developments in philosophy as well as faith.[46] The statement, then, is fully consistent with theodiceal understanding of enormity; as the intellectually rigorous coming to terms with evil, the statement is all the more effective for its careful, tentative expression, and because of that expression it is all the more consistent with the skeptical methodology of both empiricism and evangelicalism. Glibness, after all, would doom any explanatory effort, theodiceal or other, to the failures of facile assumption and premature conclusion.

Thus the Emerson of *Fate* works in and through his sense experience toward the possibility of something more in human experience than sense experience alone; he finds the means of keeping both his skepticism and his natural-spiritual vision sharp. Almost because both *Fate* and *Experience* test the efficacies of empiricism per se and evangelicalism per se, each essay not only endorses each of these methodologies the more ringingly but also intermingles them the more fully. The suggestion that *Experience* is too tough-minded to be even theodiceal goes against a view of Emerson as too optimistic to be theodiceal at all. George Santayana claims that Emerson's florid prose is quite at odds with fact,[47] and Yvor Winters complains that Emerson possesses "the gift of style without the gift of thought."[48] According to Quentin Anderson, Emerson does not accept the value of social experience and therefore has no room for evil in his theory, and although his excessive optimism is "solved" in his life by the various sorrows he faces, it returns, says Anderson, to weaken his later metaphysics.[49] Joel Porte, while increasingly "sensitive to the nuances of Emerson's thought," blames Emerson's philosophical sources for his excessive optimism.[50] "Like many others," confesses Christopher Lasch, "I used to think of Emerson as a foolish optimist," but "my rereading of his works began with *Fate*, an essay that revealed my mistake."[51] *Fate, Experience,* and for that matter all the other essays studied here, show that Emerson's tough and tender optimism is indeed well earned.

His early admirers, according to Lasch, "confused his affirmations with moral uplift, his hopefulness with a belief in progress"; it is not surprising, therefore, that as early as 1915 Van Wyck Brooks adopted a dismissive tone toward Emerson.[52] Brooks's revised view of Emerson (1932), however, is sentimental, and it does not make clear "why a more sophisticated and disillusioned generation of Americans should take any but a nostalgic interest

in the 'Orpheus' of the nation's infancy."[53] The Emerson of Orphean innocence, closely identified with American newness, remains very much alive
in Emerson studies, despite this putative Emerson's necessarily limited
appeal to anyone with emotional-intellectual maturity in the late twentieth
century. Alfred Kazin is confused: the Emerson he has recently perceived
thrilled to the "primacy that he shared with Nature and America itself,"
and Kazin's Emerson believed, too, in "self-actualization" and "rapturous
self-affirmation"; but Kazin's Emerson also showed "underlying contempt
for those who could not live up to his revelation," held that life was "indeed nothing but what the 'great man' is thinking of," took no account
of harsh material realities because of the "trust" of this "apostle of perfect
personal power" in "the spiritual life" alone, and perhaps worst of all, became an "unctuous" ex-preacher who gave the ruling establishment their
"favorite image of the literary man as someone removed from 'real' life
while remaining an embodiment of the idealism professed as the essence of
America."[54] By contrast, the Emerson I perceive successfully balances these
extremes, for his blend of nature with Anglo-American culture anchors his
development of a less psychologically than empirically evangelically real-
ized self whose rapturous affirmation makes room for all people to aspire
to greatness through revelation, and since his quest for spiritual perfection
is precisely dependent on material reality, this ex-preacher illustrates (that
is, embodies actual-ideal involvement in) Anglo-American sensibility.

SEVENTEEN

Language Method

Emerson, by apprehending the importance of culture, seems to anticipate Postmodern theory. He writes in *Circles* that "the things which are dear to men at this hour are so on account of the ideas which emerged on their mental horizon, and which cause the present order of things." [1] He adds that "a new degree of culture would instantly revolutionize the entire system of human pursuits." "Such a proposition," as Richard Poirier observes, "could be expected from Nietzsche and Foucault." [2] Granting the precocity of Emerson's proto-theory, and however much one may marvel at his insights into paradigm shifts, [3] I argue, nevertheless, that his aesthetic assumptions are not so much "cultural" or even mind-based, as "natural" or ground-based. They are more methodological than theoretical in kind.

"The ideas which emerged on Emerson's mental horizon," specifically, are in large part the ideas/ideals of sensation put forward by Wesley and Edwards in their Lockean mode. On the basis of the essays that I have emphasized so far, and on the basis of *Nature* in addition, I infer that the "things" "dear" to Emerson at the "hour" in which he lived include both natural and spiritual objects raised to concepts and to words. Derivable not only from *The Poet* but also from his practice in general, his understanding of language is not so much theoretical or top-down as method-built. His philosophically theological theme refers to his words on one side and on the other to extra-conceptual reality, for his thought-thing world underlies, verifies, makes resonant, and unifies the sign systems of empiricism and evangelicalism to which he is drawn. By these systems, and by what he regards as their points of reference, that is, natural and spiritual things, he is perennially renewed; and if his literary universe is too large for his late twentieth-century readers to swallow, it is nonetheless sufficiently accommodating for even them to expatiate in.

Emerson's empirical perspective on language acknowledges what Wordsworth, in tough-minded Lockean mood, calls "the sad incompetence of human speech."[4] Just as Locke's *Essay*, 3, is more confident about the relation of ideas to sense experience than about the relation between ideas and words, so *The Over-Soul* emphasizes "character" more than "tongue" (911). By eliding language, that is, by doing without the intervention of words, character "evermore tends and aims to pass into our thought and hand, and become wisdom, and virtue, and power, and beauty" (911). Thus the essence of character, "the action of the soul," is "oftener in that which is felt and left unsaid, than in that which is said in any conversation" (915). This preverbal-nonverbal empirical reality underlies Emerson's dictum that "no answer in words can reply to a question of things" (918). "Words," as he says in *Nature*, "are finite organs," for while they "break, chop, and impoverish" thought, and while they "cannot cover the dimensions of what is in truth," "an action," by contrast, "is the perfection and publication of thought" (843).

Just as Locke devotes a quarter of the *Essay* to linguistics, so Emerson devotes a long chapter of his manifesto, that is, *Nature*, 4, to "Language," and just as Emerson's empirical perspective includes tough-minded understanding of language, so it includes recognition of linguistic potential. The chapter's opening indicates in no uncertain terms the full and precise use that his methodology of language makes of empiricism: "Words are signs of natural facts. . . . Every word which is used to express a moral or intellectual fact, if traced to its root, is found to be borrowed from some material appearance. *Right* originally means *straight; wrong* means *twisted. Spirit* primarily means *wind; transgression,* the crossing of a *line; supercilious,* the *raising of the eye-brow*" (834). To "supercilious" Emerson clearly prefers "raising of the eyebrow," because "supercilious," by dint of abstraction, is too far removed from nature, and concrete words, by contrast, are sufficiently nature linked to be fully referential.

"The scholar of the first age," he writes in *The American Scholar*, "received unto him the world around him; brooded thereon; gave it the new arrangement of his own mind, and uttered it again" (861). Such Lockean utterance makes "the theory of books . . . noble" (861), for language is lofty only to the extent that it approximates experience. "Life," announces

The American Scholar, "is our dictionary," for "authors we have in numbers," to wit, Nathaniel Parker Willis, James Fenimore Cooper, and Washington Irving, "who have written out their vein, and who, proved by a commendable prudence, sail for Greece or Palestine, follow the trapper into the prairies, or ramble around Algiers to replenish their merchantable stock" (866). Thus close to experience, words work back through the idea not only to things but also to people; or as *The Over-Soul* puts it, "Who can tell the grounds of his knowledge of the character of the several individuals in his circle of friends? No man. Yet their acts and words do not disappoint him" (918). *The American Scholar* puts it even more succinctly: "instantly we know whose words are loaded with life, and whose not" (865).

Emerson most fully applies his understanding of the empirical potential of language to *Nature*, where he declares that "a work of art is an abstract or epitome of the world" (833). (See Wesley's most characteristic "empirical" genre, his abstracts or epitomes of such broadly experiential treatises as Edwards's *Religious Affections* and Peter Browne's *Procedure, Extent, and Limits of Human Understanding*.) "Parts of speech," *Nature* continues, "are metaphors because the whole of nature is a metaphor of the human mind" (837). *Nature* adds that "the imagination may be defined to be the use which the Reason makes of the material world" (846).

"Language," Emerson concludes in *The Poet*, "is fossil poetry" (932), a form beautiful in that it is only at a relatively direct remove from life. Such principles, from the beginning of his career to its height, illustrate the no less empirical for being sometimes subjective grounding of his "theory" of literature. "The true philosopher and the true poet," he writes in *Nature*, "are one" (848), and what *Nature* says abstractly, *Self-Reliance* says concretely, that the writer is or should be an empiricist: "My book should smell of pines and resound with the hum of insects. The swallow over my window should interweave that thread or straw he carries in his bill into my web also" (895).

Emerson's evangelical perspective on language also acknowledges "the sad incompetence of human speech." Insofar as his experiential faith emphasizes immediate revelation, his faith is wary of any kind of mediation, including language. *The Over-Soul*, for its part in his expression of faith, is careful to declare that "language cannot paint" the "great soul" of which "every man" is "at some time sensible" (912). Although the Over-Soul "pervades and contains us," and hence relates to us as experientially as pos-

238

sible, this Emersonian equivalent to the Holy Spirit is "too subtle" for mere language to define or measure (912). Although humankind seeks various answers from the Over-Soul or God, "an answer in words is delusive," for "never a moment" did the "sublime spirit" of Jesus speak in "*patois*" (917). The paraphrase of Christ's message in *The Divinity School Address*, "would you see God, see me; or, see thee, when thou also thinkest as I now think" (879), amounts to an endorsement of direct, nonverbal spiritual experience. This endorsement, in turn, leads Emerson to his logical but still rather shocking objection that God's own language, that is, traditional revelation or the Bible, hinders one's knowledge or experience of God: "The idioms of [Christ's] language, and the figures of his rhetoric, have usurped the place of his truth; and churches are not built on his principles, but on his tropes" (879).

Distinguishing among kinds of language, however, Emerson prefers religious idioms, finding them superior even to empirical language. *The Divinity School Address*, while admonishing "the man who speaks as books enable" to "hush" (he "babbles"), proclaims that "every man" who opens his door to the "angels" of courage, piety, love, and wisdom will have "the gift of tongues," that is, will in effect enjoy the glad afflatus of glossolalia (881). The address also teaches that the perceiver of spiritual things must report on what he sees, for "always the seer is a sayer" (881). Whether a given utterance is inspired will be easy to tell, for "only [the spirit of prophecy which is innate in every man]," according to *The Over-Soul*, "can inspire whom it will, and behold! their speech shall be lyrical, and sweet, and universal as the rising of the wind" (911). By the same token, anyone who has "not found his home in God"—notice the especially evangelical ring of this phrase from *The Over-Soul*—will reveal himself as lost by his very "forms of speech, the turn of his sentences, the build, shall I say, of all his opinions" (919). "We but half express ourselves," warns the Emerson of *Self-Reliance*, and that same Emerson, after lamenting that we "are ashamed of that divine idea which each of us represents," instructs us "bravely . . . [to] speak the utmost syllable of [our] confession" (890).

At its best, then, language expresses spiritual experience. As Emerson puts it in *The Divinity School Address*, "the soul's worship is builded," not only on canvas and in stone and music but also "clearest and most permanent" in "words" (881). The address brings much of Emerson's evangelical view of language into focus, for he tells the ideal preacher what to say and how to say it. Insofar as such a preacher is "a newborn bard of the Holy Ghost" who acquaints people with "Deity" by drawing on his own experience (886), his words, despite their inevitable imperfections, make him an effective instrument of evangelism, a kerygmatic/pragmatic appealer to the congregational kind of audience, whether indoors or out. The address defines "the institution of preaching" as "the speech of man to men"—compare this with Wordsworth's definition of the poet as "a man speaking to men" in the preface to *Lyrical Ballads*—and enjoins Emerson's preachers as Wesley's *Address to the Clergy* (1756) enjoins his, namely, to "speak the very truth, as your life and conscience teach it" (888). Emerson wants their language to forsake the formulaic and the conventional for the experiential and the genuine.

Thus his understanding of language is broad enough to include and be informed by experiential "epistemology," and thus, too, his evangelical as well as empirical language method features accessibility with sophistication. Although sophistication characterizes Postmodern language theory, the current critical climate is anything but accessible. It may be instructive to compare and contrast the Emerson I discern with the Emerson discerned by Postmodern criticism.

Poirier speculates that "Emerson is the kind of writer who invested too heavily in his bargain with the common reader—his inheritor Frost is surely another—so that he has somehow dissuaded his own countrymen from taking him as complexly as, say, the Germans take their Goethe or the English their Dr. Johnson."[5] But Poirier rejoices that Emerson, although "the type of popular writer," "escapes all of his own platitudes." " 'Genius,' " Poirier points out, "is commonly assumed to involve a mastery of the codes and signs by which a culture structures itself." He adds that "it therefore also offers a clue to any latently subversive content that these codes and signs might have accumulated during their long passage through many histories." Thus the strongest evidence for Emerson the talented writer is that "he wrote in such a way as simultaneously to affirm and to call into doubt his own individual authority over language." He calls into doubt, for example, "the very existence in language of the individual self even while he famously affirms it."

I would only add that any affirmation and doubt in Emerson's language is built into his empirical-evangelical worldview, so that his affirming and doubting theory of self, for example, is both sufficiently complex and quite understandable. When "genius" asserts itself in language, writes Poirier, the result is a "productive multiplication," a "thickening of possibilities which are a challenge to those clarifications of purpose and design on which public and institutional life prides itself." Although Poirier regards Emerson's "proverbial wisdom" as an "embarrassment," he is sure that Emerson himself felt the "potentially deadening" effect of his aphorisms even as he "thrilled" at "their promise to echo down the centuries." Poirier's Emerson has the wit to realize that since "life is totally subordinated to language systems," resistance can come only "from within the discourse already believed to be utterly ubiquitous and, in its effects, claustrophobic." He uses "words having to do with the enterprise of American capitalism (the self 'relies because it works and is,' for example) in order to claim virtues for exactly those human attributes which the business ethic finds antithetical." All of this is well and good.

I would add, however, that Emerson can escape from empiricism into evangelicalism, or vice versa, without being too clever about it, for empiricism and evangelicalism, after all, are not mutually exclusive but subsumable under, reconcilable through, the rubric of experience. While Emerson may indeed think that "life is totally subordinated to language systems," he thinks, too, that language systems are themselves subordinated to particular worlds outside them. These empirical-evangelical frames of reference, their experiential combination of presence with mystery, mean for Emerson that the echoing promise of his aphorisms is not only in addition to but also part of the proverbial wisdom on which he draws. His wisdom, at any rate, is both conventional and alive. It is rarely embarrassing. He finds "productive multiplication" and a "thickening of possibilities" even within public and institutional life. His genius is to recognize the grounding of that life in both nature and worlds "elsewhere."

Poirier places Emerson in the context of Foucault and company. Applying the theory of Foucault to the practice of Emerson, Poirier observes that "the discovered plight of 'genius' in the clutches of language becomes consistent with a recognition of a need for cultural change of great magnitude, a change, let us say, as would bring about an end to man as that figure is represented to ourselves." Poirier accordingly compares Emerson's subversion of capitalistic language to Foucault's subversion of antihomosexual legalisms.[6] I suggest, though, that Emerson's subversiveness is more prophetic than quasi-Marxist. The natural-cultural construct

241

within which he operates, his empirical-evangelical, scientific-millennial vision seeks to facilitate the sea-change of humankind from biological creature into spiritual dreamer. Thus the "plight" of Emerson's genius is its privilege.

Poirier's emphasis on Emerson's most characteristic usages as a language "elsewhere," like Bishop's emphasis on Emerson's "tonal puns" and Packer's on his "contempt for intelligibility,"[7] overlap with deconstructionist assumptions. Although Derrida and Freud think that jokes and puns are important,[8] J. L. Austin argues that they are "merely minor aberrations 'parasitic' on more ordinary language usage."[9] Van Leer, in accordance with Austin more than with Derrida and Freud, concludes that "my own sense of Emerson's intentional (though not necessarily conscious) ironies" is "conservative, meaning to show Emerson's deconstruction of others' positions without giving him over totally to linguistic indeterminacy."[10]

Emerson's ironies, perhaps, can be self-directed without being self-deconstructing, for after the manners of Locke's and Wesley's searches for linguistic plainness in conjunction with the satisfying complexity of language, Emerson's language usage remains ordinary at the same time that his "puns" emerge as important. His playful language is significant for reasons not so much of Freudian self-reference or of Derridean suspended reference as of Emerson's belief in the linguistic resonance he hears along the continuum that joins natural and spiritual concepts to natural and spiritual things. Thus "tonal puns" become plays of empiricism on evangelicalism and vice versa: "contempt for intelligibility" becomes a love of mystery; and a "language elsewhere" not only displaces nuances from one idiom to another but also refers to the spirit world. Without claiming that Emerson brings language to heel, then, I suggest that he calls it into account, for while his empirical-evangelical viewpoint thickens verbal texture and exploits irony, it does not surrender to the irony of irony.

Critics, while admiring one or another facet of Emerson's linguistic "genius," sometimes doubt whether his powers of language are quite in balance, but what George Santayana terms the "kindly infidelities" of language[11] may well be a good way to think of Emerson's combination of the genial appeal of language with its slippery treachery. While *infidelities* is not quite *le mot juste* for his religious as well as skeptical practice, *kindly* seems just right for his skepticism that leads to knowledge and faith.

Emerson's generally praiseworthy anticipation of Nietzsche, according to Poirier, is flawed. The "tone" through which he strikes his pre-Nietzschean note is "at once so gingerly and placid, so confident," that it is not close enough to Nietzsche, who, by Poirier's implication, is admirable only in that he is spicy, agitated, and, while not diffident, skeptical to the point of nihilism. Emerson's tone, in Poirier's words, is "confused by its own geniality," [12] but while his tone may indeed be too placid, one does not mind it for being gingerly, confident, and genial. It is not so much "confused" or hopelessly out of step with the late twentieth century as placeable on the optimistic but not naive ground of Locke, Wesley, and Edwards.

Perhaps it is advisable, then, to cherish Bloom's view of Emerson as "a necessary resource in a time beginning to weary of Gallic scientism." Bloom's Emerson "knew," and never forgot, "that the only literary and critical method was oneself." This may sound too subjective to be consistent with my point of view. Neither empiricism nor evangelicalism allows for a complete self-centeredness. Bloom is surely right, however, to feature Emerson's prayer that God may "fire the heart with his presence." He is correct, too, in relegating to a lesser importance in the Emersonian schema Emerson's nostalgia for the "God of rhetoric," which, as "the Gallic Demiurge, Language," is still found, unfortunately (in Bloom's opinion), in the "academies." [13]

Earl Wasserman, speaking of the relative merits of poetry and prose, calls the language of prose "unyielding," for he believes that the separation of sentences into subject and predicate is more rigid in prose than in poetry. He studies the unsuccessful effort of Shelley's prose, distinct from his poetry, "to capture in the unyielding dualistic language of discourse the paradox inherent in his monistic interpretation of the internal and external." [14] Since the times of Shelley and Wasserman, "monistic interpretation" has fallen out of favor; among such Postmodernist methodologies as new historicism, feminist criticism, and deconstruction, "the unyielding dualistic language of discourse" is not so much a problem to be solved as an opportunity to be celebrated. Literature now yields the *fröhliche Wissenschaft* of semantic hare chasing, the aporia of meanings in suspension, for "meaning" is what Terry Eagleton calls "the result of a process of division or articulation, of signs being themselves only because they are not some other sign." [15] When "two diametrically opposed terms" are "suddenly brought together," writes Roland Barthes, "the impossible conjunction . . . occurs," and Barthes adds that "meaning," properly "statutorily based on difference," is thus unfortunately "abolished: there is no more meaning, and this subversion is fatal." [16] While Barthes's poststructuralism thus devalues unity as debilitating, Emerson's prose, like the poetry if not the prose of Wasserman's Shelley, values unity as the reciprocal, heartening marriage of opposites, for Emerson answers in the affirmative "whether, seeing these two things, fate and power," or empiricism and evangelicalism, "we are permitted to believe in unity" (*Fate*, 343). His linguistic legacy of accessibility with sophistication contributes a salutary as well as unusual value to language study in general, for his empirical-evangelical approach to aesthetics (as well as to the writing of belletristic prose) yields just what is needed at the present time to relieve the uniformity of sophisticated debate about multiplicity in literary theory and practice.

Recapitulation and Cadenza

According to Stanley Fish, poststructuralist "theory" does not "govern practice from above" but "rests on induction from past experience,"[1] and empiricism and evangelicalism, similarly, are not modes of abstract contemplation but ways of knowing. "Originally *theoria* meant seeing the sights, seeing for yourself, and getting a world view," and E. V. Walter adds that "the first theorists were 'tourists'—the wise men who traveled to inspect the obvious world. Solon, the Greek sage whose political reforms around 590 B.C. renewed the city of Athens, is the first 'theorist' in Western history." This *theoria* "did not mean the kind of vision that is restricted to the sense of sight. The term implied a complex but organic mode of active observation—a perceptual system that included asking questions, listening to stories and local myths, and feeling as well as hearing and seeing. It encouraged an open reception to every kind of emotional, cognitive, symbolic, imaginative, and sensory experience."[2] Similarly, the "theories" of Tennyson and Emerson do not govern practice from above but, like the Wesleyan-Edwardsean, Anglo-American sensibility of which they form a part, rest on inductions from what this Anglo-American diptych of letters forcefully claims as its natural-spiritual experience. This "experience" appears palpable on the page.

The empirical-evangelical link between Tennyson and Emerson illustrates the tendency in England and the United States to set oneself apart from and even against Continental stripes of criticism and philosophy. The homegrown inductive character of Anglo-American philosophical theology, for example, underscores the difference between Anglo-American character and the deductive temper of the post-Cartesian Continent. A blend of extra-Anglo-American *methodologies,* however—or of theories in Walter's sense of the term—influences my *method* of criticism. I emulate the eclectic example of M. H. Abrams, who does not so much turn abstruse modes of literary contemplation to practical use as he locates ways of knowing within "abstract" critical modes.[3] Broad areas of agreement between Slavic-linguistic and Francophiliac currents of language study and my own criticism serve to recapitulate my argument in this book. Bakhtinian criticism, deriving from the Russian M. M. Bakhtin (who spent time in Byelorussia), new historicism, deriving from Michel Foucault (a "guru of *franglais*"), and deconstructive criticism, deriving from Jacques Derrida (another such guru), entertain demonstrably "religious" as well as appropriately philosophical views of experience. My empirical-evangelical stance, accordingly, shares much in common with and acquires much from these modes that inform and even sometimes underlie my method.

Bakhtin, who contributed to Polish-Czechoslovakian linguistics, argues along with Baudouin de Courtenay, Nikolai Kruszevski, Lev Vygotsky, Sergej Karcevskij, Jan Mukarovsky, and Roman Jakobson that "I can mean what I say, but only *indirectly,* at a second remove, in words I take and give back to the community according to the protocols it establishes. My voice can mean, but only with others: at times in chorus, but at the best of times in a dialogue."[4] Just as Bakhtin predicts that "every meaning will have its homecoming festival,"[5] so my empirical-evangelical antiphony brings home, recovers, diverse meanings. The poststructuralist venue of Bakhtinian dialogism, according to R. B. Kershner, seeks "knowledge" in "a form of relationship between or among different languages," and the "knowledge" won by my dialogue of the empirical with the evangelical reflects, if not precisely the "comic," as Bakhtin's experiential code would have it, then "joy and affirmation" through "energy, dynamism, and continuity in the heart of change" (Kershner's phrasing).[6] Just as Bakhtin is interested in "the spoken world of folk-consciousness," so also do Wesley, Edwards, Tennyson, and Emerson participate in that world.

Not much Bakhtinian "carnivalization," of course, inheres in my method, for I indulge in more "authoritative utterance" than "mockery, crowning and decrowning of fools, billingsgate, nonsense, and the degrading of everything held noble or holy" (Kershner's phrasing). The "carnival-

istic," however, not only undermines but also coexists with the "authoritative," and the coexistence of empiricism with evangelicalism, distinct from
any undermining of the one by the other, assures (after a struggle against
the possibility of such undermining) the abidingly rich, because fully experiential, authority shared by works of Wesley, Edwards, Tennyson, and
Emerson. James B. Twitchell's sufficiently Bakhtinian study of *Carnival
Culture* suggests that the carnivalistic and the authoritative are mutually
exclusive. Twitchell argues that "the vulgar is not 'the best that has been
thought and said' because it is too important to be thought and said";
thus he devalues the Arnoldian ideal of written art as the "high culture"
saying of thought.[7] Twitchell assumes, or seems to, that the images of tele-
vision conquer or obliterate, more than coexist with or undermine "high
culture." My concept of empiricism-cum-evangelicalism, by contrast, is
not without its Bakhtinian interplays, that is, its exchanges between high-
and low-culture force-fields.

The challenges thus exchanged between scientific method and experiential faith, that is, between substantive thought and spiritual desire, feed
into and benefit from natural-spiritual expressions by Wesley, Edwards,
Tennyson, and Emerson. All four include carnival touches within their
authoritative utterances. What is seen and heard is as important as what
is thought and written, but what is thought and written, though "recollected in tranquillity" (see Wordsworth's preface to *Lyrical Ballads*) and
positioned at a remove from point-blank immediacy, is as compellingly
experiential, as almost point-blank as what is seen and heard. What is seen
and heard, in turn, is not far from the "high culture" of belletristic form
and content, for even Jane Austen, as Twitchell admits, was originally a
"carnie." In the Wesleyan-Edwardsean, Tennysonian-Emersonian chronotope, at any rate, ideas/ideals of sensation operate along an experiential
continuum that joins what is naturally and spiritually seen and heard to
what is naturally and spiritually thought and written. While a given point
on this continuum can be so distant from another as to make the points
seem all but unrelated, the continuum's spiritual as well as natural integrity, its graceful as well as grace-like quality, remains sufficient for at
least these two diptychs of Anglo-American letters—if not for such other,
largely belletristic diptychs as Eliot/Melville and Browning/Dickinson—
to preserve their theistical and spiritually immediate world pictures intact.
Despite the "discontinuities" that make for ironic disparity, and despite

247

the specific strains and stresses in the composite voice of Tennyson and Emerson, this more lyrical than narrative/dramatic duo accomplishes theistical/spiritually immediate preservations, that is, grounded yet aspirant world pictures. The natural-spiritual breathing of the duo, perhaps only because of the still-popular precursor-diumvirate Wesley/Edwards, holds in abeyance any desperate whistling in the dark that would come later.

The "literariness" of the American Renaissance, according to David S. Reynolds, "resulted from the whole of the socioliterary context," that is, from not only "the sensational discourse of pornographers and of the penny press, fiction by and for women, and humor in almanacs and press" but also tracts and sermons "straightforwardly and sympathetically considered (and not rejected so much as assimilated and transformed)." "American writers," Reynolds continues, "followed a roughly similar career pattern of early experimentation with popular modes followed by self-conscious mixture of the modes, the stylization of the modes in highly complex literary texts, and sometimes in late career a recoil away from the purely literary toward other forms of expression."[8] In this connection one thinks of the similarly Bakhtinian synergism of professional learning and "dime-novel" lore in Umberto Eco's *Foucault's Pendulum* with its "papery honeycomb" of "Derrida-ism" and intellectual "cleverness" and its clear understandings that "life is represented better by bad music than by a Missa solemnis" and that "history is closer to what Sue narrates than to what Hegel projects."[9]

In the Bakhtinian connection, too, one thinks of the synergism of *les belles lettres* with *les bonnes lettres,* that is, of the illuminating juxtaposition of Tennyson/Emerson and their elite culture with Wesley/Edwards and their popular culture. Dialectically and antiphonally, if not synergistically, the "author-itative" figures of Tennyson and Emerson relate to the hardly less learned or literary but rather more carnivalistic figures of Wesley and Edwards, who, although hardly humorous, and although certainly not pornographic, are sufficiently comic or festive in their encouragements of spiritual autobiography, hymn-singing, mass-appeal religion, and, significantly, women.[10]

New historicism, the "cultural construction of texts, authors, and readers," is comparable to the "nominalism" of fourteenth-century scholasticism.[11] Both methodologies regard the particular as radically real. An affinity between particularists Tennyson and Emerson and new-historicist if not nominalist methodology naturally suggests itself. William of Ockham's determination to preserve "the prerogative of divine creative fiat (as opposed to emanation)" led him to apply his famous "razor" to empirical theorizing: "nothing should be assumed that does not need to be assumed in accounting for a particular fact at hand." [12] Like the great new-historicist guru/cultural anthropologist Clifford Geertz, new historicists do not appeal to human nature but rest content with "thick descriptions" of particular cultures. [13] Thus, despite Ockham's theological goals, ethics might seem to have no place in either new-historicist or nominalist-scholastic methodology. As John D. Cox puts it, "the sine qua non of ethical analysis and action is the recognition of generic continuity." "Two particular situations" must be understood as "the same *kind* of situation" if responsible action is to be carried over from one case into the other. [14]

Cox, applying his point to Paul de Man's early defense of Nazism, observes that "de Man's actions might well be defended as an instance of nominalist ethics. For radical nominalism would deny continuity between de Man's situation in the 1940s and his situation later in the United States: being radically particular situations, they admit of no comparison by which to evaluate de Man's action. Moreover, a radical nominalism might well deny that Paul de Man was the same agent in both places and could therefore be held morally accountable at Yale for what he did during World War II. Yet this is not how de Man wished to be seen himself." [15]

At the same time that new historicists "develop a sophisticated anthropological framework . . . intended to explain their moral commitments as culturally relative," they "accentuate" what Cox calls "the moral force of their analysis," that is, their liberal democratic values. Frederick Crews, among others, makes the similar point that, despite what they say, "social constructionists" actually subscribe to "a presumed state of nature," namely, the "politically correct position . . . guiltless of sexism, racism, [and] economic individualism." [16] Thus new historicists (among whom Cox counts himself) need to realize that they take an ethical position whether they want to or not; "committed we indeed are," declares Cox, "whether we like it or not, and we therefore need to give careful attention to the basis of our commitments and to what follows from them."

Since Tennyson and Emerson, despite their particularism, are under no illusion of being without an ethic, have no desire to be without one, and do not even think it possible to be without one, they lend themselves to the new-historical methodology of Cox. Their versions of Ockham's razor do not shave as closely as that razor shaves now, for like Ockham, Tennyson and Emerson were surrounded by what Cox calls "structures of belief that preserved the faithfulness of God as an essential element of theorizing." Ockham's razor "has now shorn away the creative faithfulness of God and indeed God himself, leaving to our worldly philosophizing an affirmation of the particular but nothing more." Cox thus yearns for a less efficient razor, one that would make even new historicists more akin to the believing, not exclusively particularist authors considered here.

The new-historicist search by Stephen Greenblatt for "insight into the half-hidden cultural transactions through which great works of art are empowered"[17] parallels my argument for the greatness of not just *les belles lettres* but even *les bonnes lettres,* that is, of not just Tennyson and Emerson but even Wesley and Edwards. My argument has emerged from the hardly point-blank but always propitious transactions between Wesley and Edwards on the one hand, and Tennyson and Emerson on the other. What Greenblatt calls the "shared codes" of culture informs my cultural poetics, too. But my notion of influence is especially particularist.

In the "void" between literary text and historical context, there is (according to Alan Liu) no " 'influence' (subject acting causally)"; instead, there is only "the marginalized and consciously figural intentionality underlying all New Historicist conceits of culture."[18] My "Old Historicist" conceit, by contrast, assumes an intentionality both consciously literal and finally central. Although "old historicists" have much to learn from new-historicist questions of revolutionary politics, the new-historical emphasis on "authority and subversive counterforces," and on "power and the abuse of power," is too narrow.[19] I harbor nostalgia for what I have sought to show, namely, the Anglo-American occurrence if not the general possibility of empirical-evangelical emphasis on "Holy Spirit" experientialism.

Because Liu is "embarrassed" at what he calls "the marginality of literary history now," he seeks to "change" his embarrassment into "special bravura: a thrown-glove *why not?* " He explains that "even when a New Historicist study internalizes a paradigm as its centerpiece rather than its opening, the paradigm retains a throw-away quality": "Serendipitous and adventitious—always merely found, always merely picked up—these models compose a *bricolage* substituting for what was once more methodical *narratio* or presentation of facts in history of ideas. . . . The Paradigms of the New Historicism bare a shy rashness, a supremely cavalier *why not?*

assertive of their marginality."[20] Perhaps a "thrown-glove *why not?*" moti-vates my clinging to philosophical theology. While I have acquired enough new-historical sophistication to be assertive, if not rash and cavalier, I in-sist, however, on retaining the intellectual-historical *narratio*. (One might bristle at Greenblatt's knowing dismissal of the "conventional pieties" of "source study," since liberal-democratic "pieties" influence his method.[21])

New historicism and my view of Tennyson and Emerson attempt to highlight the problematic relationship between culture and text. "A New Historicist paradigm," Liu declares, "holds up to view a historical context on one side, a literary text on the other, and, in between, a connection of pure nothing." This is "not far removed at base from the etymological wordplay of deconstruction," for "as deconstructive 'catachresis' is to refer-ence, so subversion [in texts] is to power [in culture]."[22] Edward Pechter accuses new historicists of making the text "unambiguously dependent" on its "ideological and historical situation"; culture in new historicism, accord-ing to Pechter, is a much too "unambiguously determining . . . stable point of reference."[23] My empirical-evangelical paradigm holds up a Wesleyan-Edwardsean context on one side, texts by Tennyson and Emerson on the other, and, in between, a connection of achieved mutuality. Greenblatt, describing the relation between ideology and text as "a subtle, elusive set of exchanges, a network of trades and trade-offs, a jostling of competing rep-resentations, a negotiation between joint-stock companies,"[24] parallels my conception of the relation between Wesley and Edwards on the one hand and Tennyson and Emerson on the other. "Negotiation" and "competing representations," however, do not come as near describing this relationship as "trade-offs," "trades," and "exchanges" do.

Deconstruction, quite apart from the debate over Paul de Man's out-spoken advocacy of fascism during the Nazi occupation of Belgium,[25] is on the defensive just now. There is growing impatience with and opposition to it. The Eighteenth Alabama Symposium on English and American Litera-ture, for example, held at the University of Alabama on October 1–3, 1992, weighed in against one or another flaw in deconstructive theory; M. H. Abrams, Frederick Crews, Ihab Hassan, Nina Baym, John Searle, David Lehman, and others participated in "The Emperor Redressed: Critiquing Critical Theory."

The distinction between hard- and soft-core deconstruction in David Lehman's *Signs of the Times: Deconstruction and the Fall of Paul de Man* parallels my own distinction between deconstruction as abstract theory/ideology and deconstruction as method. Lehman writes:

> By hard-core deconstruction I mean precisely the academic orthodoxy associated with de Man and his disciples. It is "hard" in the sense of being putatively rigorous (or rigid, depending on your viewpoint) and defiantly difficult to follow. It is programmatic. It asks to be taken as something more than a critical method—something like an antitheological theology. By contrast, soft-core deconstruction is an elastic critical concept and is meant to be used with a lighter touch; a synonym might be "practical" or "applied" deconstruction. It differs from hard-core deconstruction in having a strictly provisional value and an utterly pragmatic function; its use does not imply the critic's subscription to deconstructive doctrine in any larger sense. Soft-core deconstruction may serve to describe virtually any form of critical interpretation that is concerned with the tricky relations between language and meaning, between what is said and what is hidden, in a text. It refuses the mandatory trip to the linguistic abyss but retains the sense of deconstruction as a devastating critique, an expose, an unmasking—what the journalist is getting at in describing the effect of Lloyd Bentsen's showstopping line in his vice-presidential debate with Dan Quayle. Finally, soft-core deconstruction in this broad sense eschews the idea that reality is "inexpressible and incommunicable" but retains the deconstructive alertness to conundrums, logical contradictions, enigmas, and ironic reversals.[26]

Lehman, in his quotation of Philip K. Dick's novel *Valis* (1981), implies a "soft-core," lighthearted deconstruction of deconstruction itself; Dick, Lehman points out, writes the same sentence two ways: "GOD IS NO WHERE./GOD IS NOW HERE."

On the perhaps too diverse bases of rationalistic logic and skeptical empiricism, John M. Ellis exposes Derrida's "inflexibility and prejudgment" amid his only apparent "subversion" of tradition and authority. Ellis, denigrating the issue of logocentrism, points out how philosophers have long known that categories of meaning are not independent of language. Ellis scores an intriguing double hit: first, Derrida's "writing precedes speech" grants priority to "high" culture and is thus ethnocentric; and second, deconstruction's rhetoric of repression, liberation, and enslavement has more to do with a crusade than with logical debate and so is not as scientific as it claims.[27]

Especially unkindly treated, because of its supposed predictability and clichés (for example, "all perception is already experienced as signs"), is the deconstructionist, latest phase of J. Hillis Miller's remarkably adaptive career.[28] Miller declares that "I'm still looking for and would be glad to find some solid ground to stand on,"[29] but theologian-critic David Jasper entertains little hope of finding solid ground in Miller's work. Jasper judges Miller's predictably Derridean position as inferior to the aggressively non-Derridean yet sufficiently rigorous stance of Paul Ricoeur:

> In a much publicized recent debate (TLS October 9–15, 1987, pp. 1104–5) J. Hillis Miller argued against Paul Ricoeur that "there is no such thing" as "experience of being in the world and in time prior to language." But what Miller . . . regard[s] as axiomatic is denied by Ricoeur's insistence on the ontological foundation of language—that there is an "outside-the-text" to which language refers.[30]

Irving Massey, attacking Miller for slipups and inconsistencies, notices that Miller goes against his own axiom, Derridean in origin, that there is nothing outside language; Miller, Massey points out, argues not only that the "something liberated" by a William Carlos Williams poem is "beyond or between the words," but also that Williams's imagination is "a natural force that goes beyond nature."[31]

Perhaps the most courageously personal attack on deconstruction in recent years is Brian McCrea's *Addison and Steele Are Dead: The English Department, Its Canon, and the Professionalization of Literary Criticism*. Not only does McCrea show in detail how the "techniques of clarity" practiced by Addison and Steele make them "the loudest voices of eighteenth-century culture"; he also links the stilling of their voices with the rise of the special, decidedly nonpublic languages and techniques of modern critical theory. Derrida, according to McCrea, is neither good nor bad so much as inevitable in the current context of professionalization. Derridean neologisms, for example, are indispensable for the autonomy and hence the power of English studies. Though aware that "theorists, critics, and scholars all profit within the common enterprise," McCrea laments that we have lost "the ability to treat literature as a public, moral, emotional phenomenon." This lament is the opposite of dry, academic writing. McCrea is requisitely judicious: "The turn to theory, older professors need to understand, is a sign of strength, not of weakness or heresy," he observes, and he adds that "younger professors need to understand that the turn to theory can come only after a field has become institutionalized and professionalized, only after, in the case of criticism, men from [William Lyon] Phelps to [William K.] Wimsatt won a place for the English department in the university." But McCrea does not duck the question of value, that is, of whether Derrida *should* be inevitable: "Will we allow authors their signs," he asks, "or will we ingeniously prove that all those signs are 'without truth present'?" He answers his own question; he will enter "the community that gives value to the sign."[32]

McCrea finds appeal in the Slavic-linguistic "we own meaning" as distinct from the intentionalist "I own meaning" or the Derridean "no one owns meaning."[33] This does not mean that he will end up using such "we own meaning" portmanteau-words as heteroglossia, chronotope, and dialogism. Indeed, by way of indicating the refreshing if idiosyncratic direction of his work, he ends his book by asking, forthrightly, "How dare Nietzsche tell me that the signs of love I shared with my grandfathers were empty?"

Thus, along with such an Addison- and Steele-like essayist as Samuel Pickering, McCrea will make English studies accessible and public once again. Kevin L. Cope calls McCrea's *Addison and Steele Are Dead* "the most conscience-piquing book of this decade" and adds that it "offers a whiff of moralized air in the deodorized rooms of modern academe."[34] Pickering, besides being a scholar of children's literature and a specialist in nineteenth-century fiction, is the real-life hero of *Dead Poets Society* and the near-sole reviver of the familiar essay for our time.[35] Pickering the movie inspiration and Pickering the essayist may well make Pickering the scholar even better known, but his *John Locke and Children's Books in Eighteenth-Century England* has enjoyed the honor of a second printing.

Daniel T. Jenkins and Donald Davie, in *Literature and Theology*, offer their especially pertinent second thoughts about deconstruction.[36] In a bold exchange of views, they confront the challenge posed by deconstruction to Protestant faith in general and Protestant aesthetics in particular. Jenkins, identifying simplicity, sincerity, and purity as hallmarks of "Puritan style," remembers that no less a Protestant than Kierkegaard believes that "purity of heart is to will one thing":

Seeing things steadily and seeing them whole, we have no need for
covering things up, either by deviousness and guile or by elaborate
surface decoration which may possibly conceal defects. "Everything
is what it is and not some other thing" may have been said by an
Anglican bishop but it was no accident that he was educated in a
Dissenting academy in Isaac Watts's time. Having courage through
justification by faith to submit our inward parts to scrutiny by the
light of truth, we can dare to let our yea be yea and our nay be nay.[37]

Jenkins has in mind Anglican bishop and some time Presbyterian Joseph
Butler, who preached that "Things and Actions are what they are, and the
Consequences of them will be what they will be: Why then should we
desire to be deceived? As we are reasonable Creatures, and have any Regard
to ourselves, we ought to lay these Things plainly and honestly before our
Mind, and upon this, act as you please, as you think most fit; make that
Choice and prefer that Course of Life, which you can justify to yourselves,
and which fits most easy upon your own Mind."[38]

Davie, rather than just holding up his end of the debate and "making
whatever concessions are called for," responds by pushing some of Jenkins's
points "a little further":

What Daniel Jenkins does not care to bring out is that at the present
time most if not all influential students of language declare this [i.e.,
the belief that "we can dare to let our yea be yea and our nay be nay"]
to be an impossibility, based on an unacceptably naive understanding of how language works—in particular, on a failure to understand
how our language uses us, more than we use it. The deservedly well-
regarded poet Geoffrey Hill has an essay, "Our Word Is Our Bond,"
which argues—so far as I understand it, for it is dense and difficult—that our word never *can* be our bond, since it is not in the
nature of language to be thus in the service of any one speaker's inten-
tions. The authorities that Geoffrey Hill cites and draws on for this
view are mostly English. But far more generally influential among
us are certain French thinkers who, as disseminated among us by
their translators and epigones, may be called "the gurus of *franglais*."
They are many, but the names most often genuflected to are those
of Jacques Lacan, Jacques Derrida, and Michel Foucault. They differ widely among themselves. But they speak with one voice when

they tell us that we do not command language, because language commands us; that our yea can never be yea, nor our nay be nay, because our language—whether English or French or whatever other—mutinously refuses to be thus univocal.[39]

"Nay," to be sure, is used to "express negation, dissent, denial, or refusal," but the word is also "occasionally used as an introductory word, without any direct negation; used to introduce a more correct, precise, or emphatic statement than the one first made" (*Oxford English Dictionary*). Not even psychologically and actually Protestant Emily Dickinson finds it simple to let her nay be nay:

> "Nature" is what we see—
> The Hill—the Afternoon—
> Squirrel—Eclipse—the Bumble bee—
> Nay—Nature is Heaven—
> Nature is what we hear—
> The Bobolink—the Sea—
> Thunder—the Cricket—
> Nay—Nature is Harmony—
> Nature is what we know—
> Yet have no art to say—
> So impotent our Wisdom is
> To her Simplicity.
> (number 668)[40]

The Protestant goal of simplicity is Emily Dickinson's goal too, but do the "nays" of lines 4 and 8 negate, or do they emphasize, lines 1–3 and lines 5–7? The poem finally achieves a simplicity, namely, the radical interidentification of the physical senses with the spiritual sense. The language of the poem, however, does not lose sight of the gulf between nature and spirit, for although Emily Dickinson's nay is indeed nay, her nay is nay with a distinct awareness of the complex difference between mere univocity and precise gradations of meaning. Her nay is not so much the everlasting nay of Thomas Carlyle as it is the oddly affirmative, more ordained than contingent nay of slant truth-telling.

Casting about for a French thinker "whom English Protestants cannot afford to ignore," Davie comes up with Jacques Ellul, who writes that "for our society and our epoch" and "for our intellectual or bourgeois groups" (whom Jenkins wittily calls "lumpen-intelligentsia"), Derrida, Lacan, and Foucault are correct; but this is "a sociological observation rather than something linguistic or psychoanalytic." Ellul, as quoted by Davie, sustains impassioned thought:

> In our day, in this place, a sort of social discourse flows endlessly and is repeated twenty hours out of every twenty-four, expressed by individual mouths. The discourse is completely anonymous, even though it may sometimes be affirmed with force and conviction by a particular individual. . . . The word has become anonymous and therefore has no importance, since its only reality involved the meaning of two living persons who needed to know and recognize each other and to exchange something. Words are just wind. They pass by and have no importance: as long as no one puts the weight of his entire life behind the word he speaks, how can one take one statement more seriously than any other? The rupture between the speaker and his words is the decisive break. If a person is not behind his words, it is mere noise.[41]

Ellul's statement in its implications for authors compares with George Steiner's with regard to readers. Steiner, eloquently calling on the reader to "read as if" the text has meaning, employs the fullest extent of intuition and moral imagination: "If we wish to meet the challenge of autistic textuality or, more accurately, 'anti-textuality' on grounds as radical as its own, we must bring to bear on the act of meaning, the full force of moral intuition. The vitally concentrated agencies are those of tact, of courtesy of heart, of good taste, in a sense not decorous or civil, but inward and ethical. Such focus and agencies cannot be logically formalized. They are existential modes. Their underwriting is . . . of a transcendental kind. This makes them utterly vulnerable. But also 'of the essence,' this is to say, essential."[42] Distracted by "poststructuralist textuality," "the theoretical suppositions of reading and writing," and "issues of undecidability and play," the literary establishment is anything but interested, perhaps, in such issues as value-laden judgment and choice,[43] but change is at hand.

Davie casts about again, and comes up with the British-Protestant poet Basil Bunting, who places his modest yea and nay here and there among his Protestant verse forms. Thus Bunting preserves what Davie regards as the salutary heritage of Protestant antiorder; dissent, or the slogan that

"God is the dividing sword," is Bunting's watchword (quoted by Davie). One need not look so far afield as Bunting, however, for Protestant-like and simple but intellectually rigorous and anything but simple-minded authors who reveal that word is bond and yea yea, not because language is univocal—it is multilayered—but—with apologies to Derrida and in line with Locke as well as the Bible—because it is referential. One need look no further for such authors than the familiar Wesley, Edwards, Tennyson, and Emerson.

My method of criticism, then, unlike Derrida's theory, upholds tradition, authorship (if not authority), and reasoning of a flexibly sense-based, a posteriori kind. I am not so much interested in language-centered subversion of meaning as I am intent on nature- and spirit-grounded proliferation of meaning. Along my continuum from Wesley and Edwards to Tennyson and Emerson I include a perhaps ethnocentric but decidedly nonelitist element of "low" culture. While I claim no scientific basis for the liberating qualities of empirical-evangelical methodology, I include science along with religion in my debate as well as crusade. Creatures of reason as well as belief can avoid debates no more than crusades.

The ground of experience is a sufficiently solid basis on which to read works that might not otherwise coinhere. Tennyson and Emerson hold to preverbal or even nonverbal experience, but since they regard language also as experience, they link words to sense perception and the spiritual sense. The particular but public languages and techniques of empirical-evangelical method make Wesley, Edwards, Tennyson, and Emerson among the loudest, clearest voices of eighteenth- and nineteenth-century England and America. The truest power and autonomy of English studies can come from recognizing these particular, public voices as moral and emotional phenomena.

Thus, if we allow that the "signs" of Tennyson and Emerson entertain a "truth present," we can counterbalance the Derridean "no one owns meaning" with the intentionalist "I own meaning" and the Slavic-linguistic, if not new historicist, "we own meaning." Methodologically rigorous as well as (refreshingly?) idiosyncratic, we can revive the humanity if not the humanism of English studies. We can cast a wide net once again.

The simplicity, sincerity, and purity of Tennyson's and Emerson's styles are owing not just to their Protestant but also to their empirical-evangelical aesthetic. Without being univocal and, indeed, while exemplifying playful irony, they "will one thing" in that their minds and hearts encounter objects of a spiritual as well as natural kind. Their unembellished, lucid, and revealing styles yield more than one meaning, but these meanings are discoverable, if not straightforward, and interrelatable, if not synthesizable. If their yeas are not yeas and their nays not nays, if their understandings of how language works are anything but naive, their spiritual as well as natural lives are sufficiently behind their words to preserve their empirical-evangelical intentionalities intact.

Their Anglo-American, distinct from Slavic/French, understandings of language evince all the force and conviction of their particular individualities. Sufficiently in control of their languages, putting the weight of their lives behind the words they speak, they evince more than Arnoldian, because capaciously empirical-evangelical, "high seriousness." Their works, without being merely chaotic, are sufficiently pluralistic in tone and point of view to avoid the closure of too much order. I hasten to emphasize, notwithstanding these demurrers to deconstruction as theory, that deconstruction as method is much more "constructive" than Davie, Jenkins, McCrea, Massey, and Ellis seem to think.

Miller, by speaking philosophically and theologically of what language points to, avoids, if only unintentionally, deconstruction's formalistic excess. A personal statement made by Miller at the University of Florida Convocation, September 18, 1992, identifies the two chief reference points of his life as science and religion. In some ways this statement is as surprising as Georgi (formerly Eduard) Shevardnadze's recent conversion to Greek Orthodoxy, for, without exactly being a palinode, the statement smacks of method more than theory.[44] In Miller's hands the procedure of deconstructive poststructuralism proves especially supple.

"Thinking Like Other People," the title of Miller's statement, responds specifically to the question, "How can Miller so admire Matthew Arnold?" What can the Victorian inspector of the English public schools, who seems to epitomize a conservative advocacy for Western European tradition as "the best which has been thought and said in the world," have to do with Miller? Miller, after all, promotes a radical critical method that uncovers contradictions and gaps in the texts of Western European literature. He advocates a reformed curriculum. Miller confesses that his Protestant upbringing taught him to search out answers for himself, to eschew commentaries and translations in favor of earning his own interpretations of original texts; and his training in physics, describing data with detailed precision, helped him "explain" anomalies in nature. Maintaining these scientific/Protestant standards of judgment, even as he faces powerful and uncanny passages in literature, he finds that Matthew Arnold, as much as Empson, Burke, Poulet, Derrida, and de Man, maintains such standards. If Arnold does not exactly scrutinize disorientations, disruptions, discrepancies, conflicts, and contradictions, he nonetheless exemplifies rigorous/ "scientific" and reverential/"religious" methodologies. He honors tradition and reveres powerful touchstones.

If one consequence of Derridean method is that "the rationality and authoritativeness of the book are out," a more positive consequence is that we "surrender voluptuously" to the "surfaces of language" and "joyously collaborate" with its anarchy to "start semantic hares running in all directions."[45] Philosophical/theological as well as literary readers of Derrida may think of themselves as starting *conceptual* hares running in all directions. Deconstruction has been useful to religious thinkers whose ontological commitments, reminiscent of Ricoeur's to language, only *seem* inimical to Derrida. William G. Doty, Charles Winquist, Thomas J. J. Altizer, Mark C. Taylor, Garrett Green, John C. Sherwood, G. Douglas Atkins, Clarence Walhout, Robert Detweiler, and Wesley A. Kort, among others, are critics/theologians who either make deconstruction compatible with religion or downright Christianize it.[46] Derrida, in Jasper's view, "never denies that there is, in a sense, a centre," for Derrida not only completes the Nietzschean project but also "suggests a new project, described by Frank Lentricchia as 'to uncover the nonontological reincarnation of the signifier within cultural matrices which . . . in their moment of power, use the signifier, take hold of it, establish dominance over it in order to create truth, value and rationality.'"[47] Jasper is irritated at Don Cupitt, who, more in the *mold* of Derrida than genuinely *like* him, is merely "a good old-fashioned poststructuralist" (Jasper's phrase) lacking in Derrida's complexity and subtlety.

We have learned much from the "gurus of *franglais.*" I can well understand the antideconstructionist meditation of Alison Lurie who, as a creative writer or, in poststructuralist parlance, mere dead author, has every right to be shaken at being written out of existence. "Appropriately," she writes, "the texts studied by deconstructionist critics are approached without interest in their particular authors, as if they were the work of either an ignorant artisan or an anonymous arachnid." [48] Derrida himself, however, is not especially de-author-izing; neither are the best of his epigones.

Consider, for example, the intriguing, especially pertinent case of Gregory L. Ulmer. For him, Derridean grammatology exceeds the linear teleology of "the Book" in order to be "pictographic (related to hieroglyphics)" and "homonymic (related to the signature effect of the author who unconsciously signs himself or herself in a particular work)." [49] Ulmer reminds us that puns and wordplays reveal the authorial unconscious; although "the anecdote inscribed in a theoretical text" is told "not in reference to a prior life, but as part of a 'speculative' structure—the *mise en abyme*—a double take in which the narrative development of the event has formal, conceptual, explanatory consequences," Ulmer is ultimately interested in "outlining the place of the idiosyncratic individual in a generalizable discourse formation." [50] Thus the methodologically Derridean Ulmer, who conceives, after all, of "*applied* grammatology," [51] cultivates the authorship, the homonymic signature-effects, and the life-inscriptions of the *critic*.

The very least that I can learn from Ulmer, therefore, is to read myself into, in, and out of my own criticism. Although any Ulmer-esque "mystory" (Ulmer's neologism) demands a more than George Steiner–like tact, the "mystories" of Miller and McCrea (as well as that of Ulmer) exemplify great tact. I go ahead, in any case, and run the risk (in today's self-conscious critical climate) of tactless self-indulgence. [52] My story may be more *heimlich* than *unheimlich,* and humorless self-importance is not forgivable even at tetralogy's end, but those who blush at the bare possibility of shameless navel gazing in the following statement may "stop here, or gently pass." [53]

If my critical cadenza is too idiosyncratic, it is at least justifiably testimonial, for a favorite way of speaking and writing among Locke, Wesley, Edwards, Tennyson, and Emerson is their quasi-coordinated experiential testimony. Their testimony cries out to be emulated in any study of them. Witness the analogy of psychoanalytic critics who report the results of their personal therapy sessions. On July 14, 1990, at a family reunion near the First Methodist Church of Millen, Georgia, I discovered four generations of Waldo Emerson Brantleys. It is because of my genes that Emerson is the first American of whom I would write. The combination of empiricism with evangelicalism is my birthright. My fascination with what is difficult about this topic is understandable on the Anglo-American ground of an

Anglo-Saxon branch of Brantleys who include such educators in science and religion as my father, my mother, and my brother. Another part of my homonymic reference, perhaps, is the unconscious operation of a symmetry among 1703, the year of Wesley's and Edwards's births, 1803, the year of Emerson's birth, 1903, the year of my father's birth, 1809, the year of Tennyson's birth, and 1909, the year of my mother's birth.

For purposes of illustrating the philosophical, religious, and literary implications of the characteristic form of my writing, I dip, at random, into my chapter on Emerson (I add bracketed indications of the characteristic structure): "Indeed, the skepticism of Emerson's perception-crisis is matched by his dim view [a] of experience in general [b]. Far from relying on experience as the best means of knowing what is true whether naturally or spiritually [b], he announces that ' 'Tis the trick of nature . . . to degrade today' (943), that experience is unimportantly ineffectual" (a). This passage reflects my conscious assumption that even the admittedly self-reflexive practice of bibliomancy, like all other experience, is, if not providential, far from capricious, and is more than conceivably synchronous, serendipitous, and, while not exactly self-similar according to the predilections/predictions of chaos theory,[54] reliably forthcoming. The passage illustrates for purposes of relating my form to my content and *vice versa* the chiasmus or abba structure employed throughout much of this book and all of *Locke, Wesley, and the Method of English Romanticism*. (*Wordsworth's "Natural Methodism"* and *Coordinates of Anglo-American Romanticism* are constructed according to the abab form of parallelism.) The letter chi (X), after all, implies the intercrossing or bridging of empiricism and evangelicalism, and, consistent with the principle that the near influence is always telling even when one is not fully aware of the fact, I reveal how the trope of chiasmus, as distinct from catachresis and *mise en abyme*, pervades not only much modish academic writing but also, mutatis mutandis, my writing.

Syntagms repeated in reverse order—John Mitchell's "when the going gets tough, the tough get going," John F. Kennedy's "ask not what your country can do for you; ask what you can do for your country," and Mae West's "it's not the men in my life, it's the life in my men"—offer what Thomas Mermall calls "a wide range of semantic possibilities."[55] The combination of Winston Churchill's "tears, sweat, and blood" with the folk-"improved" version, "blood, sweat, and tears," constitutes composite chiasmus with especially complex provenance. "The No to Nothing and the Nothing to Know" and "The Being of God when God Is Not Being God" constitute especially droll representatives of this rhetorical obliquity.[56] One finds it not only in new historicism but also in Derridean-theological studies of Karl Barth and Paul Tillich and in various applications of Paul Ricoeur's hermeneutic circle: "Believe in order to understand; understand in order to believe."[57] Almost as a reversal of Ricoeur's chiasmus, Wesley's career follows his own chiasmus, in effect, "understand in order to believe; believe in order to understand." His intense study of Locke (as I have argued) precedes and seems to affect his conversion, which, in turn, deepens his understanding of Locke.

Mermall, with the help of Rosalie Colie and Ernest B. Gilman,[58] traces the history of chiastic usage, a brief rehearsal of which pertains not only to the structure but also to the argument of this book. For Augustine, Montaigne, Pascal, and Kierkegaard the "contradictions" generated by chiasmus find "some ultimate resolution" (Mermall, 247). The baroque artist, through this trope, is what Gilman calls a "rational amphibian" who, "by wedging opposing perspectives into a single image," is "partially able" to "repair the split suffered by the Fall" and even to "approximate the unity of the divine mind."[59] Mermall himself links chiasmus to the always unresolvedly paradoxical imagination of both Modernism and Postmodernism. Miguel de Unamuno and Octavio Paz pioneered the commonplaces of Postmodernist idiom; Paz defines "the spirit of modernity" as "the self-destructive creativity by which post-Hegelian reason, having renounced its metaphysical ambitions, thrives on the contradictions generated by a relentless self-criticism of its foundations." "Absent" from the "agonistic paradox" of Unamuno's chiastic practice are "balance, resolution, and ultimate belief," for Unamuno, according to Mermall, "relies on the chiasmus to avoid closure, sustain tension, dissociate terms, undermine identities, generate perpetual contradiction, and affirm the eternal struggles between reason and faith, the self and the other, appearance and reality." Thus chiasmus allows Unamuno "to be all things and rest in none, to say yes and no simultaneously to momentous existential and moral questions." Unlike his "religiously disposed predecessors," who used chiasmus "within the boundaries of some kind of metaphysical serenity," Unamuno "risked touching the border of the abyss."

Although the leisured reader desirous of contemplating calculated chiasmus may practice bibliomancy on either this volume or *Locke, Wesley, and the Method of English Romanticism*, my chiasmus is more paratheoretical or neomethodological than theoretical. It is intended to pioneer post-Postmodernist usage. Although I share the "Master Trope" of Unamuno, my chiasmus has to do with the political if not intellectual climate of optimism at the present time. I write this in December 1992, when, even for prospects of economic health in the United States—a country obsessed at times by its apparent loss of a George C. Marshall type of leadership in the world—one finds optimism expressed.[60] Chiasmus need not have to do with pessimism but may promisingly consist in a "complex play on words in which dissociation and punning yield a richer meaning" (Mermall, 247). Mermall adds that the chiasmus of denotation consists simply in a "reversal, without a significant shift in meaning of the key word" or concept. Even "in these bad days"[61] of residual Postmodernist paralysis, I hark back to Kierkegaardian if not Renaissance chiasmus, which can be the means of achieving balance and of renewing resolution and ultimate belief.

In December 1989 Dan Rather described events in Eastern Europe as the post-Hegelian, post-dialectical end of history, for he had read (or heard about) Francis Fukuyama's piece in the *National Interest* of September 1989.[62] I still expect, however, the dialectic of empiricism with evangelicalism, for chiasmus is "an incipient form of . . . dialectic" that does not so much "check progressive movement toward a resolution of the contraries it generates" as enhance that very movement (Mermall). The second "a" of abba, after all, need not come full circle or effect closure so much as recapitulate prior to setting off again. Although ontogeny recapitulates phylogeny, evolution proceeds, if only by "punctuated equilibrium," and the chiasmus of incremental recapitulation similarly leads to "fresh woods, and pastures new,"[63] itself a chiasmus of the Protestant type to which I aspire and which I reinvent. Far from renouncing, like Unamuno, the dialectical "ambition" of chiasmus, and indeed by way of attempting to succeed the "rigorous" frivolity of Postmodernist chiasmus, I revive that very ambition.

Irving Massey, as long ago as 1985, complained that chiasmus formed part of the even then cliché-ridden "hardened orthodoxy" of Postmodernism.[64] If my chiasmus should seem to reflect the narcissism of small differences from other types of chiasmus or, worse, a still too predictable

formalistic excess, the self-conscious preoccupation of my formalism is as
nothing compared to the especially rigid form imposed by Vaclav Havel's
prison warden on his letter writing from jail.[65] Yet look how *his* deep
word changed his world! A contrasting because less life-related (and perhaps, therefore, more typical) formalism of our times is to be found in the
ingenious but "ludicrously programmatic" novel by Walter Abish, *Alphabetical Africa*; "the adventure Mr. Abish has set himself," observes John
Updike, "is to compose a novel of twice twenty-six chapters, of which the
first employs only words beginning with 'A,' the second words beginning
'A' and 'B,' and so on up to 'Z,' by which time the full lexical possibilities
of the English language are available; then, from 'Z' to 'A,' he moves back
down the alphabet, subtracting letters one by one until the last chapter,
like the first, is composed entirely of words beginning with 'A' "—N.B. the
highly chiastic structure of Abish's "adventure"! Updike quotes a passage
from Abish's first chapter: "Africa again: antelopes, alligators, ants and
attractive Alva, are arousing all angular Africans, also arousing author's
analytically aggressive anticipations, again and again. Anyhow author anticipates Alva anatomically, affirmatively, and also accurately." Even here,
as Updike admits, is a certain verisimilitude, a "nice rightness" of Abish's
work, for in Africa, "incantations are still potent and national boundaries
slice across tribal realities as arbitrarily as the alphabet schematizes language."[66] In my admittedly formalistically intense chiasmus of incremental
recapitulation, similarly, is the hint of a purposive because spiritual (as
well as material) dialectic to be found even now. My version of "believe in
order to understand; understand in order to believe" is "empiricism before
evangelicalism = evangelicalism with a difference."[67]

Having said a personal word, then, about the religious as well as
philosophico-literary implications of my writing form, I now give a personal word about theology. What Leonard I. Sweet calls "the maturation of
evangelical historiography" is an instance of what he calls "the phenomenon of observer-participant history." To the extent that I exemplify such
maturation, I practice such history. The new evangelicalism is defined by
Sweet as the "third force" between fundamentalism and liberalism and as
the restorer of the "didactic" to the academy "through a new version of
history as moral discourse." The early family lives of those who espouse the
new evangelicalism gave rise to that evangelicalism. Joel Carpenter, Harry

Stout, Nathan Hatch, George Marsden, Mark Noll, and Grant Wacker were all nurtured on "truths of divine whisperings, tools of biblical literacy, and techniques of doctrinal discussion," and Sweet adds that

> They all knelt at family altars. They were put to bed not just with once-upon-a-time stories, but with once-before-time Bible readings and once-in-time family prayers. Their home environments were heady with theological inquiry and heavy with moralism, a powerful combination that has spurred intellectual endeavor and creativity throughout history and has even spawned households of children driven to become intellectuals (e.g. the Wesleys and the Edwardses).[68]

What Sweet calls the "critical history" of the new-evangelical historiographers is based on their "inside-out immersion" in both the old and the new evangelical traditions. My "critical history," too, is thus grounded; I share enough of this background to be able to offer an observer-participant contribution to evangelical historiography.

I also offer, however, a philosophico-literary contribution. Is it too much to say, with Sweet, that "by posing critical distance and objective detachment from one's field of study, scientific scholarship and scientific history have led the way down terrible paths toward Auschwitz, Bangladesh, Chernobyl, Dresden, etc."? Perhaps. But with Sweet and other new-evangelical academicians, I say that since any past, "however relativized by history," remains "real and active in the present," observer-participant history need make no apologies for itself as a tool of knowing. Although I am not exactly prompted as Sweet says the new-evangelical historians are to fulfill Lucien Febvre's dictum that historians be "like the ogre in the fairy tale: roused when sniffing the scent of human flesh,"[69] the ideas I have here pursued are sufficiently *embodied* in Wesley, Edwards, Tennyson, and Emerson. This is not only because the "epistemology" of this quartet-in-letters is Lockean and therefore either sense-based or sense-oriented but also because my evangelical background (like the backgrounds of Carpenter, Stout, Hatch, Marsden, Noll, Wacker, and Sweet) gives me an eye for theology-in-persons.

New-evangelical historiography, says Sweet, is a form of *Vergangenheitsbewältigung*, defined by Sweet as "coming to terms with *and overcoming* the past by recognizing oneself as a product of the past and by mastering the history of one's own past." I underline an element of the definition not finally true, perhaps, either for what new-evangelical historians do or for what I do. One does not ever quite overcome the past. Nor does one necessarily find it entirely desirable to do so. But since "the best attacks are inside jobs," Grant Wacker's early theological rebellion makes him what Sweet calls "best able to point out the ironic and comic in fundamentalism's iconic astringencies." Sweet enjoys overcoming his own past:

> Evangelical historians' *Vergangenheitsbewältigung* is with a fundamentalist movement that, thinly scarfed in tradition, went forth to battle the elements of modernity; that explicitly denied that it was shaped by a cultural context . . .; that in varying degrees has embarrassed them, both by its anti-intellectualism and by its unfair share of leaders who, on the tracks of their souls, were creeps.

Finally, however, both Sweet and other new-evangelical historians variously refer to their methods and tones as (1) "believing criticism, . . . wise as serpents with respect to the world of thought, . . . innocent as doves with respect to the gospel" (Noll), (2) "critical perspectives . . . on traditions that [we] take seriously" (Marsden), (3) exemplifications of "both the true confessions of faith and the highest canons of critical scholarship" (Sweet), and (4) mediations "between faith and criticism" (Noll).

This betweenness, this liminality, may describe my stance even better than theirs. While Carpenter has moved from the independent Baptist faith to orthodox Presbyterianism, while Hatch has moved from the southern Presbyterian church to the Christian reformed, and while Wacker has moved from the Assemblies of God to the United Methodist Church, I am, as yet, hovering, with no little wistfulness at their having arrived, between the Southern Baptist Church in which I was brought up and United Methodism, toward which my research tends. Bill and Hillary Clinton have pulled off, between them, this very combination of denominational allegiances!

Ultimately, perhaps, one belongs to the uhr-Protestant "church" of Milton's Abdiel, who formed a sect of one. Although attracted to Arminianism in Wesley, Tennyson, and Emerson (Edwards implies it only in his most Lockean moments), I am not yet ready or willing (any more than Wesley, Tennyson, and Emerson are quite able) to throw off the Calvinism of youth. A thin scarf of Calvinism clothes the dominant, domineering fundamentalist faction of today's Southern Baptist Church. The minority moderates of this church, as none other than Harold Bloom has recently reminded us, are all that is left of whom Bloom admires, namely, the "soul-competent," Arminian as well as Calvinist descendants of Southern Baptist founder E. Y. Mullins.[70] "Infant damnation," of course, is hardly the appealing doctrine it was! But Calvinism might continue to appeal to those who find it well stated not just by Edwards but even sometimes by Wesley, Tennyson, and Emerson. It offers, at a minimum, an especially tough-minded explanation of the presence and power of evil.

I can sympathize with the need of Harry Crews to be close to but not in the Georgia he fictionalizes, but there is no need to be as far away from one's subject matter as Joyce got from Dublin. I am not necessarily committed to liminality.[71] There is a world of difference, after all, between May 23, 1738, when Wesley's heart was presumably chilly, and May 24, when it "strangely warmed." With something of Locke's subject-object spirit, then, I seek, even now, coalescences and interpenetrations of Arminianism with Calvinism. I do not wish, through invidious comparisons, to set one of these doctrinal systems over against the other. I do not abandon "both/ and" logic. Precisely consistent with my hope of experience, I cultivate the present's simultaneous deepening of the past, with its "always already" Calvinist dimensions, and promising of the future, with its Arminian as well as Lockean emphases on nurture, education, and choice.

Thus, while I greatly admire Leonard I. Sweet's emphasis on the need among "New Light" Christians to adopt a more than merely "common sense," because quite "quantum," attitude toward the relationship between scientific ethos and Christian mythos,[72] I share something of Bishop Berkeley's Lockean desire to prevent philosophical-theological knowledge from becoming the purview only of those in the Newtonian know. My version of philosophical-theological knowledge would include, alongside Sweet's magisterial meditation on physics and faith, an intellectual-emotional application of neo-Lockean as well as neo-Wesleyan-Edwardsean/neo-Tennysonian-Emersonian methodology to the natural-spiritual world of every day. Such a procedure, such an emphasis on the practical and on action in matters of religion, can be yet another weapon in the arsenal by which to avoid the quasi-rationalistic yet almost know-nothing stance that leads to addiction to religion, to defenses of biblical "inerrancy" by brandishing rather than interpreting the Book.

If I develop a "third force" of my own, a philosophical/ religious/literary force against unobservant obtuseness, it will be with the continued help of such friends as Rex Matthews on the Arminian side and Ralph Wood on the Calvinist. Kindly corresponding with me at a crucial juncture of this writing, they tried to keep me from my own obtuseness. Consider, with the indulgence of Wood, a summary of my correspondence with him. I intend, by this summary, to contribute to the public-private genre established not only by Jenkins and Davie but also by Robert Detweiler and Wesley A. Kort.[73]

Wood, Southern Baptist believer as well as theologian-critic, seeks to "deepen and toughen" what is best in the Southern Baptist tradition, which, according to him, is Calvinism. He generously sees my own work as "making a similar contribution, though in something of the opposite direction," namely, the Arminianism to be found among the social consciousnesses of such moderate Southern Baptists as Bill Moyers, Jimmy Carter, and Rosalynn Carter. Yet Wood, of course, is as far from being a fundamentalist, know-nothing Baptist as it is possible to be. Although recognizing, not only in correspondence with me but also in his published works, that Edwards "leads . . . to William James and Charles Peirce (on the secular side)" as well as to "Charles Hodge and B. B. Warfield (on the religious side)," Wood emphasizes Edwards's Calvinism per se and admires it so much that on April 4, 1986, he predicted my "greater regard for Calvin" as the result of my then-intensifying study of Edwards. This has come to pass. My "greater regard," however, is due not so much to Edwards as to Wood, whose theology, to use his own words for it, is "shaped by a recovered sense of Calvin's stress on the sovereignty of God and the prevenience of grace."[74]

Hear, at random, Wood's neo-Calvinist *mots*: "we live from our salvation and not toward it"; "we repent because we have been forgiven and not in order to be forgiven"; "faith is the one offer which cannot be refused"; and "the revolutionary thing about 'God is love' is that you cannot reverse it . . . and be speaking the truth." From Wood's point of view and with apologies to the Beatles, love is *not* "all you need." Wood is at his best in his devastating satire on the rhetoric of the self-sufficient soul, on "the folly of thinking that we belong merely to ourselves." He gets in especially good licks at ethical humanism, for example, where he speaks of "caring and sharing persons who have not a twinge of self-doubt, much less of transcendent judgment or hope." Both Wood and I greatly admired the

269

late Carlyle Marney, who, with the possible exception of Warren Carr, was the best preacher I ever heard. By exposing such glaringly self-sufficient rhetoric as Marney's announcement that "I am looking for God, and I intend to find him," however, Wood points, sadly, to Marney's abandonment of his potentially salutary red-neck Calvinism in favor of an extreme self-reliance.

Wood, then, evinces like the Flannery O'Connor he so well understands[75] an unsentimental and even hard Christian realism, with an especially fierce vision of evil. The striking modernity of Wood's Calvinism, reminiscent of Karl Barth's, is especially well suggested by his quasi-deconstructive "always already" formula that "time has already been redeemed." Grace for the Catholic, of course, is always already, but only if the priest says so. Anything else, certainly including the authority of John Calvin, to say nothing more at this juncture of the "real presences" of spiritual sense perception, may smack of human self-deception. The Jew, for whom such truths as I discern are far back and deep, may well not trust anyone who has been "saved." Speaking from where I stand, however, and despite my "second-naiveté" reminders to academe that theory is not all, I express my thanks to Ralph Wood for "always already" reviving my sense of Calvinism, and indeed for helping me overcome my uneasiness about it. Wood prepared me to value the mostly moderate, salutary Calvinism that informs Edwards's works.

Wood's emphasis, of course, lies in the comedic gospel, but he comes close to saying that the search for God in experience leads to tragedy. This stance, consistent with the antiexperientialism of the Calvinist world picture, is especially persuasive where Wood consciously (or unconsciously) uses Calvinism to apprehend the tough-mindedness that attaches to tragic art and understanding. The South, for Wood, is at once filled with a "sense of tragedy" and "Christ-haunted." "The one who has read and comprehended *King Lear*," Wood declares, "would never sign up for a seminar on 'How to be your own best friend.'" The shabby humanism of self-help manuals is "a banally *untragic* humanism" (my italics). What is bad about "coping and burn-out prevention, of stress management and marriage enrichment, of wellness training and the like" is precisely the un-tragedy of these shallow techniques. Thus, both Wood's understanding of tragedy and his Calvinism teach us that "we are not the answer to our own question," that is, that "there is no human explanation of the human condition."

Consistent with the homonymic implications of Wood's first name, his Calvinism is not finally inimical to the fully comedic, and even Arminian, understanding of experience; *Ralph* Emerson's Calvinism was in contrast with but finally yielded to his Arminianism. Although Wood says that "life is a battle already won," he also says that "God plants us amid contraries so that life will not go slack and lose interest." Although he says that "we are freed to live graciously in the world [only] because God has dealt with us graciously rather than righteously," this formulation, I suggest, calls attention to living full of grace. Although Wood says that "we long for the grace of God because we have already been found by it," this formulation raises at least the following experiential questions:

Why do we long if we have been found?
Why need we long if we have been found?
Is longing somehow consistent with being found?
Does longing not resemble the *Sehnsucht* of Romantic experientialism?
Is being found by grace so unspectacular as to escape notice?
What notice does one take of grace?
If one notices grace, does such noticing constitute a finding of, distinct from a having been found by, grace?
Must Calvinism be exclusively antiexperientialist?
Is it?

Wood speaks admiringly of Augustine's *incurvatus in se,* the self "turned futilely in upon itself, until [self] is redirected both by and toward Grace." The futurism of the latter clause, smacking of living toward one's salvation rather than from it, is much less Calvinistic and much more experiential/Arminian than Wood's "always already" formula of grace usually is.

It may be hard to believe in this deconstructing age that any two people are still corresponding in this vein. We might be back in the eighteenth century, except that such issues were not taken so seriously then! Although we are not the answer to our question and none can answer whether personal experiential religion is reconcilable with the doctrines of sovereignty and prevenient grace, I remain sure of one curious empirical fact, that Edwards and even Wesley, Tennyson, and Emerson are somehow both Calvinist and experiential/Arminian. It may be that Wood is, too, for the same reason that Arminian-Lockean, philosophically theological experientialism of the Anglo-American sort mixes with, if without quite bonding to, Anglo-American Calvinism. Where Wood speaks of the "radical Protestant insistence on the nonsacramental encounter with God in the lonely leap of faith," "nonsacramental encounter" may mean, besides "inward experience," "experience of the natural/spiritual senses."

The Harvard dissertation of Rex Matthews, who kindly sent it to me, argues that Wesley's "transcendental empiricism" is an "epistemology" both "consistent with 18th-century empiricism" and hospitable to "a kind of experience" independent of "the physical senses."[76] Although Matthews borrows the phrase "transcendental empiricism" from G. C. Cell,[77] Matthews's interpretation is his own. While some might regard phrases like "consistent with . . . but allows for" and "transcendental empiricism" as excessively oxymoronic, I have no difficulty with them for, without fudging differences or papering over the gap between sense experience and spiritual experience, I emphasize those moments in Wesley, Edwards, Tennyson, and Emerson when sense experience and spiritual experience overlap or are coterminous. Thus I derive a sufficiently academic definition of *experience* as the capacious if diaphanous net cast over philosophy and theology alike and, for that matter, literature.

No one more than Matthews, of course, realizes how precarious this strategy can be, but he writes that "transcendental empiricism" provides the "philosophical underpinning" for the doctrine of the witness of the Spirit, and although the implication of "underpinning" is to grant privilege to and make an independent variable of philosophy, the payoff for Matthews is theology. For me, the payoff for granting privilege to the equilateral triangle of philosophy, religion, and literature is an empirical-evangelical procedure of literary criticism. I thank Matthews for persuading me to take seriously a theology that is both startling and profound in its emphasis on Wesley's intellectual as well as emotional witness of the Spirit as "the normal privilege of all real Christians."

"We find ourselves," writes David Tracy, "by allowing claims upon our attention, by exploring possibilities suggested by others, including those others we call texts."[78] In this spirit I have tried to respond not only to what Tennyson and Emerson write but also to them. In Tracy's spirit, too, I have responded to an especially wide range of works and people, for a daunting "cloud of witnesses," a determined allusiveness, is perhaps particularly justified here.

Hear a final witness, the voice of Philip Larkin in his haunting, evocative concluding lines of "Church Going" (1955):

> I wonder who
> Will be the last, the very last, to seek
> This place for what it was; one of the crew
> That tap and jot and know what rood-lofts were?
> Some ruin-bibber, randy for antique,
> Or Christmas-addict, counting on a whiff
> Of gown-and-bands and organ-pipes and myrrh?
> Or will he be my representative,
>
> Bored, uninformed, knowing the ghostly silt
> Dispersed, yet tending to this cross of ground
> Through suburb scrub because it held unspilt
> So long and equably what since is found
> Only in separation—marriage, and birth,
> And death, and thoughts of these—for whom was built
> This special shell? For, though I've no idea
> What this accoutered frowsty barn is worth,
> It pleases me to stand in silence here;
> A serious house on serious earth it is,
> In whose blent air all our compulsions meet,
> Are recognized, and robed as destinies.
> And that much never can be obsolete,
> Since someone will forever be surprising
> A hunger in himself to be more serious,
> And gravitating with it to this ground,
> Which, he once heard, was proper to grow wise in,
> If only that so many dead lie round.

Precisely for the almost philosophical as well as straightforwardly theological reason of high seriousness, one is perennially attracted to the ac-
coutered but never quite wholly acculturated nor ever quite wholly effaced
church. Although dwelling in the shadow even of Larkin's nostalgic if
still-respectful belatedness, I infer from his modulations the Protestant aesthetic that nurtures a particular duo in belles lettres. Among the features
of this Larkinian-Protestant as well as Tennysonian-Emersonian aesthetic
are: the unfussy cultivation of sobriety, even after having "drunk the wine
of true inspiration" (see Romans 8, 12); the "intense artistic alertness"
brought about by vigilance, attentiveness, watching, and biding one's time
(see Ecclesiastes, Habakkuk, and Galatians); the achievement of a new

creation, if not the coming kingdom, through the challenge and stimulation of setting things in order (see the Genesis story); the expression of a discord that achieves, even in this life, resolution through reconciliation (see 2 Corinthians 6, and Philippians 2); and the untidy but extravagant reach for what lies beyond.[79] There is no better way to characterize the evangelical and for that matter empirical-evangelical aesthetic of Anglo-American Romanticism than through just such combinations of simplicity, seriousness, measure, tension, exhilaration, and adventure.

"Americans," according to Stanley Cavell, tend to "compose their theoretical works in a kind of scrip, good for exchanges at the company store but worth next to nothing in the international market."[80] My "works," if not worth much in *any* international market where the combination of empiricism and evangelicalism is a factor, may be worth something in the Anglo-American market, where it is an important factor.

One could raise the same objection to my work that Jasper Griffin raises to David Sansone's *Greek Athletics and the Genesis of Sport*. Just as Sansone finds a single origin for sporting activities, namely, "in the area of primitive sacrificial ritual," so I may appear ready to trace all Anglo-American literature to the Wesleyan-Edwardsean chronotope. What Griffin says about Sansone could be said about me, that "the inventor of an explanatory theory naturally feels more and more delight in it, the more things he can apply to it; but, by a sadly symmetrical reflex, the reader can find himself less and less convinced as he sees it used to explain everything he can think of."[81] I can certainly agree with Julian Barnes's animadversions against single-vision historiography:

> The past is a distant receding coastline, and we are all in the same boat. Along the stern rail there is a line of telescopes; each brings the shore into focus at a given distance. If the boat is becalmed, one of the telescopes will be in continual use; it will seem to tell the whole, the unchanging truth. But this is an illusion, and as the boat sets off again, we return to our normal activity: scurrying from one telescope to another, seeing the sharpness fade in one, waiting for the blur to clear in another. And when the blur does clear, we imagine that we have made it do so all by ourselves.

Barnes admits, however, that we all *do* proceed in such a manner, whether we like it or not: "We make up a story to cover the facts we don't know or can't accept; we keep a few true facts and spin a new story round them. Our panic and our pain are only eased by soothing fabulation; we call it history."[82]

I have proposed a framework for making sense of discourses that most uninitiated readers would not generally tend to connect, namely, the works of Wesley and Edwards on the one hand and the works of Tennyson and Emerson on the other. What I do, like what Barnes admits to doing, may be mere "soothing fabulation." We all feel if not the panic and the pain then at least the quiet desperation of all inquiry. I do not take more credit for any intervals of lucidity than Wesley does for his strange warming of the heart, but while I am ready to acknowledge the relativity and even the narrowness of my historical perspective, I cannot quite assign it to the merely imaginary or to illusion. I offer, therefore, no more than a strategic drawing back, a partial palinode. My historiography cultivates an at least double vision. From the palimpsest of these materials should emerge "a few true facts" intellectually as well as emotionally good for another new "tale" or two, for example, "The Experiential Irony of Emily Dickinson." My philosophically theological method of close reading, while hardly "by my own eyes inspired" (see Keats's "Ode to Psyche"), is not the slave of any other system (Blake's concept); my less fragmented than reticulated and arrayed heritage of empiricism-cum-evangelicalism constitutes the broadly experiential basis of Anglo-American Romanticism.

Notes

Prelude

1. See Denis Donoghue's review, "Bewitched, Bothered, and Bewildered," of J. Hillis Miller, *Illustration*, J. Hillis Miller, *Ariadne's Thread: Story Lines*, Frederick Crews, *The Critics Bear It Away: American Fiction and the Academy*, Morris Dickstein, *Double Agent: The Critic and Society*, and Giles Gunn, *Thinking Across the American Grain: Ideology, Intellect, and the New Pragmatism*, in *The New York Review of Books* 40 (March 25, 1993): 46–53, esp. 52.

2. Norman Maclean, *A River Runs Through It and Other Stories*, esp. 113.

3. Ralph C. Wood, "Words Under the Rocks," *The Christian Century*, January 20, 1993, 62–63.

4. See the editorial statement of the journal *Ultimate Reality and Meaning: Interdisciplinary Studies in the Philosophy of Understanding*. See also W. David Shaw, "The Fashioner of Worlds: Ultimate Reality in Tennyson," *Ultimate Reality and Meaning* 14 (1991): 245–62; and Donald Gelpi, "Emerson's Sense of Ultimate Meaning and Reality," *Ultimate Reality and Meaning* 15 (1992): 93–111.

5. Friedrich Nietzsche, *The Gay Science*, translated by Walter Kauffmann, 246. See also Melvyn New, *Telling New Lies: Seven Essays in Fiction, Past and Present*, 1, 19–23. New writes on authors as various as Nietzsche and Sterne, Swift and Mann. His epigraph is from "The S. S. *Cow Wheat*," by Isaac Babel:

"Jew," said the helmsman to me, "what will become of the children?"
"What children?"
"The children are getting no schooling," said the helmsman, spinning his
wheel. "The children will all turn out thieves."

See Isaac Babel, *The Collected Stories*, 324. *Telling New Lies*, incidentally, is dedicated to the News' sons, David and Carl.

6. See line 155 of Alexander Pope's *An Essay on Criticism* (1711). Even tough-minded philosopher/critic Thomas Hobbes acknowledges that "expressing more

than is perfectly conceived," the attempt to name the unnameable or speak the in-effable, necessitates "ambitious obscurity." See Thomas Hobbes, "Answer to Davenant's Preface to *Gondibert*" (1650), in Hazard Adams, ed., *Critical Theory Since Plato*, 216.

7. See the discussion throughout Paul Ricoeur, *Freud and Philosophy*.

8. Richard E. Brantley, *Locke, Wesley, and the Method of English Romanticism*, 168–85.

9. I quote from line 203 of William Wordsworth's "Ode: Intimations of Immortality" (1802–4).

10. I quote from William Butler Yeats's "The Fascination of What's Difficult" (1910).

11. I allude to Robert Frost's famous definition of poetry.

12. I quote from Gerard Manley Hopkins's "Spring and Fall: To a Young Child" (1880), line 8.

13. I quote from Dylan Thomas's "A Refusal to Mourn the Death, by Fire, of a Child in London" (1952), line 24.

14. I quote from William Butler Yeats's "Lapis Lazuli" (1938), line 17.

15. Robert Frost as quoted in Dana Gioia, *Can Poetry Matter?: Essays on Poetry and American Culture*, 22.

Theme and Variations

1. Richard E. Brantley, *Wordsworth's "Natural Methodism."*

2. Brantley, *Locke, Wesley, and the Method of English Romanticism.*

3. Richard E. Brantley, "The Common Ground of Wesley and Edwards," *Harvard Theological Review* 83 (July 1990): 271–303.

4. Richard E. Brantley, *Coordinates of Anglo-American Romanticism: Wesley, Edwards, Carlyle, and Emerson.*

5. Christopher Ricks, ed., *The Poems of Tennyson*, second edition, "incorporating the Trinity College Manuscripts," 2:317. All quotations from *In Memoriam* observe this edition. For a discussion of the prologue as an expression of Broad Church, relativist Christianity, see Eleanor B. Mattes, In Memoriam: *The Way of a Soul: A Study of Some Influences that Shaped Tennyson's Poem*, passim.

6. Brantley, *Coordinates of Anglo-American Romanticism*, 97–123, esp. 97–98.

7. See, for example, E. O. Wilson, *Sociobiology: The New Synthesis*.

8. See, for example, Ricoeur, *Freud and Philosophy*, passim.

9. Bloom, *The Anxiety of Influence*.

10. See the wide-ranging discussion by Jerome Bruner and Carol Fleisher Feldman, "Under Construction," *The New York Review of Books* 33 (March 27, 1986): 46–49.

11. Nelson Goodman, *Of Mind and Other Matters*.

12. Bruner and Feldman, "Under Construction," 47.

13. See W. V. Quine's review of Nelson Goodman's *Ways of Worldmaking*, in *The New York Review of Books* 25 (November 23, 1978): 17–19.

14. Roland Barthes, *S/Z*.

15. Edouard Morot-Sir, *The Imagination of Reference: Meditating the Linguistic Condition*.

16. David Locke, *Science as Writing*, passim.

17. See the discussion in Israel Rosenfield, "Mind-Reading," *The New York Review of Books* 35 (September 29, 1988): 72.

18. Ronald de Sousa, *The Rationality of Emotion*.

19. See R. C. Lewontin's review, "Fallen Angels," of Stephen Jay Gould's *Wonderful Life: The Burgess Shale and the Nature of History*, in *The New York Review of Books* 37 (June 14, 1990): 3–7. See also Wilson, *Sociobiology*; Richard Dawkins, *The Selfish Gene*; and Richard Dawkins, *The Blind Watchmaker*.

20. See Stephen Toulmin, *Cosmopolis: The Hidden Agenda of Modernity*; and the discussion in Quentin Skinner, "The Past in the Present," *The New York Review of Books* 37 (April 12, 1990): 36–37. See also Don Gifford, *The Farther Shore: A Natural History of Perception, 1798–1984*.

21. See Hans Moravec, *Mind Children: The Future of Robot and Human Intelligence*; and the discussion in Brad Leithauser, "No Loyalty to DNA," *The New Yorker* (January 9, 1989), 84–88.

22. William McKibben, *The End of Nature*.

23. See Wilson Coker, *Music and Meaning: A Theoretical Introduction to Musical Aesthetics*; Peter Kivy, *Osmin's Rage: Philosophical Reflections on Opera, Drama, and Text*; and James A. Winn, *Unsuspected Eloquence: A History of the Relations Between Poetry and Music*.

24. Michael Guillen, *Bridges to Infinity*. See also Morris Klein, *Mathematics and the Search for Knowledge*.

25. Keith Devlin, *Mathematics: The New Golden Age*.

26. Martin Gardner, "Beauty in Numbers," *The New York Review of Books* 36 (March 16, 1989): 26–28.

27. See William G. Doty, "Contextual Fictions that Bridge Our Worlds: 'A Whole New Poetry,'" *Literature and Theology* 4 (March 1990): 104–29, esp. 104–5; and Wayne Proudfoot, *Religious Experience*.

28. John J. McDermott, *Streams of Experience: Reflections on the History and Philosophy of American Culture*, 165.

29. D. G. Leahy, "To Create the Absolute Edge," with an introduction by Thomas J. J. Altizer, *Journal of the American Academy of Religion* 57 (Winter 1989): 773–89, esp. 774, 785–88.

30. See the discussion in Colin Clarke, *Romantic Paradox: An Essay on the Poetry of Wordsworth*, esp. 1.

31. Stephen Prickett, *Words and the Word: Literature, Poetics, and Biblical Interpretation*, 9.

32. See the discussion in Brad Leithauser's review, "A Master's Legacy," of Italo Calvino, *Mr. Palomar*, translated by William Weaver; and Italo Calvino, *Six Memos for the Next Millennium*, translated by Patrick Creagh, in *The New York Review of Books* 35 (September 29, 1988): 74–76.

33. See the discussion in Douglas R. Hofstadter and Daniel C. Dennett, *The Mind's I: Fantasies and Reflections on Self and Soul*; and Leithauser, "A Master's Legacy," 74–76.

34. See John Updike's review, "Small Packages," of Raymond Queneau, *Pierrot mon ami*, translated by Barbara Wright, Patrick Suskind, *The Pigeon*, translated by John E. Woods, and Emmanuel Carrère, *The Moustache*, translated by Lanie Goodman, in *The New Yorker* (July 4, 1988), 81–84.

35. Nicholson Baker, *The Mezzanine: A Novel*, esp. 9.

36. See Brad Leithauser's review, "Microscopy," of Nicholson Baker's *The Mezzanine*, in *The New York Review of Books* 36 (August 17, 1989): 15.

37. See G. E. Murray, "Young Poets in Full Flower of Their Talent," *Chicago Sunday Times*, February 14, 1982; G. E. Murray, "Questing Poets with Different Destinations," *Chicago Tribune*, December 14, 1986, section 14, 7; Richard Tillinghast, "Dragonflies and Hegel's Cows," *The New York Times Book Review*, July 13, 1986; and Thomas Swiss, "Six Poets," *Sewanee Review* 20 (Spring 1986): 307–8.

38. William Logan, *Vain Empires*.

39. William Logan, "Natural Selections," *Parnassus* 16 (1990): 72–86.

40. Samuel F. Pickering, Jr., *Moral Instruction and Fiction for Children, 1749–1820*, passim.

41. Jay Fliegelman, *Prodigals and Pilgrims: The American Revolution Against Patriarchal Authority, 1750–1800*.

42. Samuel F. Pickering, Jr., *John Locke and Children's Books in Eighteenth-Century England*.

43. I cite Donald Davie's witty nomenclature for such French exponents of poststructuralism as Jacques Lacan, Michel Foucault, and Jacques Derrida; see Donald Davie, "Nonconformist Poetics: A Reply to Daniel Jenkins," *Literature and Theology* 2 (September 1988): 163.

44. Russ Rymer, "The Annals of Science (A Silent Childhood—Part I)," *The New Yorker* (April 13, 1992), 41–81; and Russ Rymer, "The Annals of Science (A Silent Childhood—Part II)," *The New Yorker* (April 20, 1992), 43–77.

45. As quoted in Israel Rosenfield's review, "Mind-Reading," of *The Oxford Companion to the Mind*, ed. Richard L. Gregory, with the assistance of O. L. Zangwill, in *The New York Review of Books* 35 (September 29, 1988): 70–73.

46. As quoted in Martin Gardner's review, "Beauty in Numbers," of William Poundstone, *Labyrinths of Reason: Paradox, Puzzles, and the Frailty of Knowledge*, in *The New York Review of Books* 36 (March 16, 1989): 26–28.

47. See the paraphrase of Gerald M. Edelman's *Topobiology: An Introduction to Molecular Embryology*, in R. C. Lewontin's review, *The New York Review of Books* 36 (April 27, 1989): 18–22.

48. Vaclav Havel, "The Power of the Word," *The New York Review of Books* 37 (January 18, 1990): 3–8.

49. Melvyn New, *Telling New Lies*.

50. J. P. Stern, *Hitler: The Führer and the People*, esp. 49–56, 78–84.

51. Vaclav Havel, *Letters to Olga: June 1979–September 1982*, translated by Paul Wilson.

52. See the discussion in George Steiner, "Poor Little Lambs," *The New Yorker* (February 6, 1989), 103.

53. See the discussion in E. D. Hirsch, Jr., *The Aims of Interpretation*, 140–42.

54. See Lawrence Stone's review of Gertrude Himmelfarb, *The New History and the Old*, in *The New York Review of Books* 34 (December 17, 1987): 59–62.

55. See Peter Medawar, *The Hope of Progress: A Scientist Looks at Problems in Philosophy, Literature, and Science*; and Robert Nisbet, *A History of the Idea of Progress*.

56. See Stone's review of Himmelfarb's *The New History and the Old*.

57. See Christopher Fox, ed., *Psychology and Literature in the Eighteenth Century*, esp. the contribution of Michael V. DePorte, "Vehicles of Delusion: Swift, Locke, and the Madhouse Poems of James Carkesse."

58. Stephen Jay Gould, *Time's Arrow, Time's Cycle: Myth and Metaphor in the Discovery of Geological Time*.

59. Paul Fussell, *Class*, 133.

60. German Arciniegas, *America in Europe: A History of the New World in Reverse*, translated from the Spanish by Gabriela Arciniegas and R. Victoria Arana.

61. John O. Eidson, *Tennyson in America: His Reputation and Influence from 1827 to 1858*.

62. Although Edwards referred to Wesley just once, and disparagingly, Wesley rejoiced in Edwards, abridging five of his works. These abridged works of Edwards are *A Faithful Narrative of the Surprising Work of God in the Conversion of many hundred souls in Northampton; The Distinguishing Marks of a Work of the Spirit of God; Some Thoughts concerning the Present Revival in New England; A Treatise concerning Religious Affections*, in vol. 2 of *The Works of Jonathan Edwards*; and *An Account of the Life of the Late Reverend Mr. David Brainerd*. Wesley's abridgments of these works, in the order in which he abridged them, are *A Narrative of Many Surprising Conversions in Northampton and Vicinity; Thoughts concerning the Present Revival of Religion; An Extract of the Life of the Late Rev. Mr. David Brainerd*; and *An Extract from a Treatise concerning Religious Affections* (1773), in vol. 23 of *The Works of the Rev. John Wesley*.

See the discussions in Charles Rogers, "John Wesley and Jonathan Edwards," *Duke Divinity School Review* 31 (January 1966): 20–38; and Brantley, "The Common Ground of Wesley and Edwards."

63. Daniel T. Jenkins, "A Protestant Aesthetic? A Conversation with Donald Davie," *Literature and Theology* 2 (September 1988): 153, 158–59; and Davie, "Nonconformist Poetics," 163, 172.

64. See Robert M. Ryan, *Keats: The Religious Sense*; Bernard M. G. Reardon, *Religion in the Age of Romanticism*; and Prickett, *Words and the Word*.

65. See Harold Bloom, *Ruin the Sacred Truths*.

66. See Denis Donoghue's review, "The Sad Captain of Criticism," of Bloom, *Ruin the Sacred Truths*, in *The New York Review of Books* 36 (March 2, 1989): 22–24.

67. See Robert Langbaum, *The Poetry of Experience: The Dramatic Monologue in Modern Literary Tradition*; and Robert Langbaum, *The Word from Below: Essays on Modern Literature and Culture*, esp. 33–57. See also Robert Langbaum, *The Mysteries of Identity: A Theme in Modern Literature*. For more aesthetic, less philosophical connections between nineteenth- and twentieth-century Romanticism, see, for example, George Bornstein, *Transformations of Romanticism in Yeats, Eliot, and Stevens*. See also Carlos Baker, *The Echoing Green: Romanticism, Modernism, and the Phenomena of Transference in Poetry*.

68. See, besides Langbaum's work, L. J. Swingle, *The Obstinate Questionings of English Romanticism*. See also L. J. Swingle, *Romanticism and Anthony Trollope: A Study in the Continuities of Nineteenth-Century Literary Thought*.

69. Langbaum, *The Word from Below*, xiii–xiv; see also 110–29.

1. Introit

1. Friedrich von Schiller, *Letters on the Aesthetic Education of Man* (1795), in Hazard Adams, ed., *Critical Theory Since Plato: Revised Edition*, 420.

2. John R. Reed, *Perception and Design in Tennyson's* Idylls of the King, 30.

3. William R. Brashear, *The Living Will: A Study of Tennyson and Nineteenth-Century Subjectivism*, 52:60.

4. Ward Hellstrom, *On the Poems of Tennyson*, 4.

5. W. David Shaw, "The Transcendentalist Problem in Tennyson's Poetry of Debate," *Philological Quarterly* 46 (1967): 79–94.

6. James R. Kincaid, *Tennyson's Major Poems: The Comic and Ironic Patterns*, 3, 87, 104.

7. A. Dwight Culler, *The Poetry of Tennyson*, esp. 151–53. See also Elton Edward Smith, *The Two Voices: A Tennyson Study*.

8. Friedrich Nietzsche, *The Birth of Tragedy from the Spirit of Music* (1872), in Adams, ed., *Critical Theory Since Plato: Revised Edition*, 629.

9. M. H. Abrams et al., eds., *The Norton Anthology of English Literature: Fifth Edition*, 2:60.

10. Valerie Pitt, *Tennyson Laureate*, 18.

11. Robert Langbaum, "The Dynamic Unity of *In Memoriam*" (1970), reprinted in Harold Bloom, ed., *Modern Critical Views: Alfred Lord Tennyson*, 63–64.

12. Robert Pattison, *Tennyson and Tradition*, 110. For Tennyson and the Hegelian dialectic, see Richard W. Noland, "Tennyson and Hegel on War," *Victorian Newsletter* 25 (1964): 4–8.

13. Daniel Albright, *Tennyson: The Muses' Tug-of-War*, 3, 12.

14. Hallam Tennyson, *Alfred, Lord Tennyson: A Memoir*, 1:43–44.

15. Ibid.

16. William Boyd-Carpenter, "Tennyson and His Talk on Some Religious Questions," in Norman Page, ed., *Tennyson: Interviews and Recollections*, 188.

17. Sir Charles Tennyson, *Alfred Tennyson*, 249–50.

18. Boyd-Carpenter, "Tennyson and His Talk on Some Religious Questions," 186.

19. Langbaum, "The Dynamic Unity of *In Memoriam*," 58–59.

20. T. S. Eliot, "In Memoriam," *Essays Ancient and Modern*, 200–201.

21. Langbaum, "The Dynamic Unity of *In Memoriam*," 61–62.

22. See Graham Hough, "The Natural Theology of *In Memoriam*," *Review of English Studies* 33 (1947): 244–56; and Eugene R. August, "Tennyson and Teilhard: The Faith of *In Memoriam*," *PMLA* 84 (1969): 217–26.

23. Langbaum, "The Dynamic Unity of *In Memoriam*," 58.

24. Kincaid, *Tennyson's Major Poems*, 81.

25. Timothy Peltason, *Reading* In Memoriam, 12, 16.

26. Abrams et al., eds., *The Norton Anthology of English Literature: Fifth Edition*, 2:1095.

27. See Langbaum's discussion of Alfred North Whitehead's *Science and the Modern World*, in Langbaum, "The Dynamic Unity of *In Memoriam*," 57.

2. Empirical Procedures

1. Jerome H. Buckley, ed., *Poems of Tennyson*, xiii.

2. See the discussion in Langbaum, "The Dynamic Unity of *In Memoriam*," esp. 58.

3. Buckley, ed., *Poems of Tennyson*, esp. xiii.

4. See Langbaum, "The Dynamic Unity of *In Memoriam*," 63.

5. See Walker Gibson, "Behind the Veil: A Distinction Between Poetic and Scientific Language in Tennyson, Lyell, and Darwin," *Victorian Studies* 2 (1958): 60–68; and Pattison, *Tennyson and Tradition*, esp. 112. See also George R. Pot-

ter, "Tennyson and the Biological Theory of Mutability in Species," *Philological Quarterly* 16 (1937): 321–43; W. R. Rutland, "Tennyson and the Theory of Evolution," *Essays and Studies* 26 (1940): 7–29; Georg Roppen, "Alfred Tennyson," in *Evolution and Poetic Belief: A Study in Some Victorian and Modern Writers*, 66–112; James Harrison, "Tennyson and Evolution," *Durham University Journal* 64 (1971): 26–31; Milton Millhauser, *Fire and Ice: The Influence of Science on Tennyson's Poetry*; Susan Gliserman, "Early Victorian Science Writers and Tennyson's *In Memoriam*: A Study in Cultural Exchange," *Victorian Studies* 18 (1975): 277–308, 437–59; Nicolas A. Rupke, *The Great Chain of History: William Buckland and the English School of Geology (1814–1849)*, 225–30; and D. R. Dean, *Tennyson and Geology*.

6. Paul Turner, "The Stupidest English Poet," *English Studies* 30 (1949): 1–12.

7. Buckley, ed., *Poems of Tennyson*, xiii.

8. Ibid.

9. See Arthur J. Carr, "Tennyson as a Modern Poet," *University of Toronto Quarterly* 19 (1950): 361–82; Curtis Dahl, "The Victorian Wasteland," *College English* 16 (1955): 341–47; and A. H. Quereshi, "The Waste Land Motif in Tennyson," *Humanities Association Bulletin* 18 (1967): 20–30.

10. Buckley, ed., *Poems of Tennyson*, xiii.

11. Langbaum, "The Dynamic Unity of *In Memoriam*," 58.

12. A. Dwight Culler, *The Poetry of Tennyson*, 157.

13. Norman Page, ed., *Tennyson: Interviews and Recollections*, 190.

14. Ibid.

15. Ibid., 15–16.

16. For details of Hallam's death and the importance of his friendship with Tennyson, see Ricks, ed., *The Poems of Tennyson*, 2:304–15. For the relation between Hallam as depicted in *In Memoriam* and the "Arthurian" focus of other poems by Tennyson, see Cecil Y. Lang, *Tennyson's Arthurian Psycho-Drama*. Besides *In Memoriam*, Lang emphasizes *Morte d'Arthur, Ode on the Death of the Duke of Wellington*, and *Idylls of the King*.

17. Brantley, *Locke, Wesley, and the Method of English Romanticism*, 137–59, 185–200. See also Richard E. Brantley, "Keats's Method," *Studies in Romanticism* 22 (Fall 1983): 389–406.

18. Quotations of poetry, unless otherwise indicated, are from Abrams et al., eds., *The Norton Anthology of English Literature: Fifth Edition*.

19. Kincaid, *Tennyson's Major Poems*, 99–100.

20. Peltason, *Reading In Memoriam*, 78–81.

21. See the discussion of Wordsworth's "A slumber did my spirit seal" (1798) in Brantley, *Locke, Wesley, and the Method of English Romanticism*, 148–49.

22. Peltason, *Reading In Memoriam*, 24–25.

23. Ibid., 30–31.

24. Penelope Fitzgerald, Tom Paulin, Kingsley Amis, Terry Eagleton, A. S. Byatt, Seamus Heaney, Andrew Motion, Pat Rogers, Gavin Ewart, Paul Muldoon, Anthony Hecht, and Isobel Armstrong, "A Hundred Years After: Twelve Writers Reflect on Tennyson's Achievement and Influence," *TLS* 4670 (October 2, 1992): 8–9.

25. See Kincaid, *Tennyson's Major Poems*, 83–85, 89, 98–99; and A. Dwight Culler, *The Poetry of Tennyson*, 151. See also K. W. Gransden, *Tennyson*: In Memoriam, esp. 25; and Brashear, *The Living Will*, 52:92–114.

26. As quoted in Christopher Ricks, *Tennyson*, 214.

27. See, for example, the discussion in Kincaid, *Tennyson's Major Poems*, 83–84.

28. I refer to Gerard Manley Hopkins's "I Wake and Feel the Fell of Dark" (1918). "The dark night of the soul" alludes to the experience of St. John of the Cross.

29. Buckley, ed., *Poems of Tennyson*, x.

30. Kincaid, *Tennyson's Major Poems*, 83.

31. Francis P. Devlin, "Dramatic Irony in the Early Sections of Tennyson's *In Memoriam*," *Papers on Language and Literature* 8 (1972): 172–83.

32. I refer to Dylan Thomas's "The Force that Through the Green Fuse Drives the Flower" (1934).

33. I refer to Wordsworth's preface (1800) to *Lyrical Ballads* (1798).

34. Peltason, *Reading* In Memoriam, 61.

35. See Wallace Stevens's "Sunday Morning" (1915), Robert Browning's "Home-Thoughts, from Abroad" (1845), and the General Prologue to Geoffrey Chaucer's *Canterbury Tales* (ca. 1386).

36. Kincaid, *Tennyson's Major Poems*, 103.

37. Pickering, *John Locke and Children's Books in Eighteenth-Century England*, esp. 160–68.

38. See Lionel Trilling, *The Liberal Imagination: Essays on Literature and Society*, 129–59, esp. 146–47.

39. As quoted in M. H. Abrams, ed., *The Norton Anthology of English Literature: Third Edition*, 2:1080n.

40. I refer to Shakespeare's *Hamlet*.

3. Evangelical Principles

1. John Wesley, *The Journal of the Rev. John Wesley, A. M.*, Nehemiah Curnock, ed., 1:475–76.

2. Brantley, *Locke, Wesley, and the Method of English Romanticism*, 27–47.

3. Ricoeur, *Freud and Philosophy*, passim.

4. Hough, "The Natural Theology of *In Memoriam*," esp. 244–45.

5. Ricks, *Tennyson*, 222.

6. See esp. Brantley, *Coordinates of Anglo-American Romanticism*, 36–42.

7. Brantley, "The Common Ground of Wesley and Edwards," passim.

8. Peltason, *Reading* In Memoriam, 72.

9. A. C. Bradley, *A Commentary on Tennyson's* In Memoriam, 113.

10. Brantley, *Wordsworth's "Natural Methodism,"* 83.

11. Hellstrom, *On the Poems of Tennyson*, passim.

12. Page, ed., *Tennyson: Interviews and Recollections*, 190.

13. Roger S. Platizky, *A Blueprint of His Dissent: Madness and Method in Tennyson's Poetry*, 42–43. See also Ian Bradley, *The Call to Seriousness: The Evangelical Impact on the Victorians*, 23.

14. Brantley, "The Common Ground of Wesley and Edwards," 272–82.

15. Page, ed., *Tennyson: Interviews and Recollections*, 188.

16. Bernard Semmel, *The Methodist Revolution*, passim.

17. As quoted in Ricks, *Tennyson*, 212.

18. Sir Thomas Browne's *Religio Medici*, 1.21, as quoted in A. C. Bradley, *A Commentary on Tennyson's* In Memoriam, 111.

19. A. Dwight Culler, *The Poetry of Tennyson*, 168–69.

20. A. C. Bradley, *A Commentary on Tennyson's* In Memoriam, 110.

21. Joan New, "Martha," *Seneca Review* 16 (1986): 75–76.

22. Brantley, *Wordsworth's "Natural Methodism,"* 120, 133–34.

23. Ibid., 66–78.

24. Vivian R. Pollak, *Dickinson: The Anxiety of Gender*, 140–41.

25. Brantley, "The Common Ground of Wesley and Edwards," passim.

26. Buckley, ed., *Poems of Tennyson*, xi.

27. As quoted in Ricks, *Tennyson*, 221.

28. C. F. G. Masterman, *Tennyson as a Religious Teacher*, 210.

29. Peltason, *Reading* In Memoriam, 18.

30. Jerome H. Buckley, *Tennyson: The Growth of a Poet*, 125.

31. Mattes, In Memoriam: *The Way of a Soul*, passim. See also Langbaum, "The Dynamic Unity of *In Memoriam*," 75.

32. A. Dwight Culler, *The Poetry of Tennyson*, 158–59.

33. Buckley, ed., *Poems of Tennyson*, xi, xiii.

34. Harold Bloom, *The American Religion: The Emergence of the Post-Christian Nation*, 198–207.

4. Philosophical Theology

1. I allude to Shakespeare's *King Lear*.

2. I allude to Shakespeare's sonnet "Let Me Not to the Marriage of True Minds."

3. I allude to Shakespeare's sonnet "An Expense of Spirit in a Waist of Shame."

4. I allude to Keats's "Ode to a Nightingale" (1819).

5. As quoted in A. Dwight Culler, *The Poetry of Tennyson*, 167.

6. See the discussion in ibid., 166–89, esp. 167.

7. As quoted in ibid., 170–71. See also Milton Millhauser, "A Plurality of After-Worlds: Isaac Taylor and Alfred Tennyson's Conception of Immortality," *Hartford Studies in Literature* 1 (1969): 37–49.

8. I refer to Blake's description of the industrial revolution as "dark Satanic mills" in his "And Did Those Feet," which appears in the preface to his *Milton* (ca. 1804–10).

9. Friedrich von Schiller, *Letters on the Aesthetic Education of Man*, in Adams, ed., *Critical Theory Since Plato*, 419.

10. I have in mind Max Beerbohm's "Mr Tennyson, reading 'In Memoriam' to his Sovereign," which appears in Beerbohm's *The Poets' Corner* (1904).

11. See the discussion in Richard E. Brantley, "John Wesley (1703–1791)," in Donald T. Siebert, ed., *British Prose Writers, 1660–1800: Second Series*, in *Dictionary of Literary Biography*, 104:338–49, esp. 340.

12. I refer to Shakespeare's *Macbeth*, II.ii.37.

13. I refer to Shakespeare's sonnet, "That Time of Year Thou Mayst in Me Behold."

14. As quoted in A. Dwight Culler, *The Poetry of Tennyson*, 166.

15. Richard Whately's *A View of the Scripture Revelations concerning a Future State* (1829), as quoted in A. Dwight Culler, *The Poetry of Tennyson*, 170.

16. Buckley, ed., *Poems of Tennyson*, xii.

17. Boyd-Carpenter, "Tennyson and His Talk on Some Religious Questions," 186–87.

18. See Wordsworth's "Surprised by Joy" (written in 1812).

19. I refer to Byron's *Childe Harold's Pilgrimage* (1816), canto 3, stanza 34.

20. Cf. Yeats's "A Prayer for My Daughter" (1919).

21. Langbaum, "The Dynamic Unity of *In Memoriam*," 72.

22. See lines 25–26 of Wordsworth's "Expostulation and Reply" (1798).

23. See the discussion in A. G. den Otter, "The Question and *The Book of Thel*," *Studies in Romanticism* 30 (Winter 1991): 633–55.

24. See the discussion in Ricks, *Tennyson*, 226. See also Winston Collins, "Tennyson and Hopkins," *University of Toronto Quarterly* 38 (1968): 84–95.

25. Alistair W. Thomson, *The Poetry of Tennyson*, 138.

26. See the discussion by George H. Ford in Abrams et al., eds., *The Norton Anthology of English Literature: Fifth Edition*, 2:1095.

27. Kincaid, *Tennyson's Major Poems*, 103.

28. I refer to Hopkins's "The Starlight Night" (1877).

287

29. Robert Bernard Martin, *Tennyson: The Unquiet Heart*, 17–18.

30. For a discussion of the Lockean underpinnings of Charles Wesley's art, see Richard E. Brantley, "Charles Wesley's Experiential Art," *Eighteenth-Century Life* 11 (May 1987): 1–11, esp. 5.

31. See Coleridge's "The Aeolian Harp" (1796), esp. line 26.

32. I refer to the mythology in Blake's *Milton*.

33. Peltason, *Reading* In Memoriam, 148.

34. See A. C. Bradley's brave but finally muddled speculations in *A Commentary on Tennyson's* In Memoriam, 219–26.

35. Peltason, *Reading* In Memoriam, 159.

36. Ricks, ed., *The Poems of Tennyson*, 2:450.

37. Edmund Gosse, "Lord Tennyson's Eightieth Birthday," *St James's Gazette*, August 3, 1899, 7.

5. Spiritual Sense

1. I refer to Blake's *The Marriage of Heaven and Hell*.

2. John Dixon Hunt, "The Symbolist Vision of *In Memoriam*," *Victorian Poetry* 8 (1970): 187–98.

3. See Brantley, "The Common Ground of Wesley and Edwards," esp. 292–96, 301–3.

4. Abrams, ed., *The Norton Anthology of English Literature: Third Edition*, 2: 1056n. See also A. C. Bradley, *A Commentary on Tennyson's* In Memoriam, 125–36.

5. See the discussion in Martin, *Tennyson: The Unquiet Heart*, 482–84.

6. I refer to Hopkins's "Spring and Fall: To a Young Child" (1880), line 13.

6. Theodiceal Impulse

1. See Ricks, *Tennyson*, 214. Tennyson's *In Memoriam* and John Berryman's *Dream Songs*, Ricks adds, are both "on the death of friends" and both "modern equivalents of the sonnet sequence." See also Christopher Ricks, "Recent American Poetry," *Massachusetts Review* 11 (Spring 1970): 313–39, esp. 334–39.

2. A. Dwight Culler, *The Poetry of Tennyson*, 176.

3. Boyd-Carpenter, "Tennyson and His Talk on Some Religious Questions," 186–87.

4. As quoted in Page, ed., *Tennyson: Interviews and Recollections*, 187n.

5. Hope Dyson and Charles Tennyson, eds., *Dear and Honoured Lady: The Correspondence between Queen Victoria and Alfred Tennyson*, 79.

6. Philip Flynn, "Hallam and Tennyson: The 'Theodicaea Novissima' and *In Memoriam*," *Studies in English Literature* 19 (1979): 705–20, esp. 706, 719.

7. See Brantley, *Locke, Wesley, and the Method of English Romanticism*, esp. 160–68.

8. Ricks, ed., *The Poems of Tennyson*, 2:370n.

9. Peltason, *Reading* In Memoriam, 84.

10. Martin, *Tennyson: The Unquiet Heart*, 39–40.

11. See, e.g., Ricks, ed., *The Poems of Tennyson*, 2:370–72.

12. Peltason, *Reading* In Memoriam, 139. For an exploration of the section's obscurity, see A. C. Bradley, *A Commentary on Tennyson's* In Memoriam, 212–13.

13. Peltason, *Reading* In Memoriam, 17.

7. Set Pieces

1. A. Dwight Culler, *The Poetry of Tennyson*, 1.

2. Kincaid, *Tennyson's Major Poems*, 104.

3. Peltason, *Reading* In Memoriam, 108.

4. As quoted in ibid., 108–9.

5. Ibid., 110.

6. Buckley, *Tennyson: The Growth of a Poet*, 123. See also Augustine's *Confessions*, Book VII, chapter 17, section 23, in Albert C. Outler, ed., *Confessions and Enchiridion*, 151. For a full comparison of Augustine's vision with Tennyson's trance in section 95, see Percy H. Osmond, *The Mystical Poets of the English Church*, 309–10. See also Carlisle Moore, "Faith, Doubt, and Mystical Experience in *In Memoriam*," *Victorian Studies* 7 (1963): 155–69; and Mario L. D'Avanzo, "Lyric 95 of *In Memoriam*: Poetry and Vision," *Research Studies* 37 (1969): 149–54.

7. Buckley, *Tennyson: The Growth of a Poet*, 124.

8. A. Dwight Culler, *The Poetry of Tennyson*, 1.

9. Albright, *Tennyson: The Muses' Tug-of-War*, 8–9.

10. For a more positive assessment of Tennyson's iambic mastery in section 95 and throughout his work, see Vladimir Nabokov, "Notes on Prosody," in Vladimir Nabokov, ed., *Eugene Onegin*, 3:448–540.

11. A. Dwight Culler, *The Poetry of Tennyson*, 183.

12. A. C. Bradley, *A Commentary on Tennyson's* In Memoriam, 116.

13. Ricks, ed., *The Poems of Tennyson*, 2:413n.

14. See, for example, Horton Davies, *Worship and Theology in England from Watts and Wesley to Maurice, 1690–1850*, esp. 32.

15. I refer to Hopkins's "Carrion Comfort" (1885), lines 5–6.

16. I refer to Keats's "Ode to Psyche" (1819), line 33.

17. A. C. Bradley, *A Commentary on Tennyson's* In Memoriam, 192.
18. Kincaid, *Tennyson's Major Poems*, 106.

8. Language Method

1. See Dorothy Mermin's review of Herbert Tucker's *Tennyson and the Doom of Romanticism*, in *JEGP* 88 (1989): 246–48, esp. 246.
2. See the discussion in Martin, *Tennyson: The Unquiet Heart*, esp. 169–73.
3. Ricks, *Tennyson*, 224.
4. Kincaid, *Tennyson's Major Poems*, 96.
5. Thomson, *The Poetry of Tennyson*, 135.
6. For a historical as well as philosophical discussion of the Romantic fragment, see Thomas McFarland, *Romanticism and the Forms of Ruin: Wordsworth, Coleridge, and Modalities of Fragmentation*.
7. For the consistency of Romantic and Modernist fragments with the idea of revelation, see Robert Langbaum, "The Epiphanic Mode in Wordsworth and Modern Literature," in Langbaum, *The Word from Below*, 33–57.
8. Alan Sinfield, *Alfred Tennyson*, 124.
9. See the discussion in A. Dwight Culler, *The Poetry of Tennyson*, 155–56.
10. See W. David Shaw, "*In Memoriam* and the Rhetoric of Confession," *ELH* 38 (1971): 80–103; and Samuel C. Burchell, "Tennyson's Dark Night," *South Atlantic Quarterly* 54 (1955): 75–81. See also E. D. H. Johnson, "*In Memoriam*: The Way of a Poet," *Victorian Studies* 2 (1958): 139–48; and R. A. Foakes, "The Rhetoric of Faith: Tennyson's *In Memoriam* and Browning's *Men and Women*," in R. A. Foakes, *The Romantic Assertion: A Study in the Language of Nineteenth-Century Poetry*, 111–37.
11. Gordon D. Hirsch, "Tennyson's *Commedia*," *Victorian Poetry* 8 (1970): 92–106, esp. 98.
12. See the discussion in Ricks, *Tennyson*, 228–29. For other poets' uses of abba, see Ricks, ed., *The Poems of Tennyson*, 2:311–12.
13. I refer to line 14 of Keats's "Ode on a Grecian Urn" (1819).
14. Ricks, *Tennyson*, 228–29.
15. Kincaid, *Tennyson's Major Poems*, 97.
16. A. C. Bradley, *A Commentary on Tennyson's* In Memoriam, 191.
17. Ricoeur's trenchant statement merits full quotation:
The contrary of suspicion, I will say bluntly, is faith. What faith? No longer, to be sure, the first faith of the simple soul, but rather the second faith of one who has engaged in hermeneutics, faith that has undergone criticism, postcritical faith. Let us look for it in the series of philosophic decisions that secretly animate a phenomenology of religion and lie hidden even within its apparent neutrality. It is a rational faith, for it interprets; but it is a faith

because it seeks, through interpretation, a second naiveté. Phenomenology is its instrument of hearing, of recollection, of restoration of meaning. "Believe in order to understand, understand in order to believe"—such is its maxim; and its maxim is the "hermeneutic circle" itself of believing and understanding.
See Ricoeur, *Freud and Philosophy*, 22.

18. See Donald S. Hair, *Tennyson's Language*; see also the discussion of Hair in Aidan Day, "Textual Tapestries," *TLS* 4670 (October 2, 1992): 7.

19. See Brantley, *Locke, Wesley, and the Method of English Romanticism*, 19–24, 57–58, 63, 84, 95, 136, 160–68, 258n. 91.

20. Albright, *Tennyson: The Muses' Tug-of-War*, 177–78.

21. Terry Eagleton, "Tennyson: Politics and Sexuality in *The Princess* and *In Memoriam*," in Francis Barker et al., eds., *1848: The Sociology of Literature*, 104.

22. Sinfield, *Alfred Tennyson*, 118, 130, 144, 151, and also 131–33, 137, 152; Marion Shaw, *Alfred Lord Tennyson*, esp. 80–85; Ricks, *Tennyson*, 215–19; and Joanne P. Zuckerman, "Tennyson's *In Memoriam* as Love Poetry," *Dalhousie Review* 51 (1971): 202–17.

23. Sinfield, *Alfred Tennyson*, 140–41.

24. Ibid., 125.

25. See Gerhard Joseph, *Tennyson and the Text: The Weaver's Shuttle*; see also Day, "Textual Tapestries," 7.

26. Alan Sinfield, *The Language of Tennyson's* In Memoriam, 39.

27. Boyd-Carpenter, "Tennyson and His Talk on Some Religious Questions," 187.

28. I refer to Wordsworth's "Ode: Intimations of Immortality from Recollections of Early Childhood" (1802–4), lines 202–3.

29. I allude to Pope's *Essay on Criticism* (1711), lines 315–17.

30. Abrams, ed., *The Norton Anthology of English Literature: Third Edition*, 2:1042.

31. T. S. Eliot, "In Memoriam," *Selected Essays*, 291.

9. Intra-Romantic Relationships

1. Harold Bloom, "Emerson: The American Religion," in Harold Bloom, ed., *Modern Critical Views: Ralph Waldo Emerson*, 102.

2. See Brantley, "The Common Ground of Wesley and Edwards," 271–303, esp. 271. See also Brantley, *Coordinates of Anglo-American Romanticism*, esp. 36–42.

3. See Bloom, ed., *Modern Critical Views: Alfred Lord Tennyson*, 2, 9. See also Harold Bloom, "Tennyson, Hallam, and the Romantic Tradition," in *The Ringers in the Tower: Studies in the Romantic Tradition*, 145–54; H. M. McLuhan, "Tenny-

son and the Romantic Epic," in John Killham, ed., *Critical Essays on the Poetry of Tennyson*, 86–95; and Lore Metzger, "The Eternal Process: Some Parallels Between Goethe's *Faust* and Tennyson's *In Memoriam*," *Victorian Poetry* 1 (1963): 189–96.

4. Langbaum, *The Poetry of Experience*, 35–36.

5. Langbaum, *The Word from Below*, xiii.

6. Ibid., xiv.

7. Ibid., xiv, 33–57.

8. Peltason, *Reading* In Memoriam, 14–15. For Sinfield's similar tribute to Langbaum, see Sinfield, *The Language of Tennyson's* In Memoriam, 26.

9. I refer to Wordsworth's preface (1800) to the second edition of *Lyrical Ballads*.

10. Swingle, *The Obstinate Questionings of English Romanticism*, 39. Subsequent citations of this book in the text are by page number alone.

11. I have in mind the phrase "faith so mild" from Shelley's "Mont Blanc" (1816), line 77.

12. Swingle refers to Wordsworth's "Ode: Intimations of Immortality" (1802–4), lines 141–42.

13. For my favorable estimate of Swingle's book, see Richard E. Brantley, review of *The Obstinate Questionings of English Romanticism*, in *ANQ: A Quarterly Journal of Short Articles, Notes, and Reviews* 3 (July 1990): 142–45. See also David Punter's admiring review of the same book in *Studies in Romanticism* 30 (Summer 1991): 305–11.

14. For my study of Emerson as a Romantic, see Brantley, *Coordinates of Anglo-American Romanticism*, 123–39.

15. See Brantley, *Locke, Wesley, and the Method of English Romanticism*, esp. 129–200.

16. Frank Kermode and John Hollander, eds., *The Oxford Anthology of English Literature: Major Authors Edition*, 2:827n.

17. See the discussion in E. D. Hirsch, Jr., *Innocence and Experience: An Introduction to Blake*, esp. 27–29.

18. See the discussion in Brantley, *Locke, Wesley, and the Method of English Romanticism*, 129–36, esp. 134.

19. See the discussion of Yeats's *Art and Ideas* in Harold Bloom, "Tennyson: In the Shadow of Keats," in Harold Bloom, *Poetry and Repression*; see also Bloom, ed., *Modern Critical Views: Alfred Lord Tennyson*, 1.

20. Peltason, *Reading* In Memoriam, 52.

21. Patricia Ball, *The Central Self*, 176.

22. Buckley, *Tennyson: The Growth of a Poet*, 108.

23. Roden Noel, "Lord Tennyson," *Atalanta* (1892), 269–70, as quoted in Page, ed., *Tennyson: Interviews and Recollections*, 190.

24. See, for example, Peltason, *Reading In Memoriam*, 111; A. Dwight Culler, *The Poetry of Tennyson*, 163; and D. G. James, "Wordsworth and Tennyson," *Proceedings of the British Academy* 36 (1950): 113–29.

25. See Wordsworth's "The Solitary Reaper" (1807), lines 19–20.

26. See Tennyson's "Tears, Idle Tears" (1847), line 5.

27. See Wordsworth's "To a Butterfly" (1807), lines 17–18.

28. See Wordsworth's "The Sparrow's Nest" (1807), lines 17–20.

29. See Wordsworth's "The Happy Warrior" (1802), lines 59–60, 64.

30. I refer to Edgar A. Guest's "The Things that Make a Soldier Great And Send Him Out to Die" (1918), lines 3, 5.

31. Wordsworth's "Surprised by Joy" (1815), lines 6–9.

32. See Wordsworth's *Prelude*, 6.593. See also Frances Ferguson, *Wordsworth: Language as Counterspirit*.

33. See Wordsworth's "A Slumber Did My Spirit Seal" (1800), lines 7–8.

34. See Wordsworth's "Yew-trees" (1802), lines 1, 10–11.

35. See the discussion in Brantley, *Locke, Wesley, and the Method of English Romanticism*, 149–53.

36. I have in mind, from Yeats's "A Prayer for My Daughter" (1919), "How but in custom and in ceremony / Are innocence and beauty born?" (lines 61–62).

37. I have in mind Shirley Jackson's "The Lottery" (1948).

38. See Coleridge's "The Aeolian Harp" (1796), lines 49, 51.

39. A. Dwight Culler, *The Poetry of Tennyson*, 156–59.

40. See Coleridge's "Dejection: An Ode" (1802), lines 21, 38.

41. As quoted in Bloom, ed., *Modern Critical Views: Alfred Lord Tennyson*, 1.

42. As quoted in Kermode and Hollander, eds., *The Oxford Anthology of English Literature: Major Authors Edition*, 2:811.

43. See the quotation and discussion in Bloom, "Tennyson: In the Shadow of Keats"; and in Bloom, ed., *Modern Critical Views: Alfred Lord Tennyson*, 1.

44. See the discussion in Kermode and Hollander, eds., *The Oxford Anthology of English Literature: Major Authors Edition*, 2:811. With regard to the advice in Hallam's review, Bloom observes that "Tennyson forgot this too often, particularly after 1850, and perhaps he delayed his marriage and consequent domestication and institutionalization because something in him accurately feared that he would forget it."

45. See the discussion in Brantley, *Locke, Wesley, and the Method of English Romanticism*, 168–200.

46. Buckley, ed., *Poems of Tennyson*, xi–xii.

47. Nathaniel Brown, *Sexuality and Feminism in Shelley*.

48. See the discussion in Pattison, *Tennyson and Tradition*, esp. 166.

49. Bloom, *Ringers in the Tower*, 110.

50. See the discussion in Brantley, *Locke, Wesley, and the Method of English Romanticism*, 168–85.

51. See Shelley's "Mont Blanc" (1817), lines 4–6.

52. See, for example, A. C. Bradley, *A Commentary on Tennyson's* In Memoriam, 192–93.

53. See the discussion in Earl Wasserman, *The Subtler Language: Critical Readings of Neoclassic and Romantic Poems*, esp. 215–16.

54. I refer to Demogorgon's axiom in Shelley's *Prometheus Unbound* (1819).

55. Jack Stillinger, "Imagination and Reality in the Odes of Keats," in Jack Stillinger, *The Hoodwinking of Madeline, and Other Essays on Keats's Poems*, 99–119, esp. 99–100.

56. See, for example, the discussion in Buckley, ed., *Poems of Tennyson*, xi–xii.

57. For a discussion of Keats's spiritual sense, see Brantley, "Keats's Method," 389–405. See also Brantley, *Locke, Wesley, and the Method of English Romanticism*, 185–200.

58. Kermode and Hollander, eds., *The Oxford Anthology of English Literature: Major Authors Edition*, 2:597.

59. Ibid., 2:597n.

60. Review, besides section 64, sections 44 through 47.

61. For a full discussion of these two "spots of time," see Brantley, *Wordsworth's "Natural Methodism,"* 55–56, 95–100.

62. James Knowles, "Aspects of Tennyson, II," *Nineteenth Century* 33 (January 1893): 164–88, esp. 167.

63. Sinfield, *Alfred Tennyson*, 120.

64. Nowhere, to my knowledge, does Tennyson object to the American Revolution.

65. For positive assessments of the epilogue, see Thomson, *The Poetry of Tennyson*, 106; and Albright, *Tennyson: The Muses' Tug-of-War*, 213. For a negative assessment, see Kincaid, *Tennyson's Major Poems*, 109.

66. Herbert Tucker, *Tennyson and the Doom of Romanticism*, 185.

67. I mention only M. H. Abrams, *Natural Supernaturalism: Tradition and Revolution in Romantic Literature*.

68. Tucker, *Tennyson and the Doom of Romanticism*, 222.

10. *Introit*

1. See Ralph Waldo Emerson, *Selections from Ralph Waldo Emerson: An Organic Anthology*, ed. Stephen E. Whicher, 179, 303, 353; hereafter, Whicher, ed., *Selections*.

2. David Van Leer, *Emerson's Epistemology: The Argument of the Essays*, 8. For

another recent view of Emerson's Kantian epistemology, see Evan Carton, *The Rhetoric of American Romance: Dialectic and Identity in Emerson, Dickinson, Poe, and Hawthorne.*

3. See the discussion in Brantley, *Coordinates of Anglo-American Romanticism,* esp. 97–118.

4. Van Leer, *Emerson's Epistemology,* 264.

5. See the discussion in Vicki Hearne, *Adam's Task: Calling Animals by Name,* esp. 42. See also Nietzsche's *The Genealogy of Morals.*

6. See Van Leer, *Emerson's Epistemology,* 8; and Stephen E. Whicher, *Freedom and Fate: An Inner Life of Ralph Waldo Emerson.*

7. Whicher, ed., *Selections,* 179, 303, 353. See also Whicher, *Freedom and Fate,* passim.

8. See Ralph Rusk, *The Life of Ralph Waldo Emerson;* Jonathan Bishop, *Emerson on the Soul;* and Joel Porte, "The Problem of Emerson," *Harvard English Studies* 4 (1973): 89.

9. Whicher, ed., *Selections,* 179.

10. Ibid., 303.

11. See Leonard Neufeldt, *The House of Emerson,* passim. See also Christopher Lasch, *The True and Only Heaven: Progress and Its Critics,* 549.

12. Newton Arvin, "The House of Pain," in Newton Arvin, *American Pantheon.*

13. See Stanley Cavell, "Hope Against Hope," *American Poetry Review* 15 (January–February 1986): 9–13; and Stanley Cavell, "Thinking of Emerson," and "An Emerson Mood," in Stanley Cavell, *The Senses of Walden.*

14. Besides Van Leer's study of Emerson and Kant, see the discussion of Emerson and Hume in John Michael, *Emerson and Skepticism: The Cipher of the World.*

15. McFarland, *Romanticism and the Forms of Ruin.*

16. See Neufeldt, *The House of Emerson,* passim; and Michael, *Emerson and Skepticism,* passim.

17. Julie Ellison, *Emerson's Romantic Style,* esp. 76. "Freedom and fate," of course, is Whicher's phrase in *Freedom and Fate.*

18. Francis Murphy and Herschel Parker, eds., *The Norton Anthology of American Literature: Second Edition,* 1:823.

19. Cf. line 51 of Wallace Stevens's "The Idea of Order at Key West" (1935).

20. See especially Stephen J. Greenblatt, *Shakespearean Negotiations: The Circulation of Social Energy in Renaissance England.* For further discussion of theoretical criticism in Emerson studies, see chapter 17 and "Recapitulation and Cadenza."

21. I quote from the annotation to line 431 of T. S. Eliot's "The Waste Land" (1922)—"These fragments I have shored against my ruins"—in Kermode and Hollander, eds., *The Oxford Anthology of English Literature: Major Authors Edition,* 2:1420n.

22. Besides McFarland's *Romanticism and the Forms of Ruin*, see the discussion of Carlyle as a proto-Modernist in Eloise M. Behnken, *Thomas Carlyle: "Calvinist Without the Theology."*

23. See, for example, Barthes, *S/Z*.

24. Bloom, *The American Religion*, 99–100.

11. Perspective-by-Perspective Understanding

1. *The American Scholar* gets no more than passing mention in any of the critical works I cite.

2. See, for example, Sacvan Bercovitch, *The Puritan Origins of the American Self*; and Sacvan Bercovitch, *The American Jeremiad*.

3. *The American Scholar* appears, for example, in volume 1 of Murphy and Parker, eds., *The Norton Anthology of American Literature: Second Edition*.

4. Murphy and Parker, eds., *The Norton Anthology of American Literature: Second Edition*, 1:868–69. Subsequent citations of this volume are by page number alone. This edition, used in keeping with my interest in the anthologized Emerson, is based on Ralph Waldo Emerson, *The Complete Works of Ralph Waldo Emerson: Centenary Edition*, ed. Edward Waldo Emerson. Edward Waldo Emerson's edition is being superseded by *The Collected Works of Ralph Waldo Emerson*, ed. Robert Spiller, Albert Ferguson, et al., with 3 volumes to date.

5. See the discussion in Brantley, "The Common Ground of Wesley and Edwards."

6. Murphy and Parker, eds., *The Norton Anthology of American Literature: Second Edition*, 1:824.

7. See the discussion in Ann Douglas, *The Feminization of American Culture*.

8. See the discussion in David Leverenz, *Manhood and the American Renaissance*, esp. 4–5, 7, 42–71.

9. See the discussion in Brantley, *Wordsworth's "Natural Methodism,"* 25–29.

10. See the discussion in Brantley, *Coordinates of Anglo-American Romanticism*, 7–42.

12. Religious Methodology

1. For an interpretation of *The Divinity School Address* as not only deriving from but also generally agreeing with Unitarian emphases, see David Robinson, *Apostle of Culture: Emerson as Preacher and Lecturer*, esp. 123–37.

2. Van Leer, *Emerson's Epistemology*, esp. 238.

3. Curnock, ed., *The Journal of the Rev. John Wesley, A. M.*, 1:424.

4. Through careful reasoning, Locke accepts the sense-based testimony of New Testament witnesses, for he not only argues that "the Testimony of others" vouches "the Observation and Experience" of the objective world but also suggests that, in and of itself, such testimony is an avenue to spiritual as well as natural knowledge: "A credible Man vouching his Knowledge of [the Being and Existence of the thing itself], is a good proof." See John Locke, *An Essay concerning Human Understanding*, 4.16.10, ed. Peter Nidditch, 664.

5. I quote line 125 of Milton's "Lycidas" (1637).

6. Mary Moody Emerson, "Almanacks, 1802–1855" (a Houghton Library manuscript), as quoted in Phyllis Cole, "From the Edwardses to the Emersons: Four Generations of Evangelical Family Culture," *College English Association Critic* 49 (1986–87): 70–78, esp. 74.

7. As quoted in Murphy and Parker, eds., *The Norton Anthology of American Literature: Second Edition*, 1:874n.

8. Conrad Wright, "Emerson, Barzillai Frost, and the Divinity School Address," *Harvard Theological Review* 49 (January 1956): 19–43.

9. See the discussion in David Robinson's introduction to Ralph Waldo Emerson, *The Complete Sermons of Ralph Waldo Emerson*, ed. Albert J. von Frank, 1:19–20.

10. For "experience into words" as applied to another literary context, see D. W. Harding, *Experience into Words: Essays on Poetry*. For a pertinent study of evangelical homiletics in the context of homiletics in general, see, for example, James Downey, *The Eighteenth-Century Pulpit: A Study of the Sermons of Butler, Berkeley, Secker, Sterne, Whitefield and Wesley*.

11. See Thomas Jackson, ed., *The Lives of Early Methodist Preachers*.

12. Daniel Walker Howe, *The Unitarian Conscience: Harvard Moral Philosophy, 1805–1861*, esp. 161.

13. See Brantley, *Locke, Wesley, and the Method of English Romanticism*, 99–100.

14. Ibid., 129–36.

15. See the discussion in Brantley, *Wordsworth's "Natural Methodism,"* esp. 70.

16. For a view of Karl Barth as a "humorous and happy theologian not in spite of his Calvinism but because of it," and for a discreet application of his theology to the study of Flannery O'Connor, Walker Percy, John Updike, and Peter de Vries, see Ralph C. Wood, *The Comedy of Redemption: Christian Faith and Comic Vision in Four American Novelists*, esp. 35, 42–43.

17. For John Fletcher's importance to Wesley, see, for example, Brantley, *Wordsworth's "Natural Methodism,"* 11, 68, 72–73, 77, 86, 99.

18. The phrase occurs in lines 34–35 of Wordsworth's "Lines: Composed a Few Miles Above Tintern Abbey" (1798).

19. For the effect of Wesley's words about practical charity on Wordsworth's

theme of social consciousness, for example, see the discussion of Wordsworth's "The Old Cumberland Beggar" (1798) in Brantley, *Wordsworth's "Natural Methodism,"* 31–32, 106.

20. Arminian triumph is traced on the British side by Semmel in *The Methodist Revolution.*

21. See the discussion in Hirsch, *Innocence and Experience,* esp. 27–29.

22. For the general continuity between Emerson and Nietzsche, see, for example, Harold Bloom, *Kabbalah and Criticism.* See also scattered comments in Philippa Foot, "Nietzsche's Immoralism," *The New York Review of Books* 38 (June 13, 1991): 18–22.

23. See Wesley's "Address to the Clergy" (1756), and *The Arminian Magazine.*

24. For a discussion of the eighteenth and nineteenth centuries as Wesley- and Edwards-inspired apostolic ages, see Brantley, "The Common Ground of Wesley and Edwards," 271–303; and Brantley, "John Wesley (1703–1791)," 104:338–49.

25. Bloom, *The American Religion,* 23–24.

13. Suspenseful Subjectivity

1. William K. Bottorff, " 'Whatever Inly Rejoices Me': The Paradox of 'Self-Reliance,' " *ESQ* 18 (1972): 207–17.

2. Michael, *Emerson and Skepticism,* xii–xiii.

3. Thomas P. Joswick, "The Conversion Drama of 'Self-Reliance': A Logological Study," *American Literature* 55 (1983): 507–24.

4. See the discussion in Whicher, *Freedom and Fate.*

5. See Barbara Packer, *Emerson's Fall: A New Interpretation of the Major Essays,* 144–47; and Van Leer, *Emerson's Epistemology,* 258. See also William S. Scheick, *The Slender Human Word: Emerson's Artistry in Prose,* esp. 87–97.

6. I quote line 18 of Tennyson's "Ulysses" (1842).

7. See Jacques Lacan, "Of Structure as an Inmixing of Otherness Prerequisite to any Subject Whatever," in Richard Macksey and Eugenio Donato, eds., *The Structuralist Controversy: The Languages of Criticism and the Sciences of Man*; and Norman Holland, *The I.* See also Ellie Ragland-Sullivan, *Jacques Lacan and the Philosophy of Psychoanalysis,* esp. 58–67.

8. Michael, *Emerson and Skepticism,* 50–51.

9. See the discussion in Brantley, *Locke, Wesley, and the Method of English Romanticism,* esp. 107, 113, 150, 253 n. 18.

10. I allude to Wordsworth's *The Prelude,* 12.220–23, which refers to

those passages of life that give
Profoundest knowledge to what point, and how,

The mind is lord and master—outward sense
The obedient servant of her will.

11. I quote line 28 of Wallace Stevens's "Of Modern Poetry" (1940).

12. See the discussion and quotation of Oliver Cromwell in Jacob Bronowski, *The Ascent of Man*, 374.

13. Sacvan Bercovitch, "Emerson the Prophet: Romanticism, Puritanism, and Auto-American-Biography" (1975), reprinted in Harold Bloom, ed., *Modern Critical Views: Ralph Waldo Emerson*, 38.

14. As quoted in Bercovitch, "Emerson the Prophet," 38–39.

15. Wesley T. Mott, "Emerson and Antinomianism: The Legacy of the Sermons," *American Literature* 50 (November 1978): 369–97.

16. As quoted in Robinson's introduction to Frank, ed., *The Complete Sermons of Ralph Waldo Emerson*, 1:28.

17. See the discussion in Bloom, *The Ringers in the Tower*, 217–26, 291–304.

18. See the discussion in Brantley, *Wordsworth's "Natural Methodism,"* esp. 31–34.

19. See the discussion in Brantley, "The Common Ground of Wesley and Edwards," esp. 285.

20. See the discussion in Brantley, *Wordsworth's "Natural Methodism,"* esp. 127–30, 134–38, 184.

21. For a portrait of Thomas Clarkson, see Brantley, *Wordsworth's "Natural Methodism,"* 150–52.

22. Cole, "From the Edwardses to the Emersons," 73. For the importance of eighteenth- and nineteenth-century women in revival culture in America, to say nothing of their similar importance in England, see Nancy Cott, "Young Women in the Second Great Awakening in New England," *Feminist Studies* 3 (Fall 1975): 15–29; Nancy Cott, *The Bonds of Womanhood: "Woman's Sphere" in New England*; Douglas, *The Feminization of American Culture*; Mary Ryan, "A Woman's Awakening: Evangelical Religion and the Families of Utica, N.Y., 1800–1840," *American Quarterly* 30 (1978): 602–23; Mary Maples Dunn, "Saints and Sisters: Congregational and Quaker Women in the Early Colonial Period," *American Quarterly* 30 (1978): 582–601; Amanda Porterfield, *Feminine Spirituality in America: From Sarah Edwards to Martha Graham*; Barbara Epstein, *The Politics of Domesticity: Women, Evangelism and Temperance in Nineteenth-Century America*; and Laurel Thatcher Ulrich, *Good Wives: Image and Reality in the Lives of Women in Northern New England, 1650–1750*.

23. Mary Moody Emerson, "Almanacks," as quoted in Cole, "From the Edwardses to the Emersons," 76.

24. Cole, "From the Edwardses to the Emersons," 76.

25. Folder 3 of the 47 folders of Mary Moody Emerson's "Almanacks" in the Houghton Library.

26. Ibid.

27. Cole, "From the Edwardses to the Emersons," 76.

28. Ralph Waldo Emerson, *The Journals and Miscellaneous Notebooks of Ralph Waldo Emerson*, ed. William Gilman et al., 5:323–24. See also the discussion in Cole, "From the Edwardses to the Emersons," 70.

29. Cf. the argument of Eric Cheyfitz in *The Trans-Parent: Sexual Politics in the Language of Emerson*.

30. Ralph Waldo Emerson, *The Letters of Ralph Waldo Emerson*, ed. Ralph Rusk, 1:138.

31. See the discussion in Lasch, *The True and Only Heaven*, esp. 548. See also Robert Bellah, *Habits of the Heart: Individualism and Commitment in American Life*.

32. The latter phrase is Christopher Lasch's; the former is Robert Bellah's. See the discussion in Lasch, *The True and Only Heaven*, 548.

33. See the discussion throughout David Marr, *American Worlds Since Emerson*.

34. Carolyn Porter, *Seeing and Being: The Plight of the Participant Observer in Emerson, James, Adams, and Faulkner*.

35. See Harold Bloom, *Agon: Towards a Theory of Revisionism*; and Packer, *Emerson's Fall*. See also the discussion in Lasch, *The True and Only Heaven*, 550–51.

36. See, besides Lasch's *The True and Only Heaven*, his "Notes on Gnosticism," *New Oxford Review* 53 (October 1986): 14–18.

37. See the discussion in Lasch, *The True and Only Heaven*, 550–51.

14. Experience and Faith

1. William James's *A Pluralistic Universe* is based on his understanding of Spencer, Taine, Fiske, Barratt, and Clifford; see the discussion in Richard Poirier, "The Question of Genius: The Challenge of Emerson," reprinted in Bloom, ed., *Modern Critical Views: Ralph Waldo Emerson*, esp. 178.

2. I quote section 2, lines 255–56, of Alexander Pope's *Essay on Criticism* (1711).

3. Ricoeur, *Freud and Philosophy*, esp. 20–36.

4. See the discussion throughout Kenneth MacLean, *John Locke and English Literature of the Eighteenth Century*.

5. Murphy and Parker, eds., *The Norton Anthology of American Literature: Second Edition*, 1:910n.

6. See, for example, the discussion in Brantley, *Wordsworth's "Natural Methodism*,*"* esp. 79–110.

7. Murphy and Parker, eds., *The Norton Anthology of American Literature: Second Edition*, 1:820.

8. For an application of evangelical spiritual theology to literature, see "Wordsworth's Theology of the Spirit," in Brantley, *Wordsworth's "Natural Methodism,"* 66–138.

9. See, for example, the discussion in Brantley, *Locke, Wesley, and the Method of English Romanticism*, 34, 51, 62, 135.

10. See the discussion in Brantley, *Wordsworth's "Natural Methodism,"* 70–72, 127–29, 131. See also Isaac Watts, *The Works of Isaac Watts*, 1:718, 720.

11. See the discussion in Brantley, *Wordsworth's "Natural Methodism,"* 70–73.

12. See the discussion in Martha England and John Sparrow, *Hymns Unbidden: Donne, Herbert, Blake, Emily Dickinson, and the Hymnographers*, esp. 47. See also Brantley, "Charles Wesley's Experiential Art," 1–11.

13. See the discussion in Brantley, "The Common Ground of Wesley and Edwards," esp. 281.

15. Roots of Theory

1. See Lawrence Buell, "Unitarian Aesthetics and Emerson's Poet-Priest," *American Quarterly* 20 (Spring 1968): 3; and Buell, *Literary Transcendentalism*, passim.

2. Kenneth Walter Cameron, "An Early Prose Work of Emerson," *American Literature* 22 (November 1950): 332–38.

3. I quote "Poetry" (1921) by Marianne Moore.

4. See Van Leer, *Emerson's Epistemology*, 150–53, 263–64; and David Porter, *Emerson and Literary Change*, 176–80.

5. Packer, *Emerson's Fall*, 179.

6. Joel Porte, *Representative Man: Ralph Waldo Emerson in His Time*, 177.

7. For a discussion of the empirical, consciousness-oriented dimension of Freudian psychology, see, for example, Lionel Trilling, "Freud and Literature," in Adams, ed., *Critical Theory Since Plato*.

8. I quote from Wordsworth's preface to *Lyrical Ballads* (1800).

9. See, for example, the discussion in E. D. Hirsch, Jr., *Cultural Literacy: What Every American Needs to Know*.

10. See especially the account by the Methodist minister in Hamilton Holt, ed., *The Life Stories of Undistinguished Americans: As Told by Themselves*.

11. I have in mind Plato's *Ion*; see Adams, ed., *Critical Theory Since Plato*, esp. 14–15.

12. See the discussion in Brantley, *Wordsworth's "Natural Methodism,"* 33.

13. See the discussion in Stanley Fish, *Is There a Text in This Class? The Authority of Interpretive Communities*.

14. I have in mind the excerpts from Thomas Aquinas's *Summa Theologica*, in Adams, ed., *Critical Theory Since Plato*, esp. 117–19.

16. The Play of Skepticism

1. Van Leer, *Emerson's Epistemology*, 154.
2. Whicher, *Freedom and Fate*, 111–12.
3. Packer, *Emerson's Fall*, 157–59.
4. Michael, *Emerson and Skepticism*, passim.
5. Gayle L. Smith, "Style and Vision in 'Experience,'" *ESQ* 27 (1981): 85–86.
6. Van Leer, *Emerson's Epistemology*, 154.
7. Gertrude Hughes, *Emerson's Demanding Optimism*, xi.
8. Murphy and Parker, eds., *The Norton Anthology of American Literature: Second Edition*, 1:942n.
9. Abrams et al., eds., *The Norton Anthology of English Literature: Fifth Edition*, 2:60.
10. For other predominantly Late Romantic essays by Emerson, see *Nature* (1836), *The Transcendentalist* (1841), *Spiritual Laws* (1841), *Heroism* (1841), *Man the Reformer* (1841), *Friendship* (1841), *Intellect* (1841), *Art* (1841), *Nature* (1844), *Politics* (1844), *Character* (1844), *The New England Reformers* (1844), *Napoleon* (1850), *English Traits* (1856), *Wealth* (1860), *Culture* (1860), *Society and Solitude* (1870), and *Historic Notes on Life and Letters in New England* (1883).
11. Locke, *Essay*, 2.1.24, in Nidditch, ed., 118.
12. See the discussion in Brantley, *Locke, Wesley, and the Method of English Romanticism*, 144–48.
13. Ibid., 76–80.
14. See, for example, J. Hillis Miller, "The Critic as Host," in Harold Bloom, ed., *Deconstruction and Criticism*, 217–53.
15. I quote from Wallace Stevens's "Sunday Morning" (1915) and Thomas Hardy's "Hap" (1898).
16. I employ the phrase with which Henry James described death.
17. Dante Alighieri, *The Inferno: A Verse Rendering for the Modern Reader*, trans. and ed. John Ciardi, 28.
18. See lines 76–80 of Percy Bysshe Shelley's "Mont Blanc" (1817).
19. Brantley, *Coordinates of Anglo-American Romanticism*, 79–81, 96, 100.
20. Wendy Farley, *Tragic Vision and Divine Compassion: A Contemporary Theodicy*, passim.
21. Murphy and Parker, eds., *The Norton Anthology of American Literature: Second Edition*, 1:942n.
22. David W. Hill, "Emerson's Eumenides: Textual Evidence and the Interpre-

tation of 'Experience,' " in Joel Myerson, ed., *Emerson Centenary Essays*, 93–106.

23. See the discussion in Murphy and Parker, eds., *The Norton Anthology of American Literature: Second Edition*, 1:942n.

24. See Robinson's introduction to Frank, ed., *The Complete Sermons of Ralph Waldo Emerson*, 1:4.

25. Van Leer, *Emerson's Epistemology*, 150.

26. See especially Packer's chapter on "The Curse of Kehama," in her *Emerson's Fall*.

27. For a discussion of the poems of grief by Ben Jonson and Charles Wesley, see Brantley, "Charles Wesley's Experiential Art," esp. 2–3.

28. Cf. Brantley, *Wordsworth's "Natural Methodism,"* 81–85, 95–100.

29. See the discussion of Wesley's and Edwards's Lockean usage of *impulse* in Brantley, "The Common Ground of Wesley and Edwards," esp. 281–82.

30. Brantley, *Wordsworth's "Natural Methodism,"* 1–12, 66–79.

31. Cf. Brantley, *Locke, Wesley, and the Method of English Romanticism*, 109–10.

32. Brantley, *Coordinates of Anglo-American Romanticism*, 80–81, 101–3.

33. Ibid., 287–90.

34. Cf. Brantley, *Wordsworth's "Natural Methodism,"* 66–79.

35. Whicher, ed., *Selections*, 343. This edition is hereafter cited by page number alone.

36. Whicher, *Freedom and Fate*, 495.

37. See Stanley Cavell, "Thinking of Emerson," *New Literary History* 11 (1979): 166–76; and Stanley Cavell, "Genteel Responses to Kant? in Emerson's *Fate* and Coleridge's *Biographia Literaria*," *Raritan* 3 (Fall 1983): 36–61. See also Stanley Cavell, *The Chain of Reason: Wittgenstein, Skepticism, Morality, and Tragedy*.

38. Cf. Brantley, "The Common Ground of Wesley and Edwards," 292–97.

39. See, for example, the discussion in Brantley, *Locke, Wesley, and the Method of English Romanticism*, 20–21.

40. For Blake's lines on the importance of twofold, threefold, and even fourfold vision, see his letter to Thomas Butts (November 22, 1802), in Abrams, ed., *The Norton Anthology of English Literature: Third Edition*, 2:110.

41. F. Scott Fitzgerald's definition of intelligence is quoted in Michiko Kakutani's review of Anne Stevenson, *Bitter Fame: A Life of Sylvia Plath*, in *New York Times*, October 21, 1989, B14.

42. See Brantley, *Wordsworth's "Natural Methodism,"* 55–56.

43. For a discussion of Emerson's concept of surfaces in *Prudence*, see Packer, *Emerson's Fall*, 102–9.

44. For the seriousness with which nineteenth-century Britain took eschatological issues, see Michael Wheeler, *Death and the Future Life in Victorian Literature and Theology*.

45. Eliezer Schweid, "The Holocaust as a Challenge to Jewish Thoughts on Ultimate Reality and Meaning," *Ultimate Reality and Meaning* 14 (September 1991): 185–209.

46. See Ulrich E. Simon, *A Theology of Auschwitz: The Christian Faith and the Problem of Evil*; Harold M. Schulweis, *Evil and the Morality of God*; Marjorie Suchocki, *The End of Evil: Process Eschatology in Historical Context*; and Larry D. Bouchard, *Tragic Method and Tragic Theology: Evil in Contemporary Drama and Religious Thought*.

47. Richard Colton Lyon, ed., *Santayana on America: Essays, Notes, and Lectures on American Life, Literature, and Philosophy*, esp. 262–63.

48. Yvor Winters, *In Defense of Reason*, 600.

49. Quentin Anderson, *The Imperial Self: An Essay in American Literary and Cultural History*, 51–58.

50. See Joel Porte, *Emerson and Thoreau: Transcendentalists in Conflict*, passim; and Porte, *Representative Man*, xxi–xxiii.

51. Lasch, *The True and Only Heaven*, 546.

52. See Van Wyck Brooks, *America's Coming-of-Age*; and Lasch, *The True and Only Heaven*, 547. For full discussions of Emerson's early admirers, see Edwin D. Mead, *The Influence of Emerson*; and Milton R. Konvitz, ed., *The Recognition of Ralph Waldo Emerson: Selected Criticism Since 1837*.

53. See Lasch, *The True and Only Heaven*, 547; and Van Wyck Brooks, *The Life of Emerson*. For more sophisticated views of Emerson's artistry as one of reverence and wonder, see Lewis Mumford, *The Golden Day*; F. O. Matthiessen, *American Renaissance: Art and Expression in the Age of Emerson and Whitman*; R. W. B. Lewis, *The American Adam: Innocence, Tragedy, and Tradition in the Nineteenth Century*; Larzer Ziff, *Literary Democracy: The Declaration of Cultural Independence in America*; and Irving Howe, *The American Newness: Culture and Politics in the Age of Emerson*.

54. See Alfred Kazin's *An American Procession*; and the discussion in Lasch, *The True and Only Heaven*, 547–48.

17. Language Method

1. As quoted in Poirier, "The Question of Genius," 168.

2. Ibid.

3. "Sexy names," as Nicholson Baker observes, "are so often Germanic noun pairs or trios: *category mistake, paradigm shift, catastrophe theory, reader response criticism*"; yet Baker adds that "*paradigm shift* never moved anyone to tears"; for "*all* promise," this phrase offers only the rather absurd, if not the inadvisable and rather inhuman, "prospect of infinite applicability, of normally reticent colleagues from

a hundred different disciplines singing in one great lusty chorus." See Nicholson Baker, *U and I: A True Story*, 33–34.

4. For Wordsworth's concept of "the sad incompetence of human speech," see Ferguson, *Wordsworth: Language as Counterspirit*.

5. Poirier, "The Question of Genius," 166. See also 164–65, 170–71.

6. Here is Foucault as quoted by Poirier: "It is in discourse that power and knowledge are joined together. . . . There is no question that the appearance in nineteenth century psychiatry, jurisprudence, and literature of a whole series of discourses on the species and subspecies of homosexuality, inversion, pederasty, and 'psychic hermaphrodism' made possible a strong advance of social controls into this area of 'perversity'; but it also made possible the formation of a 'reverse' discourse: homosexuality began to speak in its own behalf, to demand that its legitimacy or 'naturality' be acknowledged, often in the same vocabulary, using the same categories by which it was medically disqualified." See Poirier, "The Question of Genius," 171.

7. See Packer, *Emerson's Fall*, 9–10, 18, 168; Bishop, *Emerson on the Soul*, 139; and Richard Poirier, *A World Elsewhere: The Place of Style in American Literature*, 56–70.

8. See the discussion in Jonathan Culler, *Structuralist Poetics: Structuralism, Linguistics, and the Study of Literature*, esp. 152–59.

9. See the discussions in Van Leer, *Emerson's Epistemology*, 247–48; and J. L. Austin, *How to Do Things with Words*, passim.

10. Van Leer, *Emerson's Epistemology*, 216.

11. As quoted in Poirier, "The Question of Genius," 169.

12. Ibid., 168.

13. See Bloom's introduction to his edition of *Modern Critical Views: Ralph Waldo Emerson*, 10.

14. Wasserman, *The Subtler Language*, 203.

15. See the discussion in Terry Eagleton, *Literary Theory: An Introduction*, esp. 129.

16. Barthes, *S/Z*, esp. 186.

Recapitulation and Cadenza

1. Stanley Fish, *Doing What Comes Naturally: Change, Rhetoric, and the Practice of Theory in Literary and Legal Studies*, esp. chapter 1.

2. See E. V. Walter, *Placeways: A Theory of the Human Environment*. See also Gregory L. Ulmer, "Metaphoric Rocks: A Psychogeography of Tourism and Monumentality," in Christoph Gerozissis, ed., *The Florida Landscape: Revisited*, 39–50.

3. M. H. Abrams, *Doing Things with Texts: Essays in Criticism and Critical Theory*.

4. The paraphrase is that of Michael Holquist in "The Politics of Representation," Stephen J. Greenblatt, ed., *Allegory and Representation*, 163–83, esp. 165.

5. M. M. Bakhtin, *Speech Genres and Other Late Essays*, ed. Michael Holquist, trans. Vern McGee, 170.

6. R. B. Kershner, *Joyce, Bakhtin, and Popular Literature*, 15–21.

7. James B. Twitchell, *Carnival Culture: The Trashing of Taste in America*, 10, 57.

8. See David S. Reynolds, *Beneath the American Renaissance: The Subversive Imagination in the Age of Emerson and Melville*; and Donald R. Hettinga's review of *Beneath the American Renaissance*, in *Christianity and Literature* 38 (Spring 1989): 73–74.

9. See Umberto Eco, *Foucault's Pendulum*, trans. William Weaver; and John Updike's review, "In Borges' Wake," of *Foucault's Pendulum*, *The New Yorker* (February 5, 1990), 120.

10. See Henry Abelove, *The Evangelist of Desire: John Wesley and the Methodists*; and Richard E. Brantley, review of *The Evangelist of Desire*, in *Eighteenth-Century Studies* 25 (Winter 1991–92): 250–54.

11. John D. Cox, "Nominalist Ethics and the New Historicism," *Christianity and Literature* 39 (Winter 1990): 127–39.

12. I quote from Cox's paraphrase of Ockham's procedure.

13. See, for example, Clifford Geertz, *The Interpretation of Cultures: Selected Essays*.

14. Cox, "Nominalist Ethics and the New Historicism."

15. Ibid., 133.

16. Frederick Crews, "The Parting of the Twains," *The New York Review of Books* 36 (July 1989): 39–44.

17. Greenblatt, *Shakespearean Negotiations*, 4. Ira Clark, in *Professional Playwrights: Massinger, Ford, Shirley and Brome*, supplements new-historicist methodology with social theory to explore the social and political stances of not just Caroline drama but the major Caroline playwrights.

18. Alan Liu, "The Power of Formalism: The New Historicism," *ELH* 56 (1989): 721–71, esp. 745. Liu recognizes that new historicism, like Jerome McGann's romanticizers of Romanticism, tends to be guilty of "indiscriminate cross-flow between past and present concerns," for "New Historicism" is simply "our latest Romantic ideology unable to differentiate meaningfully between then and now" (752).

19. Greenblatt, *Shakespearean Negotiations*, 7.

20. Liu, "The Power of Formalism," 721–22.

21. See E. A. J. Honigmann's review, "The New Shakespeare?" of Greenblatt's *Shakespearean Negotiations*, in *The New York Review of Books* 35 (March 31, 1988): 32–35.

22. Liu, "The Power of Formalism," 743–44.

23. Edward Pechter, "The New Historicism and Its Discontents: Politicizing Renaissance Drama," *PMLA* 102 (1987): 292–303. Especially helpful on the relations between text and culture are Hayden V. White, *Metahistory: The Historical Imagination in Nineteenth-Century Europe*; and Hayden V. White, *The Content of the Form: Narrative Discourse and Historical Representation*.

24. Greenblatt, *Shakespearean Negotiations*, 4.

25. A book entitled *Responses: On Paul de Man's Wartime Journalism*, ed. Werner Hamacher, Neil Hertz, and Thomas Keenan; and eight essays in recent issues of *Critical Inquiry* are devoted to the topic of Paul de Man's advocacy of fascism: see discussions by Denis Donoghue, "The Strange Case of Paul de Man," *The New York Review of Books* 36 (June 29, 1989): 32–37; Robert Detweiler, "Response to 'Doing "Religion and Literature" in a Postmodernist Mode,' " *Christianity and Literature* 39 (Spring 1990): 317–20; and Jon Wiener, "Deconstructing de Man," *The Nation* (January 9, 1988), 22–24.

26. See David Lehman, *Signs of the Times: Deconstruction and the Fall of Paul de Man*, 118–24. See also Howard Felperin, *Beyond Deconstruction: The Uses and Abuses of Literary Theory*; and Stephen D. Moore, *Literary Criticism and the Gospels: The Theoretical Challenge*.

27. John M. Ellis, *Against Deconstruction*, esp. 26, 74.

28. See J. Hillis Miller, *The Linguistic Moment: From Wordsworth to Stevens*; and Irving Massey's review of *The Linguistic Moment*, in *Studies in Romanticism* 27 (Summer 1988): 336–39.

29. For Miller's reply to the question whether his readings are all predetermined, see Morris Eaves and Michael Fischer, eds., *Romanticism and Contemporary Criticism*, 119. See also Karl Kroeber's review of Miller, *The Linguistic Moment*, in *Studies in Romanticism* 27 (Summer 1988): 339–44.

30. See David Jasper's review of Don Cupitt's *The Long-Legged Fly: A Theology of Language and Desire*, in *Literature and Theology* 2 (September 1988): 274–75.

31. See Miller, *The Linguistic Moment*, 338, 376; and Massey's review of *The Linguistic Moment*, esp. 338.

32. See Brian McCrea, *Addison and Steele Are Dead: The English Department, Its Canon, and the Professionalization of Literary Criticism*. Morris Dickstein, *Double Agent: The Critic and Society*, confronts the yawning gulf between poststructuralist academics and popular reviewers; the question his book raises is "how a strong sense of literature in itself can be reconciled with an equally strong sense of the place of literature in the course of history and the lives of men and women." He provides profiles of critics who bestride the gulf: Matthew Arnold, Van Wyck Brooks, H. L. Mencken, Edmund Wilson, Malcolm Cowley, R. P. Blackmur, Lionel Trilling, Northrop Frye, F. W. Dupee, Philip Rahv, George Orwell, and

Alfred Kazin. Arnold's role was "by day a mild-mannered school inspector, on weekends the scourge of barbarians and philistines—the engaged critic as double agent trying to balance art and social concern." The Arnoldian synthesis broke up into the thesis of Marxist criticism and the antithesis of New Criticism; the former has degenerated into the "bookchat" of popular reviewers, the latter into the academic solipsism of poststructuralist critics, bishops talking to bishops. It is time, according to Dickstein and McCrea, for a new synthesis. The sophisticated yet accessible empirical-evangelical dialectic of Anglo-American Romanticism historically exemplifies such synthesis.

33. See also Holquist, "The Politics of Representation," 163–83.

34. See Kevin L. Cope's review of McCrea, *Addison and Steele Are Dead*, in *South Atlantic Review* 56 (September 1991): 148–51, esp. 151.

35. Among Samuel F. Pickering, Jr.'s several collections of essays is *Still Life*.

36. Jenkins, "A Protestant Aesthetic?" 153–59; and Davie, "Nonconformist Poetics," 160–73.

37. Jenkins, "A Protestant Aesthetic?" 154.

38. Joseph Butler, *Fifteen Sermons Preached at the Rolls Chapel*, 136.

39. Davie, "Nonconformist Poetics," 163. See also Geoffrey Hill, "Our Word Is Our Bond," *Agenda* 21 (1983): 1, reprinted in Geoffrey Hill, *The Lords of Limit*, 138–59.

40. Emily Dickinson, *The Complete Poems of Emily Dickinson*, ed. Thomas Johnson, 332.

41. As quoted by Davie, "Nonconformist Poetics," 163. See also Jacques Ellul, *La Parole Humiliée*, trans. Joyce Main Hanks as *The Humiliation of the Word*, 157.

42. George Steiner, *Real Presences: The Leslie Stephen Memorial Lecture*, 15.

43. See the discussion in Patricia Ward, "'An Affair of the Heart': Ethics, Criticism, and the Teaching of Literature," *Christianity and Literature* 39 (Winter 1990): 181–92, esp. 182.

44. See the address by J. Hillis Miller, "Thinking Like Other People," in Mark Edmundson, ed., *Wild Orchids and Trotsky: Messages from American Universities*. I am grateful to Ira Clark for conversation about the address.

45. John Sturrock, "The Book Is Dead, Long Live the Book," *The New York Times Book Review* (September 13, 1987), 3.

46. See Wesley A. Kort, *Story, Text, and Scripture: Literary Interests in Biblical Narrative*; Robert Detweiler, *Breaking the Fall: Religious Readings of Contemporary Fiction*; Clarence Walhout, "Can Derrida Be Christianized?" *Christianity and Literature* 34 (Winter 1985): 15–22; G. Douglas Atkins, *Reading Deconstruction, Deconstructive Reading*; John C. Sherwood, "Derrida, Formalism, and Christianity," *Christianity and Literature* 35 (Summer 1986): 15–17; Garrett Green, *Imagining God: Theology and the Religious Imagination*; Mark C. Taylor, *Altarity*; Mark C. Taylor,

ERRING: A Postmodern A/Theology; Thomas J. J. Altizer, ed., *Deconstruction and Theology*; Charles Winquist, *Epiphanies of Darkness: Deconstruction in Theology*; and Doty, "Contextual Fictions that Bridge Our Worlds," 104–29.

47. Frank Lentricchia, *After the New Criticism*, 176, as quoted in Jasper's review of Cupitt's *The Long-Legged Fly: A Theology of Language and Desire*, 274–75.

48. Alison Lurie, "A Dictionary for Deconstructors," *The New York Review of Books* 36 (November 23, 1989): 49–50.

49. See Gregory L. Ulmer, *Applied Grammatology: Post(e)-Pedagogy from Jacques Derrida to Joseph Beuys*; and Patricia Ward, review of Ulmer, *Applied Grammatology*, in *Christianity and Literature* 36 (Spring 1987): 52–53.

50. Gregory L. Ulmer, "Teletheory: A Mystory," in Clayton Koelb and Virgil Lokke, eds., *The Current in Criticism*, 339–71, esp. 342, 344.

51. See, besides Ulmer's *Applied Grammatology*, Gregory L. Ulmer, *Teletheory: Grammatology in the Age of Video*; and Gregory L. Ulmer, *Heuristics*, forthcoming.

52. For an especially self-conscious if not unduly self-indulgent illustration of the current critical climate, consider John N. Duvall's *Faulkner's Marginal Couple: Invisible, Outlaw, and Unspeakable Communities*. Duvall, wanting to be thought a feminist, apologizes for the fact that he "will never have a baby," but makes up for the problem by proclaiming his belief that all gender differences, except for the basic "sexual hardware," are culturally constructed, and boasts: "I resolutely oppose thinking that tells me I have a more primordial bond with my male dog than with a human female because my dog and I both have testicles or that my wife's behavior can be compared to a cow's because each has a uterus." Frederick Crews calls this gratuitous remark "the trend-conscious male academic's anxiety to be considered politically unstained"; see Frederick Crews, "The Strange Fate of William Faulkner," *The New York Review of Books* 38 (March 7, 1991): 47–52, esp. 50.

53. I refer to Wordsworth's "The Solitary Reaper" (1807).

54. For the idea of self-similarity in human culture as well as science, see James Gleick, *Chaos: Making a New Science*, esp. 103, 115–16.

55. Thomas Mermall, "The Chiasmus: Unamuno's Master Trope," *PMLA* 105 (March 1990): 245–55, esp. 246. Subsequent references to this essay are by page numbers alone.

56. See Robert P. Sharlemann, "The No to Nothing and the Nothing to Know: Barth and Tillich and the Possibility of Theological Science," *Journal of the American Academy of Religion* 55 (Spring 1987): 57–74; and Robert P. Sharlemann, "The Being of God when God Is Not Being God: Deconstructing the History of Theism," in Altizer, ed., *Deconstruction and Theology*, 79–108.

57. See Ricoeur, *Freud and Philosophy*; and Liu, "The Power of Formalism," 722.

58. See Ernest B. Gilman, *The Curious Perspective: Literary and Pictorial Wit*

in the Seventeenth Century, esp. 234; and Rosalie Colie, *Paradoxia Epidemica: The Renaissance Tradition of Paradox*, esp. 260–62.

59. As quoted in Mermall, "The Chiasmus," 247.

60. See Naomi Bliven's review of Ed Cray, *General of the Army George C. Marshall: Soldier and Statesman*, in *The New Yorker* (August 6, 1990), 97–99. See also Paul Kennedy, "Fin-de-Siècle America," a review of recent books by Henry R. Nau, Richard Rosecrance, John Chancellor, and Joseph S. Nye, Jr., in *The New York Review of Books* 37 (June 28, 1990): 31–40.

61. I allude to Matthew Arnold's "To a Friend" (1849), the first line of which is, "Who prop, thou ask'st, in these bad days, my mind?" Arnold answers, in effect, "Homer, Epictetus, and especially Sophocles."

62. See Francis Fukuyama, *The End of History and the Last Man*.

63. I refer to Milton's "Lycidas."

64. See Massey's review of Miller, *The Linguistic Moment*, 336–39.

65. See Janet Malcolm's review, "The Trial of Alyosha," of Havel's *Letters to Olga: June 1979–September 1982*, in *The New York Review of Books* 37 (June 14, 1990): 35–38.

66. See John Updike's review of Walter Abish, *Alphabetical Africa*, in John Updike, *Picked-Up Pieces*, 399–402.

67. Brantley, *Coordinates of Anglo-American Romanticism*, esp. 36–42.

68. Leonard I. Sweet, "Wise as Serpents, Innocent as Doves: The New Evangelical Historiography," *Journal of the American Academy of Religion* 56 (Fall 1988): 397–416, esp. 398, 401–2, 403, 412–13.

69. As quoted in ibid., 408.

70. See Bloom, *The American Religion*, esp. 190–233.

71. For a discussion of liminality as an epistemological mode, see, for example, Victor Turner, *The Ritual Process: Structure and Anti-Structure*.

72. Leonard I. Sweet, *Quantum Spirituality: A Postmodern Apologetic*, esp. 263–302.

73. Wesley A. Kort casts a recent essay as a letter to Robert Detweiler; see Kort, "Doing 'Religion and Literature' in a Postmodernist Mode," *Christianity and Literature* 39 (Winter 1990): 193–98.

74. Wood gives credit to George Marsden's essay, "America's 'Christian' Origins: Puritan New England as a Case Study," and R. T. Kendall's essay, "The Puritan Modification of Calvin's Theology," both in W. Stanford Reid, ed., *John Calvin: His Influence in the Western World*.

75. See Wood, *The Comedy of Redemption*. See also the highly favorable assessments of *The Comedy of Redemption* by Richard E. Brantley, in *The Flannery O'Connor Bulletin* 17 (1988): 105–8; and by Frederick Crews, "The Power of Flannery O'Connor," in *The New York Review of Books* 37 (April 26, 1990): 49–55.

76. Rex D. Matthews, " 'Religion and Reason Joined': A Study in the Theology of John Wesley," Th.D. dissertation.

77. G. C. Cell, *The Rediscovery of John Wesley.*

78. See David Tracy, *Plurality and Ambiguity: Hermeneutics, Religion, Hope*; and the discussion by John G. Parks, "Losing and Finding: Meditations of a Christian Reader," *Christianity and Literature* 38 (Summer 1989): 19–24.

79. See the discussion in Jenkins, "A Protestant Aesthetic?" esp. 155–56, 158–59.

80. Stanley Cavell, "In Quest of the Ordinary: Texts of Recovery," in Eaves and Fischer, eds., *Romanticism and Contemporary Criticism*, 205.

81. See Jasper Griffin's review of David Sansone, *Greek Athletics and the Genesis of Sport*, in *The New York Review of Books* 35 (September 29, 1988): 3–4.

82. See Julian Barnes, *A History of the World in 10½ Chapters*; and the review by Michiko Kakutani of Barnes, *A History of the World in 10½ Chapters*, in *New York Times*, September 29, 1989. Compare Barnes's statement with that of Alfred Clayton, the hero of John Updike's fifteenth novel: "[Historical texts] are like pieces of a puzzle that only roughly fit. There are little irregular spaces between them, and through these cracks, one feels, truth slips. History, unlike fiction and physics, never quite jells; it is an armature of rather randomly preserved verbal and physical remains upon which historians slap wads of supposition in hopes of the lumpy statue's coming to life. One of the joys of doing original research is to observe how one's predecessor historians have fudged their way across the very gaps, or fault-lines, that one is in turn balked by. History in its jaggedness constantly tears at our smooth conception of human behavior." See John Updike, *Memories of the Ford Administration: A Novel* (New York: Knopf, 1992), 165–66.

Works Cited

ABELOVE, HENRY. *The Evangelist of Desire: John Wesley and the Methodists*. Stanford: Stanford University Press, 1990.

ABISH, WALTER. *Alphabetical Africa*. New York: New Directions, 1974.

ABRAMS, M. H. *Doing Things with Texts: Essays in Criticism and Critical Theory*. New York: W. W. Norton, 1990.

———. *Natural Supernaturalism: Tradition and Revolution in Romantic Literature*. New York: W. W. Norton, 1971.

ABRAMS, M. H., ed. *The Norton Anthology of English Literature: Third Edition*. 2 volumes. New York: W. W. Norton, 1974.

ABRAMS, M. H., et al., eds. *The Norton Anthology of English Literature: Fifth Edition*. 2 volumes. New York: W. W. Norton, 1986.

ADAMS, HAZARD, ed. *Critical Theory Since Plato*. San Diego: Harcourt Brace Jovanovich, 1971.

———. *Critical Theory Since Plato: Revised Edition*. New York: Harcourt Brace Jovanovich, 1992.

ALBRIGHT, DANIEL. *Tennyson: The Muses' Tug-of-War*. Charlottesville: University Press of Virginia, 1986.

ALIGHIERI, DANTE. *The Inferno: A Verse Rendering for the Modern Reader*. Translated and edited by John Ciardi. New York: New American Library, 1954.

ALTIZER, THOMAS J. J. Introduction to "To Create the Absolute Edge," by D. G. Leahy. *Journal of the American Academy of Religion* 57 (Winter 1989): 773–89.

ALTIZER, THOMAS J. J., ed. *Deconstruction and Theology*. New York: Crossroad, 1982.

ANDERSON, QUENTIN. *The Imperial Self: An Essay in American Literary and Cultural History*. New York: Alfred A. Knopf, 1971.

ARCINIEGAS, GERMAN. *America in Europe: A History of the New World in Reverse*. Translated by Gabriela Arciniegas and R. Victoria Arana. San Diego: Harcourt Brace Jovanovich, 1986.

ARVIN, NEWTON. "The House of Pain." In Newton Arvin, *American Pantheon*, 31–47. New York: Delcourt, 1966.

ATKINS, G. DOUGLAS. *Reading Deconstruction, Deconstructive Reading*. Lexington: University Press of Kentucky, 1983.

AUGUST, EUGENE R. "Tennyson and Teilhard: The Faith of *In Memoriam*." *PMLA* 84 (1969): 217–26.

AUSTIN, J. L. *How to Do Things with Words*. Second edition. Cambridge, Mass.: Harvard University Press, 1975.

BABEL, ISAAC. *The Collected Stories*. Translated and edited by Walter Morrison. New York: New American Library, 1974.

BAKER, CARLOS. *The Echoing Green: Romanticism, Modernism, and the Phenomena of Transference in Poetry*. Princeton, N.J.: Princeton University Press, 1984.

BAKER, NICHOLSON. *The Mezzanine: A Novel*. New York: Weidenfeld and Nicolson, 1988.

———. *U and I: A True Story*. New York: Random House, 1991.

BAKHTIN, M. M. *Speech Genres and Other Late Essays*. Edited by Michael Holquist and translated by Vern McGee. Austin: University of Texas Press, 1986.

BALL, PATRICIA. *The Central Self*. London: Athlone, 1968.

BARNES, JULIAN. *A History of the World in 10½ Chapters*. New York: Alfred A. Knopf, 1989.

BARTHES, ROLAND. *S/Z*. New York: Hill and Wang, 1974.

BEHNKEN, ELOISE M. *Thomas Carlyle: "Calvinist Without the Theology."* Columbia: University of Missouri Press, 1978.

BELLAH, ROBERT. *Habits of the Heart: Individualism and Commitment in American Life*. Berkeley: University of California Press, 1985.

BERCOVITCH, SACVAN. *The American Jeremiad*. Madison: University of Wisconsin Press, 1978.

———. "Emerson the Prophet: Romanticism, Puritanism, and Auto-American-Biography." 1975. Reprint. In *Modern Critical Views: Ralph Waldo Emerson*, edited by Harold Bloom, 31–45.

———. *The Puritan Origins of the American Self*. New Haven, Conn.: Yale University Press, 1975.

BISHOP, JONATHAN. *Emerson on the Soul*. Cambridge, Mass.: Harvard University Press, 1964.

BLIVEN, NAOMI. Review of *General of the Army George C. Marshall: Soldier and Statesman*, by Ed Cray (New York: W. W. Norton, 1990). *The New Yorker*, August 6, 1990, 97–99.

BLOOM, HAROLD. *Agon: Towards a Theory of Revisionism*. New York: Oxford, 1982.

———. *The American Religion: The Emergence of the Post-Christian Nation*. New York: Simon and Schuster, 1992.

———. *The Anxiety of Influence*. New York: Oxford University Press, 1973.

———. *Kabbalah and Criticism*. New York: Continuum, 1975.

———. *The Ringers in the Tower: Studies in the Romantic Tradition*. Chicago: University of Chicago Press, 1971.

———. *Ruin the Sacred Truths*. Cambridge, Mass.: Harvard University Press, 1989.

———. "Tennyson, Hallam, and the Romantic Tradition." In Harold Bloom, *The Ringers in the Tower: Studies in the Romantic Tradition*, 145–54.

———. "Tennyson: In the Shadow of Keats." In Harold Bloom, *Poetry and Repression*, 121–36. New Haven, Conn.: Yale University Press, 1976.

BLOOM, HAROLD, ed. *Modern Critical Views: Alfred Lord Tennyson*. New York: Chelsea House, 1985.

———. *Modern Critical Views: Ralph Waldo Emerson*. New York: Chelsea House, 1985.

BORNSTEIN, GEORGE. *Transformations of Romanticism in Yeats, Eliot, and Stevens*. Chicago: University of Chicago Press, 1976.

BOTTORFF, WILLIAM K. "'Whatever Inly Rejoices Me': The Paradox of 'Self-Reliance.'" *ESQ* 18 (1972): 207–17.

BOUCHARD, LARRY D. *Tragic Method and Tragic Theology: Evil in Contemporary Drama and Religious Thought*. University Park: Pennsylvania State University Press, 1989.

BOYD-CARPENTER, WILLIAM. "Tennyson and His Talk on Some Religious Questions." In *Tennyson: Interviews and Recollections*, edited by Norman Page, 186–90.

BRADLEY, A. C. *A Commentary on Tennyson's In Memoriam*. Third edition, revised. London: Macmillan, 1910.

BRADLEY, IAN. *The Call to Seriousness: The Evangelical Impact on the Victorians*. London: Jonathan Cape, 1976.

BRANTLEY, RICHARD E. "Charles Wesley's Experiential Art." *Eighteenth-Century Life* 11 (May 1987): 1–11.

———. "The Common Ground of Wesley and Edwards." *Harvard Theological Review* 83 (July 1990): 271–303.

———. *Coordinates of Anglo-American Romanticism: Wesley, Edwards, Carlyle, and Emerson*. Gainesville: University Press of Florida, 1993.

———. "John Wesley (1703–1791)." In *British Prose Writers, 1660–1800: Second Series*, edited by Donald T. Siebert. *Dictionary of Literary Biography*. Volume 104. Detroit: Gale Research, 1991.

———. "Keats's Method." *Studies in Romanticism* 22 (Fall 1983): 389–406.

———. *Locke, Wesley, and the Method of English Romanticism*. Gainesville: University Press of Florida, 1984.

———. Review of *The Comedy of Redemption: Christian Faith and Comic Vision in*

Four American Novelists, by Ralph C. Wood. *The Flannery O'Connor Bulletin* 17 (1988): 105–8.

———. Review of *The Evangelist of Desire: John Wesley and the Methodists*, by Henry Abelove. *Eighteenth-Century Studies* 25 (Winter 1991–92): 250–54.

———. Review of *The Obstinate Questionings of English Romanticism*, by L. J. Swingle. *ANQ: A Quarterly Journal of Short Articles, Notes, and Reviews* 3 (July 1990): 142–45.

———. *Wordsworth's "Natural Methodism."* New Haven, Conn.: Yale University Press, 1975.

BRASHEAR, WILLIAM R. *The Living Will: A Study of Tennyson and Nineteenth-Century Subjectivism.* Studies in English Literature. Volume 52. The Hague: Mouton, 1969.

BRONOWSKI, JACOB. *The Ascent of Man.* Boston: Little, Brown, 1973.

BROOKS, VAN WYCK. *America's Coming-of-Age.* New York: B. W. Heubsch, 1915.

———. *The Life of Emerson.* New York: Dutton, 1932.

BROWN, NATHANIEL. *Sexuality and Feminism in Shelley.* Cambridge, Mass.: Harvard University Press, 1979.

BRUNER, JEROME, and CAROL FLEISHER FELDMAN. "Under Construction." *The New York Review of Books* 33 (March 27, 1986): 46–49.

BUCKLEY, JEROME H. *Tennyson: The Growth of a Poet.* Cambridge, Mass.: Harvard University Press, 1961.

BUCKLEY, JEROME H., ed. *Poems of Tennyson.* Boston: Houghton Mifflin, 1958.

BUELL, LAWRENCE. *Literary Transcendentalism: Style and Vision in the American Renaissance.* Ithaca, N.Y.: Cornell University Press, 1973.

———. "Unitarian Aesthetics and Emerson's Poet-Priest." *American Quarterly* 20 (Spring 1968): 1–13.

BURCHELL, SAMUEL C. "Tennyson's Dark Night." *South Atlantic Quarterly* 54 (1955): 75–81.

BUTLER, JOSEPH. *Fifteen Sermons Preached at the Rolls Chapel.* Fifth edition. London: John, Francis, and Charles Rivington, 1797.

CALVINO, ITALO. *Mr. Palomar.* Translated by William Weaver. San Diego: Harcourt Brace Jovanovich, 1985.

———. *Six Memos for the Next Millennium.* Translated by Patrick Creagh. Cambridge, Mass.: Harvard University Press, 1988.

CAMERON, KENNETH WALTER. "An Early Prose Work of Emerson." *American Literature* 22 (November 1950): 332–38.

CARR, ARTHUR J. "Tennyson as a Modern Poet." *University of Toronto Quarterly* 19 (1950): 361–82.

CARRERE, EMMANUEL. *The Moustache.* Translated by Lanie Goodman. New York: Scribner's, 1988.

CARTON, EVAN. *The Rhetoric of American Romance: Dialectic and Identity in Emerson, Dickinson, Poe, and Hawthorne*. Baltimore: Johns Hopkins University Press, 1985.

CAVELL, STANLEY. *The Chain of Reason: Wittgenstein, Skepticism, Morality, and Tragedy*. New York: Oxford University Press, 1979.

——. "Genteel Responses to Kant? in Emerson's *Fate* and Coleridge's *Biographia Literaria*." *Raritan* 3 (Fall 1983): 36–61.

——. "Hope Against Hope." *American Poetry Review* 15 (January–February 1986): 9–13.

——. "In Quest of the Ordinary: Texts of Recovery." In *Romanticism and Contemporary Criticism*, edited by Morris Eaves and Michael Fischer, 201–15.

——. *The Senses of Walden*. New York: Viking, 1972.

——. "Thinking of Emerson." *New Literary History* 11 (1979): 166–76.

CELL, G. C. *The Rediscovery of John Wesley*. New York: Henry Holt, 1935.

CHEYFITZ, ERIC. *The Trans-Parent: Sexual Politics in the Language of Emerson*. Baltimore: Johns Hopkins University Press, 1981.

CLARK, IRA. *Professional Playwrights: Massinger, Ford, Shirley and Brome*. Lexington: University Press of Kentucky, 1992.

CLARKE, COLIN. *Romantic Paradox: An Essay on the Poetry of Wordsworth*. New York: Barnes and Noble, 1963.

COKER, WILSON. *Music and Meaning: A Theoretical Introduction to Musical Aesthetics*. New York: Free Press, 1972.

COLE, PHYLLIS. "From the Edwardses to the Emersons: Four Generations of Evangelical Family Culture." *College English Association Critic* 49 (1986–87): 70–78.

COLIE, ROSALIE. *Paradoxia Epidemica: The Renaissance Tradition of Paradox*. Princeton, N.J.: Princeton University Press, 1966.

COLLINS, WINSTON. "Tennyson and Hopkins." *University of Toronto Quarterly* 38 (1968): 84–95.

COPE, KEVIN L. Review of *Addison and Steele Are Dead: The English Department, Its Canon, and the Professionalization of Literary Criticism*, by Brian McCrea. *South Atlantic Review* 56 (September 1991): 148–51.

COTT, NANCY. *The Bonds of Womanhood: "Woman's Sphere" in New England*. New Haven, Conn.: Yale University Press, 1977.

——. "Young Women in the Second Great Awakening in New England." *Feminist Studies* 3 (Fall 1975): 15–29.

COX, JOHN D. "Nominalist Ethics and the New Historicism." *Christianity and Literature* 39 (Winter 1990): 127–39.

CRAY, ED. *General of the Army George C. Marshall: Soldier and Statesman*. New York: W. W. Norton, 1990.

CREWS, FREDERICK. "The Parting of the Twains." *The New York Review of Books* 36 (July 1989): 39–44.
———. "The Power of Flannery O'Connor." *The New York Review of Books* 37 (April 26, 1990): 49–55.
———. "The Strange Fate of William Faulkner." *The New York Review of Books* 38 (March 7, 1991): 47–52.
CULLER, A. DWIGHT. *The Poetry of Tennyson*. New Haven, Conn.: Yale University Press, 1977.
CULLER, JONATHAN. *Structuralist Poetics: Structuralism, Linguistics, and the Study of Literature*. Ithaca, N.Y.: Cornell University Press, 1975.
CUPITT, DON. *The Long-Legged Fly: A Theology of Language and Desire*. London: SCM, 1987.
DAHL, CURTIS. "The Victorian Wasteland." *College English* 16 (1955): 341–47.
D'AVANZO, MARIO L. "Lyric 95 of *In Memoriam*: Poetry and Vision." *Research Studies* 37 (1969): 149–54.
DAVIE, DONALD. "Nonconformist Poetics: A Reply to Daniel Jenkins." *Literature and Theology* 2 (September 1988): 160–73.
DAVIES, HORTON. *Worship and Theology in England from Watts and Wesley to Maurice, 1690–1850*. Princeton, N.J.: Princeton University Press, 1961.
DAWKINS, RICHARD. *The Blind Watchmaker*. New York: W. W. Norton, 1989.
———. *The Selfish Gene*. 1976. Reprint. New York: Oxford University Press, 1989.
DAY, AIDAN. "Textual Tapestries." *TLS* 4670 (October 2, 1992): 7.
DEAN, D. R. *Tennyson and Geology*. Lincoln, England: Tennyson Research Centre, 1985.
DEN OTTER, A. G. "The Question and *The Book of Thel*." *Studies in Romanticism* 30 (Winter 1991): 633–55.
DePORTE, MICHAEL V. "Vehicles of Delusion: Swift, Locke, and the Madhouse Poems of James Carkesse." In *Psychology and Literature in the Eighteenth Century*, edited by Christopher Fox, 217–31.
DE SOUSA, RONALD. *The Rationality of Emotion*. Boston: MIT Press, 1987.
DETWEILER, ROBERT. *Breaking the Fall: Religious Readings of Contemporary Fiction*. San Francisco: Harper and Row, 1989.
———. "Response to 'Doing "Religion and Literature" in a Postmodernist Mode.' " *Christianity and Literature* 39 (Spring 1990): 317–20.
DEVLIN, FRANCIS P. "Dramatic Irony in the Early Sections of Tennyson's *In Memoriam*." *Papers on Language and Literature* 8 (1972): 172–83.
DEVLIN, KEITH. *Mathematics: The New Golden Age*. Harmondsworth, England: Penguin, 1988.

DICKINSON, EMILY. *The Complete Poems of Emily Dickinson.* Edited by Thomas Johnson. Boston: Little, Brown, 1960.

DICKSTEIN, MORRIS. *Double Agent: The Critic and Society.* New York: Oxford University Press, 1992.

DONOGHUE, DENIS. "Bewitched, Bothered, and Bewildered." *The New York Review of Books* 40 (March 25, 1993): 46–53.

————. "The Sad Captain of Criticism." *The New York Review of Books* 36 (March 2, 1989): 22–24.

————. "The Strange Case of Paul de Man." *The New York Review of Books* 36 (June 29, 1989): 32–37.

DOTY, WILLIAM G. "Contextual Fictions that Bridge Our Worlds: 'A Whole New Poetry.'" *Literature and Theology* 4 (March 1990): 104–29.

DOUGLAS, ANN. *The Feminization of American Culture.* New York: Alfred A. Knopf, 1977.

DOWNEY, JAMES. *The Eighteenth-Century Pulpit: A Study of the Sermons of Butler, Berkeley, Secker, Sterne, Whitefield and Wesley.* Oxford: Clarendon, 1969.

DUNN, MARY MAPLES. "Saints and Sisters: Congregational and Quaker Women in the Early Colonial Period." *American Quarterly* 30 (1978): 582–601.

DUVALL, JOHN N. *Faulkner's Marginal Couple: Invisible, Outlaw, and Unspeakable Communities.* Austin: University of Texas Press, 1990.

DYSON, HOPE, and CHARLES TENNYSON, eds. *Dear and Honoured Lady: The Correspondence between Queen Victoria and Alfred Tennyson.* London: Macmillan, 1969.

EAGLETON, TERRY. *Literary Theory: An Introduction.* Minneapolis: University of Minnesota Press, 1983.

————. "Tennyson: Politics and Sexuality in *The Princess* and *In Memoriam.*" In *1848: The Sociology of Literature,* edited by Francis Barker et al. Essex, England: University of Essex Press, 1978.

EAVES, MORRIS, and MICHAEL FISCHER, eds. *Romanticism and Contemporary Criticism.* Ithaca, N.Y.: Cornell University Press, 1986.

ECO, UMBERTO. *Foucault's Pendulum.* Translated by William Weaver. New York: Harcourt Brace Jovanovich, 1989.

EDWARDS, JONATHAN. *An Account of the Life of the Late Reverend Mr. David Brainerd.* Boston: D. Henchman, 1749.

————. *The Distinguishing Marks of a Work of the Spirit of God.* Boston: S. Kneeland and T. Green, 1741.

————. *A Faithful Narrative of the Surprising Work of God in the Conversion of many hundred souls in Northampton.* Edinburgh: J. Oswald, 1736.

————. *Some Thoughts concerning the Present Revival in New England.* Boston: S. Kneeland and T. Green, 1742.

————. *A Treatise concerning Religious Affections*. In volume 2 of *The Works of Jonathan Edwards*. Edited by John E. Smith. New Haven, Conn.: Yale University Press, 1959.

EIDSON, JOHN O. *Tennyson in America: His Reputation and Influence from 1827 to 1858*. Athens: University of Georgia Press, 1943.

ELIOT, T. S. *Essays Ancient and Modern*. New York: Harcourt, Brace, 1936.

————. *Selected Essays*. New York: Harcourt, Brace and World, 1960.

ELLIS, JOHN M. *Against Deconstruction*. Princeton, N.J.: Princeton University Press, 1989.

ELLISON, JULIE. *Emerson's Romantic Style*. Princeton, N.J.: Princeton University Press, 1984.

ELLUL, JACQUES. *The Humiliation of the Word*. Translated from the French, *La Parole Humiliée* (Paris, 1981), by Joyce Main Hanks. Grand Rapids: Eerdmans, 1985.

EMERSON, MARY MOODY. "Almanacks, 1802–1855." Houghton Library MS.

EMERSON, RALPH WALDO. *The Collected Works of Ralph Waldo Emerson*. Edited by Robert Spiller, Albert Ferguson, et al. Cambridge, Mass.: Harvard University Press, 1971–.

————. *The Complete Sermons of Ralph Waldo Emerson*. Edited by Albert J. von Frank. With an introduction by David Robinson. Volume 1. Columbia: University of Missouri Press, 1989.

————. *The Complete Works of Ralph Waldo Emerson: Centenary Edition*. Edited by Edward Waldo Emerson. 12 volumes. Boston: Houghton Mifflin, 1903–4.

————. *The Journals and Miscellaneous Notebooks of Ralph Waldo Emerson*. Edited by William Gilman et al. 16 volumes. Cambridge, Mass.: Harvard University Press, 1960–82.

————. *The Letters of Ralph Waldo Emerson*. Edited by Ralph Rusk. 3 volumes. New York: Columbia University Press, 1939.

————. *Selections from Ralph Waldo Emerson: An Organic Anthology*. Edited by Stephen E. Whicher. Boston: Houghton Mifflin, 1957.

ENGLAND, MARTHA, and JOHN SPARROW. *Hymns Unbidden: Donne, Herbert, Blake, Emily Dickinson, and the Hymnographers*. New York: New York Public Library, 1966.

EPSTEIN, BARBARA. *The Politics of Domesticity: Women, Evangelism and Temperance in Nineteenth-Century America*. Middletown, Conn.: Wesleyan University Press, 1981.

FARLEY, WENDY. *Tragic Vision and Divine Compassion: A Contemporary Theodicy*. Philadelphia: Westminster/John Knox, 1990.

FELPERIN, HOWARD. *Beyond Deconstruction: The Uses and Abuses of Literary Theory*. Oxford: Clarendon, 1985.

FERGUSON, FRANCES. *Wordsworth: Language as Counterspirit*. New Haven, Conn.: Yale University Press, 1977.

FISH, STANLEY. *Doing What Comes Naturally: Change, Rhetoric, and the Practice of Theory in Literary and Legal Studies*. Durham, N.C.: Duke University Press, 1989.

———. *Is There a Text in This Class? The Authority of Interpretive Communities*. Cambridge, Mass.: Harvard University Press, 1980.

FITZGERALD, PENELOPE, TOM PAULIN, KINGSLEY AMIS, TERRY EAGLETON, A. S. BYATT, SEAMUS HEANEY, ANDREW MOTION, PAT ROGERS, GAVIN EWART, PAUL MULDOON, ANTHONY HECHT, AND ISOBEL ARMSTRONG. "A Hundred Years After: Twelve Writers Reflect on Tennyson's Achievement and Influence." *TLS* 4670 (October 2, 1992): 8–9.

FLIEGELMAN, JAY. *Prodigals and Pilgrims: The American Revolution Against Patriarchal Authority, 1750–1800*. Cambridge: Cambridge University Press, 1982.

FLYNN, PHILIP. "Hallam and Tennyson: The 'Theodicaea Novissima' and *In Memoriam*." *Studies in English Literature* 19 (1979): 705–20.

FOAKES, R. A. "The Rhetoric of Faith: Tennyson's *In Memoriam* and Browning's *Men and Women*." In R. A. Foakes, *The Romantic Assertion: A Study in the Language of Nineteenth-Century Poetry*, 111–37. New Haven, Conn.: Yale University Press, 1958.

FOOT, PHILIPPA. "Nietzsche's Immoralism." *The New York Review of Books* 38 (June 13, 1991): 18–22.

FOX, CHRISTOPHER, ed. *Psychology and Literature in the Eighteenth Century*. New York: AMS, 1987.

FUKUYAMA, FRANCIS. *The End of History and the Last Man*. New York: Free Press, 1992.

FUSSELL, PAUL. *Class*. New York: Ballantine Books, 1983.

GARDNER, MARTIN. "Beauty in Numbers." *The New York Review of Books* 36 (March 16, 1989): 26–28.

GEERTZ, CLIFFORD. *The Interpretation of Cultures: Selected Essays*. New York: Basic Books, 1973.

GELPI, DONALD. "Emerson's Sense of Ultimate Meaning and Reality." *Ultimate Reality and Meaning* 15 (1992): 93–111.

GIBSON, WALKER. "Behind the Veil: A Distinction Between Poetic and Scientific Language in Tennyson, Lyell, and Darwin." *Victorian Studies* 2 (1958): 60–68.

GIFFORD, DON. *The Farther Shore: A Natural History of Perception, 1798–1984*. New York: Atlantic Monthly, 1990.

GILMAN, ERNEST B. *The Curious Perspective: Literary and Pictorial Wit in the Seventeenth Century*. New Haven, Conn.: Yale University Press, 1978.

GIOIA, DANA. *Can Poetry Matter? Essays on Poetry and American Culture.* St. Paul, Minn.: Graywolf, 1992.

GLEICK, JAMES. *Chaos: Making a New Science.* Harmondsworth, England: Penguin, 1987.

GLISERMAN, SUSAN. "Early Victorian Science Writers and Tennyson's *In Memoriam*: A Study in Cultural Exchange." *Victorian Studies* 18 (1975): 277–308, 437–59.

GOODMAN, NELSON. *Of Mind and Other Matters.* Cambridge, Mass.: Harvard University Press, 1985.

GOSSE, EDMUND. "Lord Tennyson's Eightieth Birthday." *St James's Gazette*, August 3, 1899, 7.

GOULD, STEPHEN JAY. *Time's Arrow, Time's Cycle: Myth and Metaphor in the Discovery of Geological Time.* Cambridge, Mass.: Harvard University Press, 1987.

GRANSDEN, K. W. *Tennyson*: In Memoriam. Studies in English Literature, number 22. London: Edward Arnold, 1964.

GREEN, GARRETT. *Imagining God: Theology and the Religious Imagination.* San Francisco: Harper and Row, 1989.

GREENBLATT, STEPHEN J. *Shakespearean Negotiations: The Circulation of Social Energy in Renaissance England.* Berkeley: University of California Press, 1988.

GREGORY, RICHARD L., and O. L. ZANGWILL, eds. *The Oxford Companion to the Mind.* New York: Oxford University Press, 1988.

GRIFFIN, JASPER. Review of *Greek Athletics and the Genesis of Sport*, by David Sansone. *The New York Review of Books* 35 (September 29, 1988): 3–4.

GUILLEN, MICHAEL. *Bridges to Infinity.* New York: J. P. Tarcher, 1984.

HAIR, DONALD S. *Tennyson's Language.* Toronto: University of Toronto Press, 1992.

HAMACHER, WERNER, NEIL HERTZ, AND THOMAS KEENAN, eds. *Responses: On Paul de Man's Journalism.* Lincoln: University of Nebraska Press, 1989.

HARDING, D. W. *Experience into Words: Essays on Poetry.* New York: Horizon, 1964.

HARRISON, JAMES. "Tennyson and Evolution." *Durham University Journal* 64 (1971): 26–31.

HAVEL, VACLAV. *Letters to Olga: June 1979–September 1982.* Translated by Paul Wilson. New York: Alfred A. Knopf, 1988.

———. "The Power of the Word." *The New York Review of Books* 37 (January 18, 1990): 3–8.

HEARNE, VICKI. *Adam's Task: Calling Animals by Name.* New York: Alfred A. Knopf, 1986.

HELLSTROM, WARD. *On the Poems of Tennyson.* Gainesville: University Press of Florida, 1972.

HETTINGA, DONALD R. Review of *Beneath the American Renaissance: The Subversive*

Imagination in the Age of Emerson and Melville, by David S. Reynolds. *Christianity and Literature* 38 (Spring 1989): 73–74.

HILL, DAVID W. "Emerson's Eumenides: Textual Evidence and the Interpretation of 'Experience.'" In *Emerson Centenary Essays*, edited by Joel Myerson, 93–106. Carbondale: Southern Illinois University Press, 1982.

HILL, GEOFFREY. "Our Word Is Our Bond." *Agenda* 21 (1983): 1. Reprinted in Geoffrey Hill, *The Lords of Limit*. London: Andre Deutsch, 1984.

HIMMELFARB, GERTRUDE. *The New History and the Old*. Cambridge, Mass.: Harvard University Press, 1987.

HIRSCH, E. D., JR. *The Aims of Interpretation*. Chicago: University of Chicago Press, 1975.

———. *Cultural Literacy: What Every American Needs to Know*. New York: Vintage Books, 1988.

———. *Innocence and Experience: An Introduction to Blake*. New Haven, Conn.: Yale University Press, 1964.

HIRSCH, GORDON D. "Tennyson's *Commedia*." *Victorian Poetry* 8 (1970): 92–106.

HOFSTADTER, DOUGLAS R., and DANIEL C. DENNETT. *The Mind's I: Fantasies and Reflections on Self and Soul*. New York: Basic Books, 1981.

HOLLAND, NORMAN. *The I*. New Haven, Conn.: Yale University Press, 1986.

HOLQUIST, MICHAEL. "The Politics of Representation." *Allegory and Representation*, edited by Stephen J. Greenblatt, 163–83. Baltimore: Johns Hopkins University Press, 1981.

HOLT, HAMILTON, ed. *The Life Stories of Undistinguished Americans: As Told by Themselves*. 1902. Reprint. New York: Routledge, 1990.

HONIGMANN, E. A. J. "The New Shakespeare?" Review of *Shakespearean Negotiations: The Circulation of Social Energy in Renaissance England*, by Stephen J. Greenblatt. *The New York Review of Books* 35 (March 31, 1988): 32–35.

HOUGH, GRAHAM. "The Natural Theology of *In Memoriam*." *Review of English Studies* 33 (1947): 244–56.

HOWE, DANIEL WALKER. *The Unitarian Conscience: Harvard Moral Philosophy, 1805–1861*. Cambridge, Mass.: Harvard University Press, 1970.

HOWE, IRVING. *The American Newness: Culture and Politics in the Age of Emerson*. Cambridge, Mass.: Harvard University Press, 1986.

HUGHES, GERTRUDE. *Emerson's Demanding Optimism*. Baton Rouge: Louisiana State University Press, 1984.

HUNT, JOHN DIXON. "The Symbolist Vision of *In Memoriam*." *Victorian Poetry* 8 (1970): 187–98.

JACKSON, THOMAS, ed. *The Lives of Early Methodist Preachers*. Second edition. 3 volumes. London: Mason, 1846.

JAMES, D. G. "Wordsworth and Tennyson." *Proceedings of the British Academy* 36 (1950): 113–29.

JASPER, DAVID. Review of *The Long-Legged Fly: A Theology of Language and Desire*, by Don Cupitt (London: S.C.M., 1987). *Literature and Theology* 2 (September 1988): 274–75.

JENKINS, DANIEL T. "A Protestant Aesthetic? A Conversation with Donald Davie." *Literature and Theology* 2 (September 1988): 152–59.

JOHNSON, E. D. H. "*In Memoriam*: The Way of a Poet." *Victorian Studies* 2 (1958): 139–48.

JOSEPH, GERHARD. *Tennyson and the Text: The Weaver's Shuttle*. Cambridge: Cambridge University Press, 1992.

JOSWICK, THOMAS P. "The Conversion Drama of 'Self-Reliance': A Logological Study." *American Literature* 55 (1983): 507–24.

KAKUTANI, MICHIKO. Review of *Bitter Fame: A Life of Sylvia Plath*, by Anne Stevenson (Boston: Houghton Mifflin, 1989). *New York Times*, October 21, 1989.

———. Review of *A History of the World in 10½ Chapters*, by Julian Barnes. *New York Times*, September 29, 1989.

KAZIN, ALFRED. *An American Procession*. New York: Alfred A. Knopf, 1984.

KENDALL, R. T. "The Puritan Modification of Calvin's Theology." *John Calvin: His Influence in the Western World*, edited by W. Stanford Reid.

KENNEDY, PAUL. "Fin-de-Siècle America." *The New York Review of Books* 37 (June 28, 1990): 31–40.

KERMODE, FRANK, and JOHN HOLLANDER, eds. *The Oxford Anthology of English Literature: Major Authors Edition*. 2 volumes. New York: Oxford University Press, 1975.

KERSHNER, R. B. *Joyce, Bakhtin, and Popular Literature*. Chapel Hill: University of North Carolina Press, 1989.

KINCAID, JAMES R. *Tennyson's Major Poems: The Comic and Ironic Patterns*. New Haven, Conn.: Yale University Press, 1975.

KIVY, PETER. *Osmin's Rage: Philosophical Reflections on Opera, Drama, and Text*. Princeton, N.J.: Princeton University Press, 1988.

KLEIN, MORRIS. *Mathematics and the Search for Knowledge*. New York: Oxford University Press, 1985.

KNOWLES, JAMES. "Aspects of Tennyson, II." *Nineteenth Century* 33 (January 1893): 164–88.

KONVITZ, MILTON, ed. *The Recognition of Ralph Waldo Emerson: Selected Criticism Since 1837*. Ann Arbor: University of Michigan Press, 1972.

KORT, WESLEY A. "Doing 'Religion and Literature' in a Postmodernist Mode." *Christianity and Literature* 39 (Winter 1990): 193–98.

————. *Story, Text, and Scripture: Literary Interests In Biblical Narrative*. University Park: Pennsylvania State University Press, 1988.

KROEBER, KARL. Review of *The Linguistic Moment: From Wordsworth to Stevens*, by J. Hillis Miller. *Studies in Romanticism* 27 (Summer 1988): 339–44.

LACAN, JACQUES. "Of Structure as an Inmixing of Otherness Prerequisite to any Subject Whatever." In *The Structuralist Controversy: The Languages of Criticism and the Sciences of Man*, edited by Richard Macksey and Eugenio Donato. Baltimore: Johns Hopkins University Press, 1970.

LANG, CECIL Y. *Tennyson's Arthurian Psycho-Drama*. Lincoln, England: Tennyson Research Centre, 1983.

LANGBAUM, ROBERT. "The Dynamic Unity of *In Memoriam*." 1970. Reprint in *Modern Critical Views: Alfred Lord Tennyson*, edited by Harold Bloom, 61–71.

————. *The Mysteries of Identity: A Theme in Modern Literature*. New York: Oxford University Press, 1977.

————. *The Poetry of Experience: The Dramatic Monologue in Modern Literary Tradition*. London: Chatto and Windus, 1957.

————. *The Word from Below: Essays on Modern Literature and Culture*. Madison: University of Wisconsin Press, 1987.

LASCH, CHRISTOPHER. "Notes on Gnosticism." *New Oxford Review* 53 (October 1986): 14–18.

————. *The True and Only Heaven: Progress and Its Critics*. New York: W. W. Norton, 1991.

LEAHY, D. G. "To Create the Absolute Edge." *Journal of the American Academy of Religion* 57 (Winter 1989): 773–89.

LEHMAN, DAVID. *Signs of the Times: Deconstruction and the Fall of Paul de Man*. New York: Poseidon, 1991.

LEITHAUSER, BRAD. "A Master's Legacy." *The New York Review of Books* 35 (September 29, 1988): 74–76.

————. "Microscopy." *The New York Review of Books* 36 (August 17, 1989): 15–17.

————. "No Loyalty to DNA." *The New Yorker*, January 9, 1989, 84–88.

LENTRICCHIA, FRANK. *After the New Criticism*. Chicago: University of Chicago Press, 1980.

LEVERENZ, DAVID. *Manhood and the American Renaissance*. Ithaca, N.Y.: Cornell University Press, 1989.

LEWIS, R. W. B. *The American Adam: Innocence, Tragedy, and Tradition in the Nineteenth Century*. Chicago: University of Chicago Press, 1955.

LEWONTIN, R. C. Review of *Topobiology: An Introduction to Molecular Embryology*, by Gerald M. Edelman (New York: Basic Books, 1988). *The New York Review of Books* 36 (April 27, 1989): 18–22.

————. Review of *Wonderful Life: The Burgess Shale and the Nature of History*, by

Stephen Jay Gould (New York: W. W. Norton, 1989). *The New York Review of Books* 37 (June 14, 1990): 3–7.

LIU, ALAN. "The Power of Formalism: The New Historicism." *ELH* 56 (1989): 721–71.

LOCKE, DAVID. *Science as Writing.* New Haven, Conn.: Yale University Press, 1992.

LOCKE, JOHN. *An Essay Concerning Human Understanding.* Edited by Peter H. Nidditch. Oxford: Clarendon, 1975.

LOGAN, WILLIAM. "Natural Selections." *Parnassus* 16 (1990): 72–86.

————. *Vain Empires.* Boston: Godine, 1994.

LURIE, ALISON. "A Dictionary for Deconstructors." *The New York Review of Books* 36 (November 23, 1989): 49–50.

LYON, RICHARD COLTON, ed. *Santayana on America: Essays, Notes, and Lectures on American Life, Literature, and Philosophy.* New York: Harcourt, Brace and World, 1968.

MCCREA, BRIAN. *Addison and Steele Are Dead: The English Department, Its Canon, and the Professionalization of Literary Criticism.* Newark: University of Delaware Press, 1990.

MCDERMOTT, JOHN J. *Streams of Experience: Reflections on the History and Philosophy of American Culture.* Amherst: University of Massachusetts Press, 1986.

MCFARLAND, THOMAS. *Romanticism and the Forms of Ruin: Wordsworth, Coleridge, and Modalities of Fragmentation.* Princeton, N.J.: Princeton University Press, 1981.

MCKIBBEN, WILLIAM. *The End of Nature.* New York: Random House, 1989.

MACLEAN, KENNETH. *John Locke and English Literature of the Eighteenth Century.* 1936. Reprint. New York: Russell and Russell, 1962.

MACLEAN, NORMAN. *A River Runs Through It and Other Stories.* Reprint. New York: Pocket Books, 1992.

MCLUHAN, H. M. "Tennyson and the Romantic Epic." In *Critical Essays on the Poetry of Tennyson*, edited by John Killham. London: Routledge and Kegan Paul, 1960.

MALCOLM, JANET. "The Trial of Alyosha." Review of *Letters to Olga: June 1979–September 1982*, by Vaclav Havel. *The New York Review of Books* 37 (June 14, 1990): 35–38.

MARR, DAVID. *American Worlds Since Emerson.* Amherst: University of Massachusetts Press, 1988.

MARSDEN, GEORGE. "America's 'Christian' Origins: Puritan New England as a Case Study." In *John Calvin: His Influence in the Western World*, edited by W. Stanford Reid.

MARTIN, ROBERT BERNARD. *Tennyson: The Unquiet Heart.* New York: Oxford University Press, 1980.

MASSEY, IRVING. Review of *The Linguistic Moment: From Wordsworth to Stevens*, by J. Hillis Miller. *Studies in Romanticism* 27 (Summer 1988): 336–39.

MASTERMAN, C. F. G. *Tennyson as a Religious Teacher*. 1900. Reprint. New York: Octagon, 1977.

MATTES, ELEANOR B. In Memoriam: *The Way of a Soul: A Study of Some Influences that Shaped Tennyson's Poem*. New York: Exposition, 1951.

MATTHEWS, REX D. "'Religion and Reason Joined': A Study in the Theology of John Wesley." Th.D. dissertation, Harvard University, 1986.

MATTHIESSEN, F. O. *American Renaissance: Art and Expression in the Age of Emerson and Whitman*. New York: Oxford University Press, 1941.

MEAD, EDWIN D. *The Influence of Emerson*. Boston: American Unitarian Association, 1903.

MEDAWAR, PETER. *The Hope of Progress: A Scientist Looks at Problems in Philosophy, Literature, and Science*. Garden City, N.Y.: Anchor, 1973.

MERMALL, THOMAS. "The Chiasmus: Unamuno's Master Trope." *PMLA* 105 (March 1990): 245–55.

MERMIN, DOROTHY. Review of *Tennyson and the Doom of Romanticism*, by Herbert Tucker. *JEGP* 88 (1989): 246–48.

METZGER, LORE. "The Eternal Process: Some Parallels between Goethe's *Faust* and Tennyson's *In Memoriam*." *Victorian Poetry* 1 (1963): 189–96.

MICHAEL, JOHN. *Emerson and Skepticism: The Cipher of the World*. Baltimore: Johns Hopkins University Press, 1988.

MILLER, J. HILLIS. "The Critic as Host." In *Deconstruction as Criticism*, edited by Harold Bloom, 217–53. New York: Seabury, 1979.

———. *The Linguistic Moment: From Wordsworth to Stevens*. Princeton, N.J.: Princeton University Press, 1985.

———. "Thinking Like Other People." In *Wild Orchids and Trotsky: Messages from American Universities*, edited by Mark Edmundson. New York: Penguin, 1993.

MILLHAUSER, MILTON. *Fire and Ice: The Influence of Science on Tennyson's Poetry*. Lincoln, England: Tennyson Research Centre, 1971.

———. "A Plurality of After-Worlds: Isaac Taylor and Alfred Tennyson's Conception of Immortality." *Hartford Studies in Literature* 1 (1969): 37–49.

MOORE, CARLISLE. "Faith, Doubt, and Mystical Experience in *In Memoriam*." *Victorian Studies* 7 (1963): 155–69.

MOORE, STEPHEN D. *Literary Criticism and the Gospels: The Theoretical Challenge*. New Haven, Conn.: Yale University Press, 1989.

MORAVEC, HANS. *Mind Children: The Future of Robot and Human Intelligence*. Cambridge, Mass.: Harvard University Press, 1988.

MOROT-SIR, EDOUARD. *The Imagination of Reference: Meditating the Linguistic Condition*. Gainesville: University Press of Florida, 1993.

MOTT, WESLEY T. "Emerson and Antinomianism: The Legacy of the Sermons." *American Literature* 50 (November 1978): 369–97.

MUMFORD, LEWIS. *The Golden Day*. New York: Boni and Liveright, 1926.

MURPHY, FRANCIS, and HERSCHEL PARKER, eds. *The Norton Anthology of American Literature: Second Edition*. 2 volumes. New York: W. W. Norton, 1985.

MURRAY, G. E. "Questing Poets with Different Destinations." *Chicago Tribune*, December 14, 1986.

———. "Young Poets in Full Flower of Their Talent." *Chicago Sunday Times*, February 14, 1982.

NABOKOV, VLADIMIR, ed. *Eugene Onegin*. 4 volumes. London: Routledge and Kegan Paul, 1964.

NEUFELDT, LEONARD. *The House of Emerson*. Lincoln: University of Nebraska Press, 1982.

NEW, JOAN. "Martha." *Seneca Review* 16 (1986): 75–76.

NEW, MELVYN. *Telling New Lies: Seven Essays in Fiction, Past and Present*. Gainesville: University Press of Florida, 1992.

NIETZSCHE, FRIEDRICH. *The Gay Science*. Translated by Walter Kauffmann. New York: Random House, 1974.

NISBET, ROBERT. *A History of the Idea of Progress*. New York: Basic Books, 1980.

NOEL, RODEN. "Lord Tennyson." In *Tennyson: Interviews and Recollections*, edited by Norman Page, 190–91. London: Macmillan, 1983.

NOLAND, RICHARD W. "Tennyson and Hegel on War." *Victorian Newsletter* 25 (1964): 4–8.

OSMOND, PERCY H. *The Mystical Poets of the English Church*. London: S.P.C.K., 1919.

OUTLER, ALBERT C., ed. *Confessions and Enchiridion*. Philadelphia: Westminster, 1955.

PACKER, BARBARA. *Emerson's Fall: A New Interpretation of the Major Essays*. New York: Continuum, 1982.

PAGE, NORMAN, ed. *Tennyson: Interviews and Recollections*. London: Macmillan, 1983.

PARKS, JOHN G. "Losing and Finding: Meditations of a Christian Reader." *Christianity and Literature* 38 (Summer 1989): 19–24.

PATTISON, ROBERT. *Tennyson and Tradition*. Cambridge, Mass.: Harvard University Press, 1979.

PECHTER, EDWARD. "The New Historicism and Its Discontents: Politicizing Renaissance Drama." *PMLA* 102 (1987): 292–303.

PELTASON, TIMOTHY. *Reading* In Memoriam. Princeton, N.J.: Princeton University Press, 1985.

PICKERING, SAMUEL F., JR. *John Locke and Children's Books in Eighteenth-Century England*. Knoxville: University of Tennessee Press, 1981.

————. *Moral Instruction and Fiction for Children, 1749–1820.* Athens: University of Georgia Press, 1993.

————. *Still Life.* Hanover, N.H.: University Press of New England, 1990.

PITT, VALERIE. *Tennyson Laureate.* London: Barrie and Rockliff, 1962.

PLATIZKY, ROGER S. *A Blueprint of His Dissent: Madness and Method in Tennyson's Poetry.* Lewisburg, Penn.: Bucknell University Press, 1989.

POIRIER, RICHARD. "The Question of Genius: The Challenge of Emerson." In *Modern Critical Views: Ralph Waldo Emerson,* edited by Harold Bloom, 167–85.

————. *A World Elsewhere: The Place of Style in American Literature.* New York: Oxford University Press, 1966.

POLLAK, VIVIAN R. *Dickinson: The Anxiety of Gender.* Ithaca, N.Y.: Cornell University Press, 1984.

PORTE, JOEL. *Emerson and Thoreau: Transcendentalists in Conflict.* 1966. Reprint. New York: AMS, 1985.

————. "The Problem of Emerson." *Harvard English Studies* 4 (1973): 84–98.

————. *Representative Man: Ralph Waldo Emerson in His Time.* New York: Oxford University Press, 1979.

PORTER, CAROLYN. *Seeing and Being: The Plight of the Participant Observer in Emerson, James, Adams, and Faulkner.* Middletown, Conn.: Wesleyan University Press, 1981.

PORTER, DAVID. *Emerson and Literary Change.* Cambridge, Mass.: Harvard University Press, 1978.

PORTERFIELD, AMANDA. *Feminine Spirituality in America: From Sarah Edwards to Martha Graham.* Philadelphia: Temple University Press, 1980.

POTTER, GEORGE R. "Tennyson and the Biological Theory of Mutability in Species." *Philological Quarterly* 16 (1937): 321–43.

POUNDSTONE, WILLIAM. *Labyrinths of Reason: Paradox, Puzzles, and the Frailty of Knowledge.* Garden City, N.Y.: Anchor, 1988.

PRICKETT, STEPHEN. *Words and the Word: Literature, Poetics, and Biblical Interpretation.* Cambridge: Cambridge University Press, 1986.

PROUDFOOT, WAYNE. *Religious Experience.* Berkeley: University of California Press, 1985.

PUNTER, DAVID. Review of *The Obstinate Questionings of English Romanticism,* by L. J. Swingle. *Studies in Romanticism* 30 (Summer 1991): 305–11.

QUENEAU, RAYMOND. *Pierrot mon ami.* Translated by Barbara Wright. 1943. Reprint. New York: Dalkey Archive, 1988.

QUERESHI, A. H. "The Waste Land Motif in Tennyson." *Humanities Association Bulletin* 18 (1967): 20–30.

QUINE, W. V. Review of *Ways of Worldmaking,* by Nelson Goodman (Indianapolis: Hackett, 1978). *The New York Review of Books* 25 (November 23, 1978): 17–19.

RAGLAND-SULLIVAN, ELLIE. *Jacques Lacan and the Philosophy of Psychoanalysis.* Urbana: University of Illinois Press, 1986.

REARDON, BERNARD M. G. *Religion in the Age of Romanticism.* Cambridge: Cambridge University Press, 1985.

REED, JOHN R. *Perception and Design in Tennyson's* Idylls of the King. Athens: Ohio University Press, 1969.

REID, W. STANFORD, ed. *John Calvin: His Influence in the Western World.* Grand Rapids: Zondervan, 1982.

REYNOLDS, DAVID S. *Beneath the American Renaissance: The Subversive Imagination in the Age of Emerson and Melville.* New York: Alfred A. Knopf, 1988.

RICKS, CHRISTOPHER. "Recent American Poetry." *Massachusetts Review* 11 (Spring 1970): 313–39.

———. *Tennyson.* New York: Macmillan, 1972.

RICKS, CHRISTOPHER, ed. *The Poems of Tennyson.* Second edition. 3 volumes. Berkeley: University of California Press, 1987.

RICOEUR, PAUL. *Freud and Philosophy.* Translated by Denis Savage. Cambridge: Cambridge University Press, 1970.

ROBINSON, DAVID. *Apostle of Culture: Emerson as Preacher and Lecturer.* Philadelphia: University of Pennsylvania Press, 1982.

ROGERS, CHARLES. "John Wesley and Jonathan Edwards." *Duke Divinity School Review* 31 (January 1966): 20–38.

ROPPEN, GEORG. "Alfred Tennyson." In *Evolution and Poetic Belief: A Study in Some Victorian and Modern Writers,* 66–112. Oslo, Norway: Oslo University Press, 1956.

ROSENFIELD, ISRAEL. "Mind-Reading." *The New York Review of Books* 35 (September 29, 1988): 70–73.

RUPKE, NICOLAS A. *The Great Chain of History: William Buckland and the English School of Geology (1814–1849).* Oxford: Clarendon, 1983.

RUSK, RALPH. *The Life of Ralph Waldo Emerson.* New York: Scribner's, 1949.

RUTLAND, W. R. "Tennyson and the Theory of Evolution." *Essays and Studies* 26 (1940): 7–29.

RYAN, MARY. "A Woman's Awakening: Evangelical Religion and the Families of Utica, N.Y., 1800–1840." *American Quarterly* 30 (1978): 602–23.

RYAN, ROBERT M. *Keats: The Religious Sense.* Princeton, N.J.: Princeton University Press, 1976.

RYMER, RUSS. "The Annals of Science (A Silent Childhood—Part I)." *The New Yorker,* April 13, 1992, 41–81.

———. "The Annals of Science (A Silent Childhood—Part II)." *The New Yorker,* April 20, 1992, 43–77.

SANSONE, DAVID. *Greek Athletics and the Genesis of Sport.* Berkeley: University of California Press, 1988.

SCHEICK, WILLIAM S. *The Slender Human Word: Emerson's Artistry in Prose.* Knoxville: University of Tennessee Press, 1978.

SCHULWEIS, HAROLD M. *Evil and the Morality of God.* Cincinnati: Hebrew Union College Press, 1984.

SCHWEID, ELIEZER. "The Holocaust as a Challenge to Jewish Thoughts on Ultimate Reality and Meaning." *Ultimate Reality and Meaning* 14 (September 1991): 185–209.

SEMMEL, BERNARD. *The Methodist Revolution.* New York: Basic Books, 1973.

SHARLEMANN, ROBERT P. "The Being of God when God Is Not Being God: Deconstructing the History of Theism." In *Deconstruction and Theology*, edited by Thomas J. J. Altizer, 79–108.

———. "The No to Nothing and the Nothing to Know: Barth and Tillich and the Possibility of Theological Science." *Journal of the American Academy of Religion* 55 (Spring 1987): 57–74.

SHAW, MARION. *Alfred Lord Tennyson.* Atlantic Highlands, N.J.: Humanities, 1988.

SHAW, W. DAVID. "The Fashioner of Worlds: Ultimate Reality in Tennyson." *Ultimate Reality and Meaning* 14 (1991): 245–62.

———. "*In Memoriam* and the Rhetoric of Confession." *ELH* 38 (1971): 80–103.

———. "The Transcendentalist Problem in Tennyson's Poetry of Debate." *Philological Quarterly* 46 (1967): 79–94.

SHERWOOD, JOHN C. "Derrida, Formalism, and Christianity." *Christianity and Literature* 35 (Summer 1986): 15–17.

SIMON, ULRICH E. *A Theology of Auschwitz: The Christian Faith and the Problem of Evil.* Atlanta: John Knox, 1979.

SINFIELD, ALAN. *Alfred Tennyson.* Oxford: Basil Blackwell, 1986.

———. *The Language of Tennyson's* In Memoriam. New York: Barnes and Noble, 1971.

SKINNER, QUENTIN. "The Past in the Present." *The New York Review of Books* 37 (April 12, 1990): 36–37.

SMITH, ELTON EDWARD. *The Two Voices: A Tennyson Study.* Lincoln: University of Nebraska Press, 1964.

SMITH, GAYLE L. "Style and Vision in 'Experience.'" *ESQ* 27 (1981): 81–90.

STEINER, GEORGE. "Poor Little Lambs." *The New Yorker*, February 6, 1989, 101–4.

———. *Real Presences: The Leslie Stephen Memorial Lecture.* Cambridge: Cambridge University Press, 1986.

STERN, J. P. *Hitler: The Führer and the People.* Berkeley: University of California Press, 1975.

STILLINGER, JACK. "Imagination and Reality in the Odes of Keats." In *The Hood-*

winking of Madeline, and Other Essays on Keats's Poems, 99–119. Urbana: University of Illinois Press, 1971.

STONE, LAWRENCE. Review of *The New History and the Old*, by Gertrude Himmelfarb. *The New York Review of Books* 34 (December 17, 1987): 59–62.

STURROCK, JOHN. "The Book Is Dead, Long Live the Book." *The New York Times Book Review*, September 13, 1987, 3.

SUCHOCKI, MARJORIE. *The End of Evil: Process Eschatology in Historical Context.* Albany: State University of New York Press, 1988.

SUSKIND, PATRICK. *The Pigeon.* Translated by John E. Woods. New York: Alfred A. Knopf, 1988.

SWEET, LEONARD I. *Quantum Spirituality: A Postmodern Apologetic.* Dayton, Ohio: Whaleprints, 1991.

———. "Wise as Serpents, Innocent as Doves: The New Evangelical Historiography." *Journal of the American Academy of Religion* 56 (Fall 1988): 397–416.

SWINGLE, L. J. *The Obstinate Questionings of English Romanticism.* Baton Rouge: Louisiana State University Press, 1987.

———. *Romanticism and Anthony Trollope: A Study in the Continuities of Nineteenth-Century Literary Thought.* Ann Arbor: University of Michigan Press, 1990.

SWISS, THOMAS. "Six Poets." *Sewanee Review* 20 (Spring 1986): 307–8.

TAYLOR, MARK C. *Altarity.* Chicago: University of Chicago Press, 1987.

———. *ERRING: A Postmodern A/Theology.* Chicago: University of Chicago Press, 1984.

TENNYSON, ALFRED. *Poems of Tennyson.* Edited by Jerome H. Buckley. Boston: Houghton Mifflin, 1958.

———. *The Poems of Tennyson.* Second edition. Edited by Christopher Ricks. 3 volumes. Berkeley: University of California Press, 1987.

TENNYSON, HALLAM. *Alfred, Lord Tennyson: A Memoir.* 2 volumes. New York: Macmillan, 1898.

TENNYSON, SIR CHARLES. *Alfred Tennyson.* New York: Macmillan, 1949.

THOMSON, ALISTAIR W. *The Poetry of Tennyson.* London: Routledge and Kegan Paul, 1986.

TILLINGHAST, RICHARD. "Dragonflies and Hegel's Cows." *The New York Times Book Review*, July 13, 1986.

TOULMIN, STEPHEN. *Cosmopolis: The Hidden Agenda of Modernity.* New York: Free Press, 1989.

TRACY, DAVID. *Plurality and Ambiguity: Hermeneutics, Religion, Hope.* San Francisco: Harper and Row, 1987.

TRILLING, LIONEL. "Freud and Literature." In *Critical Theory Since Plato*, edited by Hazard Adams, 949–57.

———. *The Liberal Imagination: Essays on Literature and Society.* New York: Viking, 1950.

TUCKER, HERBERT. *Tennyson and the Doom of Romanticism.* Cambridge, Mass.: Harvard University Press, 1989.

TURNER, PAUL. "The Stupidest English Poet." *English Studies* 30 (1949): 1–12.

TURNER, VICTOR. *The Ritual Process: Structure and Anti-Structure.* Chicago: Aldine, 1969.

TWITCHELL, JAMES B. *Carnival Culture: The Trashing of Taste in America.* New York: Columbia University Press, 1992.

ULMER, GREGORY L. *Applied Grammatology: Post(e)-Pedagogy from Jacques Derrida to Joseph Beuys.* Baltimore: Johns Hopkins University Press, 1985.

———. *Heuristics.* Baltimore: Johns Hopkins University Press, forthcoming.

———. "Metaphoric Rocks: A Psychogeography of Tourism and Monumentality." In *The Florida Landscape: Revisited,* edited by Christoph Gerozissis, 39–50. Lakeland, Fla.: Polk Museum of Art, 1992.

———. "Teletheory: A Mystory." In *The Current in Criticism,* edited by Clayton Koelb and Virgil Lokke, 339–71. West Lafayette, Ind.: Purdue University Press, 1987.

———. *Teletheory: Grammatology in the Age of Video.* New York: Routledge, 1989.

ULRICH, LAUREL THATCHER. *Good Wives: Image and Reality in the Lives of Women in Northern New England, 1650–1750.* New York: Alfred A. Knopf, 1982.

UPDIKE, JOHN. "In Borges' Wake." Review of *Foucault's Pendulum,* by Umberto Eco. *The New Yorker,* February 5, 1990, 120.

———. *Picked-Up Pieces.* New York: Fawcett Crest, 1977.

———. "Small Packages." *The New Yorker,* July 4, 1988, 81–84.

VAN LEER, DAVID. *Emerson's Epistemology: The Argument of the Essays.* Cambridge: Cambridge University Press, 1986.

WALHOUT, CLARENCE. "Can Derrida Be Christianized?" *Christianity and Literature* 34 (Winter 1985): 15–22.

WALTER, E. V. *Placeways: A Theory of the Human Environment.* Chapel Hill: University of North Carolina Press, 1988.

WARD, PATRICIA. "'An Affair of the Heart': Ethics, Criticism, and the Teaching of Literature." *Christianity and Literature* 39 (Winter 1990): 181–92.

———. Review of *Applied Grammatology: Post(e)-Pedagogy from Jacques Derrida to Joseph Beuys,* by Gregory L. Ulmer. *Christianity and Literature* 36 (Spring 1987): 52–53.

WASSERMAN, EARL. *The Subtler Language: Critical Readings of Neoclassic and Romantic Poems.* Baltimore: Johns Hopkins University Press, 1959.

WATTS, ISAAC. *The Works of Isaac Watts.* 6 volumes. London: Barfield, 1810–11.

WESLEY, JOHN. *The Appeals to Men of Reason and Religion.* Edited by Gerald R. Cragg. Oxford: Clarendon, 1975.

———. *The Journal of the Rev. John Wesley, A. M., Sometime Fellow of Lincoln College, Oxford, Enlarged from Original MSS., With Notes from Unpublished Diaries,*

Annotations, Maps, and Illustrations. Edited by Nehemiah Curnock. 8 volumes. London: Robert Culley, 1909.

———. *The Letters of the Rev. John Wesley, A. M.* Edited by John Telford. London: Epworth, 1931.

———. *The Works of the Rev. John Wesley, A. M.* Edited by Thomas Jackson. 14 volumes. London: Wesleyan-Methodist Book Room, n. d.

WESLEY, JOHN, ed. *A Christian Library: Consisting of Extracts from and Abridgments of the choicest Pieces of Practical Divinity which have been published in the English Tongue.* 50 volumes. Philadelphia: Jonathan Pounder, 1819–27.

———. *The Distinguishing Marks of a Work of the Spirit of God,* by Jonathan Edwards. London: William Pine, 1768.

———. *An Extract from a Treatise concerning Religious Affections,* by Jonathan Edwards. In volume 23 of *The Works of the Rev. John Wesley.* 32 volumes. Bristol: J. Paramore, 1771–74.

———. *An Extract of the Life of the Late Rev. Mr. David Brainerd,* by Jonathan Edwards. Bristol: William Pine, 1768.

———. *A Narrative of Many Surprising Conversions in Northampton and Vicinity,* by Jonathan Edwards. Boston: Felix Farley, 1744.

———. *Thoughts Concerning the Present Revival of Religion,* by Jonathan Edwards. London: W. Strahan, 1745.

WHEELER, MICHAEL. *Death and the Future Life in Victorian Literature and Theology.* Cambridge: Cambridge University Press, 1990.

WHICHER, STEPHEN E. *Freedom and Fate: An Inner Life of Ralph Waldo Emerson.* 1953. Reprint. Philadelphia: University of Pennsylvania Press, 1979.

WHITE, HAYDEN V. *The Content of the Form: Narrative Discourse and Historical Representation.* Baltimore: Johns Hopkins University Press, 1987.

———. *Metahistory: The Historical Imagination in Nineteenth-Century Europe.* Baltimore: Johns Hopkins University Press, 1973.

WIENER, JON. "Deconstructing de Man." *The Nation,* January 9, 1988, 22–24.

WILSON, E. O. *Sociobiology: The New Synthesis.* Cambridge, Mass.: Harvard University Press, 1980.

WINN, JAMES A. *Unsuspected Eloquence: A History of the Relations Between Poetry and Music.* New Haven, Conn.: Yale University Press, 1981.

WINQUIST, CHARLES. *Epiphanies of Darkness: Deconstruction in Theology.* Philadelphia: Fortress, 1986.

WINTERS, YVOR. *In Defense of Reason.* New York: Swallow, 1947.

WOOD, RALPH C. *The Comedy of Redemption: Christian Faith and Comic Vision in Four American Novelists.* Notre Dame, Ind.: University of Notre Dame Press, 1988.

———. "Words under the Rocks." *The Christian Century,* January 20, 1993, 62–63.

WRIGHT, CONRAD. "Emerson, Barzillai Frost, and the Divinity School Address." *Harvard Theological Review* 49 (January 1956): 19–43.

ZIFF, LARZER. *Literary Democracy: The Declaration of Cultural Independence in America.* New York: Viking, 1981.

ZUCKERMAN, JOANNE P. "Tennyson's *In Memoriam* as Love Poetry." *Dalhousie Review* 51 (1971): 202–17.

Index

337

bridge Apostles, 75, 139; on Tennyson, 33, 63, 107, 131
Buell, Lawrence, 204
Bulwer, Edwards, 115
Bunting, Basil, 257–58
Bunyan, John, 14
Burchell, Samuel D., 290n.10
Burder, George, 14
Burke, Kenneth, 177, 260
Butler, Bp. Joseph, 30, 36, 255
Butler, Samuel, 115
Butts, Thomas, 303n.40
Byatt, A. S., 285n.24
Byron, George Gordon, sixth baron, 42, 76

Calvin, John, 197, 217, 270
Calvinism, x; and *The Divinity School Address*, 171; and Edwards, 3, 23; and election, 188; and Emerson, 164; and *Experience*, 212, 216–17, 220; and *Fate*, 212, 225, 228–29; and "mystory," 267–72; and *The Over-Soul*, 197–98; and *The Poet*, 208; and Puritanism, 310n.74; and Tennyson, 56–57
Calvinist/Arminian controversy, 78, 100, 185
Calvino, Italo, 11–12
Cambridge Apostles, 30–34, 62, 75, 118–19, 139
Cambridge University, 98, 122
Cameron, Kenneth Walter, 301n.2
Carlyle, Thomas: and Emerson, 3; and "everlasting nay," 256; and Modernism, 296n.22; and science, 33; and Tennyson, 35, 45
Carpenter, Joel, 265–67
Carr, Arthur J., 283–84n.5
Carr, Warren, 269–70
Carrère, Emmanuel, 11
Carter, Jimmy, 269
Carter, Rosalynn, 269
Carton, Evan, 294–95n.2

Cassirer, Ernst, 6, 17
Catholicism, 57, 84, 270
Cavell, Stanley, 155–56, 224, 274
Cell, G. C., 272
Chambers, Robert, 33, 103
Chancellor, John, 310n.60
Channing, W. E., 168
Chaos theory, 262
Chardin, Teilhard de, 31, 283n.22
Chartism, 148
Chaucer, Geoffrey, 47, 285n.35
Chernobyl, 266
Chesterfield, Philip Dormer Stanhope, fourth earl of, 15
Cheyfitz, Eric, 300n.29
Chiasmus, 262–65
Chomsky, Noam, 7, 17–18
Churchill, Sir Winston, 262
Cicero, 162
Clark, Ira, 306n.17, 308n.44
Clarke, Colin, 280n.30
Clarkson, Thomas, 187
Clinton, Hillary Rodham, 267
Clinton, William Jefferson, 267
Coker, Wilson, 9
Cole, Phyllis, 187–88
Coleridge, Samuel Taylor, 2; and aesthetics of fragmentation, 156; and Broad Church, 63; and Cambridge Apostles, 122; and Christian experience, 98; and *The Divinity School Address*, 170; and German idealism, 122; and *In Memoriam*, 86, 136–38, 146; and language, 123; method of, 64; and *The Over-Soul*, 194; and science, 33; and Tennyson, 63, 98; and theodicy, 98
—works of: "The Aeolian Harp," 86, 136; *Aids to Reflection*, 63–64, 136; "Christabel," 136; "Dejection: An Ode," 136–37; *Essay on Method*, 64; *The Friend*, 64; "Kubla Khan," 136; "The Nightingale," 137–38, 146; "The Rime of the Ancient Mariner," 15–16, 170

Wesley, John—*continued*
90, 220, 222; and Tennyson, 30, 51–
53, 55–56, 60, 62, 71, 109–10, 126;
transcendental empiricism of, 272; and
Wordsworth, 2, 297–98n.19
—works of: "Address to the Clergy,"
240, 298n.23; *The Arminian Magazine*,
298n.23; "An Extract from a Treatise
concerning Religious Affections," 186,
220, 222, 230; "On Living Without
God," 170
West, Jane, 16
West, Mae, 262
Whateley, Richard, 68, 74
Wheeler, Michael, 303n.44
Whicher, Stephen E., 153–155, 211, 224,
227, 229
White, Hayden V., 307n.23
Whitefield, George, 172
Whitehead, Alfred North, 32, 34
Whitman, Walt, 207
Wiener, Jon, 307n.25
Williams, William Carlos, 253
Willis, Nathaniel Parker, 238
Wilson, Edmund, 307n.32
Wilson, Edward O., 5, 8, 10, 279n.19
Wilson, Edwin G., 149
Wimsatt, William K., 254
Winquist, Charles, 260
Winters, Yvor, 184, 234
Wittgenstein, Ludwig, 155–56
Wood, Ralph C., x, 269–72, 297n.16
Woolf, Virginia, 218
Wordsworth, Catherine (daughter of
William), 132–33, 219
Wordsworth, Dorothy (daughter of
William), 131–32
Wordsworth, William, 136; and *The
American Scholar*, 163; and *The Divinity
School Address*, 173; and Emerson, 237;
epiphanic mode of, 128; and *Experi-
ence*, 216, 218–19; and *Fate*, 233; and
fragmentation, 156; lyrics of, 20; and
The Over-Soul, 201; and *The Poet*, 205–

6; realism of, 206; and *Self-Reliance*,
182; spiritual theology of, 301n.8; and
Tennyson, 35, 39, 42, 46, 48, 50, 52,
70, 75–76, 79, 107, 113, 125, 146–
47; and Wesley, 2, 297–98n.19; wise
passivity of, 201
—works of: "Expostulation and Reply,"
79, 131; "The Happy Warrior," 132;
"I Wandered Lonely as a Cloud,"
147; "Lines: Composed a Few Miles
Above Tintern Abbey," 133–34, 173;
"My Heart Leaps Up," 17, 48; "Ode:
Intimations of Immortality," xiii, 42,
48, 113, 125, 133–35, 216; "The Old
Cumberland Beggar," 297–98n.19;
preface to *Lyrical Ballads*, 46, 129, 206,
240, 247; *The Prelude*, 35, 46, 50, 52,
54, 107, 131–33, 147, 182, 218, 233,
237, 293n.32, 298–99n.10, 305n.4;
"She Was a Phantom of Delight," 70;
"A Slumber Did My Spirit Seal," 39,
133, 284n.21; "The Solitary Reaper,"
131, 261; "The Sparrow's Nest," 132;
"Steamboats, Viaducts, and Railways,"
205; "Surprised By Joy," 75–76, 132–33,
218–19; "The Tables Turned," 163; "To
a Butterfly," 131–32; "We Are Seven,"
16; "Yew-trees," 133
Wright, Conrad, 297n.8

Yale University, 249
Yeats, William Butler: and Emerson, 156;
and *Experience*, 214; on Hallam, 138; and
Tennyson, 56, 77, 137; on Wordsworth
and Tennyson, 130–31
—works of: "The Fascination of What's
Difficult," xiii; "Lapis Lazuli," xiii, 137;
"A Prayer for my Daughter," 56, 77,
135; "The Second Coming," 156

Ziff, Larzer, 304n.53
Zoroaster, 223
Zuckerman, Joanne P., 291n.22